THE
WORLD
GUIDE TO
BEER

HOW TO RECOGNIZE THEM · WHERE TO FIND THEM · THE BREWING STYLES · THE BRANDS · THE COUNTRIES · WHEN TO DRINK THEM

EDITED BY

FULLY ILLUSTRATED IN COLOUR · THE RARE BREWS · THE CLASSIC BREWS · THE HISTORY

A QUARTO BOOK

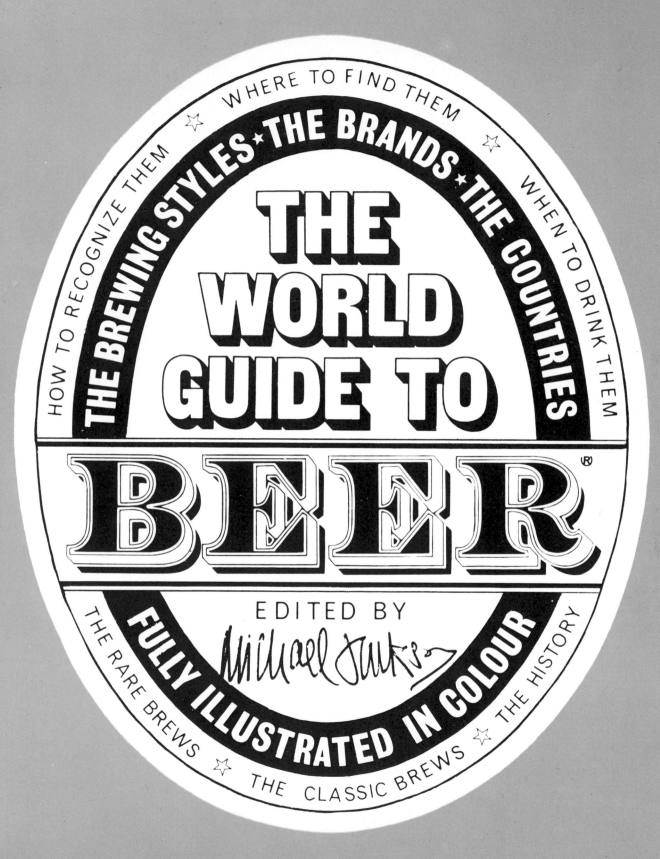

HOW TO RECOGNIZE THEM ✩ THE BREWING STYLES ✶ THE BRANDS ✶ THE COUNTRIES ✶ WHEN TO DRINK THEM ✩ WHERE TO FIND THEM

THE WORLD GUIDE TO BEER®

EDITED BY

Michael Jackson

THE RARE BREWS ✩ FULLY ILLUSTRATED IN COLOUR ✩ THE HISTORY ✩ THE CLASSIC BREWS

RUNNING PRESS
PHILADELPHIA, PENNSYLVANIA

**Beer-lovers in every continent have taken
time and trouble to help make this book possible.
I would especially like to thank the following:—**

Professor Dr Ludwig Narziss, Director, Lehrstuhl und Institut für Technologie
der Brauerei, Weihenstephan, Bavaria.

Dr L. Neumann, Versuchs- und Lehranstalt für Brauerei in Berlin.

M Marcel Melis, Faculteit voor Landbouw Wetenschap, Hévérlé-Leuven, Belgium.

Professor Anthony Rose, Department of Microbiology, Bath, England.

Père Théodore, Abbaye Notre Dame de Scourmont, Belgium.

Communauté de Travail des Brasseurs du Marché Commun.

Hans Leewens, Lamot, Belgium.

Poul J. Svanholm, President, United Breweries, Copenhagen.

Alan Bullock and colleagues at Guinness in Ireland,
Britain and all over the world.

Sandy Hunter, Belhaven Brewery, Scotland.

Tony Duckworth, Bass Production, Burton-on-Trent, England.

Frank Baillie, author of *The Beer Drinker's Companion*.

Test Achats magazine.

Dennis Flanagan, Editor, *Scientific American*.

Robert McFadden, *New York Times*.

Chet Gardner, United States Brewers' Association.

Alistair Smith, Australian Associated Brewers.

Brewers and their trade associations all over the world.

I would further like to thank for their help in my
research and the preparation of the text:
Sergei Shantyr, Jaroslav Kořán, Tad Kopinski,
Lyn Shepard, Marianne Liefländer, Susan van Tijn, Patrick Roper,
Jan Sjöby, Norman Jackson, Vernon Leonard.

A QUARTO BOOK

First American Edition published by Prentice-Hall, Inc. (1977)
© Copyright 1977 Quarto Limited
ISBN 0-89471-166-0

All rights reserved. This edition published in
the United States by Running Press, 38 South
Nineteenth Street, Philadelphia, Pennsylvania
19103.

Filmset in Britain by William Clowes (Beccles) Ltd.
Printed in Hong Kong by
Leefung-Asco Printers Limited

Edited and written by Michael Jackson.

Art Director Robert Morley.

Editorial Assistant Philippa Algeo.
Art Assistant Moira Clinch.
Editorial Consultant Rolf Hellex.

Photography by Pavel Fošenbauer, Helena Wilsonová, Jan Ságl,
John Wyand, Trevor Wood, Ian Howes,
Stefania Ciesielska, Felix Jansen, David Brinson,
Iain Macmillan, Michael Freeman, Roger Daniels,
John Burke.
Maps and charts by Q.E.D.
Brewery illustration by Robert Micklewright.

THE NUMBER of imported beers available in the United States has dramatically increased since this book was first published, and a good few of them were introduced to the American market by *The World Guide to Beer*. Within the U.S. brewing industry, there have been important changes, too. The most striking, though of little interest to the discriminating drinker, has been the advance of Miller, no longer the folksy brewery nostalgically remembered on the cover of this book. Simultaneously, Schlitz, despite a marked improvement in its products, has ceased to make Milwaukee famous. A happier development has been the emergence of a new generation of high-quality beers, led by Henry Weinhard's, from Oregon. Also in the West, tiny new breweries like New Albion, De Bakker and Sierra Nevada have reintroduced naturally-conditioned ales to the U.S. If other events have somehow been missed, if the odd birth, death or marriage among breweries has fallen somewhere between my notebook and my typewriter, it is not for lack of my caring. I have attempted more hazardous tasks, but none more difficult. Brewers can be helpful far beyond the call of self-interest, and for that I set out my heartfelt thanks elsewhere, but they can also be irrationally secretive. Depending upon their inclinations, the less helpful brewers are apt to brandish the mashing-fork and talk about their history, or to lyricize about their "modern and well-equipped plant." Worthwhile information is harder to come by. Some of the brewers whose products I most admire have been recalcitrant to the point of discourtesy. I have made every effort, nonetheless, to do justice to their beers. This book was not written for brewers, though I hope they will find it interesting, and perhaps even useful. It is a book for the beer-drinker. Similar books have been written about the beers of individual nations, but such a wide-ranging coverage of the beer-drinking world has not been attempted before. There is much more to say about the great brewing nations, and about the lesser ones, but authors – like brewers – have to find a balance. After completing a labour no less weighty than this one, Samuel Johnson reminded his readers: "In this work, when it shall be found that much is omitted, let it not be forgotten that much likewise is performed."

Where would we be without Dr Johnson? He liked his taverns, too, but he didn't have to drink while he was writing.   M.J.

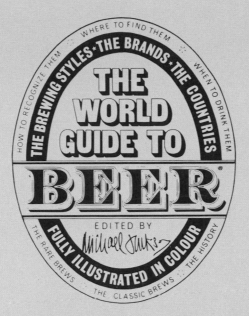

THE WORLD GUIDE TO BEER

WHERE TO FIND THEM
THE BREWING STYLES • THE BRANDS • THE COUNTRIES
HOW TO RECOGNIZE THEM
WHEN TO DRINK THEM
EDITED BY
FULLY ILLUSTRATED IN COLOUR
THE RARE BREWS
THE HISTORY
THE CLASSIC BREWS

Contents

A high and mighty liquor

King Wenceslas of Bohemia persuaded the Pope to revoke an order banning brewing during the thirteenth century. The Bohemian hops and Moravian barley on the left were photographed at the Urquell Brewery, in Pilsen, Czechoslovakia.

A MAN WHO DOESN'T CARE about the beer he drinks may as well not care about the bread he eats. Beer may have been man's staple diet before bread was invented, and these two staffs of life are as comparable as they are closely related. Each can offer an everyday experience or a rare pleasure. In each case, what we seek is a measure of what we deserve.

This was understood by the tribes who came from the East and brought brewing West with them. The *Kalevala*, the national epic of Finland, manages to describe the creation of the world in 200 verses, but requires 400 in which to explain the origins of beer. No wonder Julius Caesar described it as "a high and mighty liquor." King Wenceslas felt much the same way. He instituted the death penalty for anyone who exported cuttings from Bohemia's precious hops. In consequence, Bohemian hops are today prized the world over. The drinker also has good cause to be grateful to the Elector of Bavaria for his pure-beer law, which is still rigidly followed throughout West Germany. Having abandoned the tumbrel, the pillory and the ducking-stool as a punishment for inadequate brewers, the British have been forced to find more sophisticated means of exerting pressure. Their movement to protect and extend Britain's unique brewing tradition has become Europe's most successful consumer campaign.

In both Germany and Britain, traditional styles of brewing are gaining ground. Sales of *Berliner Weisse* and *Süddeutsche Weizenbier* are on the increase in Germany; so are those of naturally-conditioned *bitter ale* in Britain. Beer is at one and the same time becoming more local and more international. George Orwell, who once bemoaned the limited availability of draught *stout* would be astonished to see how widely the black Irish brew is sold today. *Trappiste* beer from Belgian abbeys is on sale in Britain and France; beer from Alsace in North America. While half the world drinks the famous Dutch and Danish brands, their tiny rivals are fashionable in the Netherlands and Denmark. In North America, even San Francisco *steam beer* makes a comeback. *Business Week* probes beer-drinking habits in the executive suite and at the cocktail party. *New York* magazine, *Esquire*, *Oui* and various metropolitan newspapers carry out panel-tests to decide which beer tastes best.

The adventurous consumer is confronted with a bewildering array of beers, each claiming to be the best, the original, or the strongest. For the travelling man or woman, the choice is even wider, and the opportunity greater to sample indigenous specialities which are as much a part of their native countries as the cuisine or scenery.

Chauvinism and prejudice can colour these choices. Drinkers from one country often dismiss with contempt the beers of another without wholly understanding what is available, where it can be found, how it should be served, and why it is worthy of appreciation.

They miss much.

The Elector William IV of Bavaria issued his famous Purity Order to brewers in 1516. This law, the Reinheitsgebot, today protects drinkers throughout Germany. By the eighteenth century (below), brewing was already an important industry.

The art of the brewer

FOR ALL THE PAINSTAKING research that has been done on the subject, brewing remains less of an exact science than it is an art. "Only recently have we begun to understand what a remarkable art it really is," wrote microbiologist Professor Anthony Rose in the *Scientific American* in 1959. "The brewmaster, by trial and error, has been manipulating some of the subtlest processes of life."

Contrary to the worst fears of the drinking man, the basic procedure of brewing has not changed since medieval times; the differences are in scale and refinement. The mechanics of brewing are remarkably simple, yet the natural process which is unleashed is mightily complex. The mash tun, the brew-kettle and the fermenting vessels do not reveal much to the naked eye, but within them is contained a ceaseless turmoil of invisible activity. Throughout this chain-reaction, each circumstance affects all that follows. The permutations and possibilities are infinite.

In the end, it takes palate, judgement, experience, perhaps intuition, to make a truly good brewer, much as it does a cook. The skills of the brewer and the cook are closely allied, and neither can be attained solely by the book. In each case, the quality and balance of the ingredients, the variables of time and temperature, the attention to detail, the expenditure of patience, can produce quite different results from the same recipe and equipment.

The basic recipe and method for the brewing of beer is straightforward: Barley is turned into malt; the malt is "cooked" in hot water; hops are added as an agent of flavouring and preservation; yeast is introduced to bring about fermentation.

These materials are always present. Yeast is essential, even if it manifests itself in a "wild" form, as in the unique case of the "spontaneously-fermenting" beers brewed in Belgium. Hops are always used, sometimes in the form of the natural flower, sometimes compacted into pellets or reduced to an extract. The latter method is less wasteful, but beers produced with hop-extract never seem to have quite the aroma and tang of those brewed with the natural cone. Beer-critic Frank Baillie has written that they are "like meat without salt." The hop is central to the character of beer.

Neither hops nor yeast are ingredients. They are agents of flavouring and preservation, and of fermentation. Beer is made with them, but not from them. Beer is made from barley-malt and water. The latter ingredient was once of great importance in the location of breweries, since different waters produce different beers. Today, breweries can balance their waters by adding various salts, but no such techniques were available when names like *Pilsener*, *Münchener*, *Dortmunder* and *Burton* gained their richly-deserved places in the geography of beer-drinking.

Barley-malt is the "soul of all good beers," says brewer Andrew J. Steinbuhl, of Anheuser-Busch. In the brewing of Budweiser, his company claims to use more malt per barrel than any other brewer in the United States. Barley-malt is ever present, though in many countries it is augmented by cheaper grains and sugars. Adjuncts can also help to create a lighter palate, but beers brewed solely from barley-malt have a cleaner and fuller flavour than those produced with the addition of other grains; the word "beer" probably originates from the Anglo-Saxon *baere*, meaning barley; beer is commonly understood to be a beverage made from barley; if other grains are used, perhaps this should be noted on the label, which it rarely is.

In Germany, Switzerland and Norway, barley is the only grain permitted. A single, special exception to this rule is made in the case of the traditional wheat beers which are local to some parts of Germany. In Finland and the Isle of Man (a self-governing dependency of Britain), barley is the only grain permitted, but sugars may be added. The use of sugar as a fermentable material, and to influence flavour and colour, was legalized in Britain in 1847, under pressure from growers and traders in the Caribbean colonies. In the United States, where corn (maize) is the common adjunct, Budweiser takes pride not only in its high proportion of barley-malt, but also in its preference for rice as an adjunct. This ingredient is announced with a flourish on the label or can, and the brewery claims that rice contributes to the "distinctly crisp taste" of the world's biggest-selling beer.

Malting

BEFORE MALTING, barley is stone-hard; afterwards, though its appearance is much the same, it has acquired a pleasantly biscuit-like flavour and consistency. The purpose of this metamorphosis is to render soluble the starches which are contained in the seed of the barley. The change is brought about gently, and with some skill by the caring maltster. First, a controlled germination is induced by the steeping of the barley in water. In a traditional maltings, the grain is spread on the floor during this period, which may last for a week or ten days. The traditional maltster walked barefoot so as not to damage the grains, which might then become mouldy. Today, the whole process is more likely to take place on a "moving couch," the *Wanderhaufen* system. The germination is arrested by drying, and the malt may be roasted if a dark beer is to be produced. Normally, the final temperature is between 80 and 110 degrees Centigrade (176–230°F). Roasted malts are sometimes known as *Vienna malts,* though that city has long ceased to be famous for its reddish-amber beers. In Bavaria, and notably in the town of Bamberg, malts are smoked to give a distinctive flavour to the beer. The character of the malts available, the way in which they have been treated, and the type of beer to be produced, all influence the details of the processes which follow. Malt is sieved, and milled into *grist* before the brewing process begins. If other grains are used as adjuncts, they are simply rendered soluble by pre-cooking.

Brewing

THE FIRST STAGE of the brewing process is the feeding of the malt and any other grain adjuncts into a vessel known as the *mash tun*. There, it is mixed with hot water, forming a porridge-like *mash*. The object of this process is to convert the starches of the malt into fermentable sugars.

At its simplest, mashing takes place by *infusion,* in much the way that tea is made. This infusion might be carried out at a temperature of 65–68 degrees Centigrade (149–154°F) for one or two hours. A more widely-used method is *decoction,* which brings about a more exhaustive conversion of the starches. This starts at a lower temperature, perhaps 35°C (95°F), and lasts much longer. Portions of the mash are removed, heated to a higher temperature, then replaced, gradually increasing the temperature of the whole until it reaches perhaps 76°C (168°F). Traditionally, a decoction mash could go on for five to six hours.

Where the infusion method is used, the vessel may have a slatted base, which can be opened to filter out the liquid, while retaining the spent grains. (They are no longer required, but are sold as livestock feed.) If decoction is used, the mash is filtered in a separate vessel, called the *lauter tun*. Today, a variety of modifications and refinements are possible, and the difference between the infusion and decoction systems is becoming less distinct.

The clarified mash is known as wort, and this is the liquid from which beer is brewed. (Much the same sort of liquid is the basis of whisky-distilling.) The wort is fed into a

Some brewers do their own malting. The towers and cowls which decorate their rooftops are often flues and vents used in the drying of the malt. The example on the left is in England. Malt is dried on the floor, as shown in a Czech brewery (bottom).

brew-kettle, where it is heated to boiling point. Depending upon the type of beer to be produced, the wort may be boiled for not less than an hour, and occasionally as long as two-and-a-half hours. Heat is most commonly applied by steam or hot water under pressure, though some brewers still use direct fire. The Stroh brewery, in Detroit, makes a point of its "fire-brewing." Direct flame, from oil-burners, is used on copper kettles. Stroh claims this helps produce a beer with a "uniquely smooth flavour." Other brewers talk about "a good, rolling boil." The level of heat applied is of great importance, since the boiling process brings about great changes in the nature of the wort. Copper has traditionally been used in the manufacture of the kettles because it conducts heat efficiently, and is not especially vulnerable to scaling. Stainless steel is also used, because it is easier to clean. Sometimes, the design of the kettles employs both metals. Brew-kettles are often referred to simply as "coppers," and they can occasionally be seen, in all their tall, shining glory, through massive windows in breweries. They can look like the artefacts of some lost, yet advanced civilization, simultaneously both ancient and modern. Perhaps they help remind the passing beer-drinker that his favourite beverage is the product of a craft with durable traditions and rituals.

Some brewers add a red alga called *chondrus crispus,* or Irish moss (carragheen), to clarify the wort. Rather more important, the hops are normally added at this stage, whether in whole or pellet form. If hop extracts are used, they may be added later, but this practice is falling out of fashion. The properties of the hop, and the precise way in which it brings such delicate flavour and aroma to beer, are still not entirely understood. The chemistry of hop resins has been described as "an organic chemist's dream – or nightmare, according to one's point of view," by Professor Anna M. Macleod, of the Department of Brewing and Biological Sciences at Edinburgh's Heriot-Watt University.

After brewing, the spent hops are removed by one of several systems available. The hopped wort is then cooled before being passed to the fermentation vessel, where the yeast is added.

Fermentation
BEER-STYLES fall into two distinct brackets, and they do so because there are two techniques of fermentation. This great divide appeared for reasons of history and geography. For centuries, the only yeasts

known to brewers were of the type which rise to the surface during fermentation. The behaviour of the substance which we know as yeast was accepted, but not understood. English brewers head-scratchingly named it *godisgood*. The fermentation did not always proceed as planned, and beer frequently went sour, especially during the summer. In some places, notably Switzerland, this was blamed on "beer witches."

It was eventually observed that, if beer could be kept at low temperatures, it did not go sour. This was possible where there were caves, and especially if natural ice was plentiful. It was also noticed that, if the casks of beer were stored in caves packed with ice, the yeast gradually settled to the bottom of the brew. The beer was therefore much clearer, and did not have to be "skimmed" before sale. This technique of *bottom-fermentation* seems to have first been mentioned in 1420, in the minutes of the Munich town council. The records of various other German cities mention the technique from time to time after that date. The method became popular in areas where there were caves, and natural ice. The foothills of the Bavarian Alps were an ideal location for bottom-fermentation brewing.

Only with the development of artificial refrigeration during the 1800s did bottom-fermentation become a universal technique. In the same period, the behaviour of yeast was being explained, notably by Pasteur. Brewers had new scientific resources at their disposal; they also had new markets, brought about by the emergence of the German customs union as a dominant trading bloc in Continental Europe, the birth of the railways, and the growth of the industrial cities. The first brewers to adopt a methodical and mechanized approach to bottom-fermentation, in Munich, Vienna and Pilsen, were able to attain a far wider reputation than would have been possible in earlier times. The clarity of the beer produced by bottom-fermentation, and the quality of the water at Pilsen, helped the Bohemians produce a golden-coloured brew which was something of a novelty at the time. The clarity and colour of beer became an important factor in sales as pewter and stoneware drinking vessels (even leather and wood) were challenged by mass-produced glass. Germany was big enough to accommodate both methods of fermentation, and still does, but the future direction of brewing all over the world was affected by the popularity of beers from Bavaria, Bohemia, Vienna, and later Dortmund and Copenhagen.

Beers produced in this way traditionally began their period of fermentation at about 5.0 degrees Centigrade (41°F), then were permitted to reach about 9.0° Centigrade (48.2°F), before returning to 5.0 degrees. Today, warmer cycles may be used, such as 7.0–12.0–7.0. This *primary fermentation* can last for a week, or even two. Then comes the critical phase of *secondary fermentation*. This is sometimes referred to as "aging," "maturing," "ripening," or "conditioning." Or it is simply known as "lagering." The German word *lager* means "store," and all bottom-fermented beers may be generically described as *lager* beers. Some brewers still store their beers in caves, and natural ice was still used well into the 1920s, but refrigerated cellars and tanks are more common. At whatever temperature brewing ends, lagering starts, but the beer will soon be cooled by its surroundings, to one or two degrees Centigrade, or down to zero (32°F). Traditionally, beer was lagered for up to nine months. Some brewers still claim to lager for several months, and four or five weeks is common in countries which care about their beer. During this period, a slow further fermentation of the more stubborn sugars takes place, finally producing a brew of the required palate. Sometimes this fermentation is stimulated by the addition of some younger beer, or partially-fermented wort. This traditional process is known as krausening. When the beer reaches condition, it is filtered. In the United States, Anheuser-Busch uses beechwood chips to create a filter.

Top-fermented beer is quite different. This technique continues to be used in Germany, Belgium and Northern France in the production of several prized specialities, but it is most widely associated with *ale,* a style of beer indigenous to England. Ales are available throughout the British Isles, and to a lesser extent in North America.

Primary fermentation of ales takes place at higher temperatures (15–20°C; 59–68°F), traditionally for about a week, but their period of maturation at the brewery lasts only for a few days, and certainly not for months. Instead of being krausened, they are *primed* with sugar. Although some intentionally-sweet ales are thus produced, the first object of priming is to stimulate secondary fermentation. The cask is then *bunged* (sealed), and the natural carbonation builds up inside. In some cases, the sweetness of the sugar is counteracted by *dry-hopping*. This means that a handful of whole hops is dropped into the cask. No more sophisticated measure than "a handful" is used, and one famous English brewer reports that the job is invariably carried out by a fat lady.

The brewery

No two breweries are alike. Although the basic principles of brewing are the same everywhere, the actual appearance and working of the equipment varies according to the preferences of the brewer and the designs which were available at the time of its installation. Most breweries have a mixture of old and new equipment. Traditionally, breweries were often built to a "tower" layout. The raw materials could then be stored at the top, and flow down through the building as they were transformed into the finished product.

1 The basic raw material of brewing is *malt*, which is first fed, via sieves, into a mill.

2 The *mill* grinds the malt, and the resultant material is known as grist.

3 The grist is fed into the *mash-tun*, along with hot water. A porridge-like mash is formed in this vessel. If the infusion method is used, only one vessel is required, but most of the world employs the decoction system, in which the mash is passed between two vessels. A stirring device aids the mashing process.

4 If the decoction system is used, a further vessel is employed to clarify the mash. This is known as a *lauter tun*. Rotating blades thin-out the mash, so that the maximum amount of liquid can be passed through the holes in the base. The clarified liquid, known as wort, is then passed to the brew-kettle.

5 Hops are added to the wort in the *brew-kettle*, and it is then boiled. This is the actual process of brewing.

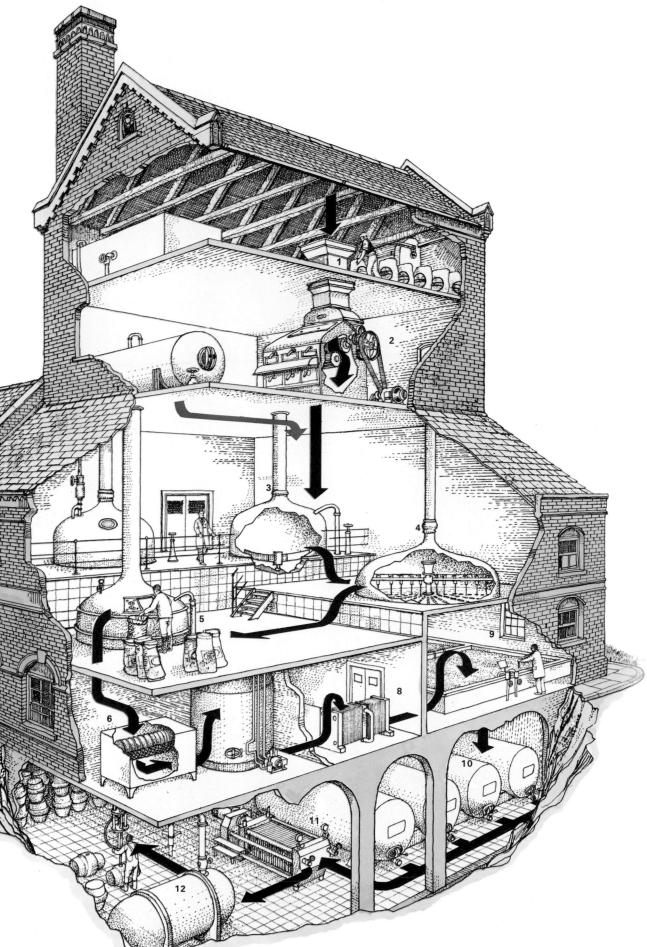

6 After brewing, the hops are removed. Several methods are used. The principle shown here is a *hop-extractor*, which squeezes the hops along a screw. It is rather like a sophisticated lemon-squeezer. The clarified wort passes through a sieve underneath the screw.

7 The wort is then passed to a device called the *whirlpool*, where unwanted protein is removed. The wort passes quickly through the whirlpool and the protein is left behind by centrifugal force.

8 The wort is then passed through a *cooler*, so that it can be brought to a temperature suitable for fermentation. This temperature varies according to the type of beer which is being produced.

9 Yeast must be added before fermentation can proceed. This takes place in the *fermentation vessel*.

10 After its period of primary fermentation, the wort is then passed to *conditioning tanks*, where it is allowed to age. Although this period of storage has given its name to lager-brewing, top-fermented beer also has to be matured — albeit for shorter periods — before it can leave the brewery.

11 In most cases, the mature beer is then passed through a *filter*, though some of the classical top-fermented beers are left unfiltered, so that they may continue to condition in the cask or bottle.

12 After filtration, the beer is passed to a *holding tank*, ready to leave the brewery, whether in the cask or the bottle.

Ice was still being cut to cool lagering cellars as late as the 1920s. The icemen shown here were at work in Livonia. Overground "cellars" sometimes had to be used, notably in the United States. The natural caverns in the bottom picture are at the Budapest brewery.

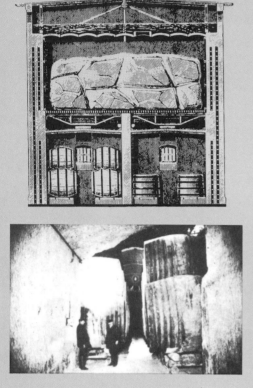

This handful heightens the hop aroma of the classically-bitter English ale. Finally, isinglass "finings," derived from the swimbladder of the sturgeon, are added to clarify the beer. "The origin of this practice is as obscure as the effect is beneficial," according to Professor Macleod.

Traditional English ale is not filtered, and there are good reasons why not. It is deliberately despatched from the brewery in an "unfinished" condition, so that secondary fermentation may continue while it is in the cellar of the pub. It must stand in the cellar of the pub for at least 48 hours before it is tapped, and then be consumed within two days. As long as it is not tapped, the beer will keep for a month, though the high turnover of draught beer in Britain renders such a long storage period unlikely.

Pasteurization

PASTEUR WAS A MIXED blessing for the beer-drinker. He helped brewers understand the nature of fermentation, and for this we should be most grateful. After Pasteur, there were fewer bad brews, and some interesting new ones. The less happy aspect of his work was the process which followed, and which bears Pasteur's name.

Pasteurization stabilizes beer, but undoubtedly damages its palate. Some beers suffer much more from pasteurization than others, but none emerges unscarred. Pasteurization also interferes with the natural carbonation of beer, which then has to be restored and "balanced" afterwards, though this can be done with gases reclaimed from the fermenting tanks. In most countries with a great beer-drinking tradition, pasteurization is unpopular, though Denmark is an exception. In Germany, neither draught nor bottled beer is pasteurized unless it is for export. In Britain, *Real Ale* is unpasteurized. In the United States, much of the draught beer is unpasteurized. In most parts of the world, there is a 50–50 chance that beer sold on draught will not have been pasteurized. The availability of draught beer indicates a high turnover, and therefore a fast sale. In those circumstances, stability is less important than it is where a bottle may stand in a bar or store for many months. No amount of filtration can remove all the fermentable materials from beer, nor can it prevent oxidation in the bottle.

Even when draught beer is pasteurized, it usually undergoes a less debilitating process than that applied to bottled beers. Draught beer is usually *flash-pasteurized* with steam for 20 seconds, while bottles may spend an hour going through a hot-water spray. The latter process, *tunnel-pasteurization,* provides a more certain sterilization, but causes greater damage to the palate. Bottled beers are also more likely to contain additives to prolong "shelf-life." Since these additives may damage the beer's froth, further substances have to be included to ensure "head-retention." Far worse tricks were employed by brewers in medieval times, and still are by wine-bottlers, but none of them do much for the confidence of the drinker.

On draught or in the bottle

BECAUSE IT IS LESS likely to have been pasteurized, and because its carbonation is less likely to have been "balanced" before packaging, draught beer is preferred by most discriminating drinkers. There are exceptions to this rule. In Britain, draught Guinness is pasteurized, while the bottled version is not. Irishmen, used to unpasteurized draught Guinness in their own country, often switch to bottles when they go to Britain.

Just as draught beer is usually popular in countries with a great brewing tradition, so canned beer is rarely seen in those nations. In Denmark and Canada, objections to the can are environmental. In Germany, they are purely practical – canned beer has to be pasteurized, and that is a critical drawback. Some American and Australian beers seem to survive canning reasonably well, but then there is the question of location: What is tolerable on a hot summer's day at Surfers' Paradise or Miami Beach would hardly suit a country pub in Sussex or a beer-garden in Munich. There is a time and a place for everything.

Which beer?

THERE WAS once a famous advertising slogan which proclaimed, quite simply: "Beer is best." It didn't say which.

To quench a thirst, there's nothing quite like a *Berliner Weisse*. Since its cloudy counterpart in Louvain vanished from sight, Belgians are left with the choice of a *gueuze*, from Brussels, or a *Hoegaardse Wit*. On a hot day in Hamburg, there's always an *alster-wasser*, though that's hardly the same thing. The Tropical thirst can be slaked by an acidic style of strong *stout*, but British and Irish drinkers had best settle for a *black velvet*. Although no American brew has quite the tang of a *steam beer*, the New World's more conventional styles should not be dismissed. The light, everyday brews of the United States are excellent thirst-quenchers, even if they lack the full flavour which Europeans expect from a beer. American Budweiser is more quenching than its Czech inspiration, because the Bohemian beers are so well-hopped. This dryness of palate ensures that one glass of *Pilsener* will soon demand to be followed by another.

There is surely no *aperitif* like a well-hopped beer. After work in the evening, Dutchmen spend what they call the "happy hour" at a cafe. The troubles of the day have faded long before the tram or train reaches their home neighbourhood, and the appetite has been awakened for a leisurely dinner. One of the more vinous *Trappisten* a *Dublin stout* or a *Burton bitter* has the commuter ravenous by the time he gets home.

An *India Pale Ale* goes well with a Bangalore curry, and just as handsomely with the hearty dishes of Northern Europe, though there are those who prefer the less bitter palate of a *Dortmunder* with their dinner. The *Dortmunder*, only lightly hopped, not too aromatic, yet not too bland, substantial without being heavy, has just the right balance for a mealtime beer. The Belgians make some very acceptable *table beers*, but they are really intended for the children.

As a *digestif*, nothing rivals a *Kölsch*, which can only easily be found in Cologne or Bonn, except perhaps a *krieken-lambic*, which belongs to the area around Brussels. It depends whether you were eating *mettwurst* or mussels. In Munich, drinkers abandon their year-round *helles* or October *Märzen* to sample the May *bock*, but a really strong *doppel* works wonders in winter weather. A beer called *Winter Warmer* is produced by a London brewer, and he is well placed to know about weather. At the end of the day, a strong, short beer makes an excellent nightcap. *Scotch ale* has its late-night devotees, but there's nothing to beat *Russian stout*.

The classical beer-styles

BEERS FALL INTO three broad categories: those which are top-fermented; those which are brewed with some wheat content (they are also top-fermented); and those which are bottom-fermented. There are certain classical examples within each group, and some of them have given rise to generally-accepted styles, whether regional or international. If a brewer specifically has the intention of reproducing a classical beer, then he is working within a *style*. If his beer merely bears a general similarity to others, then it may be regarded as being of their *type*. Such distinctions can never be definitive internationally, since the understanding of terminology varies between different parts of the world:—

Bottom-fermented

Münchener. The internationally-accepted name for a dark-brown, bottom-fermented beer which is malty without being excessively sweet. The name arises from the development of this style in Munich in the second half of the 19th century. In its home city, such a beer would be specified as a *dunkel*, to distinguish it from the more common golden-coloured *helles*. In either colour, *Münchener* beers are still characterized by their malty palate. Alcoholic content by volume: 4·0–4·75 per cent. Dark *Müncheners* should be served at cellar temperatures. *Helles* should be gently chilled.

Vienna. An amber-coloured, bottom-fermented beer of above-average strength. The designation *Vienna* for this style is now found only occasionally, notably in Latin America. In Germany, Spain and some other countries (though not Austria) a *Vienna*-type beer is known as a *Märzen*. In its home country, Vienna's traditional style is recalled by the *spezial*. Alcoholic content by volume: 5·5. Serve at cellar temperature.

Pilsner/Pilsener. Beyond doubt the world's most famous beer-style. Outside of Czechoslovakia, usually spelled *Pilsener*, or abbreviated to *Pils*. The spelling *Pilsner* is associated with the original brewery at Pilsen (in Czech, Plzeň), Bohemia. The beer developed there in 1842 is known in Czech as Plzeňský Prazdroj, and in German and English as Pilsner Urquell. These names mean, "the original . . . the source of all Pilseners". It is a pale golden-coloured beer of 12·0 degrees Balling, with a characteristically well-hopped palate. Bohemian hops are used. Imitators of this style should properly prefix their brand-names with their own place of origin, as in Bitburger-Pils, a well-liked German version. Some German *Pilseners*, especially those from the North, are even drier than the original. In other countries, the term *Pilsener* is often used very loosely indeed. Alcoholic content by volume: 4·5–5·0 per cent. Serve chilled, but not below eight degrees Centigrade (46°F).

Ur-, Urtyp, etc. A beer claiming to be the original of its style. In Germany, such claims are likely to be valid; elsewhere, they may be spurious.

Dortmunder. A bottom-fermented beer less well-hopped than a *Pilsener* but drier than a *Münchener*. Slightly fuller in colour than a *Pilsener*, and sometimes described as a "blonde" beer. Also known in Germany as *Export*, though in Belgium this term indicates a beer of much lower density. The Belgians and Dutch use the abbreviation *Dort* when they imitate the German style. Alcoholic content by volume: more than 5·0 per cent. Serve gently chilled.

Lager. All bottom-fermented beers are *lagers*. This is a generic term, though it is sometimes applied to the most basic bottom-fermented brew produced by a brewery. In Britain and the United States, the majority of *lagers* are very loose local interpretations of the *Pilsener* style.

Bock. A strong bottom-fermented beer originating from Lower Saxony, but now more strongly associated with Munich. Most countries' *bock* is dark-brown in colour, but Germany has many paler examples. The style has seasonal associations, with the month of May (*Maibock*), and with autumn. Often labelled with a goat symbol. *Bock* means a male goat in various Germanic languages. Beer should have a density of not less than 16·0 degrees Plato. Alcoholic content by volume: not less than 6·0 per cent. Serve at room temperature or lightly chilled, according to taste.

* In Belgium and France, by some gross act of peversion, Bock has come to mean a beer of medium-to-low strength.

Doppelbock. Extra-strong bottom-fermented beer first brewed by Italian monks in Bavaria. At least 200 examples are produced in Germany. By convention, brand-names end in the suffix -*ator*. Their density should not be less than 18·0 degrees Plato, and may be as high as 28·0. Alcoholic content by volume: 7·5–13·0 per cent. Serve at room temperature or lightly chilled, according to taste.

Wheat beers

(Süddeutsche) Weizenbier. A wheat beer originating from Bavaria. Also extensively produced in Baden-Württemberg. Has a considerably higher density (12·4–14·0) than the famous *Berliner* style of wheat beer. Many interesting variations on the style are available. Alcohol content by volume: 5·0 per cent or higher. Serve at cellar temperature or gently chilled, with a slice of lemon.

(Berliner) Weisse. "The Champagne of the Spree." Classical, refreshing wheat beer originating from Imperial Berlin. Low density, in the region of 7·0–8·0 degrees Plato. Alcohol content by volume: 2·5–3·0 per cent. Serve at cellar temperature, with essence of woodruff or raspberry juice.

Gueuze-Lambic (Brussels). Unique "spontaneously-fermenting" wheat beer from the Senne Valley, West of Brussels. A blend of vinous *lambic* wheat beers. *Lambic* may also be drunk in its natural state, or as a *kriek* cherry beer. There is also a tradition of conventionally-fermented wheat beers to the East of Brussels, of which a notable survivor is *Hoegaardse Wit*. Alcohol content by volume usually not less than 5·0 per cent. Serve at cellar temperature.

Top-fermented

Saisons. Naturally-conditioned *ale*-type top-fermented summer beers indigenous to Walloon Belgium and French border area. Alcohol content by volume around 5·0 per cent. Serve at cellar temperature.

Trappiste. Extra-strong, naturally-conditioned, top-fermented *ale*-type beers produced exclusively in five Belgian abbeys and at a sixth in The Netherlands. Many similar *bières de l'abbaye*, or *abdijbieren* are produced by conventional commercial brewers in Belgium. Within the range of *Trappiste* beers is a remarkable sub-group, the golden-coloured *Triple* style. In Germany and Austria, *klosterbräu* and *stiftsbräu* beers do not have their own exclusive styles. The alcohol content of Belgian *Trappiste* beers varies, but is usually in the range of 6·0–8·0 per cent by volume. Serve at room or cellar temperature, with reverence.

Kölsch (Cologne). Unique local top-fermented style of Cologne-Bonn metropolitan area, where it is produced by about a dozen breweries. Distinctively pale, golden colour. Alcohol content by volume just under 4·5 per cent. Serve at cellar temperature, with German sausages.

(Düsseldorfer) Alt. Distinctive copper-coloured top-fermented beer which is the principal brewing style of Düsseldorf, Münster, and some other towns of North Rhineland and Westphalia. A second-cousin to English *ale*, but less vinous in palate. Alcohol content by volume more than 4·0 per cent. Serve at cellar temperature. Sometimes laced with fruit.

Brown beers. The most distinctive dark-brown beer is the top-fermented *Provisie* of Oudenaarde, in Belgium, with its subtly dry-sweet palate. *Brown ale* is a traditional beer-style in Britain, and bottom-fermented equivalents exist in many other countries, notably Belgium and The Netherlands. Brown beers are often very sweet. Alcohol content by volume varies from the medium-strong (Provisie has about 6·0 per cent) to the minimal, which is more common. Serve at room temperature.

Ale. Generic term for English-style top-fermented beers. Usually copper-coloured, but sometimes darker.

Mild ale. A distinctive draught beer popular in the Midlands and North-West of England, though available in most parts of the country. Often dark-brown, with a caramel palate, but "pale" (copper-coloured) *mild* is also brewed. By British standards, only lightly hopped. Usually the cheapest *ale* available. Alcohol content by volume: 2·5–3·5 per cent. Serve at room or cellar temperature.

Bitter ale. The national drink of England. A distinctive, copper-coloured, draught beer, much more heavily hopped than most styles from elsewhere in the world. Some-

times extremely bitter; often full-bodied and malty. Notably low carbonation. Alcohol content by volume: 3·0–5·5 per cent. Serve at room or cellar temperature.

(Burton) Pale Ale. Although draught *bitter* beers are sometimes described as *pale ale*, the term is most commonly used to designate the bottled equivalent. In its naturally conditioned form, *pale ale* from Burton is a rare classic. It is a lively beer, faintly acidic, with a strong tang of hops. This type of beer is also sometimes known as *India Pale Ale*, a name dating from the days of great colonial trade. The term *light ale* is used to describe similar beers, usually of a slightly lower gravity. In this instance, "light" refers to strength rather than colour. A similar *sparkling ale* can be found in Adelaide, Australia. France has *Irish Russet Ale*. All of these beers are copper-coloured. The term "pale" was originally intended to distinguish beers of this type from the black London *porter*. Strength varies, but a good-quality *pale ale* is likely to have about 5·0 per cent alcohol by volume. Serve at room temperature.

Porter. Originally a local London beer made with roasted, unmalted barley, well hopped, and blended. In Britain, it has been superseded by the similar *Bitter Stout,* a drier and creamier blend. *Porter* continues to be brewed, but by bottom-fermentation, in many other countries. Traditionally, it was a beer of modest strength. Modern-day examples range from 5·0 per cent alcohol by volume to 7·5. Serve at room temperature.

Bitter Stout (Dublin). The national beer of Ireland. The definitive example of bitter stout is produced by the world-famous Guinness brewery, of Dublin, whose name is protected as a registered trademark. Thus the term "Guinness" can be applied only to stouts produced by this company and its associates. The characteristic Guinness stouts have a distinctive palate, more bitter than that of any comparable beer, though several other brewers have products of a similar style. Beers which aspire to the *bitter stout* style can be found in regions as far apart as the Caribbean, West Africa and the Indian Ocean. This type of brew is also sometimes described as *extra* or *double stout*. Alcoholic content by volume varies considerably, from less than 4·0 per cent to more than 7·0 per cent. Beers in this style express their flavour

best at room temperature, but in hot weather they may also be served chilled, preferably with Champagne.

Milk stout. Also known as *sweet stout*, which better describes its palate. A faintly lactic English *stout*, with a low alcohol content. Serve at room temperature.

Russian Stout. An extra-strong and highly-individualistic fruity *stout* originally marketed in St Petersburg. Still brewed in London by the Courage group, to an alcohol content of more than 10·5 per cent by volume. Comparable brews are usually styled as *barley wines*, though most of them are slightly less strong. Draught strong beers are often called *old ales*, and range from 8·0 per cent by volume down to about 6·0. Serve at room temperature.

Scotch Ales. Historically, Scotland was noted for strong beers. Today, the term *Scotch ale* is more commonly used in Belgium and France than in its native islands. Clearly, the *auld alliance* survives. The Scots call a short, strong beer a *wee heavy*. Traditionally, heavy and light were the Scottish counterparts of *bitter* and *mild*. The strength of beer is described in Scotland according to its one-time value in shillings per cask. The half-forgotten British pricing symbol of a stroke-and-dash is used to indicate "shillings". In the East of Scotland, a low-gravity 54-shilling beer was produced for harvest time, followed by a 60/- *mild*, a 70/- *bitter* and an 80/- *best bitter*. The West had no harvest beer, but used the rather different scale of 80/-, 90/- and 120/- for its regular brews. Today, *Scotch ales* vary in gravity. The strongest are those marketed in Belgium, with 7·0 per cent or more alcohol by volume. Serve at room temperature.

Steam Beer. In the late 1800s, many mechanized breweries incorporated the word "steam" in their names, but the adjective stuck in the San Francisco Bay area. There, it became associated with a curious style of brewing which was a hybrid between top and bottom-fermentation. This process produced a beer with a very lively head, and the pressure released when the casks were tapped was dubbed "steam". The city still has one brewery producing the distinctive style known as *steam beer*. Alcohol content by volume: 5·0 per cent. Serve at room temperature.

The hop

As a climbing plant, the hop has to be tied to a pole and trained. The cones have then to be harvested with care. The methodical approach was demonstrated (below) in a growers' guide produced in the 1500s, in England.

BEER BREWED ONLY WITH GRAIN tastes thick and sticky. For centuries, man has used a variety of plants, herbs and spices to season his beer, to help clarify it, and to preserve it. A typical example is juniper, which is still used by home-brewers in Norway. Coriander, rosemary and other aromatic herbs were also employed, in a mixture known as a *gruit*. Another traditional flavouring, the bay leaf, contains some of the same essential oils that are present in the hop. Brewers learned by trial and error which plants produced the best results. Perhaps its superficial resemblance to the grapevine helped draw attention to the hop as a plant which must surely be useful in the preparation of a potable drink. The shapes of plants have fostered far more remote notions than that, often with coincidentally happy results. Were it not shaped like a man, the therapeutic properties of the ginseng root might never have been discovered. In the case of the hop, a more contemporary association might be with marijuana, since both belong to the family *Cannabinaceae*.

Hops were known to the early civilizations, and Pliny's study of natural history mentions them as a garden plant. He knew the hop as a plant whose young shoots were eaten in spring – like asparagus – and this custom is still sometimes observed in areas where it is grown. Apparently the hop grew wild among willows "like a wolf among sheep," and thus the Romans called it *Lupus salictarius*. This was the origin of its botanical name, *Humulus lupulus*. The ancients may have used hops in beer. Records of the Jews' captivity in Babylon refers to a *sicera* (strong drink) *ex lupulis confectam* ("made from hops"). This drink prevented leprosy.

More persistent references to the cultivation of hops do not appear until the eighth and ninth centuries A.D., when gardens are mentioned in Bohemia, the Hallertau district of Bavaria, and various parts of Charlemagne's Europe. It is not clear whether the hops thus grown were employed in brewing, though documents from the year 822 suggest that monks from Picardy certainly brought this technique with them when they established the abbey of Corbay on the upper Weser, in Northern Germany.

As cultivation became more widespread, the plant was generally known by names deriving from the Old High German *hopfo*. Wherever hopped beer was introduced, in Germany and beyond, there was the likelihood that it might meet with suspicion or outright hostility. The use of hops presented an unfamiliar challenge to established brewers, and to people whose livelihood de-

pended upon the cultivation and sale of other plants employed in the making of beer. The Flemings exported hopped beer across the Channel in the very early 1400s, but the use of the plant by English brewers was viewed with horror. Even after Flemings settled in Kent to cultivate the plant there a century later, it took many years for its merits to be generally accepted.

Kent has become a world centre for the study and breeding of hops, and has given birth to such famous varieties as Brewer's Gold and Northern Brewer, which are also extensively grown in other parts of the world. The hop thrives in all the areas where it was first commercially grown. Flanders has its Alost and Poperinge hop-gardens; Germany grows more hops than any other country, especially in the Hallertau; and even German brewers prize Bohemia's Saaz hops, from around the town of Žatec. The cultivation of hops was introduced into North America in the very early 1600s, and it was later reported that they grew "fair and large" and thrived well in the New Netherlands and Virginia. Today, the United States is second

only to Germany in the volume of its hop-growing, and production is centred on Washington State. Wild hops from Manitoba were interbred with Kent hops in the early part of this century to improve the vigour of the British varieties. Hops are also grown on a large scale in the Soviet Union, and in Japan and Tasmania, where a variety called Late Cluster is especially popular.

In Europe, a certain amount of international tension has been caused by the sex-life of the hop. Only the female, with its cone-like flower, is used in brewing. Being a perennial, it can be propagated from cuttings, and seeds are not needed. Therefore, the male is at best redundant and at worst a nuisance. It is not cultivated, but it can still manifest itself in the wild. It disseminates wind-borne pollen which fertilizes the seed in the female, adding weight to the cone without doing anything to improve the beer. In fact, the fertilized seeds cause problems in the clarification of bottom-fermented beer.

In Continental Europe, the wild male hop has been outlawed and exterminated, but the British take an altogether different view on this issue. Seeded hops do not present such problems in the production of British-style top-fermented beers. Furthermore, some of the British hop varieties ripen more quickly, fully and evenly if they have been fertilized. This suits Britain's short summer and her very full-flavoured hoppy beers. The "harmonization" of agricultural policies is a central feature of planning within the European Economic Community, but the British will not easily forgo their independence on a matter such as this.

The flower of the female hop is popularly known as a cone, and technically described as a strobile. Each strobile is made up of overlapping bracteoles, the "petals". At the base of each bracteole is the seed. Both the base of the bracteole and the seed bear sticky yellow glands containing the chemical compounds which the brewer needs. The glands produce resins and essential oils which provide aroma and bitterness, and the bracteoles contain tannin, which helps clarify the brew. Although the chemistry of the hop is immensely complicated, the alpha acids within it, also known as humulones, are of particular importance. They provide the bitterness, while also having a rather secondary role as an antiseptic and preservative.

The hop itself is preserved by being dried with hot air. This was once done in picturesque oast-houses, but they have largely given way to less individualistic buildings even in the most tradition-conscious hop-growing areas.

Actual size

Strobile

Seed

The hop as used in brewing is the female plant. In the wild, its seeds are fertilized by wind-borne pollen from the male plant. In most countries, the male has been eradicated, so that the female is not fertilized.

Resin glands

Bracteoles

Humulus lupulus

THE COMMON HOP

Barley

Barley corn

Embryo

Outer husk

Endosperm

Basal bristle

Broken awn

Hordeum vulgare

TWO-ROWED BARLEY

A WILD GRASS called *Hordeum spontaneum* seems to have been the principal ancestor of barley, but it is likely that man learned to cultivate the cereal long before he was able to write. His first purpose in doing this may well have been to brew beer. By the time man had the ability to record his history, about 3,000 years before Christ, brewing was already a sophisticated industry. Early Babylonian texts actually discuss the suitability of different barleys for different types of beer. Man had decided that raw grain was not especially palatable, and had somehow developed the process of malting in order to remedy this defect. The Ancient Egyptians recorded that they first baked the malted grain into loaves, which they then crumbled in water to make a brewing mash. The process was described in 23 scenes depicted in reliefs on graves, and pieced together in *Bier und Bierbereitung bei den Volkernder Urzeit*, by Dr E. Huber, published in 1926. The question, *Did man once live by beer alone?* was subsequently raised in a paper compiled by several experts for the *American Anthropologist* in 1953.

The idea that beer may have pre-dated bread is not unreasonable. It is difficult to make acceptable bread with barley, because the gluten content of the grain is low, and the loaves do not hold together very well. Clearly, this didn't matter if they were to be crumbled, anyway, for the purpose of brewing. Barley's unsuitability for baking is one factor in its long and continuing history as a brewing grain. Beer can be brewed, though less easily, with wheat, but that grain makes excellent bread. Thus the brewer and the baker have been able to pursue their crafts in a perfectly complementary way.

Barley is also the grain most suitable for malting. When germination begins, the shoot of the developing plant travels inside the grain and is protected by it for several days until it emerges at the far end. In wheat and rye, the shoot sprouts straight out of the grain and can easily be damaged or broken during malting. An even greater advantage is barley's ready response to warmth, which makes malting a simpler operation than it is where other cereals are used.

Without having been malted, the grain cannot be fermented. Its starches have first to be broken down into their component sugars. The corn, or seed, of the barley is a spindle-shaped structure with a protective outer husk. Compared with huskless cereals such as wheat, germinating barley is normally reasonably free from mould growth, and this characteristic is another advantage offered by the grain. The husk also provides a useful

Friezes depicting the entire brewing process have been found in Egyptian tombs. Similar relics exist from Mesopotamia. There are exhibits at the City Museum of Munich, the British Museum, and the Metropolitan Museum, in New York.

filter aid during traditional methods of wort-separation. Inside the husk is the tiny embryo of the plant, supporting itself from food reserves in the form of a relatively much larger endosperm. It is these food reserves which the brewer needs. They include large polysaccharide molecules which are broken down by the action of enzymes produced during malting into maltose and dextrin. It is principally the maltose which is later converted by fermentation into alcohol and carbon-dioxide, while the dextrins are important in supplying fullness of flavour to the beer.

These biochemical processes are extremely complex. Their ability to proceed properly depends upon the skills of the plant-breeder, the farmer, the maltster, the microbiologist and the brewer. The task of all concerned is made no less difficult by the fact that the chemical composition of both barley and hops varies significantly according to the soil and season.

Good malting barley must be free from excessive moisture, which can be caused by premature harvesting; it should be sweet-smelling, and not musty; it should have a low proportion of skinned or broken grains, which attract fungoid infection; and it should have a high proportion of starch to protein. This last, and most important, requirement can be established if the grain is mealy and opaque, rather than translucent.

Only the best of barley is employed in brewing, while about nine-tenths of production finds other uses, mainly in cattle-foods. There are three principal races of barley, distinguished according to the number of rows of grain in each ear. Two-rowed barley is the most widely grown, especially in Central and Western Europe. In warm climates, six-rowed barley is also found. Good malting samples are produced in the West of the United States, in Chile, Australia and the Mediterranean region. Four-rowed barley is grown in cold Northern climates, but its high protein content makes it less suitable for brewing.

Yeast

TO THE NAKED EYE, yeast is a yellowish, viscous substance, familiar to people who bake or brew at home. Under the microscope, a sample of yeast is a clump or chain of tiny fungus organisms which can convert sugars into alcohol. If the skin of a fallen fruit is broken, the yeast in the air will immediately set to work on it, and the pulp will start to ferment. Since ancient times, man has observed that this process of fermentation can be made to produce a potable drink from almost anything. Wild yeasts flourish on the skins of grapes, and thus lie in wait for the process of wine-making. Once barley has gone through the various processes which liberate its sugars, it is also amenable to attack from yeast.

The earliest brewers merely permitted this to happen naturally, and hoped that this extremely unpredictable process would produce a drinkable brew. There is, though, evidence from early pictograms that they knew that an outside agent was at work in the fermenting vessels, and that this substance could be recovered from the dregs of the brew. At least one archaeologist has claimed that some primitive form of yeast-selection was being carried out in 1440 B.C. Since the Jews noted that they had time to bake only unleavened bread before they fled from Egypt, it follows that they knew how to leaven it.

Medieval brewers knew the substance by a variety of names, and recognized that it was

required to ensure fermentation, but they did not know how it worked. Yeast was first viewed under a microscope in 1680 by the Dutch scientist Anton van Leeuwenhoek. In the 1700s and 1800s, the work of French chemists Lavoisier and Gay-Lussac furthered knowledge in this area, but it was not until 1857 that Pasteur was able to explain fully the workings of yeast. At this stage, the distinction between top and bottom-fermenting yeasts had already been made, though they were thought to be all part of a common species, transformable one into the other in suitable conditions. Liebig talked about "ordinary frothy yeast" and the "precipitated yeast of Bavarian beer." Yeast from Bavaria was taken to Denmark by Jacob Christian Jacobsen, the founder of Carlsberg, and it was in the laboratory there that Emil Hansen was able to show that there were different species and strains. Nearly all

the yeasts used in the production of fermented drinks belong to the genus *Saccharomyces*, but different species are required for different beverages. Single-cell strains of *Saccharomyces Carlsbergensis*, named in recognition of Hansen's work, are used by most bottom-fermenting brewers. Top-fermenting brewers employ the closely-related *Saccharomyces cerevisiae*, but they may use more than one strain. *Saccharomyces cerevisiae* is also used by bakers.

Modern brewers have the facilities to raise cultures under laboratory conditions, but they still use yeast recovered from the fermenting vessels. This is stored at low temperatures, and may simply be "pitched" by the drum into the next brew.

Yeast is so active that its behaviour can cause great problems for brewers. It is a living organism, and may suddenly choose to behave in an erratic fashion. Or wild yeasts may get into the brew. In these circumstances, a massive cleaning and sterilizing operation has to be mounted, and extreme cases may demand that new yeast is procured from another brewery. Although yeast's job is to act as an agent of fermentation, it also influences taste, and the types of alcohol which it produces can affect the potential of a beer to cause hangovers. Its behaviour has caused difficulties in even the most scientifically-run of modern breweries, and sometimes these problems defy solution for years. If a brewer has the right yeast culture, he is a happy man.

The beer lands

IF GOD'S EARTH were a tidier place, the Seine might join the Danube, and separate the beer-drinkers from the wine-drinkers. Or perhaps the Alps might join the Carpathians. Either line would need straightening out a little if it were not to exclude hugely important areas on each side, but they provide a rough guide to the way in which Europe's thirst divides. Beer is the drink of Northern Europe, but it has also become the drink of North America and of the world. Beer is brewed in Rwanda and Burundi, in Paraguay and Peru, in New Caledonia and in the Seychelles.

West Germany has far more breweries than any other nation, and perhaps as many as the rest of the world put together. Its variety of beer-styles is challenged only by those to be found in Belgium and Britain. The Germans are also the biggest drinkers per head, closely followed by the Czechs, the Australians and the Belgians. The figures vary from year to year, but the same countries usually feature. In volume of production, the size and economic profile of the United States puts it ahead, with West Germany, Britain and the Soviet Union close behind.

The world's biggest brewer is Anheuser-Busch, famous for its Budweiser brand, followed by the beer that made Milwaukee famous. Japan's Kirin, another brewer with massive sales in its home market, is climbing fast. Again, figures vary from year to year, but Kirin and Heineken are always close. Although Heineken dominates its own home market, the population of The Netherlands is hardly sufficient to support a world-ranking brewery. Heineken is the world's biggest exporter of beer, though its figures include production at overseas breweries. Its sales would be challenged by Carlsberg and Tuborg, from an even smaller country, if their figures were combined under the banner of their joint parent-company. The two Danish concerns are now linked as United Breweries of Copenhagen. United Breweries would look even bigger in world terms if it were linked to Carling O'Keefe, of Canada. Although they are wholly separate corporations, both have the backing of the Rupert Group, from South Africa. Another world-ranking brewery which does not appear in the top ten is Guinness, from the Republic of Ireland. Guinness does not include as "exports" that part of its output which is produced by associate companies. Nor does it include Harp, in which it has a controlling interest. Allied Breweries, which does appear in the list, markets a great many beers in Britain, and has the controlling interest in Skol internationally.

20

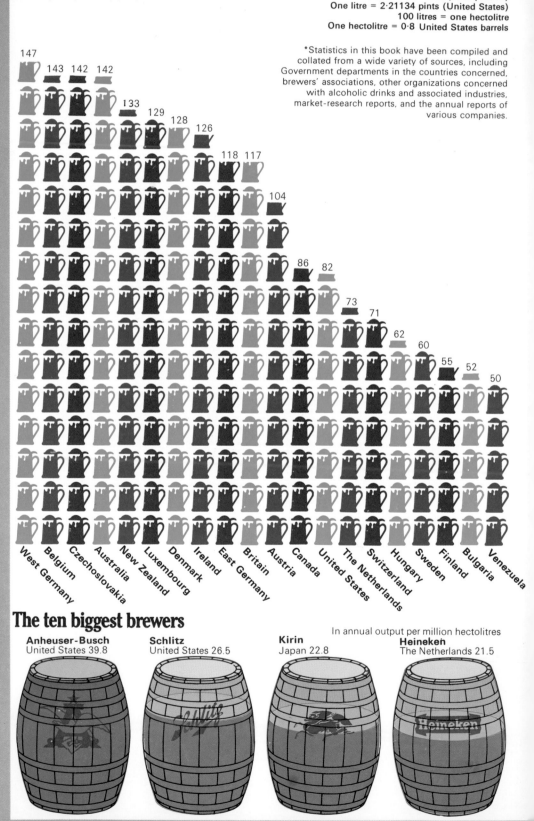

The top twenty beer-drinking nations
Consumption per head, per year, in litres

One litre = 1·7598 pints (British)
One litre = 2·21134 pints (United States)
100 litres = one hectolitre
One hectolitre = 0·8 United States barrels

*Statistics in this book have been compiled and collated from a wide variety of sources, including Government departments in the countries concerned, brewers' associations, other organizations concerned with alcoholic drinks and associated industries, market-research reports, and the annual reports of various companies.

147 — West Germany
143 — Belgium
142 — Czechoslovakia
142 — Australia
133 — New Zealand
129 — Luxembourg
128 — Denmark
126 — Ireland
118 — East Germany
117 — Britain
104 — Austria
86 — Canada
82 — United States
73 — The Netherlands
71 — Switzerland
62 — Hungary
60 — Sweden
55 — Finland
52 — Bulgaria
50 — Venezuela

The ten biggest brewers
In annual output per million hectolitres

Anheuser-Busch United States 39.8
Schlitz United States 26.5
Kirin Japan 22.8
Heineken The Netherlands 21.5

The top twenty brewing nations

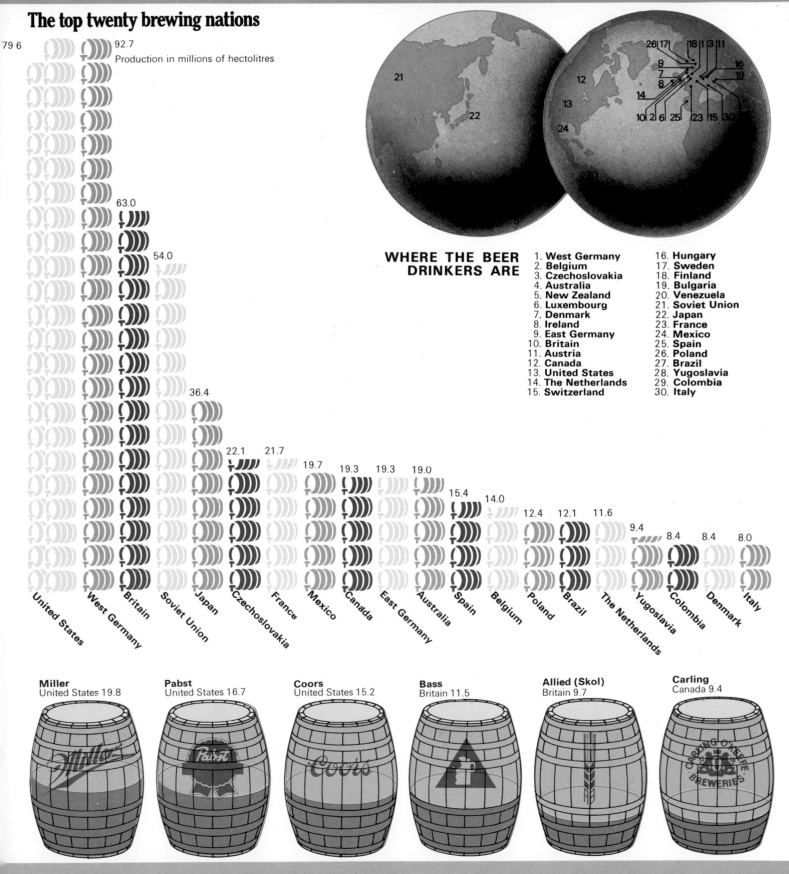

79 6   92.7
            Production in millions of hectolitres

WHERE THE BEER DRINKERS ARE

1. West Germany	16. Hungary
2. Belgium	17. Sweden
3. Czechoslovakia	18. Finland
4. Australia	19. Bulgaria
5. New Zealand	20. Venezuela
6. Luxembourg	21. Soviet Union
7. Denmark	22. Japan
8. Ireland	23. France
9. East Germany	24. Mexico
10. Britain	25. Spain
11. Austria	26. Poland
12. Canada	27. Brazil
13. United States	28. Yugoslavia
14. The Netherlands	29. Colombia
15. Switzerland	30. Italy

63.0
54.0
36.4
22.1 21.7
19.7 19.3 19.3 19.0
15.4 14.0
12.4 12.1 11.6
9.4
8.4 8.4 8.0

United States · West Germany · Britain · Soviet Union · Japan · Czechoslovakia · France · Mexico · Canada · East Germany · Australia · Spain · Belgium · Poland · Brazil · The Netherlands · Yugoslavia · Colombia · Denmark · Italy

Miller
United States 19.8

Pabst
United States 16.7

Coors
United States 15.2

Bass
Britain 11.5

Allied (Skol)
Britain 9.7

Carling
Canada 9.4

How strong is beer?

DRINKING MEN have a thirst for mythology, and in many countries the brewers are all too ready to service this need. Fanciful claims are legion, yet – except in those countries where legislation demands otherwise – facts are curiously elusive. It is cheaper to brew a weak beer, but more profitable to persuade the drinker that it is magically potent.

The strongest beer in the world is *Kulminator,* from Kulmbach, in Bavaria, with an alcohol content of 13·2 per cent by volume. Germany, Belgium and Britain all have strong beers which run at about 10·0 per cent by volume. These beers are thus comparable in strength with a regular French or German wine, yet they are drunk in far larger glasses. No one pours himself half a pint of Riesling, or 33 centilitres of Claret. Even the 17-centilitre "nip" bottle favoured for very strong beers in Britain contains rather more than the average wine-glass. Spirits vary in alcoholic content, though most of them have something between 35·0 and 55·0 per cent by volume; but they are not drunk by the half-pint, either. Measures vary from country to country, but a small bottle of very strong beer usually contains more alcohol than a large glass of hard liquor. In Britain, a 17-centilitre *Gold Label* beer is slightly stronger than a double Scotch. Not all countries have such strong brews, but beers in the 7·5–8·5 range are rather more common. In fact, it is difficult to brew beers of a higher strength than this, because the alcohol produced at

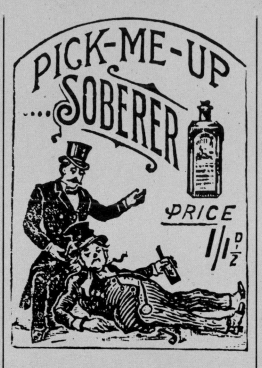

this point kills the yeast, and therefore arrests fermentation. Special yeasts, and very slow fermentations, have to be employed. The resultant beers make a marvellous restorative on a very fresh spring morning or a cold winter's evening, but they are too malty to be quenching, and too heavy to be drunk in quantity.

The nearest thing to a world standard beer-strength would be about 5·0 per cent by volume. This is true of Germany, despite the existence there of many stronger speciality beers. It is also true of the United States, despite restrictive laws in some areas. English ales usually stand at around 3·5–4·0 per cent by volume, though the British drinker takes his beer in larger quantities than is normal in most countries. In the Northern nations of Europe, the availability of beer is restricted as its strength increases. In Iceland, no beer for local consumption may have more than 2·25 per cent alcohol by weight.

In North America, laws vary from State to State. Regular beer is limited to a maximum of 3·2 per cent alcohol by weight in Colorado, Kansas, Minnesota, Ohio, Oklahoma, and Utah. Most of these States have provisions under which outlets can be specially licensed to sell beers of a higher alcoholic content. "National" brewers produce two different alcohol levels at different plants, depending on local laws.

So long as strong beers are readily available when they are required, the drinker has no cause to complain about weak ones. Alcoholic strength is not a measure of quality. A beer of 3·0 per cent alcohol by volume may be an ideal thirst-quencher on a hot day, especially if several glasses are likely to be found necessary. *Berliner Weisse* may have an alcohol content of 3·0 per cent or less, but it remains one of the world's classic beer-styles.

How strength is expressed

IF TWO BOTTLES of the same beer are bought in different places or at different times, they are likely to have different levels of alcohol content. The condition of the beer changes in the bottle, even if it has been pasteurized, and it is affected by time and temperature. When the consumer-magazine *Test Achats* carried out a costly analysis of beers available in Belgium, the results produced discrepancies which were barely credible. When they can be established, brewers' specifications provide the best means of classifying beers.

It is, at best, a confusing business, since different brewers and different countries use different systems. Nor do these systems have lateral relationships.

Alcohol-by-volume is an easy way of expressing a beer's strength. So is alcohol-by-weight, which produces a lower figure, because alcohol is lighter than water. Some countries have their own local systems, which are used in the assessment of duties. Belgium is a case in point, and its degree-system tends to provide at first glance a slightly optimistic view of beer-strengths. Most of these systems are based on the amount of fermentable material which is used in the production of the beer. This is known as its *density* or *gravity*. The British refer to *original gravity* to distinguish this measure from that taken after fermentation, which they call *specific gravity*. The density of water is rated at 1000 degrees, so that a beer with an original gravity of 1038 will have 38 parts of fermentable material. This gives only a rough guide to alcoholic strength, which could be around 3·8 per cent by volume, but could be a few points to either side. A more widely-used wort-extract system is the one devised by Balling in 1844, and this is gradually being superseded by the similar Plato method as an international standard. Densities expressed in degrees Balling or Plato produce similar, though not always identical, figures.

The relationship between any such measure and alcoholic strength depends upon the extent to which the wort has been fermented in the production of the beer. This is known as the rate of *attenuation*. There are odd cases, such as malt-extract "beers," where a wort of a high density is only slightly fermented, to produce a low-alcohol brew. More frequently, beer is attenuated to 75 or 85 per cent of its capacity, and a simple rule-of-thumb measure can be applied: The alcoholic strength by weight is likely to equal about a third of the Plato figure.

The world's "average" beer is probably a rather mild approximation of the *Pilsener* style, with an original gravity of 1050, a Plato density of 12·0–12·5, a content of 4·0–4·5 per cent alcohol by weight, and something around 5·0 per cent by volume. The more widely available among the strong beers might have an original gravity of 1070, a Plato density of 19·0, a content of 6·5–7·0 per cent by weight, and 8·0–8·5 per cent by volume.

"Say when"

The world's beers

Brews
and drinking-styles,
nation by nation

Czechoslovakia

CZEKOSLOVAKIET

CONNOISSEURS THE WORLD over have a particular regard for Czech beers, often citing the original *Pilsner Urquell* brew. The *cognoscenti* might also drop the name of the *Budvar* beer, from České Budějovice, whence came the American *Budweiser* name. Neither of these legendary brews represents even half of the story. The history of beer in Bohemia, Moravia and Slovakia is lavish and long.

All three ingredients in Czech beer enjoy a special reputation, but none more than the hops, which are internationally renowned. Chronicles say that hops were cultivated in Bohemia as early as 859 A.D., and the first evidence of their export dates back to 903. From 1101, they were shipped down the Elbe to the famous Hamburg hop market, the *Forum Humuli*.

The first mention of brewing in the Czech territories is in the 11th-century foundation charter of the Vyšehrad church. In this document, the first Czech king, Vratislav II, decreed that his estates should pay a hop tithe to the church. The first Czech brewery was built at Cerhenice in 1118. This enterprise was in defiance of an order prohibiting brewing, on pain of excommunication, which had been issued by the Bishop of Prague, St Vojtěch. The order was mercifully rescinded by Pope Innocent IV when King Wenceslas

interceded on behalf of his God-fearing and beer-loving people in the 13th century.

The good kings of the 13th century issued edicts that new towns should be planted in the virgin countryside of Bohemia, and endowed these royal settlements with important privileges. Not only were the towns granted autonomy and self-defence, they were also licensed to practise their trades within a radius of one mile. Every citizen had the right to brew and sell beer within this one-mile limit. Among these beer-producing towns were Pilsen, České Budějovice, Žatec and Prague. Breweries were also built during this period in Moravia, which is equally well known today for its fine and flavoursome wines. The oldest references to brewing in Slovakia date back to the 1300s. One brewery there, in Levoca, was already producing 2,000 hectolitres annually in the 13th century, an astonishing output for that period. The brewery stayed in business until 1967.

The Holy Roman Emperor Wenceslas of Bohemia was a friend of the drinking man. He ordered that Burgundy vines be cultivated in Bohemia, while simultaneously forbidding the export of hop cuttings. Several times over the centuries, such edicts were issued in order to protect the precious plant,

A beer-drinker's Odyssey might begin on the river Vltava (below), in Prague. Down-river flows the Elbe, and the hop-route to Hamburg. Up-river is České Budějovice, while Pilsen lies on a tributary. Czechoslovakia proclaims its brewing traditions with bold simplicity (facing page). *Tmavé* means "dark," and *Světlé* indicates "pale."

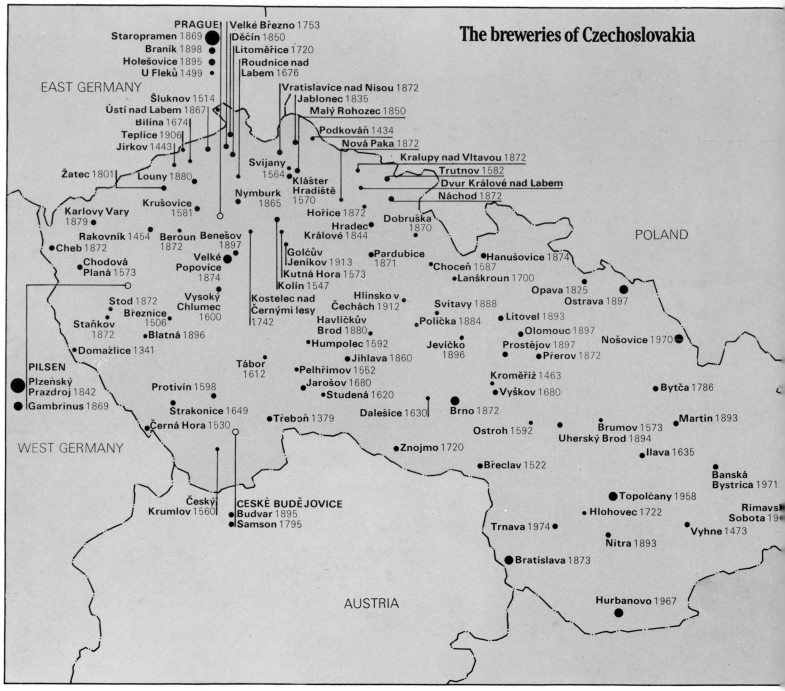

The breweries of Czechoslovakia

PRAGUE
Staropramen 1869
Braník 1898
Holešovice 1895
U Fleků 1499

Velké Březno 1753
Děčín 1850
Litoměřice 1720
Roudnice nad Labem 1676

EAST GERMANY

Šluknov 1514
Ústí nad Labem 1867
Bílina 1674
Teplice 1906
Jirkov 1443

Vratislavice nad Nisou 1872
Jablonec 1835
Malý Rohozec 1850

Podkováň 1434
Nová Paka 1872

Žatec 1801   Louny 1880
Svijany 1564

Kralupy nad Vltavou 1872
Trutnov 1582
Dvur Králové nad Labem
Náchod 1872

Krušovice 1581
Nymburk 1865

Kláster Hradiště 1570

Karlovy Vary 1879

Hořice 1872
Dobruška 1870

POLAND

Rakovník 1454   Beroun 1872   Benešov 1897
Cheb 1872
Chodová Planá 1573

Hradec Králové 1844

Golčův Jeníkov 1913
Kutná Hora 1573
Kolín 1547

Pardubice 1871
Hanušovice 1874
Choceň 1587
Lanškroun 1700

Opava 1825
Ostrava 1897

Velké Popovice 1874

Vysoký Chlumec 1600

Kostelec nad Černými lesy 1742

Hlinsko v Čechách 1912
Svitavy 1888
Polička 1884

Litovel 1893
Olomouc 1897

Nošovice 1970

Stod 1872
Březnice 1506
Staňkov 1872
Blatná 1896
Domažlice 1341

Havlíčkův Brod 1880
Humpolec 1592
Jihlava 1860

Jevíčko 1896
Prostějov 1897
Přerov 1872

Tábor 1612
Pelhřimov 1552
Jarošov 1680
Studená 1620

Kroměříž 1463
Vyškov 1680

Bytča 1786

PILSEN
Plzeňský Prazdroj 1842
Gambrinus 1869

Protivín 1598
Strakonice 1649
Černá Hora 1530

Třeboň 1379

Dalešice 1630
Brno 1872

Ostroh 1592
Brumov 1573
Uherský Brod 1894

Martin 1893
Ilava 1635

WEST GERMANY

Znojmo 1720
Břeclav 1522

Banská Bystrica 1971

Český Krumlov 1560

CESKÉ BUDĚJOVICE
Budvar 1895
Samson 1795

Topolčany 1958
Hlohovec 1722
Trnava 1974
Nitra 1893

Rimavská Sobota 19
Vyhne 1473

Bratislava 1873

AUSTRIA

Hurbanovo 1967

An elaborate system of controlled pressure is used to serve Pilsner at the Golden Tiger, in Prague. Veteran drinkers say this cafe serves the best Pilsner in the capital. Visitors to Czechoslovakia will also want to visit the town of Pilsen itself.

with the death penalty as the ultimate deterrent. There were still scoundrels who thought it worth risking this fate, but the cuttings which they smuggled never produced hops of the same quality when they were implanted in other lands.

Probably the first attempt to compile all the knowledge about beer was made in 1585 by Thaddeus Hájek of Hájek, personal physician to the Emperor Rudolf II. In his book *De cerevisia eiusque conficiendi ratione, natura, vivibus et facultate opusculum,* he describes the history of beer-making, methods of brewing different types of beer, and the importance of beer as a health-giving beverage.

The Bohemian tavern was born in the 1600s, and became famous throughout Europe. Many citizens who had brewing privileges preferred simply to cultivate their hops or malt their barley, then supply their

The lager lands

Brewery output

- ● Output over 1 million hectolitres
- ● Output over 500,000 hectolitres
- ○ Output over 100,000 hectolitres
- · Below 100,000 hectolitres

Dates shown after breweries indicate year of foundation

Czechoslovakia

MUNICH
The Bavarians had long been familiar with bottom-fermentation, but the scientific approach of Spatenbräu's Sedlmayr helped the style achieve worldwide ascendancy.

PILSEN
Although he pre-dated the lager revolution, the technical advances introduced by Poupě prepared his country for a new era in brewing.

VIENNA
The Viennese brewer Dreher worked closely with his great Bavarian contemporary. It may have been in Klein-Schwechat that the first modern lager was brewed.

●Poprad 1812

Velký Šariš 1967

Michalovce 1867

Košice 1857●

HUNGARY

PILSEN

CZECHOSLOVAKIA

WEST GERMANY

VIENNA

MUNICH

AUSTRIA

---

materials to a master of the beery art. He would then provide them with beer, which they would tap and sell on their own premises. In Prague New Town, there were at least 30 of these tap-rooms on the Charles Square, even though only five or six of them actually brewed beer.

The Falstaffian code of these taverns became famous throughout Europe, and was named "Franta's Rules" after a tap-room in Pilsen. One of Franta's Rules said that there should be no limits to the consumption of food or drink, because it is better to live well and die quickly. Another said that people should stay in bed all day on Sunday so that they could feast and drink longer in the evenings, carrying on until they had exhausted their week's pay.

The beers of Bohemia were already equally famous. The Italian physician Guarinoni recommended the beers of Žatec, Rakovník and Slaný. In his *Cosmographia,* Sebastian Münster praises the white beer of Hradec Králové and the Old Ale of Prague. The Bavarians imported Bohemian wheat beer, which they sold at twice the price of the local product. The Bohemians already had a March beer, called Březňák, which was presumably the forerunner of the Bavarian *Märzen.* They believed that in spring, the awakening force of nature had a beneficial influence on fermentation.

A wide range of beers was available. Wheat, barley and occasionally oats were used. In addition to the cherished hop, Bohemian brewers flavoured their beers with spices and herbs such as juniper, nutmeg, oak leaves, bay berries, lime blossoms and cloves. Some beers were brewed quickly, others were matured for a long time. The final brew might be "white," golden or "red," sweet or bitter. There was a selection.

Beer was used to pay off the Swedish Army when they threatened to pillage the stronghold of Kutná Hora, during the Thirty Years War. Elsewhere, breweries were ravaged along with everything else. Most of Pilsen's city brew-houses were torn down to make fortifications, and recovery was slow. But recovery came in the end.

Today's renown rests on a remarkable renaissance in brewing during the 1700s and 1800s. These years saw the disappearance of wheat beers, and the introduction of far more advanced brewing techniques. One of the world's great brewers, František Ondřej Poupě, has a place in Czech history for his work in the late 1700s. He introduced the use of thermometers and other measuring instruments, and carved out the path which was to be pursued by Sedlmayr in Munich during the 1800s. The immense success of the new bottom-fermentation brewery which

27

Czech students pick the famous hops. Harvesting by hand may, indeed, affect quality, since mechanical harvesting can cause the hop to lose some of its resin glands. An ancient oast house stands (right) at Dubá, North of Prague.

was opened at Pilsen in 1842 introduced a further change in brewing styles. Home-brewing went into decline during this period, and now-famous breweries were set up by joint-stock companies in České Budějovice, Smíchov, Brno and elsewhere.

In the 20th century, concentration of production has paralleled that in other countries. As part of this process, six large new breweries, each with an annual production of more than half a million hectolitres, were built during the 1950s and 1960s. There are still more than 100 breweries in Czechoslovakia, and 24 of their brands are exported to all five continents. The home-market is huge. Annual consumption in the beer-drinking heartlands of Bohemia and Moravia is more than 160 litres per capita, and the figures for Slovakia have increased tenfold since the Second World War.

Hops are cultivated in about 400 villages of Northern Bohemia, particularly around Žatec, Roudnice, Úštěk and Dubá a Tršice. The sole variety grown, exported to at least 65 countries simply as the "Bohemia Hop," is the Zatec Red. This derives from a strain cultivated in 1865 by Krištof Semš. The quality of the Czech hop cannot be wholly explained by botanist, biologist or chemist, but beer-drinkers find the evidence in the palate. It could be the soil, the temperature or the rainfall. Or it could be, as patriots and romantics point out, that most of the hops are still harvested by the delicate hands of young girls.

Malts are all made exclusively from barleys of native origin. The best are considered to come from Haná, a fertile region in the middle of Moravia with a warm climate and a long tradition of barley cultivation.

The waters used for brewing in Czecho-slovakia are considerably softer than those in many other centres of brewing. The water from which Pilsen beer is brewed has only $1 \cdot 6n$ degrees of hardness; the České Budě-jovice water has $4 \cdot 0°n$; most of the other Czech and Slovak beers are brewed from water no harder than $8 \cdot 0°n$. These compare with waters of $15 \cdot 0°n$ in Munich, $38°n$ in Vienna and $42°n$ in Dortmund.

Czech beers have a high content of absorbed carbon dioxide, which gives them a dense and long-lasting "head." Local connoisseurs like a lively beer – one with plenty of "soul," as they put it. Most of the beer in Czechoslovakia is drunk in taverns, rather than at home. Often, the most popular establishments are the least costly and least pretentious. The food available is likely to be limited in range, but very hearty. Beer goes very well with the national cuisine, and

is sometimes used in soups and in the rich sauces which accompany the hefty servings of meats, game and fish. A tavern is more likely, though, to be judged by its beer. The Czech drinker is most anxious about the care which is applied to the keeping and serving of beer, and may well choose his tavern by the suitability of its cellar. The best cellars are considered to be the medium dry and airy gothic vaults which are especially common to Prague.

The milieu is gregarious, the discussions forthright, the subjects anything which arouses the heart or mind, with a strong dash of football, ice-hockey and politics. Sociabili-ty is fuelled by the beer. The Czechs have a lot to say on this topic. They say that water is for frogs. They say that the second glass of beer praises the first and calls for a third. A Czech folk-song puts it another way:

Wherever beer is brewed,
Life is very good.
Let us go and drink our fill
Till the sun comes over the hill.

All types of beer are normally drunk from heavy glass mugs which contain half a litre. Occasionally, especially in the more expen-sive restaurants, half-litre tumblers are used. Taverns and country inns often display a selection of mugs, jugs and ceramic and wooden tankards belonging to regular guests. Sometimes there is a boot-glass, known in Czechoslovakia as a *tuplák*, which is used on festive occasions and for drinking contests.

Draught beers

IN CZECHOSLOVAKIA, "draught beer" might loosely be taken to mean not only a brew which is available on tap, but also one of modest gravity. "Draught" beers may also be available in the bottle. A *bière ordinaire*, which can be drunk in fair quantity to quench a powerful thirst, is most necessary. Some workers in Czechoslovakia, including steel-workers and miners, are allowed in certain circumstances to drink on the job.

Most brewers produce a light-coloured draught of seven or eight degrees Balling, and the differences between these beers are minimal. In general, they have a fresh, clean taste, and are mildly hopped.

The ten-degree light-coloured draught is a quite different proposition. Some drinkers even prefer these ten-degree beers to the various types of more ambitious brew. Ten-degree light beers are full-bodied, with a tangy, bitter aftertaste, but their palates vary considerably. There is a considerable range of such beers, and experienced Czech drinkers say they can identify the brewery at the first swallow.

Although Slovakia and Moravia have some very acceptable light draughts, the favourites among the ten-degree beers include those produced by Gambrinus, in Pilsen, and Prague's Staropramen and Braník breweries. Staropramen's ten-degree draught has a slightly yeasty palate, and the Braník brew has a full flavour which is almost spicy.

THERE MAY BE a good variety of palates among the light-coloured draughts, but there is an even greater selection of dark draught beers. The seven and eight-degree beers have a mild palate, with a caramel aftertaste, but the ten-degree version is again the most interesting.

The ten-degree dark draughts are sometimes known as "black" beers, although they range in colour from garnet red to brown. Most of them are made with dark and aromatic malts of the Bavarian type, though a few are brewed with pale malts and artificially coloured. Despite their unassuming gravities, they can be dangerously inviting beers. There are dozens from which to choose, but each part of Czechoslovakia has its own favourite.

In Prague, a popular dark ten-degree draught is *Pražanka*, from the Holešovice brewery. This is a sweetish beer, with a strong caramel taste. Northern Bohemia has its *Starovar* (Old Brew), from the local brewery in the hop town of Žatec. The brewery has a beer in the same category called *Chmelar* (Hopgrower). Western Bohemia's *Černý kozel* (Black Billy Goat) is hardly a *bock*, despite its name. This beer, from the Staňkov brewery, has a full roasted-malt palate. Southern Moravia's *Brodňanka*, from Uherský, is deceptively mild.

Perhaps the most seductive is *Dalila*, from the Samson brewery of České Budějovice. They say it puts hair on your chest . . .

Brewers are fond of the elephant as a symbol of strength, and the model on the left starred in an open-day at the Holešovice brewery in 1908. Despite such weighty displays, Holešovice is best-known for a brew of modest density, its ten-degree Pražanka. Prague's largest brewery, Staropramen, also has a popular brand among the low-density "draughts."

Lager

THE CLASSIC *Pilsner Urquell* and *Budvar* beers are in the 11–12° classification, the group loosely regarded in Czechoslovakia as "lager" beers. Although the famous examples of the style are pale, their golden colour has an extra lustre. Czech drinkers talk about the "spark" or "flame" of light refracted in the glass. These are full-bodied beers, with the characteristic hoppy bitterness, and a thick, creamy head.

The mantle was thrust upon Pilsen. Its citizens had long been unhappy with the standard of the local top-fermented beers, and those with brewing rights asked the city government in 1839 for permission to build a new brewery. By happy chance, the Pilsen water turned out to be ideal for a pale bottom-fermented beer, which was what the new brewery produced when it opened in 1842. Nine kilometres of cellars cut into sandy rock provided a perfect temperature for the maturing of the beer, which takes place in oak barrels lined with "Canadian

The renown brought to Czechoslovakia by beers like the original Pilsner (top) is reflected in the country's social ambience. Even the window at the cafe on the left proclaims the majesty of the barleycorn. Pilsner may have no rivals, but it has many contemporaries.

How "Bud" was born

These bizarre camping cabins in a Prague park were once lagering tanks at the Budvar brewery in České Budějovice. In those days, the town was called Budweis. The beer was thus popularly known as Budweiser. Such was the fame of "Budweiser" beer that Adolphus Busch used the name to describe the Bohemian-style brew which he launched in the United States in 1876. When the Bohemians exported their own beer to the Americas, they called it Crystal, to avoid confusion.

resin" to seal out the "woody" flavour.

In the first year of production, only 3,600 hectolitres were brewed, but the new beer quickly drove all its rivals out of town, and soon it was set to conquer other cities. In the 1850s, Pilsner was readily available in Prague, Mariánské Lázně (Marienbad), Karlovy Vary (Carlsbad) and Teplice. In 1856, it arrived in Vienna, which quickly became one of its biggest markets. Munich, Berlin, London and Paris followed. By the 1870s, Pilsner was already a famous name throughout Europe, and many large cities had establishments devoted exclusively to its sale. When brewers in other countries began to brew bottom-fermented beers which they described as *Pilsners*, the word *Urquell* ("original source") was added to the name. In Czechoslovakia, the famous golden beer is described similarly, as *Plzeňský Prazdroj*.

The first important award presented to *Pilsner* beer was made in 1863, at the Hamburg International Exhibition. At the end of the century, the brew won Papal approval. It was prescribed to Pope Leo XIII as an aid to digestion. In the last days of the Second World War, the brewery was heavily damaged during air-raids on the Skoda works, but production returned to normal within a few years. The accolades have continued, and President Saragat of Italy presented the *Premio Europeo Mercurio d'Oro* in 1970. Today, *Pilsner* beer is exported to 90 countries.

The best place to sample the beer is in its home town, at the famous *U Salzmanů* taproom, but there are also several celebrated *Pilsner* ale-houses in Prague. A tailor called Pinkas founded the first *Pilsner* ale-house in Prague a year after the brewery opened.

Since then, *U Pinkasů* has been a Mecca for beer-drinkers, and some of its habitues can down ten litres or more at one sitting. Despite being quite a small place, *U Pinkasů* takes delivery of more than 6,000 barrels, each containing 100 litres, every year.

Some older drinkers claim that the best *Pilsner* in Prague is at *U zlatého tygra* (The Golden Tiger), while *U kocoura* (The Tom Cat) has its devotees. There are many such places in Prague's Old Town and Lesser Town. Drinkers who like roast pork and dumplings with their *Pilsner* opt for *U Schnellů* and *U dvou koček*, both well known for their typical Czech kitchens.

Urquell is not the only pale lager to come from Pilsen. A very similar beer of this type, with a considerable export sale, is brewed by the city's Gambrinus brewery. This beer is called *Světovar*, with the rather mundane English-language name "Worldsbrew."

Despite the well-earned fame of *Pilsner Urquell*, there are Czech drinkers who would walk over hot coals for *Budvar*, the beer of České Budějovice (*Budweis* was its German-language name). This attitude was shared by the Czech King Ferdinand, who had beer from České Budějovice delivered to the royal court in 1531. Since then, it has cherished the soubriquet, "The Beer of Kings." Budvar's soft water comes from wells which plunge 320 metres underneath the brewery. The beer is paler than *Pilsner*, with a very characteristic bouquet, a mild yet hoppy palate, and a slightly sweet after-taste.

In 1876, the name *Budweiser* was adopted by the American brewer Adolphus Busch. When the Czech brewery later wished to export to the New World, this caused problems, and the Budvar beer had to be given another name. For a time it was sold in the United States as *Crystal*, hardly an original name for a beer, but now the two companies largely manage to avoid each other's markets. *Budvar* still calls itself, with some justification, "The Original Budweiser." The two beers are rather different, but the Czech "original" can be sampled in a curiously Transatlantic setting at the *Hard Rock Café*, an American-style hamburger house in fashionable Piccadilly, London. Despite the American problem, a great deal of the beer produced at the Budvar brewery is exported. Nonetheless, the characteristic bitter-sweet brew can be tasted in some dozens of ale-houses and restaurants in South Bohemia. At České Budějovice, the ancient Meat Market *(Masné krámy)* ale-house is a lively spot for a Czechoslovakian original Bud.

Special beers

The Tatra mountains (left) give their name to some interesting beers, both light and dark. The "tmavé" lager style (right and above) can be found all over the country.

In Prague, Budvar's "headquarters" is the restaurant *U Medvíků* (The Little Bears), which was itself a brewery in the Middle Ages. Among the specialities of the house are some old Czech and South Bohemian dishes which have colourful names and remarkable flavours, like Master Vok's Rib or *Táborská bašta*, a filling meal of old Czech dumplings and different kinds of meat.

A great many awards have been attracted in the post-War period by the Old Spring *(Staropramen)* beer, produced by a brewery in the Prague industrial district of Smíchov. Until then, this brewery had failed to gather the reputation enjoyed by its illustrious counterparts, despite having been in business since 1869. The Staropramen brewery, with any annual production of 1,350,000 hecto-litres, is the biggest in Czechoslovakia. Its pale lager is full-bodied, sparkling and fresh, with a mild but well-hopped palate. This is a typical example of the style, widely available throughout the country.

The Slavic deity *Radhost* or *Radegast*, the god of hospitality, gave his name to a mountain in the Beskids and to a lager from the Nosovice brewery, in Northern Moravia. Perhaps the Southern Moravians prefer the Old Brno beer *(Starobrno)*, from that city's local brewery, or *Hostan*, named after a famous medieval brewer. *Hostan* is the pride of Znojmo, where it is produced by the local brewery, despite this being the heartland of a rich wine district.

The Slovaks have *Tatran*, which takes its name from the mountain range. This lager is produced by the Poprad brewery, in the foothills of the High Tatras.

There are also many fine lagers in the 11° classification. Among Bohemia's best are

Karel, named after Charles IV, and brewed in Karlovy Vary (Carlsbad); Golden Horse *(Zlatý kuň)*, from Beroun; and Plane Tree *(Platan)*, from Provitín. South Moravians favour Hedgehog *(Ježek)*, from Jihlava; and Slovakians commend Chamois *(Kamzík)*, from Poprad, and *Cassovar*, from Košice.

ST THOMAS', in Prague's Lesser Town, was once an Augustinian monastery brewery, and beer was produced there until the 1950s. Today, *U Svatého Tomáše* is one of Prague's most atmospheric ale-houses, with vaults, nooks and crannies, and a hall called The Cave. The beer served there is an interesting lager from the local brewery in the Braník district of Prague. Although its 12° gravity does not justify the description, this beer is called Braník *Special*. It is available in both pale and dark versions, the latter of which marries an unusually deep and reflective colour with a tangy palate.

There are fewer dark lagers than pale brews, but some of them enjoy a considerable reputation. A very well-liked example is the *Kapucín* from North Bohemia's Vratislavice brewery. This velvety beer has a deep reddish-black colour, and is remarkable for a slightly sweet palate and a faintly bitter aftertaste. The dark version of Old Brno *(Starobrno)* lager is yet deeper in colour, and has a more markedly bitter aftertaste. Sweeter palates are provided by the dark lagers from the Central Bohemian Vysoký Chlumec brewery, and the Garnet *(Granát)* of South Moravia's Cerna Hora brewery. The Slovak favourites have a mild palate, and an emphatic flavour of browned malts. Good examples are the dark lager from the local brewery in Nitra, and the *Šíravar* from Michalovce.

THE BAVARIANS have the *Platzl*, in Munich; the Bohemians have *U Fleků*, in Prague. The Bohemians could argue that they have the best of this admittedly-rich comparison. Not only is *U Fleků* a remarkable and lively ale-house, dating back to 1499, it also brews its own beer. It is a home-brew house in the true sense that its beer is available nowhere else. On a pleasant evening, all 900 seats at *U Fleků*, including those in the beer-garden, are quickly occupied. Happily, there seems to be no limit to the number of determined drinkers who can find themselves a space at the bar to enjoy a few *Flek* beers and a slice or two of the delicious fried-toast savouries which are a local snack.

The dark beer of *U Fleků*, with its delicate caramel palate, is a 13° brew. Beers of this gravity and more – sometimes quite a lot more – are classified as "Specials." These brews usually have a notable bouquet and a rich palate. Among the other much-appreciated 13° dark specials are the *Chodovar*, from the brewery of the same name in West Bohemia, and the Black Pheasant *(Černý bažant)*, from the same Slovakian brewery which produced Golden Pheasant.

One degree up the scale, the Billy Goat *(Kozel)* beer of Velké Popovice, Central Bohemia, is one of the best-regarded 14° dark specials. This beer has a malty sweetness not dissimilar from that of the traditional *Münchener*. Another 14° favourite is Alderman *(Konsel)*, from Litoměřice, in North Bohemia. This has a malty caramel palate, with a bitter-sweet hop flavour. Devotees of dark beer also like The Spark *(Jiskra)*, from Hradec Králové, in East Bohemia. Distinctive malts give a characterful full-bodied flavour to this brew. Among the Slovak dark specials, *Cassovar* (also called *Marina*), from Košice, is something of a favourite.

The medieval ale-house called The Vulture *(U supa)*, in Prague, serves a pale fourteen-degree special from the city's Braník brewery. Beer has been tapped at The Vulture since the 14th century, and today's malty brew is worthy of the tradition. Its head is so creamy that it can be cut with a knife.

All of the pale specials are 14° brews. There are about two dozen of them, all well attenuated and matured, with palates which are to varying degrees malty, and usually medium-hopped. Two of the more strongly-hopped examples are named after mythological creatures. The good-humoured spirit of the Krakonoše mountains gave its name to a beer produced by the Trutnov brewery in East Bohemia. Krakonoš has a clear, fresh flavour and a hoppy aftertaste. The stuffed crocodile which hangs at the gates of Brno

At street level, the face of Old Prague . . . and a heavy hint that it might be time for an evening drink. Behind those brightly-lit windows, the convivial pleasures of 900 drinkers, not to mention the savoury delights of U Fleků. In Gothic cellars typical of Prague, a dark brew is prepared exclusively for drinkers at the tavern. It is the last true home-brew house in the Czechoslovakian capital.

Among the "special" beers of Czechoslovakia are brands with densities ranging from 13·0 to 20·0 degrees. At the top end of the range is the estimable Martinsky Porter.

town-hall is transmogrified into a dragon by the local brewery. Brno Dragon (*Brněnský drak*) has a rich taste and a distinctive hop bitterness. More historical colour provides a backdrop for the pale special of the Vyhne brewery, in Central Slovakia. This brewery was founded by the Knights Templars in 1372, and a member of this religious military order is depicted on the label of the *Sitňan* special. Two other well-liked pale specials in Slovakia are the Pearl (*perla*) of the Ilava brewery, and *Velký Šariš* from the brewery of the same name.

The miners of Ostrava, in Northern Moravia, favour a 16° dark special called *Ondráš*, which is brewed locally. This brew is rather sweet, but with a slightly bitter after-taste. The other 16° specials are uncompromisingly creamy and caramel in their palate.

The Holy Trinity of special beers are three high-gravity dark brews. Although these three Czech beers are far stronger than the stouts of Ireland, their palate is not dissimilar. In Pilsen, the Gambrinus brewery produced a rich, full-bodied 18° beer called *Diplomat* (for some reason, the name was

changed from the original *Senátor*), with a delicious well-hopped palate. This brew, which is extensively exported, tends to be available only in first-class hotels and restaurants. It is, of course, most readily found in the town of Pilsen. A 19° porter-style beer is made at Christmas in Pardubice, East Bohemia. *Pardubický Porter* has a strong roasted-malt palate, and an even more pronounced bitterness. This individualistic brew, one of several seasonal and anniversary beers which are produced in Czechoslovakia, is available only at Christmas. It may be tasted at two ancient Pardubice ale-houses, the Stork (*U čápa*) and the Green Frog (*Zelená žába*).

The strongest beer brewed in Czechoslovakia is a porter made in the Central Slovak town of Martin. This 20° *Martinský Porter* is a heavy but reflective dark brew, with a fine taste of charred malts, and a well-hopped palate. The powerful brew has been known to appear in Bratislava, but a journey to Martin may be necessary.

In Czechoslovakia, such journeys are eminently worthwhile . . .

Germany

The biggest of them all . . . no nationality drinks as much beer as the Germans do, and no State displays quite the enthusiasm which is shown by Bavaria. A giant thirst is satisfied at Munich's Mathäser Bierstadt (left).

IN MOST COUNTRIES of the world, drinkers look to Germany as the prime brewing nation. Not only do the Germans drink more beer than the people of any other nation, with a consumption of nearly 150 litres per head each year, their influence has been central to the development of brewing in many other parts of the world. Even in the first century A.D., Tacitus observed of the Germany, rather sniffily: "Their beverage they prepare from barley or wheat, a brew which slightly resembles an inferior quality of wine."

It is some years since anyone has been so disdainful about German beer – or German wine, for that matter. Germany nudges far enough into Southern Europe to grow fine white wines in vast quantities, yet its greatest contribution to the bars and dining-tables of the world is as the biggest nation of the beer-drinking North.

The people of the "wine lands" in Germany's South–West (the Rhineland Palatinate, the Saar, Baden-Württemberg) are among the richest in small breweries; the people of Frankfurt drink their local cider (*apfelwein*) in the shadow of the Henninger brewery's barley silo (a tower, with a restaurant on top); the people of Hamburg drink their schnapps with a "chaser" of beer. Throughout Germany, the customs and folklore are redolent with beer.

In Munich, elevenses (*Brotzeit*) consists of beer, with bread, butter and *wurst*. Beer is served with lunch and dinner – and at "cocktails" in the evening. The evening drink (the *Dämmerschoppen*) might accompany a card-game, skittles or choir-practice. Beer is for May Day, Father's Day, and birthdays. It is for the roof-raising, the house-warming, and the first day in a new job. On the latter occasion, the new boy must make his entrance (*seinen einstand geben*) by buying drinks all round.

Such occasions are small beer compared with some of the festivals which erupt all over the country at different times of the year, or with the pre-Lenten *Fasching* (Carnival) in the Catholic areas of Southern Germany and Rhineland. During *Fasching*,

Wherever there's a festival, there's beer. Early in November, to the South of Munich, a village called Benediktbeuren celebrates St Leonhard's Day. He is the patron saint of horses . . . and Löwenbräu pays an equine tribute.

The brewing-towns of Southern Germany

1,000 costume celebrations are held in Munich, and the impact is similar for several surreal days in major Catholic cities like Cologne.

At an altogether more formal level, a Munich-based fraternity called the International Beer Convention exists to carry out research projects, hold competitions and gatherings, with a view to upgrading the social ethos of beer-drinking. The members of this officially-registered fraternity call themselves "The Notables." New members have to be guaranteed by two sponsors, and they receive a medallion and blazon at their induction ceremony. Most of The Notables are professional men, though only a minority have any involvement in the brewing industry. The Convention is a quite independent body.

The culture of beer is a serious matter, but the quality of the brew itself is more important. Germans recognize this. More than the beer-drinkers of any other nation, the Germans protect their palate, not to mention their palette of brews. German beer is not pasteurized, unless for export. Although every German has his firm favourites and his pet hates, he simply does not have to contend with the difficulties faced by drinkers in some neighbouring countries. Nor have regional styles of brewing been eliminated; in some cases, they flourish more than ever.

Germany has suffered from attempts to create a "national" beer, but the drinker has resisted this more strongly than his counterparts in other countries. Although financial backing for Löwenbräu, of Munich, Schultheiss, of Berlin, and the Dortmunder Union Brewery comes from the same Bavarian Hypotheken Bank, the three continue to produce beers in their cities' own quite distinctive styles. Much the same can be said of the other two major brewery groupings, established in a fit of diversification by the food-based Oetker conglomerate and the Reemstma cigarette firm.

There remain at least a dozen major regional beer-styles, several of them top-fermented, and a whole cabinet-full of more offbeat brews. At least five different styles are brewed in Bavaria alone, with further major types in Berlin, Dortmund, Düsseldorf and Münster, and Cologne. Even before the war, the North–Eastern part of Germany had less to offer in the way of major styles, and that remains the case, though *Berliner* and *Pilsener* beers are common East of the border.

The laws governing beer protect purity, designation of origin, and strength. Each of the various styles fits into one of three broad brands indicating gravity: there is low-gravity *Schankbier* (7·0–8·0 degrees Balling, and 2·0–3·0 per cent alcohol by weight); regular *Vollbier* (11·0–14·0 gravity, 3·5–4·5 alcohol); and strong *Starkbier* (not less than 16·0 per cent gravity and often far more; not less than 5·0 per cent alcohol, and commensurately stronger).

If Germany is the world's most famous brewing nation, then Bavaria is its cellar, and Munich its beer-garden. Of the 1,600 breweries in the Federal Republic, a thousand are within the borders of its great southern state. Only a handful of Bavaria's breweries are in Munich, and Nürnberg has considerable historical claims as a rival brewing city, but

Mother's beer... and Mumme's

IT USED TO BE DUBBED as the beer for the nursing mother, but *Malzbier* has made something of a sprightly comeback in a health-conscious age. This roasted-malt brew has a rich flavour, and is rather sweet, but has a minimal alcoholic content (0·5 to 1·0 per cent). Its origins are probably rooted in the times when beer

was less of a drink than a food. Today, it has become popular as a nutritious drink among sportsmen and outdoor types. It is perhaps the only German beer-type in which there are truly national brands. Henninger *Karamalz* is widely available, and several brewers have a joint brand called *Vitamalz*. Some malt brews are sweetened with sugar but, under trades description laws, they may not be described as beer.

In the year when Christopher Columbus discovered America, the German brewer Christian Mumme produced a very high gravity, non-hopped beer to be taken by sailors on long voyages. This style won great renown, and was equally famous in Britain. Paradoxically, it was eventually driven from the high seas when the British started producing their own similar brews. The British still have Mather's *Black Beer*, in Yorkshire, as a memory of the style. This is a non-fermented malt extract, and the same applies to the German *Mumme*, which survives in its home town of Brunswick (Braunschweig). *Mumme* is available in the *Ratskeller* and other restaurants there. It is mixed with pale beers (as is Köstritz Black Beer, in East Germany) or drunk as a tonic.

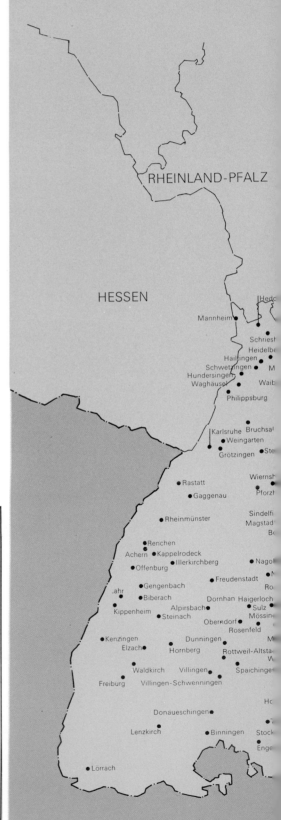

RHEINLAND-PFALZ

HESSEN

Mannheim
Schr[...]
Heidelbe[...]
Hailfingen
Schwetzingen
Hundersingen
Waghäusel
Waibl[...]
Philippsburg

Karlsruhe   Bruchsal
Weingarten
Grötzingen   Ste[...]

Rastatt
Gaggenau
Wiernsh[...]
Pforzh[...]

Rheinmünster
Sindelfi[...]
Magstad[...]
Be[...]

Renchen
Achern   Kappelrodeck
Offenburg   Illerkirchberg
Nago[...]

Freudenstadt
.ahr   Gengenbach
Biberach   Ro[...]
Dornhan   Haigerloch
Kippenheim   Alpirsbach   Sulz
Steinach   Mössin[...]
Oberndorf
Rosenfeld
Kenzingen   Dunningen   M[...]
Elzach   Hornberg   Rottweil-Altsta[...]
W[...]
Waldkirch   Villingen   Spaichinge[...]
Freiburg   Villingen-Schwenningen

Donaueschingen
Ho[...]

Lenzkirch   Binningen   Stock[...]
Enge[...]

Lörrach

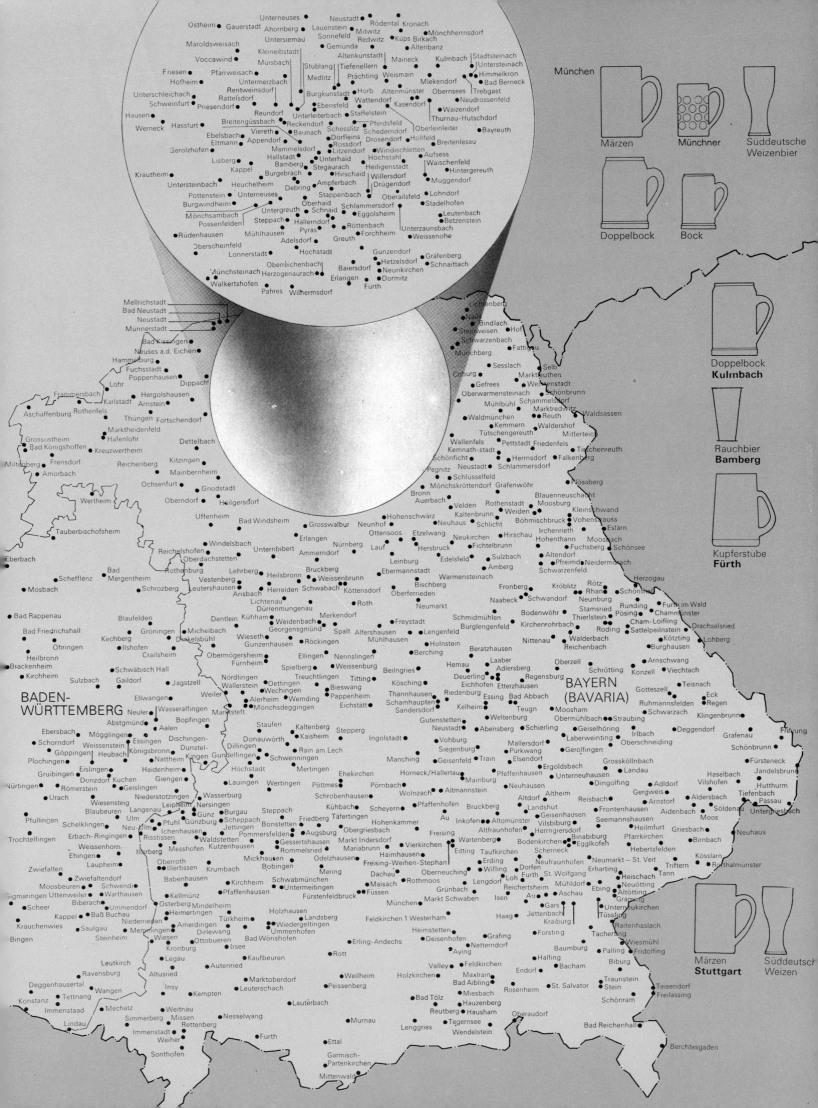

München

Märzen Münchner Süddeutsche Weizenbier

Doppelbock Bock

Doppelbock
Kulmbach

Rauchbier
Bamberg

Kupferstube
Fürth

Märzen
Stuttgart

Süddeutsch
Weizen

BADEN-WÜRTTEMBERG

**BAYERN
(BAVARIA)**

A blossoming hop industry

Hop-markets like the one at Nürnberg thrived when crops determined prices. The industry became more organized (right) in the 1930s. The South has five main growing areas.

Hersbruck

Jura

Spalt

Hallertau

Tettnang

GERMAN HOPS

The choicest varieties of hops grow well on the soil of Germany. Their reputation covers the whole world. Their aroma and flavour guarantee the brewing of the finest beers

Information in regard to supplies obtainable only through

Ausfuhrgesellschaft der Deutschen Brauwirtschaft m.b.H.
MÜNCHEN 27
Vilshofenerstraße 8

own. Not that they lack style. In 1975, a 27-year-old Franciscan nun from Mallersdorf, near Munich, passed her brewmaster's examination. Her mark was the highest among 30 male and worldly students. Sister Doris subsequently became brewmaster of the Mallersdorfer Klosterbrauerei, producing some well-regarded beers.

One of the earliest abbey breweries may have been at Weihenstephan, Freising, where the Benedictines recorded that they grew hops in 768. Hop-gardens are mentioned in records from several parts of Germany during the eighth and ninth centuries, though the evidence as to precisely when they were first used in brewing is less than conclusive.

Today, Germany is the world's largest producer of hops, and most of the cultivation takes place in the south. Bavaria has famous hop-gardens to the north of Munich, in the Hallertau, and near Nürnberg, at Spalt and Hersbruck. There are also gardens in the Jura, near Stuttgart, and at Tettnang, near the Bodensee.

The blossoming of Bavarian beer was not achieved without opposition from wine-growers. Brewing was prohibited "for ever" by the city of Würzburg in 1434. Like England's King Canute, the city fathers were unable to stem the tide.

Yet a greater cause for celebration, and one for which today's beer-drinkers have reason to be thankful, was provided by the Elector of Bavaria in 1516. Beset with debts arising from military campaigns, the Elector sought to develop the brewing industry as a source of taxable revenue. To further the reputation of the Bavarian brew, he issued a Purity Order, the *Reinheitsgebot*. This Order established that the ingredients of Bavarian beer be only malted barley, hops and water. This was subsequently amended to allow for wheat beers. The guaranteed retention of this law was a condition of Bavaria's entry into the Republic in 1919. Thus the *Reinheitsgebot* became the most famous of Germany's many laws on the purity of beer. The importance attached to this stipulation may be judged from the loftiness of the other conditions with which it was accompanied: that Bavaria continue to have separate representation at the Vatican, and that the suffix "Free State" remain in use. A quarter of a century later, the Bavarians neglected to ratify their membership of the post-war German Federal Republic, so the continued existence of "Free State" border markings remains appropriate.

The single-minded zeal of the Bavarians is

the state and its capital are barely divisible in beer lore. Breweries the world over, including a good few elsewhere in Germany, affect to be somehow Bavarian. There are beers which label themselves as being "Bavarian" from Norway to New Zealand, from Canada to Colombia. Even the Russians named one of their beers "Red Bavaria," presumably inspired by the state's Communist interlude of 1918–1919.

Today's Bavarians are considered to be an arch-conservative people, but the worldwide renown of their beers was won by a whole series of revolutionary changes, each of which made an important contribution to the history of brewing.

The first of these revolutions was brought about by an Act of God. Bavaria was originally devoted to wine, being the south-

ernmost part of Germany, with a temperate climate. Then a series of frosty winters hit the vineyards, and drinking habits had to be radically changed.

Happily for the Bavarians, their abbeys were already experienced in the brewing of beer. Unlike wine, beer provided welcome nutrition during Lent and other periods of fasting. As a result of this tradition, beer is still sometimes known in Germany as "liquid bread."

Germany still has at least a dozen active abbey breweries, mainly in Bavaria. These breweries produce a range of conventional German beer styles, with a bias towards the higher-gravity brews.

Unlike the Belgian abbeys, with their *Trappiste* beers, the German "cloister" breweries do not have a distinctive mode of their

Old ale . . . perhaps it was a very drinkable brew in Roman times, but today it is a solidified syrup. Germany's oldest beer is aging yet further in a museum. The purity law (detail below) is preserved at the Bavarian State Library, in Munich.

also evidenced in their adherence to the *Reinheitsgebot* even when they are producing beers for export to other countries, a philosophy which is not necessarily shared by brewers elsewhere in Germany. Such is the cost of brewing in this purist fashion that German beers are truly a luxury in many other parts of the world. Their snob-appeal has been further assured by the haughty performance of the Deutschmark. Such matters are of less consequence to the German brewers, with their hugely appreciative home market, than they are to their counterparts in some neighbouring countries to whom exports are crucial. When Munich's

famous Löwenbräu brewery mooted the idea that they might be excused the *Reinheitsgebot* in respect of exports, the suggestion was quashed amid some embarrassment. Purity may be less readily preserved when the good name of Munich's beers is licensed to brewers in other countries but, with that caveat, the words of a famous advertisement holds good: "If you run out of Champagne, open the Löwenbräu." This advice appears to be well taken, since Löwenbräu is one of Germany's biggest exporters of beer.

Small wonder that the Germans view with some amusement the suggestion from other

schencken/vnd verkauffen das füran allenthalben in airff dem Lannde/zů kain lain Gersten / Hopffen/ vn sölle werdn̄. Welher aber überfaren vnnd nit hallten richzöbrigkait / daſſelbig lich/ so offt es geschicht /

New brew . . . the beers of today are studied at the brewing faculty in Weihenstephan, Bavaria. The laboratory there has isolated 400 flavour compounds in beer, but as yet can identify only 150. Weihenstephan helps several breweries with quality control.

EEC countries that they themselves use the *Reinheitsgebot* as a protectionist measure against imported beers. Meanwhile, two EFTA states have long followed the example of the *Reinheitsgebot* in their own brewing industries: Norway by law, and Switzerland by voluntary convention.

The Bavarians are not above recognizing their debt to others. In the City Museum of Munich, an Ancient Egyptian wood-carving shows brewing being carried out. Another exhibit is a monument dedicated by a Roman beer-trader who served in the Rhine Navy. An etching by Martin Schongauer, dated 1480, is one of the first pictorial presentations of hops. The 78-hectolitre vat from the Nürnberg city brew-house was used in turn by all the members of the local guild, and the deeds and ledgers of the Munich brewers were kept in a magnificent inlaid chest. The permanent exhibition is a museum within a museum. Regular thematic exhibitions are also held.

The oldest surviving beer in Germany is a thick black syrup inside a vessel found when a Roman castle was excavated at Alzey, in the Rhineland Palatinate. The beer, and the oldest beer-jug in Germany, are on show at the local museum in Alzey. They are believed to date back to the fourth century.

ir wöllen auch sonderlichen/
rn Stetten/Märckthen/vñ
Pier/ inerer stückh / dañ al=
ser/ genomen vñ geprauch
vnsere Ordnung wissentlich
rde / dem sol von seiner ge=
Pier/ zustraff vnnachläß=
ommen werden. Redoch wo

Müncheners

THE HEADIEST PERIOD in Bavarian brewing was the 19th century, with the blossoming of the Sedlmayr Spatenbräu concern. Spatenbräu, still one of the great breweries of Munich, was something of a clearing-house for advances in knowledge during the 19th century, especially between the 1820s and 1870s. Gabriel Sedlmayr the Younger established an astonishing record of innovation, co-operating with brewers in Britain, Austria, Denmark and The Netherlands. Sedlmayr pioneered the use of steam power in breweries, collaborated with Carl von Linde in the development of refrigeration, and – most important of all – was associated with Pasteur and others in the study of fermentation. Although Sedlmayr did not invent bottom-fermentation, he was its greatest protagonist, and it was his work which did most to make *Münchener* a household word among beer-drinkers.

The burgeoning of the Munich breweries took place against a background of growing industrial capitalism in Europe. Simultaneously, a vast new market was being created by the emergence of a German empire which

Original Müncheners . . . dark (dunkel) and pale (hell). The pale was pioneered by Paulaner, but Hofbräuhaus and Spatenbräu also have their claims. Hacker-Pschorr (facing page) is another of Munich's great brewing names.

united Bavaria with Prussia. The dark, malty bottom-fermented *Münchener* became a standard beer-type, along with the copper-coloured *Wiener* and the golden, hoppy *Pilsener*.

The term *Münchener,* when it is used in other parts of the world, usually indicates a beer which aspires to the traditional dark style. Ironically, the same mode has all but vanished from the city of its origin. Although Munich's basic beers (and those of Bavaria as a whole) remain characteristically malty, they have become progressively paler since the Paulaner brewery introduced its *helles* (light) brew in 1928. Today, Munich's everyday beer is light in colour, but the drinker still feels the need to spell out his requirements. If he wants just an ordinary beer, he refers to it as a *helles*, as if in deference to Munich's dark and noble past. The custom of ordering a beer as a *helles* also spread to other parts of Germany. Thus, even in rendering obsolescent the classically dark *Münchener* tradition, the Bavarians introduced the word *helles* to the beer-drinker's vocabulary.

The Bavarian Brewmaster

Munich's master brewer was Gabriel Sedlmayr (left) of the Spatenbräu brewery. His pioneering work helped make the city, and the State of Bavaria, synonymous with bottom-fermented beers as the style's popularity spread throughout Europe. The group photograph, taken during the late 1800s, shows Sedlmayr's three sons (in the front row) with senior members of the Spatenbräu staff. The fame of Bavarian beer is celebrated in a lithograph produced in 1854 by an artist called von Benscler. The caption says: "A good beer is, indeed, the best of pleasures." The lithograph is exhibited in the City Museum, Munich.

Märzenbier

TRADITIONALLY, brewing had to be carried out in the winter, because the warm summer weather interfered with the fermentation processes. When the last of the winter season's beer was brewed each year in March, it was made a little stronger than usual, so that the alcohol content would preserve it through the summer months. By the end of summer, if any stocks of this "March beer" remained, they were ceremonially consumed, to make way for new brews. By then, the beer would have been very well fermented, and very strong.

The brewing of the last winter beer each March was rendered unnecessary by Sedlmayr's work on refrigeration, yet he also ensured that the *Märzenbier* tradition would be observed by future generations of beer-drinkers. He continued to brew a stronger beer to be ceremonially drunk at the end of summer, and his example was followed by his competitors. Sedlmayr gave his *Märzenbier* an unusual light-brown colouring, perhaps with an eye to the popular beers produced by his friend Anton Dreher, the great Viennese brewer.

While today's *helles* beer might have an alcohol content of about 3·5–3·9 per cent, a *Märzenbier* will be in the region of 4·5. *Märzenbiers* are fermented from a gravity of at least 13 degrees Balling in Bavaria, and not less than 12·5 in Baden-Württemberg. Bavaria's *Märzenbiers* are ceremonially downed at the famous Munich *Oktoberfest,* and those of Baden-Württemberg at Stuttgart's similar autumn event, the *Canstatter Wasen*.

The Munich *Oktoberfest,* the world's greatest beer-drinking celebration, was first held on the city's "village green" in 1810, to honour the Bavarian Queen Theresia (wife of King Ludwig). Today, the green is known as the *Theresienwiese* (Theresia's meadow), and the beer is accordingly dubbed the *Wiesenmärzen.* Each year, more than two million litres of *Wiesenmärzen* are served under canvas by the *Wiesenwirts* (marquee landlords), who start the celebration by holding a procession to the meadow. The

For the purist, the stoneware stein (right). The three-litre giant comes out occasionally, but the litre and half-litre sizes are more common. The half-litre size is shown in a traditional shape and a more modern version. The smallest stein holds a quarter-litre. The glasses hold, in descending order of size, one litre, 50cl, 40cl, 30cl, 25cl, and 20cl. *Following page:* Steins in action at the Oktoberfest, in Munich.

The other 'Oktoberfest'

Lord Mayor taps the first cask, watched over by Schwanthaler's "Bavarian maiden" statue, and the aplomb with which he carries out this ritual can affect his future civic credibility.

The *Oktoberfest* was originally a country fair, with a horse-race as its star attraction. The exhibitions of horses and cattle, the rifle-shooting contests, the merry-go-rounds, the brass bands and folk-dancing, the side-shows and freaks, gradually spread themselves until the event reached proportions which fill every hotel-room in the area with visitors from all over the world. Over the years, the event broadened to include a wide variety of performances and displays, including the presentation of new inventions (Edison's phonograph was a famous example). Its central theme is, nonetheless, the drinking of the *Märzenbier,* accompanied by pig's heels (*haxen*), roasted chickens (*hendl*), sausages and sauerkraut.

The prime rival to the *Oktoberfest* is the autumn fair of Stuttgart, which is held in the riverside district of Cannstatt. While the Müncheners call their meadow the *Wiesen* (or, in the Bavarian accent, the *Wies'n*), the people of Stuttgart call theirs the *Wasen*. Hence their fair is known as the *Canstatter Wasen*. This event was started in 1818, by the King of Württemberg, and its agricultural origins are more evident than those of the *Oktoberfest*. The symbol of the fair is a pillar of autumn fruits, about 25 metres high, a sort of thanksgiving totem for the harvest. Every third year, there is also an agricultural show, with several hundred exhibitors. Stuttgart can offer as a centrepiece for its festivities Germany's biggest fairground. Like the *Oktoberfest,* the Stuttgart celebration has its favourite savoury specialities, notably fried cockerels (*göckele*). There are four huge marquees, each accommodating about 4,500 drinkers.

At the *Oktoberfest, Märzenbier* is still commonly drunk out of the traditional one-litre *mass* (measure), though the *halbe* (half-litre) no longer meets with derision. Until the 1960s, the *mass* and the *halbe* were the everyday drinking vessels of Bavaria, but they were eventually overtaken by the 40-centilitre glass. At the *Canstatter Wasen,* the *halbe* is common, though the 30-centilitre glass is the regular drinking-vessel of Baden-Württemberg. Even this glass is gradually being replaced by the 25-centilitre vessel used in the rest of Germany. Until the 1960s, beer was often served in simple stoneware steins, decorated with the name of the brewer, but they, too, have largely fallen out of use.

From its earliest days, the Stuttgart fair has been a popular event. The royal proclamation (right) in 1818 clearly caught the Swabian imagination. The fair is held at the end of September and beginning of October.

In 1857, Napoleon III was among the royal party (top) at the fair. More than a century later, the event retains its agricultural theme, and the column of fruit is still its symbol (left).

Bock and doppelbock

PEOPLE WHO DRINK strong beer may subsequently fail to enunciate words properly. They may also muddle the memories of the events which have befallen them. This has to be taken into account when episodes of beer mythology are considered. The abbreviation and corruption of Einbeck is a case in point, though the people of Lower Saxony may consider the mistreatment of the town's name to be fair exchange for more than 600 years of beery fame.

Einbeck, not far from Hanover, was once the most famous brewing city in Europe, and probably the world. It grew from an estate into a Hanseatic city during the 13th century, at a time when the principal occupations of its inhabitants were the weaving of linen and the brewing of beer. Elsewhere, the brewing of beer for sale was largely in the hands of either abbeys or ducal courts, but the city fathers of Einbeck licensed their citizens to carry out the trade, in return for taxes which were levied on production. Whenever they wanted to produce a batch of beer, these privileged citizens were visited by the town's brewmaster, who brought with him all the necessary equipment. The architectural style of old Einbeck still recalls this period: houses were built with high doors, so that the brewing vessel could be brought through; there were large, well-aired lofts for the storage of grain; and spacious cellars for the maturing beer.

Martin Luther was given Einbeck beer as a wedding present by the city of Wittenberg, and received a barrel from the Duke of Brunswick to fortify him during the Diet of Worms, such was the fame of the brew.

Einbeck beer was exported to major Hanseatic cities throughout Germany and the Baltic, including Hamburg, Riga and Stockholm, and is even reputed to have reached

The animated bocks . . . the goat has become the symbol of the style. The Rosenbrauerei, at Kaufbeuren, to the west of Munich, hangs tiny goats round the necks of its two bock bottles.

Jerusalem. The horse-teams which hauled the beer to the ports were escorted by mercenary soldiers to guard against bandits, and the brew was given a high alcoholic strength to preserve its condition during these long journeys.

These eventful days are recalled in a small museum at today's thriving Einbecker Brauhaus, which is owned by the DUB-Schultheiss group. The Einbecker brewery produces more than half a million hectolitres a year, including a Ur-Bock which provides, at least in name, a reminder of past glories.

Paradoxically, the long-term renown of

Einbeck owes less to the present-day beers of Lower Saxony than it does to those of Bavaria. It was a Duke of Brunswick who took Einbeck beer to the South. He transported several casks of the brew to Munich for his wedding party when he married the daughter of a Southern German aristocrat. The beer proved so popular that wedding guests began to order it for themselves, and a master brewer was eventually hired from Einbeck to produce the beer locally. With the passing of the years, and the vagaries of the Bavarian accent, the name became *Oanbock* (according to a dictionary of 1789), and then simply *Bock Bier*.

Einbeck beer was one of the early products of the Hofbräuhaus, in Munich, which was set up as a Court brewery by the Elector William of Bavaria in 1589. The Hofbräuhaus has encountered its moments of notoriety since, but it survives as a proud Munich institution: a brewery, drinking-place and restaurant in the heart of the city, owned by the Bavarian State. The Hof-Bräu (*H-B*) beers are well known, and include a couple of *bock* brands.

Under German beer law, a brew described as a *bock* must have a gravity of not less than 16 degrees Balling. Historically, *bock* beers were made with roasted malts. Today, pale *bocks* are increasingly fashionable, but the brew remains extremely rich and malty-tasting. Breweries all over Germany produce *bock* beers, but the style is strongly associated with Bavaria.

The Elector of Bavaria furthered the *bock* legend when he invited to his land Italian monks from the order of St Francis of Paula during the Counter-Reformation period. These monks took up the custom of brewing, and in 1780 the Court gave them permission to sell their beers to the public. They produced an even stronger beer, and the style eventually became known as *doppel* (Double) *bock*. The brothers of St Francis of Paula named their beer Salvator, after the Saviour, and one of today's *doppelbock* brews is its direct descendant. During the Napoleonic period, the Paulaner monastery brewery passed into the hands of the State, and it was later leased to a private company. That concern grew into one of Munich's great breweries, Paulaner-Salvator-Thomasbräu, which still brands its name on a celebrated *doppelbock*.

The Salvator was originally brewed for the saint's day of the monastery, and St Joseph's Day (March 19) is still the beginning of Munich's *Frühjahrsbierfest* (springtime beer celebrations). The lore of Munich holds that a strong beer at this time is especially

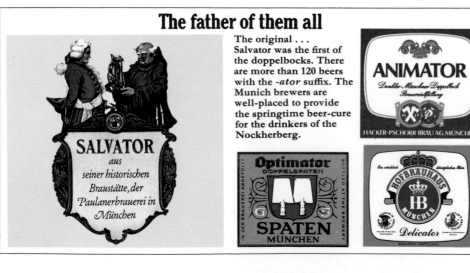

The father of them all

The original . . . Salvator was the first of the doppelbocks. There are more than 120 beers with the *-ator* suffix. The Munich brewers are well-placed to provide the springtime beer-cure for the drinkers of the Nockherberg.

The beer of Martin Luther

At the Diet of Worms, Martin Luther was fortified with Einbeck beer . . . and his portrait was used on the label in the earliest days of exports to the United States.

Although Einbeck beer has been brewed since 1351, it was not bottled until the mid 1800s. This original bottle, still corked, was found in Einbeck in 1965.

Earlier exports went by the cask, on drays which were given an armed guard. This dray from the Einbeck museum is perhaps more robust than it looks. It may have travelled thousands of miles . . . on journeys running as far as Stockholm and Amsterdam.

beneficial to the health, and a celebratory drink or two is known as "the springtime beer cure." The first glass of the season is presented to the Prime Minister of Bavaria with the ceremonial invocation, *Bibas princeps optime*. There are official receptions, functions and informal celebrations in the famous beer-gardens of the Nockherberg area, the city's brewery quarter.

Such festivities receive a further lease of life with the Maytime celebrations, and some breweries produce a *Maibock*.

A *Bockbier* celebration is held in Hanover during the autumn, and in several other places the mythology of this beer-type has leapt from the early part of the year to the later season. Since *bock* means billy-goat in German, it is sometimes regarded as a seasonal beer for the season of Capricorn, which straddles Christmas. Most German breweries produce a *bock* or *doppelbock* gift-package at Christmas, and these are popular presents, especially for business clients.

Neighbouring countries further confuse the mythology of *bock* beer. The Dutch *bock*, which is strongly associated with the goat symbol, aspires to the German style in its gravity and palate. So do the Danish, Swiss and Austrian derivations, but the Belgian and French *Maibock* and *bock* beers are low-gravity brews which have not the remotest claim to the name. Their designation seems to be derived from the size of bottle in which they are provided, or the glasses from which they are drunk.

Although the original *doppelbock* was Salvator, there are many more. In Munich alone, Löwenbräu has its Triumphator; Spatenbräu its Optimator; the Hofbräuhaus its Delicator; Augustiner its Maximator; and Hacker-Pschorr its Animator. There are more than 120 beers registered with the *-ator* suffix which has become the traditional attachment to the *doppelbock*, and all are required to have a gravity of not less than 18 degrees.

The strongest beer in the world is a *doppelbock* brewed in Kulmbach, not far from Bayreuth, in the Northern part of Bavaria. The Kulminator of the Erste Kulmbacher brewery has a density of 28 per cent, and an alcoholic strength of 13·2 per cent by volume. It is brewed with pale malts, but the enormous concentration of fermentable solids produces a mellow brown colour and a very rich, malty palate. The high density is achieved by a technique of concentration during which the beer is partially frozen so that water can be extracted, a method reminiscent of that used in the production of some sparkling wines.

Der Bock-Keller in München.

Berliner Weisse

Brewery in Brandenburg, 16c.

SINCE MAN FIRST BREWED, he seems to have found barley the most agreeable grain from which to produce his malts. Barley is the easiest of grains to malt, and in the basic community the brewer could take all he needed without depriving the baker, who preferred other cereals.

Not that things were always so well ordered. Sometimes brewers had to make do with what was available, taking into account climate and soil, or to reap from fields of mixed cereals. Even in the 19th and 20th centuries, home-brewers in Norway are recorded as having used rye and oats, though the resultant beers are said to have been unpleasantly bitter. Sometimes a solution was found in the mixing of two different grains to find the right balance.

The practice of brewing with a mixture of barley and wheat is said to have gained its first great popularity in both Britain and Bohemia, and to have spread to Germany from those two regions. Although Belgium still has its different indigenous styles of wheat beer, one in the Senne valley and the other in Hoegaarden, Germany is without question the world's greatest producer of such brews. Germany also has two very popular styles of wheat beer, of which *Berliner Weisse* ("White") is undoubtedly the most famous.

This classic beer-type belongs to Northern Germany. It seems to have first flowered in Hamburg, and then been further nurtured in Hanover by the great 16th-century brewer Cord Broyhan. Wheat beer became a favoured Prussian style under Frederick Wilhelm, "the soldiers' king." He even had his son –

later to become Frederick the Great – trained as a master brewer. Frederick Wilhelm pronounced that "beer is the best for our climate," thus taking a sideswipe at the grapy habits of the southern Germans. In fact, the beer which he favoured had such qualities that it hardly met with their disapproval.

The light and vinous quality of *Weisse* beer made it popular among visitors, and immigrants, from wine-drinking countries. The beer won notable affection in the Huguenot refugee quarter of Berlin, and it has on occasion been dubbed as the brewers' answer to Riesling. The sparkle of *Berliner Weisse* has led to loftier comparisons, too. Napoleon's occupying forces are said to have referred to it as *le Champagne du Nord*. A handsome soubriquet, but Berliners may prefer the more civically-minded description, "the Champagne of the Spree."

The *Berliner* beer is more of a pale, golden brew than a white one, but its fine colour provided a splendid contrast to the dark products of Munich when the two great capitals were competing fiercely to quench the thirst of a newly united Empire. The success of the *Weisse* brews encouraged the Bavarian brewers in the further development of their own wheat beers, while their influence in the Prussian capital helped ensure that Berlin retains even today a strong *Bock* tradition. After Bavaria and Lower Saxony (the Einbeck state), Berlin is Germany's third great centre of *bock* brewing.

"White" is a particular misnomer for a beer which is usually drunk either red or green. However delightful they may find the beer itself, visitors from other countries are apt to be shocked by these colours, but Germans are equally surprised at the thought of drinking a *Berliner Weisse* without a *schuss* (a dash of raspberry juice) or *Waldmeister* (essence of woodruff). This custom may derive from the popularity of such flavours in Germany's traditional springtime punch, the "May Bowl." Or their use may simply have originated from the days before hops were the commonly accepted agent of flavouring and preservation in beers. Even in the 19th century, it was recorded that a Berlin brewer called Josty continued to flavour his beer with herbs rather than hops.

Sweet woodruff, which is becoming the more popular of the two flavours, is known to botanists as *asperula odorata*. It grows only in Europe and Mediterranean Africa, and has historically been most widely used in Germany and Austria. Woodruff has been employed in perfumes; as a tonic; in tea; and in wines and liqueurs as well as beer.

The famous English expert Gerard said in the 16th century: "It is reported to be put into wine to make a man merrie, and to be good for the hart and liver." The tradition thrives among Berlin's beer-drinkers, and at least one brewer has used the red of the raspberry, the pale amber of the natural drink, and the green of the *Waldmeister* to project a "traffic-light" advertising theme.

Berliner Weisse is a tender, but seductive, beer. It has a gravity of only about eight degrees Balling, but is very fully fermented. The beer is brewed from three parts of barley malt to one of wheat, and fermented on top. A second fermentation is induced by the addition of a lactobacillus, and the beer is conditioned in the bottle. Fermentation and conditioning take place at the relatively warm temperature of about 20°C (68°F). Traditionally, bottles were buried in the warm earth for several months to mature.

The mature brew has a full and fruity bouquet, and the beer is extremely popular as a refreshing summer drink. The flavour and condition of the beer can best be enjoyed at between 10° and 15°C (50–60°F), at which gentle temperature it is surprisingly quenching. It must be poured carefully so that the sediment does not enter the glass and impair the colour. The dash of juice is also added slowly, so that the beer does not froth in too excitable a manner. Sometimes, again to the astonishment of the uninitiated, this colourful combination is then enjoyed with the help of a straw.

Berliners colloquially refer to their drinking-glass as a *molle* (bread mould), perhaps in subconscious memory of the historic links between brewing and baking. For them, the *molle* is a symbol of the beer-drinking culture. *Berliner Weisse* is most often drunk out of the huge, bowl-shaped stemmed glasses which are favoured by the city's Schultheiss brewery. Even at the turn of the century, Schultheiss was Germany's biggest brewer, and that position was consolidated when the company was joined by Dortmunder Union Brewery in the 1970s. The other great brewer of *Berliner Weisse* is the city's Kindl brewery, which prefers a less typical "belly-shaped" glass. *Weisse* beer is still brewed in the East, and is widely available in German cities other than Berlin. It is also exported, but only on a very small scale, being such a lively brew.

It is perhaps best enjoyed, though, in a café on the famous Kurfürstendamm, or in one of the big beer palaces which are another of Berlin's characteristic contributions to beer-drinking habits.

Berliners get the green light

With a touch of poetic licence, one brewer symbolized the three versions of Berliner Weisse as traffic lights. Bowl-shaped glasses are customarily used. The one on the left is the most basic shape. Woodruff (right) is the most popular flavour. It is a plant of between four inches and a foot (10–30cm) in height, which grows in deciduous or mixed woodland.

Süddeutsche Weizen

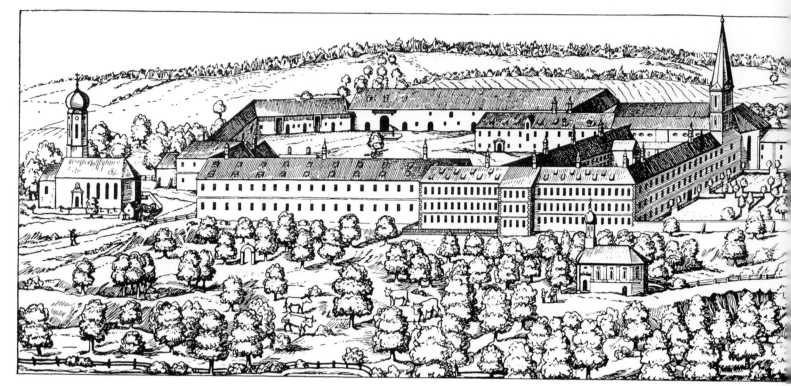

ANYTHING THE NORTH GERMANS can do, the South Germans can do better. Or equally well. Or in a quite different style. The Prussians could give the royal seal of approval to their *Weisse* beers, and the Bavarians could do the same for their equally old and quite different *Weizenbiers*. The Northern *Weisse* beer has a lineage which stretches beyond Hanover and Hamburg, and tenuously to Britain. The Southern *Weizenbier* came from Bohemia, and may have been brought there by Slavonic tribes.

The differences are greater than that. They are two wholly separate and distinct styles.

While *Weisse* is a low-gravity beer (and classified thus as a *Schankbier*), *Weizenbier* has a density of not less than 12·4, and sometimes nearer 14 degrees (and is thus a *Vollbier*). While *Weisse* is so called because of its pale colour, *Weizenbier* means, uncompromisingly, "Wheat Beer." Only a quarter of the malts in *Weisse* are made from wheat, but *Weizenbier* is made with not less than a third wheat malts, and often far more. Sometimes the brewer uses twice as much wheat as barley.

Like the Northern brew, the Southern beer is top-fermented, and only very lightly hopped. Its fruity palate is also very malty, yet it remains sharply refreshing. It is sparkling and full-bodied, a very individualistic beer-type, brewed with all the sensitivity and quality which the German brewer can

so readily muster. Fruit juices and essences are not normally added to the South German brew, but a slice of lemon enhances the fruity tang. *Weizenbier* is normally drunk out of a very tall, vase-shaped glass.

The robust tradition of *Süddeutsche Weizenbier* is a splendid by-product of tricky times at the *Hofbräuhaus*. Only 15 years after opening this establishment to produce brown barley beers, the Elector of Bavaria decided in 1603 that he must take over all rights to make wheat brews in his Duchy, ostensibly to protect supplies of the grain. As all other brewers were thus banned from producing this type of beer, the Elector's product had some exclusivity. He further manipulated its marketing by forcing some publicans to take his beer against their wishes. The Elector had the authority to license the sale of beer, so it was not easy for publicans to argue with him.

Further *Hofbräuhäuser* were also set up in other Bavarian towns and cities to expand sales of royal beer. As the centuries rolled drunkenly by, and various armed conflicts brought about the need to raise more taxes, some of these *Hofbräuhäuser* were sold, complete with all brewing rights. More and more brewers were licensed to produce *Weizenbier* until it was freely available throughout the Duchy, becoming one of Bavaria's distinguished national beers.

The beer's popularity has also been boosted since the earliest days by its reputation

as a tonic, or even a medicine. Like many beliefs which are deeply embedded in folk history, this tale may well have sound foundations. *Weizenbier* has a particularly high content of vitamin B_2, as lactoflavine, in its yeast. Just as the low-carbohydrate qualities of *Berliner Weisse* may have contributed to its growth in popularity during the late 1960s and 1970s, so the same may hold for the tonic properties of *Weizenbier*. Prosperous Germany is a health-conscious society, and the yeasty magic of *Weizenbier* must have helped Bavarian wheat brewers achieve a quadruple increase in its sales during the same two decades.

Purists like to know before they order a *Weizenbier* that the yeast has not been filtered out, and a good many Bavarian brewers make a point of indicating that this vital ingredient has not been removed. These brewers use terms like *Hefeweizen* ("Wheat beer with yeast") to describe their products. A good example is the small local brewery at Graming, near Altötting, which specialises in wheat beers. At the other end of the scale, the huge Löwenbräu brewery, of Munich, has a *Hefe-Weizenbier*.

Other brewers adopt exactly the opposite practice. They produce *Hefefrei* ("Yeast-free") beers. The drinker who likes a sparkling glass then needs to take less trouble when he pours his beer. The yeast is in the beer during brewing, of course, but it is then removed by filtration. Good examples

The abbey of Weihenstephan had already been brewing for 500 years when the engraving below was made. Today, the State brewery there (below, right) produces some fine beers, including a Weisse, a Weizenbock and a Weizenbier.

Stuttgart's top six

In contrast with the bowl-shaped glass used for Berliner Weisse, a very tall, vase-like vessel is preferred for the South German wheat beer, with its distinctive full flavour.

The people of Stuttgart regard Weizenbier as a local style, and their Sanwald brewery specializes in top-fermented beers, with six wheat brews.

are produced by the specialist wheat-beer brewery at Erding, and the State brewery at Weihenstephan.

There are many colourful and ambitious variations on this great Bavarian theme. Many brewers produce bottom-fermented wheat beers which they call *Lager-Weisse*; there are strong *Weizenbocks,* of not less than 16 degrees, a fine Bavarian combination of beer-styles; and potent wheat beers of springtime strength, not less than 18 degrees, which are known as *Weizen-Frühjahrsstark-bier*.

Such delights are usually the product of Bavarian brewers, and especially those in the "Old Duchy" area close to Munich. As the description *Süddeutsche Weizenbier* suggests, the style is also popular in Baden-Württemberg. Beer-drinkers in Stuttgart are quite ready to claim *Weizenbier* as their own on the basis of the example produced by the Sanwald brewery, which specialises in top-fermented beers. Northern brewers are also increasingly taking up the style, and a notable example is the huge Henninger concern, of Frankfurt.

As if such a dizzying variety of wheat beers were not enough, these brews are also mixed with lemonade to produce a drink which is colloquially known as *Russ.* A similar drink made with ordinary beer is called a *Radlermass* (cyclists' beer). Cyclists are presumably expected to get very thirsty, but not to get drunk.

Where the brewer is king

Many cities of old Germany had their own
municipal breweries. If the city concerned
was the capital of a duchy or kingdom within
Germany, it would have a "royal" brewery.
Today, many such breweries survive under the
ownership of the State in which they are located.
No *Bürgerliche* brewery, no *Staatsbrauerei*, no
Köningliches Hofbräuhaus is more famous than the
one in Munich, which is now owned by the
State of Bavaria. The Hofbräuhaus in Munich
has experienced its moments of notoriety, but
it is also credited with having been a pioneer
in the brewing of both bock and *Süddeutsche
Weizen* styles. The Hofbräuhaus brewery (far right)
is on the Inner Weinerstrasse. Its wooden
lagering casks (left) bear witness to its antiquity. For
more than three hundred years, the beers of the
Hofbräuhaus were marketed at what a magazine
published in 1903 called "a grim, dingy tavern."
The same magazine reported on extensive
modernizations to the tavern, reproducing an
engraving (far left) of the "new" East Courtyard.
The photograph on the right shows the present-day
main frontage, facing on to the thoroughfare known
as the Platzl. The Hofbräuhaus tavern remains the
most famous drinking-place in Munich.

Pilsener-style beers

THE TOWN OF PILSEN is in Bohemia, which is a part of Czechoslovakia, not Germany. Bohemia's eventful history has, though, been mightily influenced by its giant neighbour and the cultural links run deep.

Pilsen has been a beer-producing town since the Wenceslas kings ruled Bohemia, but its modern renown dates from the early introduction of Bavarian bottom-fermentation techniques into a new municipal brewery in 1842. This marriage of Bohemian and Bavarian skills produced a beer paler than any which had been seen before, and with a remarkable hop bitterness. The new beer quickly became famous not only throughout Bohemia and the other territories of the Austro–Hungarian Empire, but also in the German states. *Pilsener* became the most fashionable imported beer in Imperial Berlin, and the style was imitated by brewers all over Europe.

Fame was a mixed blessing for the Pilsen brewery. The sales of the *Pilsener* beer exceeded all the original, and humble, expectations – but the imitators were diluting its reputation. The brewery took its worries to the High Court, where a judgment worthy of Solomon was reached. While it was decided that *Pilsener* might well suggest a style rather than a town of origin, it was decreed that the true source of beer must always be incorporated in the name. An example from those days which still flourishes in East Germany is *Raderberger-Pilsener*.

The fashionability of *Pilsener*-style beers is as strong today as ever it was, and growing. The original product from Czechoslovakia sells half a million hectolitres each year in Germany, by far the biggest import in an understandably chauvinistic beer market. Meanwhile, the biggest segment of German brewers' own output is in *Pilsener*-style beers.

It is odd to see the Münchener brewery which bears the historic Sedlmayr name promoting its *Spaten-Pils* as "our best beer," or the Dortmunder breweries reducing output of their own eponymous product in favour of *Pilsener*-style beers. Perhaps because habits and instincts die hard, the South German brewers still produce a *Pilsener* which is maltier than the description might properly suggest, but those in the North offer some excellent examples of the style.

The cachet which attaches to *Pilsener* beers is also awarded by drinkers to those brewers who produce well-regarded brands as their house speciality. The Simon brewery at Bitburg, in the Rhineland Palatinate, is one such example. Its *Bitburger-Pils,* selectively distributed, has brought great renown to the company. Much the same applies to *König-Pilsener,* from Duisburg, and *Pils-Krone,* from Dortmund's Wenker brewery.

This latter brewery even extended the *Pilsener* cult to the cocktail circuit, by helping produce a novel beery tidbit. The Kronen brew is used instead of water in the baking of a *Pilsener Loaf,* thus reuniting two of man's earliest arts.

All three are privately-owned companies, and a fourth such example is the Stauder brewery, of Essen, which also produces a fine *Pilsener.* The Stauder brewery also has its own private collection of more than 100,000 drip-mats. Worth a detour, as Michelin would say, but a viewing should be booked by telephone.

Further North, the Hanover brewery of Herrenhausen advertises its *Pilsener* as having been "lagered for five weeks," and two of the Hamburg breweries have subsidiaries which produce notable examples of the style. A Holsten subsidiary evocatively describes its contribution as *Moravia-Pils.* Bavaria-St Pauli (a Hamburg brewery, despite its name) has a subsidiary in German Friesland, at Oldenburg, producing *Jever Pilsener.* This is superbly well-hopped and dry beer, at its best when chilled to about eight degrees centigrade (46°F).

Pilsener-style beers make a splendid aperitif, and are increasingly popular as a mealtime drink.

Imitation can be a fine flattery. Pilsen should be proud.

Among Germany's popular "Pils" brews, a great favourite is that produced at Bitburg. The brewery's foundation features in a frieze (far left) which tells the story of Bitburg's cosmopolitan past. *Following page:* Dortmund takes the Pils track.

The brewing-towns of Northern Germany

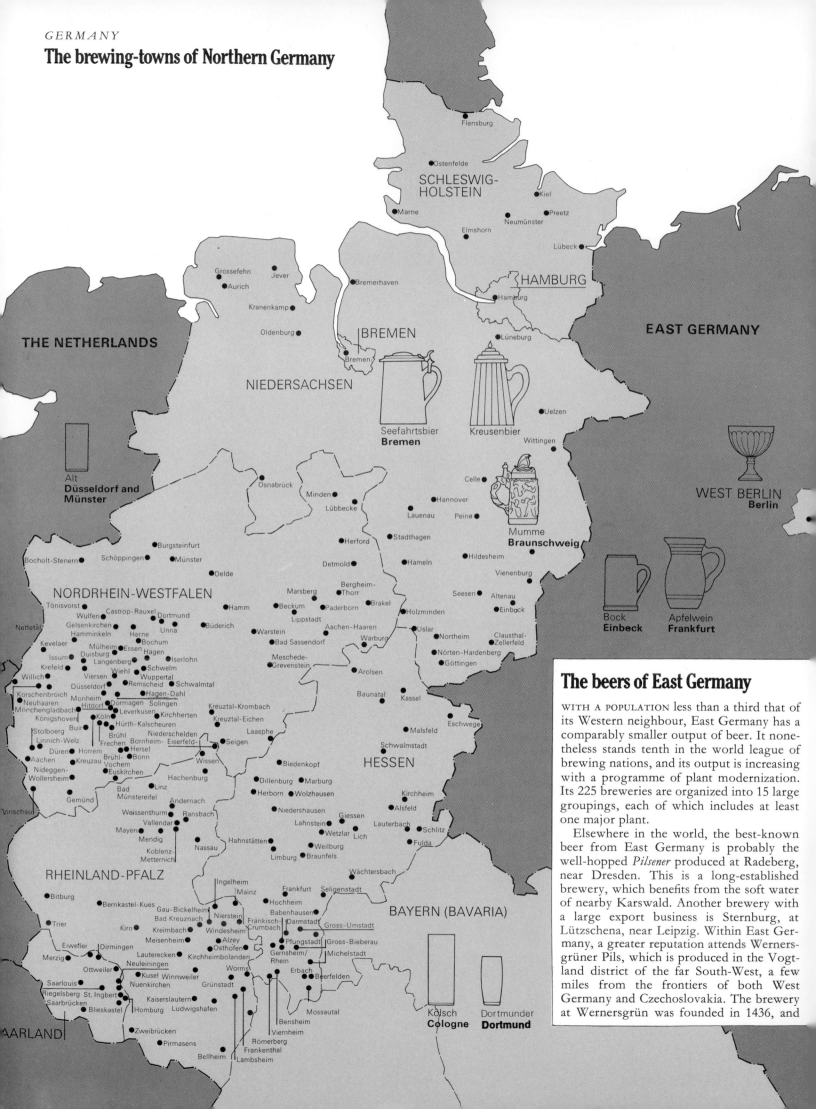

SCHLESWIG-
HOLSTEIN

Flensburg

Ostenfelde

Kiel

Marne
Neumünster
Preetz

Elmshorn

Lübeck

HAMBURG

Grossefehn
Jever

Aurich

Bremerhaven

Hamburg

THE NETHERLANDS

Kranenkamp

Oldenburg

BREMEN

EAST GERMANY

Lüneburg

Bremen

NIEDERSACHSEN

Uelzen

Wittingen

Seefahrtsbier
Bremen

Kreusenbier

Celle

Osnabrück

Minden

Hannover

WEST BERLIN
Berlin

Alt
**Düsseldorf and
Münster**

Lübbecke

Lauenau

Peine

Mumme
Braunschweig

Herford

Stadthagen

Burgsteinfurt

Detmold

Hameln

Hildesheim

Bocholt-Stenern
Schöppingen
Münster

Oelde

Vienenburg

Marsberg

Bergheim-
Thorr

Seesen
Altenau

NORDRHEIN-WESTFALEN

Hamm
Beckum
Paderborn
Brakel

Holzminden

Einbeck

Tönisvorst
Wulfen
Castrop-Rauxel
Dortmund
Büderich
Lippstadt

Aachen-Haaren

Uslar

Clausthal-
Zellerfeld

Bock
Einbeck

Apfelwein
Frankfurt

Nettetal
Gelsenkirchen
Hamminckeln
Herne
Unna
Warstein

Bochum

Bad Sassendorf

Warburg

Northeim

Nörten-Hardenberg

Kevelaer
Mülheim
Essen
Hagen
Iserlohn

Meschede-
Grevenstein

Göttingen

Issum
Duisburg
Langenberg
Schwelm

Arolsen

The beers of East Germany

WITH A POPULATION less than a third that of its Western neighbour, East Germany has a comparably smaller output of beer. It nonetheless stands tenth in the world league of brewing nations, and its output is increasing with a programme of plant modernization. Its 225 breweries are organized into 15 large groupings, each of which includes at least one major plant.

Elsewhere in the world, the best-known beer from East Germany is probably the well-hopped *Pilsener* produced at Radeberg, near Dresden. This is a long-established brewery, which benefits from the soft water of nearby Karswald. Another brewery with a large export business is Sternburg, at Lützschena, near Leipzig. Within East Germany, a greater reputation attends Wernersgrüner Pils, which is produced in the Vogtland district of the far South-West, a few miles from the frontiers of both West Germany and Czechoslovakia. The brewery at Wernersgrün was founded in 1436, and

Krefeld
Viersen
Wiehl
Wuppertal
Remscheid
Schwalmtal

Willich

Baunatal

Kassel

Korschenbroich
Monheim
Hagen-Dahl

Neuhaaren
Hitdorf
Dormagen
Solingen

Mönchengladbach
Leverkusen
Kirchherten

Kreuztal-Krombach

Königshoven
Köln
Hürth-Kalscheuren

Kreuztal-Eichen

Stolberg
Buir
Niederschelden
Eschwege

Linnich-Welz
Brühl
Frechen
Bornheim-
Eiserfeld-

Laasphe

Düren
Horrem
Hersel
Seigen

Malsfeld

Aachen
Kreuzau
Brühl-
Vochem
Bonn
Wissen

Schwalmstadt

Nideggen-
Wollersheim
Euskirchen

Biedenkopf

HESSEN

Hachenburg

Tonschau

Bad
Münstereifel

Dillenburg
Marburg

Kirchheim

Gemünd
Andernach

Herborn
Wolzhausen

Alsfeld

Weissenthurm
Ransbach

Niedershausen

Lauterbach

Mayen
Vallendar

Lahnstein
Giessen

Schlitz

Mendig
Nassau

Wetzlar
Lich

Fulda

Koblenz-
Metternich

Limburg
Weilburg
Braunfels

RHEINLAND-PFALZ

Hahnstätten

Wächtersbach

Ingelheim

Frankfurt
Seligenstadt

Bitburg

Mainz

Hochheim

Bernkastel-Kues

Gau-Bickelheim
Nierstein

Babenhausen

BAYERN (BAVARIA)

Trier

Bad Kreuznach

Fränkisch-
Crumbach
Darmstadt
Gross-Umstadt

Kirn
Kreimbach
Windesheim

Pfungstadt
Gross-Bieberau

Eiweller
Dirmingen
Meisenheim
Alzey
Osthofen

Michelstadt

Merzig
Lauterecken
Kirchheimbolanden

Gernsheim/
Rhein

Neuleiningen

Erbach
Beerfelden

Ottweiler
Kusel
Winnweiler

Worms

Saarlouis
Nuenkirchen
Grünstadt

Riegelsberg
St. Ingbert

Kölsch
Cologne

Dortmunder
Dortmund

Saarbrücken
Kaiserslautern

Blieskastel
Homburg
Ludwigshafen

Mossautal

SAARLAND
Zweibrücken

Bensheim

Pirmasens

Viernheim

Römerberg
Frankenthal
Lambsheim

Bellheim

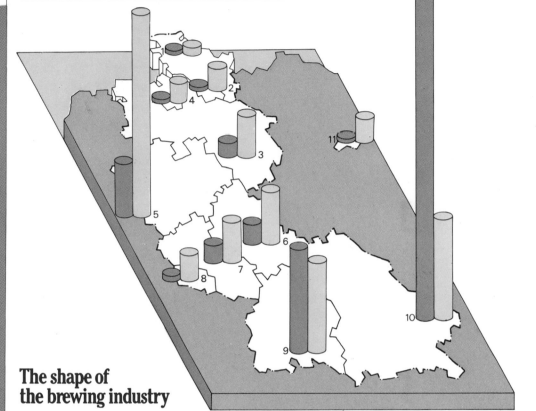

		Percentage of Germany's breweries State by State	Percentage of beer output State by State
1	Schleswig-Holstein	0.37 *(6)*	0.9
2	Hamburg	0.24 *(4)*	2.9
3	Lower Saxony	1.96 *(32)*	5.5
4	Bremen	0.37 *(6)*	2.4
5	North Rhine-Westphalia	7.40 *(121)*	29.4
6	Hesse	3.00 *(49)*	7.5
7	Rhineland Palatinate	2.20 *(36)*	5.8
8	Saarland	0.67 *(11)*	2.6
9	Baden-Württemberg	14.49 *(237)*	12.6
10	Bavaria	68.58 *(1,122)*	27.7
11	West Berlin	0.72 *(12)*	2.7

The shape of the brewing industry

today has a capacity of 650,000 hectolitres. The East Germans describe Wernersgrün as "our biggest brewing village."

The South-West, and especially the Thüringen region, is the country's traditional brewing area but several new breweries were commissioned in the North during the 1960s and 1970s. The breweries at New Brandenburg, Schwerin and Rostock belong to this generation. Until the late 1950s, East Germany had to import all of its hops, but it is now virtually self-sufficient. The centre of the hop industry is Halle, with 700 hectares.

The price of expansion has been the introduction of agitated batch-fermentation and lagering periods of days rather than weeks. The most widely-available beers are pasteurized *Pils*, and the *Reinheitsgebot* is not applied. Premium beer brewed without the use of additives is known as *Pilsator*.

The *Märzenbier* of the East is similar to its Western counterpart, sometimes of a marginally higher density, and usually unfiltered, with a yeasty sediment. *Bock* beers have a density of 16·0 degrees or more, but are less well attenuated than their Western counterparts. They are most commonly pale, but dark examples can occasionally be found. *Porter,* a style not normally found in West Germany, is brewed in the East. It has a density of 18·0 degrees, and salt is added to help create the characteristic palate. This style is intended to resemble a medium English *stout*, though the connection is tenuous. East German drinkers are apt to mix *porter* with *Pils* in a sort of Teutonic Black-and-Tan, though the anguished brewers protest that this ruins the palates of both. A twelve-degree *schwarzbier* (black beer), produced with dark malts, is also mixed with lighter brews. This affectionately-regarded style is local to the small town of Bad Köstritz, between Jena and Gera. Like their Western neighbours, the East Germans have *malz* beer, but this is sometimes "enriched" with sugar, in which case it is known as *doppelkaramelbier*. East Berlin also has its own *weissbier*. As in the West, this is a celebrated speciality.

Dortmunders

DORTMUND IS GERMANY'S biggest brewing city. It was given brewing rights as a free city by the Emperor in 1293, at a time when there was only a very limited interest in beer elsewhere in Germany.

A most colourful history attended the Dortmund brewers' rise to eminence. Their beer gained such popularity in medieval times that it was exported for sale in other Westphalian towns like Münster, Bielefeld and Minden. These towns, wishing to protect their own brewers and the revenue which they produced in taxes, protested to Dortmund by ultimatum. Dortmund is said to have responded by providing its beer transports with armed escorts. Legend has it that the other towns then sent posses to ambush the transports and shoot holes into the casks. If the sharp-shooters were then apprehended by the Dortmunders, mythology insists, they were drowned in beer.

The original brew of the city was top-fermented from wheat, but this was eventually supplanted by barley beer, and bottom-fermentation was introduced by the Kronen brewery in 1843. A great deal of anxious experimentation followed before the Union brewery produced in the 1870s the style of beer which has become associated with the city. Bismarck "turned for consolation" to the Dortmunder Union beer. On one occasion, he met the brew-master, praised his work, and expressed envy at his income.

The ordinary beer of Dortmund is sometimes known as *lager*, though this is less of a drinker's term in Germany than a brewer's (and signifies different things in different countries). The true *Dortmunder* beer, which is identified elsewhere in the world by the city's name, is locally described as *Export* (because it was originally brewed to a sufficient strength to travel, bearing in mind the continuing trade with other cities).

Compared with the famous *Münchener* beers of the day, this *Dortmunder* had a very light golden colour, though it is fractionally deeper in shade than *Pilsener*. While *Münchener* beers are pronouncedly malty, and the *Pilseners* very well hopped, *Dortmunder* once again falls neatly between the two. It is sometimes described as the "Cool Blonde" beer: mellow, but not without a certain bite, full-bodied and satisfying. *Dortmunder* should have a gravity of not less than 12·5 degrees, and usually 13·0 or more, producing an alcohol content of about 4·0 per cent. Dortmund drinkers expect their beer to be served at between nine and ten degrees Centigrade (48–50°F), with a good "head."

The barman will usually pour slowly at first, into the side of the glass, then straighten and speed his action to produce the *schöne blume*. A simple, non-stemmed glass is used, though it curves inwards slightly at the top to help retain the head.

For those people who like the *Dortmunder* palate but prefer a lower-gravity beer, the Wenker Kronen brewery has produced a very well attenuated brew which they call *Classic*. This is served in Vichy-style "dinner-look" bottles, and high-stemmed glasses.

Such elegance is a mite away from the expression "as solid at Dortmund," which is used to describe the city. Dortmund is even more of a brewing town than Berlin or Munich, where beery fame is shared with a colourful history as capital cities and centres of culture. Dortmund's most important job has been to quench the thirsts of steelworkers, miners, and the like, in industrial Rhineland and Westphalia. Such was the bombing during the war that there are even few mementoes of its long history as a brewing town. The best reminder is undoubtedly the carving of a beer-drinker supping from a cask, in the choir stalls of the Marienkirche.

The brewers of Germany held a great convention in Dortmund in 1964, but the event has not been repeated. Not that a visitor could ever be in doubt about the city's trade. It is barely possible to leave the railway station without encountering the cluster of Dortmund breweries: Dortmunder Actien and Dortmunder Union in Rheinische Street, the Thier, Hansa, Ritter and Wenker Kronen breweries.

More is the pity that their output seems to be shifting away from their city's own indigenous style.

His cup runneth over

Singers are apt to become dry-throated, and choristers at the Marienkirche can only have their thirst agonizingly sharpened by this Dortmund cameo in their midst.

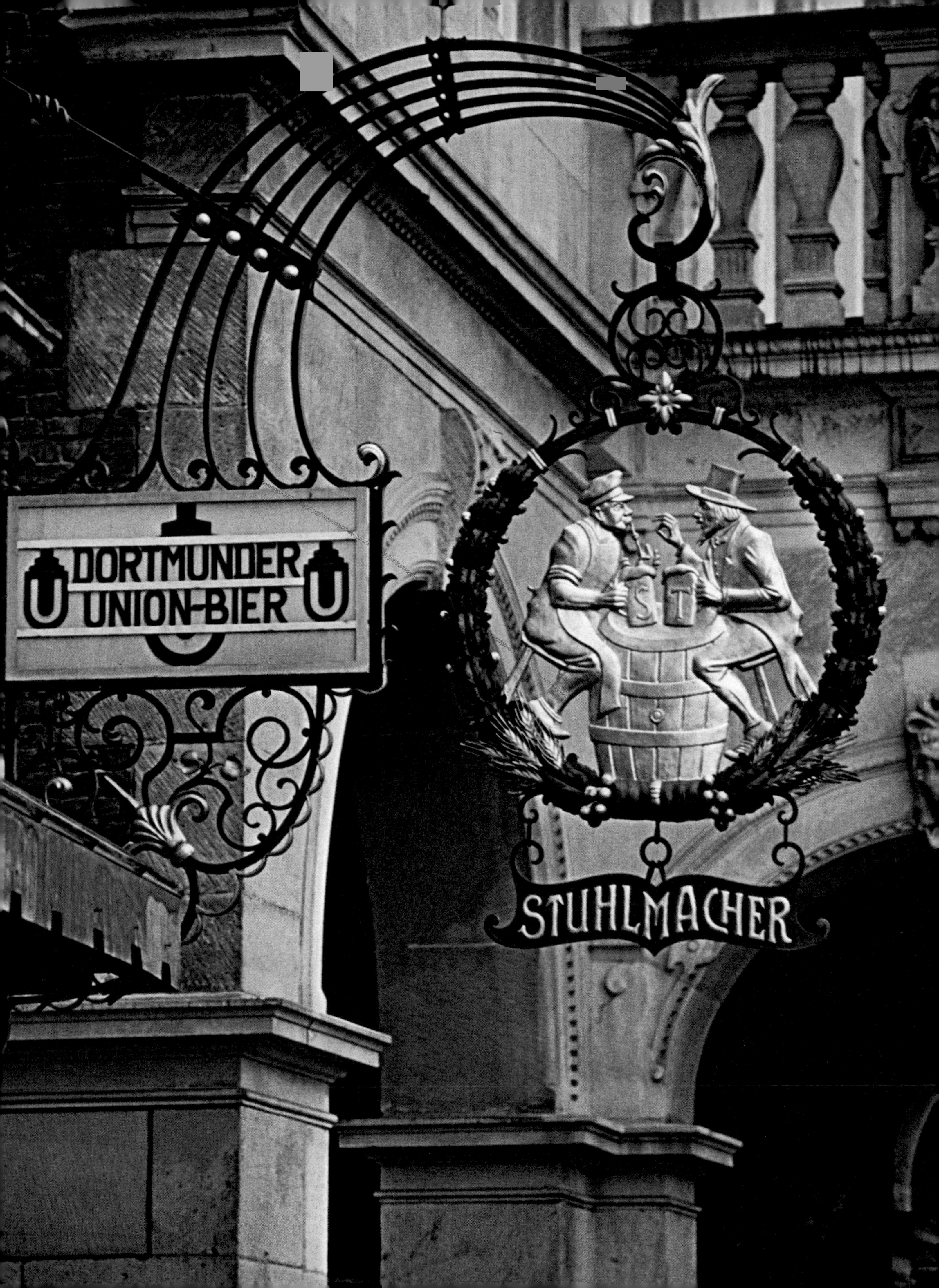
DORTMUNDER
UNION-BIER
STUHLMACHER

Kölsch

THE DRUNKEN GOD Dionysos probably feels quite happy embedded in the mosaic floor of Cologne's Roman museum. The city always had plenty of treats for the discerning drinker, and it still has. When the Romans made Cologne a Colonial capital (hence the English-language spelling of its name), they were likely seduced by the grapes of the Rhine. Today's drinker still has that choice, but he may prefer the German spelling of the city's name and its adjectival derivative, *Kölsch*. The latter is a beer, top-fermented but golden in colour, which is unique to Cologne. Kölsch is also the basis of a local craft tradition in brewing.

The Roman museum took 2,000 years to arrive. Next door, the magnificent Gothic cathedral was started in 1248 and finished in 1880. Just across the road, at 12 Am Hof, the *Cölner Hofbräu* tavern probably had its roots in the 15th or 16th century.

The *Hofbräu,* better known by the business name of P. J. Fruh, is supplied with *Kölsch* beer by its own brewery. The biggest of its several rooms was once the brewhouse. It is typical of several such Cologne taverns. Beer is tapped from the wood as fast as it will pour, and carried on specially-designed trays by waiters in the customary uniform of

**Whichever the brewery,
a narrow, straight glass
is used for Kolsch.**

blue pullovers and leather aprons. The waiters are known locally as *Köbes,* which may be a familiar contraction of Jakob. The tables are of scrubbed wood, and the atmosphere briskly convivial. Local snacks include "half a hen," which turns out to be a wedge of cheese with a roll. Or "Cologne caviare," which is a type of blood-sausage. Or mettwurst, which is the sausage equivalent of steak tartare, served with lots of onions.

A short walk away, the small Sion brewery

has its own tavern at 5–12 Unter Taschenmacher, also specializing in *Kölsch*. An even smaller brewery, *Päffgen,* of 64 Friesenstrasse, produces *Kölsch* solely for its own tavern. It is, in the truest sense, a home-brew house.

There are about a dozen breweries, some of them very small, in Cologne and its metropolitan area. Few German cities have so many. Some of the breweries, like Küppers *Kölsch* and Richmodis *Kölsch,* incorporate the civic beer-style in their names. The law on designation of origin ensures that only members of the Cologne Brewers' Union may produce *Kölsch,* though they encompass nearby Bonn. Germany's Federal capital has, however, only one brewery.

The Cologne brew is notably pale, with a slightly lactic but clean and refreshing palate. It is customarily served at about ten degrees Centigrade (50°C) in extremely narrow, straight glasses. Although these glasses are more than 13 centimetres high, they usually show only about two centimetres of "head;" *Kölsch* is not a very gassy beer. It has a gravity of 12 degrees, an alcohol content of about 3·7 per cent, and is strongly hopped. It is said to aid digestion, and Kölners swear by its healthy properties.

The restaurants and taverns of old Cologne proclaim their civic loyalties loud and clear. The Cölner Hofbräu tavern (left and above) offers a taste of the city in the glass and on the plate. There is nothing quite like half a hen.

Düsseldorfer Alt

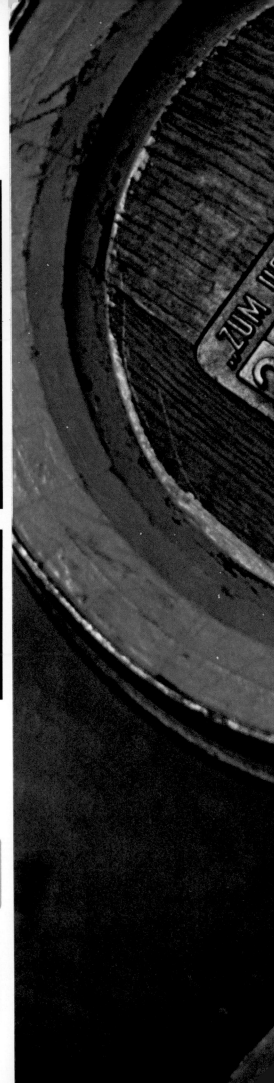

THE ROMANCE which attaches to some of Germany's brewing cities may have skirted Dortmund, but it has entirely missed Düsseldorf. Yet this bustling city, better known elsewhere in the world as a thriving commercial centre, produces one of Germany's most pronounced brewing styles.

When Dortmunders and others were experimenting with the new bottom-fermentation technique, the Düsseldorfers decided to stay with the tried and trusted top-fermentation method. Thus, now that bottom-fermentation is near-universal, the Düsseldorf brew is sometimes known by Germans as "the other beer." More formally, it is known as the "old" beer, though *Alt* might just as aptly be interpreted to mean "ale."

Although its palate is emphatically German, *Altbier* is not dissimilar in style from the British and North American ales, and it even more clearly resembles Belgian top-fermented beers like the Antwerp De Koninck brew.

By German standards, it is a dark beer, and is sometimes described as such, though its colour is really a deep, reflective copper. *Altbier* is brewed with dark malts, and very well hopped. It has an aromatic, slightly fruity, bitter-sweet taste, a gravity of 12·5 degrees, and an alcohol content of 3·5 per cent. *Altbier* is typically drunk from small cylindrical glasses, no more than 12 cm high, and should be only lightly chilled.

Home-brewing remains a tradition in Düsseldorf, much to the delight of *Altbier*

There are a good many well-liked altbiers produced in Rhineland (examples, right), and none more popular than those from the home-breweries of Düsseldorf. Little about the exterior of Zum Üerige (top) suggests what good things might be found inside, though a stained-glass window (above) recalls a splendid tradition. The typically copper-coloured, creamy beer is brewed on the premises (far right).

The home-brew houses of Northern Germany, whether they produce Kölsch or alt, are apt to serve their beer from wooden casks, by gravity. One cask may decant as many as 200 glasses in an hour. With beers such as these, a waiter's life can be a busy one.

73

Lest the Düsseldorfers become too proprietorial about their altbier, the town of Münster stakes its claim in elaborate and colourful fashion. The drinkers who have endorsed the table at Pinkus Müller's home-brew house no doubt share the sentiment.

drinkers. The home-brew houses are: Im Füchschen, at 28 Ratingerstrasse, in the old town; Zum Üerige, at 1 Bergerstrasse, also in the old town; and Ferdinand Schuhmacher, 123 Oststrasse, in the city-centre. At the other end of the scale, the biggest of the *Altbier* brewers in Düsseldorf is Schlösser, which has a very old local tradition, despite its now being a part of the Schultheiss group. Not far from Düsseldorf, there are the well-known Hannen *Alt* breweries at Korschenbroich, Willich and Mönchengladbach; the popular Rhenania *Alt* brewery at Krefeld, and Diebels *Alt* at Issum.

Despite the Düsseldorfers' proprietorial attachment to their *Altbier,* the same style is claimed by several other towns in North Rhineland and Westphalia. Münster is the other main *Altbier* town, and has a famous home-brew house called Pinkus Müller's. With an old "beer-kitchen," flagstone floor, Dutch wall-tiles, open fireplace and a collection of pewter tankards, Pinkus Müller's is one of Münster's favourite meeting-places. They say that, if you haven't seen Pinkus Müller's, you haven't seen Münster. The town is also famous for its custom of making the traditional fruit punch of spring and summer with beer, the *Altbier* Bowl.

The beers of Franconia

THE DRY SOIL of the Nürnberg area is unfavourable for the growing of wine, and this district has one of Germany's oldest and most active brewing traditions. Nürnberg had a pure-beer law in 1303, more than 200 years before the famous Bavarian *Reinheitsgebot* Munich was declared. Two casks of local beer were the sole freight when the first railway train in Germany ran from Nürnberg to nearby Fürth in 1835. Soon afterwards, the Nürnberg brewer Georg Lederer was associated with Sedlmayr and Dreher in their work on bottom-fermentation.

Today, the Lederer brewery is part of Nürnberg's Patrizier group, which also controls the Mailaender Bergbräu concern, of Fürth. This latter brewery produces a copper-red beer which is intended to evoke the district's past glories. The colour of the beer is reminiscent of that seen in German and Flemish paintings, and it is known as *Kupferstube*. It is a malty, bottom-fermented brew, of *Vollbier* gravity (12·8 degrees Balling), coloured with smoky, roasted malts.

This *Kupfer* beer is available at several restaurants in the area, including one near the castle gates of Nürnberg.

Wheat beer was once a great tradition of Nürnberg. The Royal Wheat Brewery was taken over by a private company in the 17th century, and this traditional beer now resides in the hands of Brau AG Nürnberg, the city's other brewer. Some fine *doppelbocks* are also brewed in the area for Franconia's many springtime and autumn fairs and festivals.

The biggest beer-festival of Franconia is the *Bergkirchweih* at Erlangen. The town has numerous natural beer-cellars in the Castle Hill, where the festival is held each Whitsuntide. For the festival, additional marquees are erected, and a special *Kirchweih* brew, of 13·9 degrees, is produced. At Michaelmas, a major festival is held over two weekends at Fürth, with processions, folk-dancing and bands.

Glories present (right) and past . . . the beer train rolls through Franconia. The Royal Brewery (bottom) passed to Brau A.G., while Reifbräu is today owned by Patrizier.

Bamberger Rauchbier

THE TRICKS of the brewer's craft, as practised by early man, have not altogether been forgotten. When the sun was not strong enough to dry his malt, the primitive brewer lit a fire. Home-brewers in some very rural areas continued to use the technique well into the 19th century, long after commercial companies had turned to hot-air kilns.

When the primitive fire-drying method is used, not only is the malt partially roasted, it is also permeated by the smoke. This leaves an aromatic "smoked" flavour. The same applied when peat fires were used to dry malt in the production of whisky.

The smoked-malt tradition survives particularly strongly, though no one knows why, at three breweries in the historic town of Bamberg, in the Northern part of Bavaria. The malt for these beers is dried over a fire of moist beech-wood logs. Devotees say that at least three jugs of the resultant *Rauchbier* must be drunk before the taste can be acquired, and some drinkers never come to terms with it. This seems a lily-livered attitude in a country famed for its smoked meats, fish and cheese. Smoked beer is the perfect accompaniment to such delights.

This exotic product, of *Vollbier* gravity, is produced by bottom-fermentation at Schlenkerla brewery; the Christian Merz brewery specializes in the style; and the Greifenklau brewery produces yet a third Bamberg *Rauchbier*.

Bamberg, once the home of the Holy Roman Emperor, remains rich in history. One of the best-known *Rauchbier* taverns is a 300-year-old establishment in Sandstrasse which is still regularly painted with pure ox-blood.

The smoked-malt
palate is given to a
whole range of beer
styles at the Heller
"Schlenkerla" brewery.
Beech-wood logs (inset)
are burned in the
smoking process, and
a tavern in the town
specializes in the
resultant rauchbiers.

The Schützenfest

THERE ARE *Schützenfests* throughout Germany, and in emigrant communities all over the world. In Australia, an Adelaide brewery produces a different style of *Schützenfest* beer every year. A *Schützenfest* was originally a gathering of the town's "sharpshooters," an historic civic vigilante body which grew into a ceremonial order. Today, such celebrations are beer-festivals.

The biggest *Schützenfest* is in Hanover, throughout the first week in July. The customary drink is a *Lüttje Lage* (a "little one"), which is an especially small beer accompanied by a *korn* (schnapps). The two drinks are not taken as a beer-and-chaser, but simultaneously. The small beer-glass is held between the thumb and forefinger, and the *korn* between the third and fourth fingers of the same hand. The perfect execution of this trick requires dexterity, practice and luck.

The beer in the glass might well be the celebratory *Broyhan Alt,* a light and malty beer named after the city's famous 16th-century brewer. *Broyhan Alt* is produced by Lindener Gilde, one of four Hanover breweries, which was originally a civically-supported co-operative of home-brewers. In the 17th century, a third of the population of Hanover was in the brewing trade, even though the sagacious city fathers restricted brewing rights to owners of fire-proof houses. The malt might be over-roasted, the

kettle might boil away, but Hanover would not burn.

Lindener Gilde is now a private company, but the city's Wülfel brewery remains a co-operative, under the ownership of publicans. Such is the brewing tradition of Hanover that Lindener Gilde holds a civic reception on an historic theme each year, and there is a further formal celebration to tap the new *bockbier* at the beginning of November.

How to drink a little one

Hanover's most famous brewer gives his name to a proud local beer, Broyhan Alt. Ambitious Hanoverians swallow their beer with a simultaneous schnapps. This trick takes considerable dexterity. First, the proper grip must be applied, then comes the careful raising of the glass to the lips, and finally the sublime swallow. Prost!

The Hanseatic tradition

UNLIKE SOME of its contemporaries, modern Germany has no dominant metropolitan city. This is to its great advantage. Each big city has its own role in German life, and none can legislate for the habits of the others. So it always was. In Hanseatic times, Germans said that Lubeck was the storehouse, Lüneberg the salt-house, Cologne the wine-house, and Hamburg the beerhouse.

During the brewing months, the entire shipping fleet of Hamburg was loaded with beer for export, and there were frequent pirate attacks on the port. During one assault on Hamburg, the citizenry defended the port with such gusto that the brewers provided 10,000 litres of beer to help fortify them. Some of this beer was boiled and poured over the attackers.

Because their beers were destined for long sea journeys, the brewers of Hamburg seized upon the preservative qualities of hops. The Hamburg brewers were pioneers in the use of the plant, and the tradition of well-hopped beers survives in the North today. So does the export tradition, but Hamburg can no longer claim to be Germany's brew-house. The city's fortunes suffered during the Thirty Years War, and its contribution to the lore of brewing in the centuries since then has been rather less colourful. Hamburg remains one of the biggest brewing centres in volume, but it now has only three breweries. Of these, Holsten – which also has a brewery in

Kiel – is the major exporter. The city's sole speciality is *Alsterwasser,* a shandy, which is named after the famous lake in the centre of Hamburg.

The momentum of history has been better sustained by the other great port city of the North, Bremen. The brewers there had an established trade throughout the North Sea and Baltic during the 13th century, and their exports soared during the industrial growth of the late 1800s. Today, the Bremen

Seefahrtbier
(Malzertract 40%)

nur aus bestem Malz und Hopfen, unter Ausschluß irgend welcher Ingredienzien gebraut. Wirkt nicht magensäuernd, hält sich Jahre lang. Reconvalescenten, schwächlichen, blutarmen und magenleidenden Personen (à ½ Aleflasche 60 ₰ excl. Glas) bestens empfohlen.

Wilhelm Remmer,
Bierbrauereibesitzer,
Bremen.

beer brewed by Beck's is the biggest German export brand, and one which is notably fashionable in the United States. Beck's had considerable involvements in the Far East before the Second World War, but now the company brews only in Germany. Its sole product is a full-bodied and well-hopped golden-coloured brew of 12·0 degrees, which is sold in a distinctively shouldered green bottle. The beer is pasteurized for export, and is also available in cans, a means of packaging which is rarely used in Germany. The associate firm of Haake-Beck, also in Bremen, serves the local market.

Two historic specialities of Bremen are kept alive by Haake-Beck. One is an unusually yeasty, light, bottom-fermented brew, which throws a sediment. This *Kreusenbier* is served only in selected taverns.

The other speciality derives from the high-gravity beer originally brewed for ships' crews. This beer was also drunk ceremonially each year, at winter's end, when a formal dinner was held to send the port's skippers off on their new season at sea. This *Schaffermahlzeit* was held on the second Friday of February, and the custom continues, with a ceremonial assembly at the *Ratskeller* under the auspices of Bremen's Senate. Eminent guests are invited to smoke white clay pipes; they dine on a mariners' meal of dried fish, kale and smoked pork; and *Seefahrtsbier* is brewed specially for the occasion. The brew is less of a beer today than a malt-extract, but it is alleged to taste as good as ever when it is sampled out of the customary pewter tankards.

Wenn nicht bald
ener bitt, fret ick
de Metten selber

Erste kulmbacher
Bejer

Hamburger
Oberalter
Der würzige Klare.

Deichgraf

Rum

Leevsten

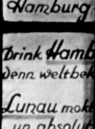
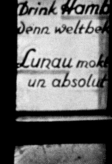

SEIT

Hamburg

Een Tass Kaffee
un ick bün wedder
kandidl.

Drink Hamb
Denn weltbek

Lunau mok
un absolut

Mein free

100 Jahre
Röpe
Kaffee
1833–1933

Ne wollne Büx, ne Deern in
und Balle Grog — dann
Arm
ward di warm

Vel Glück!
Keen Kummer!
wünscht di

Hein Sommer

Where the Germans drink

VIENNA HAS ITS COFFEE-HOUSES, England its pubs, and Southern Germany its beer-gardens. In the warmer South, "below" the river Main, Germans like to spend the early evening drinking out of doors. There are beer-gardens in the southern part of Hesse, in Baden-Württemberg, and most especially in Bavaria. A beer-garden is a place in which to relax thoughtfully under the shadow of the chestnut trees, to be part of the peaceful scene made famous by painters like Liebermann and Menzel.

There are more than 100 beer-gardens in Munich alone. The biggest, with about 7,000 seats, is the *Hirschgarten,* near the Nymphenburg Castle. This garden can serve 18,000 litres of the highly-regarded Augustiner beers in a single evening. The same brewery also owns the *Augustinerkeller,* which seats 5,000 people. *Keller* merely signifies that the beer is kept in a cellar, not that the actual drinking is in some sort of basement.

Imitation *bierkellers* in other countries are really modelled on a quite different institution, the beer-hall. While the beer-garden is notable for its quietude, the beer-hall is notable for its noise. Once again, drinkers can be accommodated by the thousand, but there is also room for brass-bands, singing and swaying. Just as each Munich brewery has its *biergarten,* so each has its *bierhalle.* The Augustiner and Pschorr *bierhallen* are good examples, but the *Mathäser Bierstadt* is said to be the biggest. This hall, in Bayerstrasse, serves Löwenbräu beer.

Munich also has something of a running beer-festival in the cabaret on the *Platzl,* with singers, folk-dancers and the like. Surprisingly, the excellent beer served at this tavern on the square is brought from out of town. It is produced by the family firm of Inselkammer, in the pretty little brewery village of Aying, 40 miles away.

North Germany has no institution with quite the regional character of the Southern drinking places. *Restaurants* and *bars* are universal, and described in the same Anglo–French way, but there is an ever-proliferating confusion of terminology.

There are beer-cellars in Hamburg, but they are not known as such. They are called *Wirtschaften,* which is simply a broad term throughout Germany for any type of drinking place. *Wirt* means landlord or host. Sometimes a *Gasthaus* (inn) is familiarized by its regular patrons into a *Gastwirtschaft.*

A *Wirtshaus* has much the same meaning, though the description has a tinge of implicit criticism. It is said of a wastrel that "he spends his pay in the *Wirtshaus.*" Most of the other names for drinking-places have similarly opprobrious undertones. A *Pinte* is a rough, simple drinking-place. A *Kneipe* is a matey meeting-place, though the name originally indicated a student drinking school. A *Destille* has more Hogarthian undertones. It is a Berlin expression for a hard-drinking spot which specializes in spirits.

Name your poison...

LOTS OF GERMANS have the surname Biergans. They may well prefer the first syllable to the second, which means "duck," but their name has nothing to do with Germany's national drink. When the revolutionary French armies occupied the Aachen region, a local man changed his name from Peter Hans to Pierre Jean. When the French left, this name was gradually re-Germanised to Pierjeans, and then Bierjans or Biergans. Even the suburb of Bierstadt, in Wiesbaden, got its name from the word *Bär* (bear), rather than beer. There are, though, plenty of other *Bier* names which might hang out for alcoholic origins.

Bierstedt is half way between Wolfsburg, in Lower Saxony, and the East German town of Salzwedel. Bierbergen is in Lower Saxony, in the triangle formed by Peine, Hildesheim and Salzgitter. One road from Osnabrück, Lower Saxony, to Minden, Westphalia, passes through Bieren. Further South, near Betzdorf, there is a place called Biersdorf. There is another Biersdorf in the Rhineland Palatinate, near Bitburg, and further West lies Bierendorf. There's a Bierbach in the Palatinate near Zweibrücken, and another in Hesse, near Darmstadt. In the Saar, near Trier, is Bierfelden, and on the Swiss border is Bierbronne, near Waldshut. In Württemberg, near Saulgau, there is Bierstetten; on the Southern bank of the Neckar there is Bierlinger; on the Jagst, Bieringen. Bavaria has Bierwinkl, Bierhütte, Biering, and Bierdorf. The road sign on the left (from Fürth) is fair warning.

In the beer-gardens of
Munich, serving styles
have altered little over
the centuries (far left).
Nor have the customs of
the Stammtisch (below).
The glass holds four
litres, and is customarily
passed to the left.
Purists say it should
be held with one hand.

Social approval is much more readily accorded to the *Stammtisch,* the large table which is reserved on different evenings of the week for various drinking fraternities. Such groups were originally trade guilds, which met to attend to their business affairs, to arrange debates, social events, parades and the like. One of the first *Stammtische* was for the sailing masters of Königsberg, Prussia (now Kalingrad).

A fraternity in Freiburg, Baden-Württemberg, is said to have more than 600 years of unbroken existence. Many *Stammtische* are nothing more than weekly meetings of sports buffs, or merely friends and neighbours. The *Stammtisch* is the ritualization of a weekly drink together, and there is unlikely to be any formal membership. The *Stammtisch* table, usually the best in the house, is marked out with a pennant, and protected against "intruders" by the landlord.

Every fifth German male of beer-drinking age belongs to a *Stammtisch,* according to research carried out by the German Brewers' Association. Thirty-nine per cent of *Stammtisch-Brüder* said they met to play cards, and 73 per cent said they regarded it as an opportunity to discuss politics. The spirit of the *Stammtisch* is convivial and male, though the customary beery singing and joke-telling do not appear to have been mentioned in the survey. Thirty-one per cent of regulars said that the *Stammtisch* was a chance to be among men – and 46 per cent of their wives responded that they were glad to have their husbands out of the house at least once a week.

For the decorous drinker...

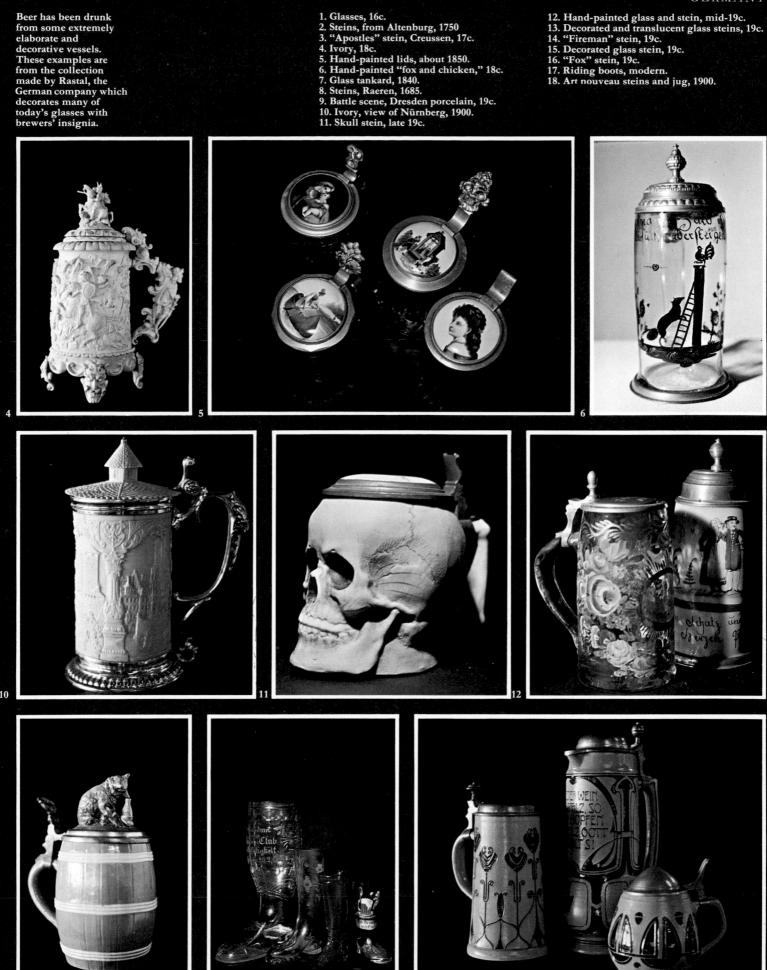

Beer has been drunk
from some extremely
elaborate and
decorative vessels.
These examples are
from the collection
made by Rastal, the
German company which
decorates many of
today's glasses with
brewers' insignia.

1. Glasses, 16c.
2. Steins, from Altenburg, 1750
3. "Apostles" stein, Creussen, 17c.
4. Ivory, 18c.
5. Hand-painted lids, about 1850.
6. Hand-painted "fox and chicken," 18c.
7. Glass tankard, 1840.
8. Steins, Raeren, 1685.
9. Battle scene, Dresden porcelain, 19c.
10. Ivory, view of Nürnberg, 1900.
11. Skull stein, late 19c.

12. Hand-painted glass and stein, mid-19c.
13. Decorated and translucent glass steins, 19c.
14. "Fireman" stein, 19c.
15. Decorated glass stein, 19c.
16. "Fox" stein, 19c.
17. Riding boots, modern.
18. Art nouveau steins and jug, 1900.

4

5

6

10

11

12

16

17

18

Scandinavia and the North

There have been many cross-currents in the beer-cultures of Europe's Far North. Despite their differences, Iceland, the three Scandinavian countries, and Finland, share many experiences. The long-ship drinking vessel (left) dates from 1699.

MOST OF THE WORLD'S brewers pay constant homage to Carlsberg, of Denmark. They do so by describing the yeast which they use in their own breweries as *Saccharomyces Carlsbergensis*. This species of yeast, used by all bottom-fermentation brewers, is named after Carlsberg because it was first isolated there, as a result of determined research, in 1883. Carlsberg is one among more than 20 producers of "taxable brews" in Denmark (see Pages 94–95), but it has a special place in the history of beer. This renown was won more by brewing achievement than by Carlsberg's equally remarkable record of philanthropic work.

Perhaps it is because of such Danish attainments that brewers in some other parts of the world are apt to give their beers spuriously Nordic names, decorating their labels with Viking symbols and the like. Or perhaps such copyists merely wish to be associated with the broader legend of Scandinavian brewing. Just as Carlsberg is not the only brewer in Denmark, but the largest, so Denmark is not the only brewing nation in Europe's North, though it is by far the most productive. Historically, its beery mythology is shared with the several nations of the North which are loosely tied together by the rest of the world in a package labelled "Scandinavia." Some of these nations have considerable claims to the beer-drinker's attention.

Home-brewing was long an important part of the folk-culture of Norway and Sweden – beer was produced especially for winter festivals and family feasts – and the traditions go much further back than that. Finland's national epic manages to accommodate the creation of the world in two hundred verses, but requires four hundred in which to explain the creation of beer. The sagas of Iceland (a country where it is now difficult to obtain a beer) reveal that the Vikings brewed a strong drink from barley. They called this beverage *aul*, which later evolved into the Danish and Swedish word *öl*, the Norwegian *øl* and the English *ale*. After drinking *aul*, the Vikings used to go *berseark*, which may explain why they were held in some fear and awe by the rest of Europe. When Eric the Red entertained some of his fellow-mariners to Yule in Greenland, he recorded his concern about the hospitality he could offer. This anxiety was met by the brewing of some beer.

Habits change. Drinks have their ebb and flow. In the early 1700s, beer lost popularity in face of competition from spirits, which had been introduced to the Nordic countries from Germany. One response was to combat the flood of spirits by trying to brew a more attractive quality of beer. As in Britain (*vidé* Hogarth), beer was seen as a natural and healthy beverage, while spirits were the curse of the working classes. Another, more drastic, solution came later in the shape of strict controls on alcohol. A legacy of those days remains in the restrictive drinking laws of Iceland, Norway, Sweden and Finland. Each of these countries retains, nonetheless, its brewing industry. Norway has its own *Reinheitsgebot*, and Finland has a similar law. Scandinavia may have changed somewhat since the Viking days but, as the warriors might have said in euphoric mood, *aul* is not lost.

On dry ice

The convivial scene above, from a medieval Icelandic manuscript, depicts "drinking guests." In times past, the serving of beer was a central part of Icelandic hospitality. Today, things are sadly different. Only "near beer" or malt extract can legally be served. The law says that no beer may contain more than 2·25 per cent alcohol by volume. The locally-brewed Polar Beer (right) is nominally for export only. In practice, the determined drinker manages to get his hands on beer when he wants to.

THE BREWERY EGILL SKALLAGRIMSSON LTD.

POLAR BEER

REYKJAVIK · ICELAND

Mack
Tromsø

Bodø
Bodø

Pripps/Top
Gällivare

Lapin
Tornio

Till/Nyckel
Luleå

Mallasjuoma
Oulu

Till/Norrlands
Umeå

Wårby
Sollefteå

Oivi
Iisalmi

Till/Östersunds
Östersund

Dahls
Trondheim

Hartwall
Vaasa

Raninin
Kuopio

NORWAY

SWEDEN

FINLAND

Hartwall
Lappeenranta

Pripps
Sundsvall

Pyynikki
Tampere

Mallasjuoma
Heinola

Sinebrychoff
Pori

Mallasjuoma
Lahti

Till/Bockens
Bollnäs

Lillehammer
Lillehammer

Hansa
Bergen

Pripps
Mora

Sinebrychoff
HELSINKI

Hamar
Hamar

Pripps
Torsby

Till/Bockens
Gävle

Frydenlund Schou
Ringnes
OSLO

Grängesbergs
Grängesberg

Risingsbo
Smedjebacken

Hartwall
Turku

Moss
Moss

Aass
Drammen

Kopparbergs
Kopparberg

Wårby
Vårby

STOCKHOLM
Pripps
Bromma

Lundetangen
Skien

Borg
Sarpsborg

Pripps
Arboga

Tou
Stavanger

Grans
Sandefjord

Pripps
Göteborg

Åbro
Vimmerby

Christianssand
Kristiansand

Fredrikstad
Fredrikstad

Sandwalls
Borås

Nässjö
Nässjö

Arendal
Arendal

Falken
Falkenberg

Banco
Skruv

Appeltofftska
Östra
Halmstad

DENMARK

Pripps
Tingsryd

Pripps
Malmö

Denmark

THERE NEVER WAS a Mister Carlsberg. There was a Christian Jacobsen, who set the pace for his descendants in the matter of better beer. What followed amounted to a remarkable sequence of achievements not only in brewing but also in micro-biology. Christian Jacobsen left his parents' farm in Jutland during the 1700s to seek his fortune in Copenhagen, and soon established himself as a brewer. He was one of the first Danish brewers to use a thermometer instead of testing the heat by dipping his elbow in the brew. His son Jacob Christian further challenged the frontiers of brewing science. He was anxiously aware of the demand for better beer in Denmark. At that time, Denmark's beers were top-fermented wheat brews of less-than-consistent quality. Europe was getting on its feet again, after the Napoleonic wars, and there was already a fashion among the prosperous in Denmark for the new beers being brewed in Munich. Jacob Christian went to study at the Sedlmayr brewery in Munich, and on his return succeeded in producing a drinkable brew in his mother's wash-copper.

With far greater understanding of such matters than was common among his contemporaries, Jacob Christian realised that he needed the original Sedlmayr yeast if he was to obtain a really satisfactory product. Thus came about one of the most celebrated episodes in the history of brewing. It took place in 1854, at a time of great advances in science, when Pasteur was unfolding the mysteries of fermentation, and Balling explaining the chemistry of yeast.

By stagecoach, Jacob Christian Jacobsen set out in that year for Munich. It was, in those days, an interminable journey. He persuaded his old workmaster to provide him

Among the elaborate decorations which bring such colour to the "New Carlsberg" brewery, none is more imposing than the Elephant Gate. The theme was celebrated in advertising, and still features in a popular beer-brand.

The revolutionaries

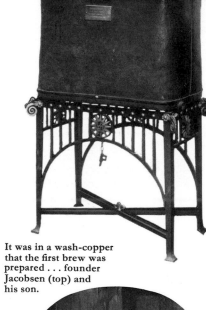

It was in a wash-copper that the first brew was prepared . . . founder Jacobsen (top) and his son.

A pioneering approach brought its rewards, and the reconciliation of the Jacobsens in the twentieth century set the seal on the expansion of Carlsberg. Theirs became the most famous name among the breweries of the Northern nations.

The world's first cultivation of a pure yeast culture was carried out at Carlsberg by Emil Christian Hansen in the equipment shown below. Today, his system is used all over the world.

with a couple of pots of yeast, and set off home. He carried the pots of yeast in his stove-pipe hat. At every single resting-place on the long road, he had to get out of the coach and pump water on the yeast to keep it alive.

He succeeded, and used the yeast to brew Denmark's first acceptable bottom-fermented beer, which he aged in storage cellars under the city ramparts. He had been given royal licence to use these cellars, and the local retailers announced his product as "the first lager beer from Mr Jacobsen's vault under the ramparts." With money inherited upon the death of his mother, Jacobsen bought land in the Copenhagen suburb of Valby, and built a bigger brewery there. The land was close to Denmark's first railway line, which was being laid at the time, and the local water was particularly favourable. The new brewery was on a hill, a *berg*, and Jacobsen named it after his five-year-old son *Carl*. On November 10, 1847, the first *Carlsberg* beer was brewed. A few decades later, this brewery would become known as Old Carlsberg, because the young son had grown up, argued with his father, and started an independent brewery of his own, called New Carlsberg.

The missionary zeal with which Jacobsen pursued the scientific aspects of brewing knew no bounds. His friends and working acquaintances included Pasteur, Sedlmayr, the Austrian brewer Dreher, and the French brewer Eugene Velten, of Marseilles. All four brewers were on the executive committee of the International Brewing Congress in Vienna, in 1873, where Professor Carl von Linde presented his celebrated paper on refrigeration. Two years later, Jacobsen set up the famous Carlsberg Laboratories, devoted not only to research in brewing, but also to serve as an endowed institute for the pursuit of scientific activities in the interests of the country. A year after that, the Carlsberg Foundation was established "to benefit science and honour the country."

Perhaps it takes one revolutionary to recognize another. Towards the end of his life, Jacobsen employed a young scientist called Emil Hansen, who had previously done some work at New Carlsberg. It was an historic appointment. In his new job at the Carlsberg Laboratory, Hansen furthered the work of Pasteur, and soon made one particularly important advance. He isolated the first single-cell yeast culture. His next step was to establish which species produced good beer and which did not. Another famous Danish brewery, Tuborg, was having trouble with its brews. After being bottled for a few days, the beer fermented to a point where it was thick and unpleasant. Hansen was able to show that Tuborg was using two "bad" yeast species along with one "good" species. At the Old Carlsberg brewery they were having problems, too. Sometimes the beer smelled bad, and was excessively bitter. Hansen discovered that there were three "bad" species of yeast at work, and one "good" species. Doubts were expressed about his findings, but he pressed ahead with an experiment using the "good" species in 1883. The experiment was a success.

Scepticism persisted for some time in Germany, Britain and France, for Hansen had contradicted some of Pasteur's theories, but the master himself entertained no such doubts. At the recommendation of Pasteur, Hansen was awarded a gold medal by *La Société d'Encouragement Pour l'Industrie Nationale* in Paris.

The "Little Mermaid" statue is popularly regarded the world over as a symbol of Copenhagen. It was originally donated to the city as a work of art by Carl Jacobsen, and was one of many such gifts. The Mermaid has been sited in the entrance to the harbour since 1913. The statue is the work of sculptor Edvard Eriksen.

The philanthropists

THE FIRST GRAND GESTURE of philanthropy was a mere foretaste. Many tycoons of the late 19th and early 20th centuries were philanthropists, but none quite like the Carlsberg Jacobsens. Not only did the philanthropy of Jacobsen precede that of Carnegie and John Rockefeller, it also took an exceptional form. The establishment of the Carlsberg Laboratories as an endowed institute was only a beginning. Nor did the giving stop with the Carlsberg Foundation for the advancement of science. The provision of money to restore Frederiksborg Castle after a catastrophic fire, and to establish a National History Museum there, was by no means all. For the grandest gesture came upon the death of Jacob Christian Jacobsen, in 1887. His will revealed that he had left his entire brewing business to the Foundation. The trustees of the Foundation were to be the proprietors of the brewery. They had inherited, as a source of funds, a large and thriving business.

The year before he died, Jacobsen and his son Carl had ended their bitter quarrel. The son was to continue the expansive tradition of philanthropy. Given the size of Carlsberg today, it is ironic that the original dispute between the two men was over the size of production. Jacobsen the father felt that quality would suffer if production went beyond 3,500 hectolitres a year, and the son disagreed. The son was leased a separate new brewery at Carlsberg, in which to produce top-fermented beers of the English type, but the potential of this market did not satisfy him. The tenancy was terminated, and Carl set up his own lager brewery, right alongside his father's, and in direct competition. There followed several years of lawsuits, and an angry silence between the two men. Carl's wife and daughter finally brought father and son together. "I'm inclined to believe that J. C. sacrificed his ascetic manufacturing ethics in recognition of Carl's overwhelming and convincing foresight," wrote the distinguished Danish journalist Carsten Nielsen, in a tribute on Carlsberg's first 125 years.

They called J. C. Jacobsen "The Captain." His son, a wildly temperamental and dandyish extrovert, of iron will and independent mind, was known as "The Brewer." Not only in his brewing skills did Carl take after his father, he inherited the same intellectual and social attitudes. His own brewery was alive with architectural delights, not least the famous decorative gate carved in the shape of two elephants. He set up a fund in 1879 to pay for public squares and gardens in the city, and added to the towers of Copenhagen's skyline by providing a spire for St Nicholas Church, and building the Jesus Church. A world-famous donation to his native city was the Little Mermaid statue on Copenhagen's harbour promenade.

Being an art-lover, Carl Jacobsen assembled a considerable private collection of paintings, sculptures and antiques, which he housed in an annexe to his private mansion. Today, this annexe is used as the Carlsberg Museum, and is open to the 150,000 people who visit the breweries each year. It contains paintings depicting scenes from Carl Jacobsen's time, rarities and curios received as gifts by the family, and early posters.

A large part of the family's personal art collection was given to the nation by Carl Jacobsen and his wife in 1884. This gift was made after the royal collection of sculpture had been devastated in a fire at Christiansborg Castle. The collection, much expanded, is now housed in a magnificent museum on Copenhagen's Western Avenue which was built by the City and the State of Denmark with the family's help. The museum, called the Ny Glyptothek, houses major works by Rodin, including *The Thinker*, no less than

Vahine no te Tiare — J. Gauguin '91

From the collection of the Ny Carlsberg Glyptothek . . . the Impressionist Alfred Sisley's "Waterworks at Bougival," painted in 1873; an Egyptian Pharaoh, and a Greek head from the Sixth century B.C.; Gaugin's famous "Vahine no te Tiare"; and the sculpture "The Water Mother," symbol of fertility, by Kai Nielsen.

73 sculptures by Degas, and works by artists like Gaugin, Monet, Corot, Bonnard and Millet. Some of these works were bought for the museum by the New Carlsberg Foundation, which was set up by Carl Jacobsen in 1902. Just as the original Carlsberg Foundation, set up by his father, was endowed to benefit the sciences, so the New Carlsberg Foundation, set up by Carl Jacobsen, was created to support the arts. Apart from its donations to the Ny Glyptothek, the Foundation has also helped finance the purchase of works by Titian, Tintoretto, Hals, Tiepolo and Goya for Denmark's State Museum of Art. Gifts to the oddly-named Louisiana museum of modern art, at Humlebaek, not far from Elsinore, have included works by Karel Appel, Jean Arp, Corneille, Alberto Giacometti, Barbara Hepworth and Henry Moore, among many others.

The Old and New Carlsberg Breweries were amalgamated in 1906, the profits from both enterprises to be used to fund the Foundations for art and science. In 1914, Carl Jacobsen died. He had said, "I care not for flowers on my coffin when so many people lack fuel for their hearths." Fifty years after the original bequest of the old brewery to the Carlsberg Foundation, a further gesture was made in 1938. "The Carlsberg Bequest to the Memory of Brewer J. C. Jacobsen" was devised to provide short-term assistance for various causes, especially in the performing arts. The Bequest has funded tours by the Danish Royal Ballet, and overseas visits by the Royal Theatre, Radio Symphony Orchestra and so forth. In 1961, the Carlsberg Foundation offered to pay for the erection and equipping of a Planetarium, which was built during the early 1970s.

The winner of the Nobel Prize for chemistry in 1972, Dr Christian Anfinsen, was an "old boy" of the Carlsberg Laboratory. Over the years, the Carlsberg Foundations have supported innumerable quests for knowledge: exploration in Greenland, a study of the mysterious migrations of the eel, geological surveys of the sea-bed (hence the naming of the Carlsberg Ridge, in the Indian Ocean), archaeological excavations all over Asia (which have benefitted the Danish National Museum, and museums in the countries concerned), ethnographic studies of peoples like the Tuareg, the building of a reflecting telescope in Chile, and countless other works.

During 1969 and 1970, Carlsberg was amalgamated with Tuborg, Denmark's second largest brewing concern. The two companies had been co-operating since the turn of the century, and their merger was intended, among other things, to form a unified brewing concern to compete in the expanding European Common Market. At that time, the European Community was preparing for Denmark's entry, along with Britain and the Republic of Ireland, all three of them great brewing nations. Such considerations may have muffled concern about Carlsberg's unusual commercial status in regard to a merger of this sort. Furthermore, Tuborg had become part of a group of brewing interests assembled worldwide with the backing of the Rupert Group, of South Africa. Whatever liberal Danes thought about the South African connection, they were perhaps reassured by the Rupert Group's innovative record in philanthropic and artistic ventures, as exemplified by the Peter Stuyvesant Collection of paintings. The first concern was that Carlsberg should remain a philanthropic organization, and this was, in fact, ensured by law. The Carlsberg Foundation is legally obliged to hold at least 51 per cent of the joint stock company which was formed in the amalgamation. The earnings derived from these shares – the Carlsberg segment of United Breweries – continue to be used for the support of the sciences and the arts.

The beer-styles of Denmark

BECAUSE DENMARK played such a part in the popularization of *lager* brewing, and because the world is so well acquainted with Denmark's own version of *Pilsener* beer (milder, less dry, than the original), it is easy to assume that the country has no other brewing styles. This is far from the truth. The Danes have a variety of beer-types and sub-groups, and most brewers produce a considerable number of brands.

At one end of the scale, there exist dark malt *ales* with a very high gravity and a very low alcohol content (up to 27 degrees Balling, and less than 2·25 per cent by weight). At the other end of the scale, there are Easter and Christmas brews, and *stouts*, with an alcohol content by weight of more than six per cent (about 7·5 per cent by volume). Between the two, there is a wide selection of pale and dark beers, some top-fermented but most of them bottom-fermented, with low, medium, and medium-to-high alcohol contents. Although Denmark's everyday beers have the same alcohol content as those produced elsewhere in Continental Europe, and the country has some very distinguished stronger brews, it has nothing in regular

production which is quite comparable with the German *doppelbock*, the Belgian *Trappiste* or the most potent of the British *barley wines* for alcohol content.

Being by far the largest group, United Breweries (Carlsberg and Tuborg) produces the most brands. Between them, Carlsberg and Tuborg have more than 15 brands in the Danish market, which are exported to different parts of the world under almost 30 names. A further ten brands are produced in Denmark for export only, and this does not include beers which are brewed in about 15 other countries by either company or their associates. The list of brands produced in the home market by Carlsberg and Tuborg gives a fair impression of the range of styles which is available.

In Denmark, beers are classified by the tax authorities according to their alcoholic content. Some specialist small brewers produce only low-alcohol beers within the tax-free classification, but these styles are also included in the range of most conventional breweries.

There are two distinctive styles in tax-free beer, both known by anachronistic names.

White ale (*hvidtøl*) may in the distant past have meant a low-gravity wheat brew, but it now indicates a tax-free normal beer with a medium density and a low alcoholic content. The *hvidtøl* produced by United Breweries has a density of 12·1 degrees Plato, and an alcohol content by weight of 1·3 per cent. Paradoxically, United Breweries' *hvidtøl* is a dark, or *mørkt* brew. It is therefore a "dark white ale." The group also produces a *lys* ("light-coloured") *white ale*. This brew has a density of 7·7 degrees Plato and an alcohol content of 2·0 per cent by weight. The other tax-free beer-style is *ships' ale* (*skibsøl*). This was originally a well-hopped, high density beer which was brewed to retain its condition during long journeys. Today, it is a low-alcohol brew, dark in colour, with a smoky roasted-malt palate. Tuborg *skibsøl* has a density of 7·0 and an alcohol content by weight of 1·9 per cent.

More conventional beers with an alcohol content of less than 2·25 per cent are graded as Class II. Carlsberg has a *let Pilsner* in this category (*let* means "light" in the sense of weight or content). Beers with an alcohol content higher than 2·25, but a density of

Most Danish breweries produce a selection of different beer styles. Hardly surprisingly, United Breweries of Copenhagen has the widest range, including all the typical Danish styles. Its brand-names include Carlsberg, Tuborg and Kongens Bryghus (Royal Brewery). The latter is abbreviated to "K.B."

One of the world's classic examples of advertising illustration, entitled simply "Thirst," was produced for Tuborg in a poster competition in 1900. The poster has been in use ever since. The artist was Eric Henningsen.

less than 10·75 Balling, are rated as Class I. These include Carlsberg Hof and Green Label (*Grøn*) Tuborg, both of which have a density of 10·7 and an alcohol content of 3·7 by weight. Both are *Pilsener*-type beers, though they are rather low in alcohol by the normal standard of the style. In the same category are two *Münchener*-style beers, Old (*Gamle*) Carlsberg and Red Label (*Rød*) Tuborg.

The beers most comparable with *Pilseners* elsewhere fit into Class "A" (density higher than 10·75, but less than 13·0). In the case of United Breweries, these are Carlsberg Gold (*Guld*) Export (11·7 degrees Plato; 4·0 per cent alcohol by weight) and Gold Tuborg (12·7; 4·6).

Stronger beers, with a density of more than 13 degrees Balling, are rated as Class "B." These include the light-coloured Elephant Beer (16·0 degrees Plato; 5·7 by weight), Tuborg F.F., or Fine Festival (17·4; 6·2), and Tuborg's Easter *Påskebryg* (17·4; 6·2). Also within this category is a distinctive amber beer, Carlsberg '47 (sometimes known simply as C47). The name commemorates 1847, the year when Carlsberg was founded, and the beer is intended to be reminiscent of the brews produced at that time. Carlsberg '47 has a density of 16 degrees Plato and 5·5 per cent alcohol by weight. Golden-coloured *lagers* like those brewed today were not produced in Denmark until the late 1880s or early 1890s, and this innovation was made by Tuborg. The amber *Vienna* tinge of '47 is unusual in Denmark, but the more common *Münchener* darkness is manifested in another strong beer, Carlsberg *Påskebryg* (18·1; 6·2). The range of stronger beers also includes Gammel Porter, a sweetish "Imperial" *stout* (18·8; 6·1).

Among the most notable export beers from United Breweries are Carlsberg '68, which is the equivalent of Elephant Beer; Carlsberg 19BC, a *Münchener*-style beer of 18·2 degrees Plato (6·3 per cent alcohol by weight); and the famous Carlsberg Special Brew (19·0 Plato; 6·8 per cent by weight).

The nearest thing to international brands are the two Gold Label beers, sometimes known as De Luxe. All-malt beers are exported to Germany, and in one instance (Tuborg Lager) to Britain. The brand exported to Britain has a density of 7·4 Plato, which is similar to that of the Tuborg Pilsner and Carlsberg Pilsner brands which are brewed locally there. Britain also has a locally-brewed Tuborg Gold (11·0) and Carlsberg Export Hof (10·5). Tuborg (11·0) is brewed under licence in the United States, and Carlsberg (10·5) in Canada.

The small breweries of Denmark

This collection of Danish costumes is just one theme from several series of illustrated labels produced by the small Lolland-Falsters brewery, in Nykøbing. The labels appeared on Class "A" beers (10·75–13·0 degrees).

WITH A POPULATION of only five million, and two famous breweries holding 80 per cent of the market, it follows that the 20-odd small brewers of taxable beer in Denmark are very tiny indeed. Even two members of this select band are owned by United Breweries: the Elsinore firm of Wiibroe, and North Jutland's Neptun Brewery, at Silkeborg.

The Elsinore firm's considerable range of light *lagers* was formerly crowned by a beer called Hamlet, but the prince has now been usurped by Nanook of the North. *Nanok* means polar bear, and this brand is the strongest of the brewery's light-coloured *lagers*, with a density of about 16 degrees Plato, 5·5 per cent alcohol by weight, and 6·5 by volume. The brewery also produces an unusually strong *Münchener* and an admirable Imperial Stout (both 18·0 Plato; 6·0 alcohol by weight; 7·5 by volume). The Wiener Ale is less interesting than it sounds, being a low-alcohol light *lager*. Neptun has a lesser range, though it is one of the few Danish breweries to use the term *bock*. The designation is in this instance attached to a beer of 5·6 per cent alcohol by weight.

The biggest independent brewery is Ceres, in the university town of Århus. This company's range includes a strongish imitation *Dortmunder* (5·5 per cent by weight; 6·9 by volume) and a hoppy Danish *stout* (6·6 per cent by weight; 7·5 by volume). With breweries in three other towns, Ceres describes itself as "the second among the Danish brewing enterprises."

Another mighty minnow is Albani, in Odense, the town where Hans Christian Andersen was born. Albani counters Elephant Beer with its own Giraffe brand (15·4 Plato; 5·7 per cent by weight). The brewery also produces a *porter* (19·5; 5·7), an Easter *Påskebryg* (17·0; 6·2) and a *Julebryg* Christmas beer (15·4; 5·3). *Julebryg* ("Yule Brew") beers are usually strong, while a Jule Øl is normally a low-alcohol tax-free brand. Special beers are also produced by some breweries at Whitsuntide (*Pinse*), and often for anniversaries of the firm itself or its home town.

Nordic folklore is well served by the brewing industry. In Northern Jutland, there is an Odin brewery, in Viborg, and a Thor brewery, in Randers. Thor has a Thunder Beer brand, but this name has been given to a fairly ordinary light-coloured *lager*. A less Nordic, but equally colourful name emanating from this brewery is Kasket Karl, which is also a light-coloured *lager* (10·7). A *kasket* is a worker's flat cap, and the beer is named after a syndicated newspaper cartoon character better known by his original English name of Andy Capp. Thor's strong beer (16·0 Balling) is known by the name of Buur, a word which has no meaning, though it is perhaps reminiscent of the similar Bear (Bjerne) beer brewed by Harboe.

The last word on animals and beer must come from the small Lolland-Falsters brewery, named after the two linked islands which are its local market. This brewery has produced colourful series of illustrated labels in much the way tobacco companies used to issue cigarette cards. One series, on the regular light-coloured *lager* (10·75 Balling) was made up of wild animals. It included polar bears, giraffes, tigers, and suchlike beery creatures.

Even in Denmark, it can be time for a tiger.

A wide variety of traditions and images is invoked by Denmark's brewers. Imperial Stout may have its origins in Britain's Baltic trade with St Petersburg (Copenhagen was on the route). The Münchener is a strong beer with an original gravity of 1072. The Dortmunder sounds another German echo, while the Bock has to keep company with a giraffe and Albani's Easter lambs and chicks, not to mention Father Christmas.

A cottage industry

DANISH BREWERS all pasteurize their beers, with the exception of one firm, Faxe. This brewery, about 30 kilometres South of Copenhagen, is independent not only in the sense of its ownership but also in its business policies.

Some of the country's grander brewers describe themselves as Purveyors of Beer to the Danish Royal Court; Faxe, a family-controlled company with 6,000 additional shares in public hands, describes itself as Purveyor of Beer to the Danish People.

The confrontation between Faxe and the brewing "Establishment" became a public one when the industry's joint body started an advertising campaign to publicize the Danish standard beer bottle. All bottles are returnable in Denmark. Because all breweries use the same bottle, it can be returned to any of them, which makes life easier for all concerned, including the consumer. The other breweries did not accept that their standard bottle would not safely contain Faxe's unpasteurized beer. Faxe, however, insisted on marketing its own bottle. Fermentation of unpasteurized beer can make a bottle explode if it is not sufficiently durable. Faxe was also concerned about the effect of light on the beer, and preferred a bottle of darker glass. The brewery claimed that it had done its best to avoid complicating the bottle-return system; Faxe certainly did not wish to be seen as anti-consumer.

On the contrary, the consumer took Faxe's side. The confrontation attracted attention to the existence of Faxe's unpasteurized brands, as well as casting the company as an underdog. Because the public tends to support the underdog, and since discerning drinkers like their beer unpasteurized, sales of Faxe soared. In some places, supplies became difficult to obtain.

Despite being in the bottle, the unpasteurized brand is called Faxe Fad (Draught) in the home market. An unpasteurized beer is exported to Germany, Austria and Switzerland in cans, a form of packaging which is not favoured in Denmark on environmental grounds. Faxe produces several other beers, some pasteurized, most of them dry and hoppy in character.

As a maverick, Faxe remains outside the Brewers' Association of Denmark. Four other brewers are outside the association, though for less clearly-defined reasons: Fuglsang, Hancock, Maribo and Marrebaek. Fuglsang produces an unpasteurized beer on tap, but draught represents only about one per cent of the Danish market.

The success story of the Faxe brewery began with Conrad and Nikoline Nielsen. Their house, in the background of the top picture, was the brewery's "administration block." The house is still used, and guests are received there. The brewery's 75th birthday was celebrated with beers named after the founders.

Norway

NOWHERE HAS THE CUSTOM of home-brewing survived with such vigour as it has in Norway, where it has been a central feature of rural life since the 12th century. "Brewing occupies an important place in the economy and household traditions of Norwegian peasant society," wrote the anthropologist and sociologist Dr Odd Nordland in the late 1960s. He was writing at a time when the cinemas of Oslo were being filled by James Bond, and when the Beatles were topping the hit parade all over Europe.

Although brewing was still "an integral part of social life" in many rural districts, Nordland wondered whether this would continue to be the case. His fears were less than justified. Some people started to buy malt, rather than making it from their own barley, but the tradition thrived. In the 1970s, national statistics were showing an annual production of at least 12 million litres of home-brewed beer, and often far more. On the West Coast in particular, brewers continued to use their own barley, and produced beers far stronger than those on general sale.

The custom was deeply rooted in family life, as Nordland recorded, looking back over the years: "It was associated with a multitude of events connected with work on the farm, and with different religious and secular high days and holidays . . . Christmas, Easter and Whitsun . . . funerals, weddings and Christenings . . . the hay-making season and other important events. Everyone brewed at Christmas, no matter how poor they were. The amount of ale brewed, and its quality, added to or detracted from the local prestige of a wedding." Sometimes a dozen or more barrels would be brewed. Old people prepared malt for their funeral beer, and renewed it if they failed to die at the expected time. When a man gathered together his friends for the last time, Nordland explained, he wanted to be sure they had good beer. He quoted an old man as saying: "They will not be putting me into the ground with shame." For hay-making, on the other hand, a less strong brew was prepared. It was thirsty work, but not to be pursued when drunk.

In a throwback to pre-hop habits, other plants have continued to be used by Norwegian brewers during the 20th century. One example is the alder, which was added to the brew in the form of finely-chopped young twigs, with plenty of sap. Even more widely used was the essence of juniper, the same plant which gave its name, in abbreviated form, to gin. Home-distilling continues to be a national pastime, despite its being illegal, and the links between the production

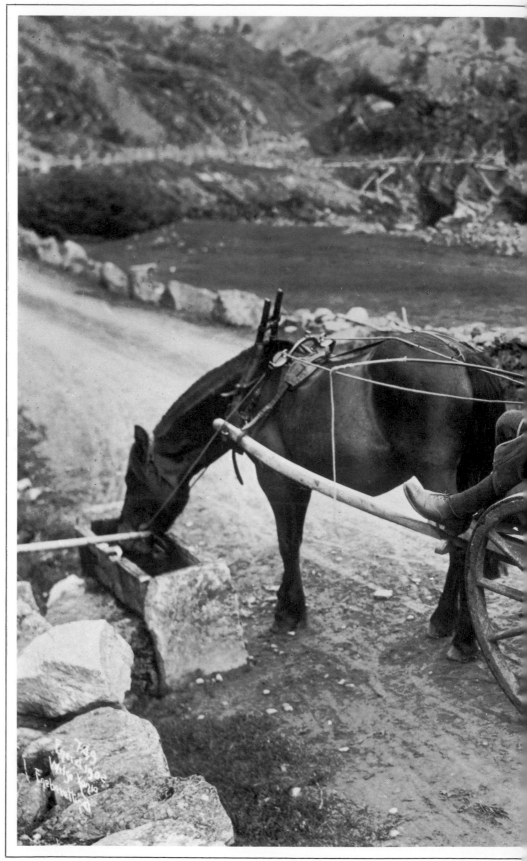

The seasons' beers

A single cask of fairly weak beer might be enough for haymakers (much the same tradition applied in Scotland), but more was required for other occasions. After the barley had been harvested (above), the malting frame (left) came into use. In the nineteenth century, every farm had its own brewing equipment.

Traditions survive and thrive. A wedding (above) might require two or three casks of beer. The master of ceremonies, in the centre of the picture, serves the ale. A ceremonial cup (below) might be used at a funeral. It is a courtesy to talk about the beer rather than less happy topics.

Rural images extend to the labels of Norway's commercial brewers (below), though the industry is proud of its modern plant. "Bavarians" and "bocks" feature in Norway . . . "Pilsners" and "Porters" are among Sweden's souvenirs (right).

of spirits and of beer are thus consolidated. (Whisky is distilled in its native countries from a wort which is much the same as un-hopped beer.) "There are still many people familiar with the brewing of juniper ale, especially in the coastal areas near Bergen," wrote Odd Nordland. He also noted its popularity in the smaller industrial towns by the shores of the Oslo Fjord. Historically, Norway provided much of the juniper for the great gin-distilling industry of The Netherlands, trading the berries for supplies of the finished product. With some irony, home-brewers of juniper ale sometimes call their beer *Bols*.

Juniper beers and home-brewing lie at odds with the Norwegian pure-beer law and the strict controls on the sale of alcohol. About ten per cent of Norway's population cannot buy beer in their home district be-cause the local municipality forbids it. In many other communities, beer can be ob-tained only from a special liquor shop. The State has 80-odd liquor shops, concerning themselves especially with spirits and im-ported beers. The most restrictive areas are the West and South coasts; the most liberal the East, the inland areas and the half-dozen main cities. There are more than 400 drinking places which serve spirits. Many of these are restaurants, though it is permissible to drink without eating; some are simply bars.

Norway has a non-alcoholic beer called, appropriately, Zero. A low-alcohol beer (2.2 per cent by volume; Tax class I) is called Brigg, after the sailing vessel. This may be an allusive attempt to associate the beer with Denmark's *skibsøl*, though the etymology can hardly be the same.

Except in the case of Zero and Brigg, beer may not be advertised. The advertising of tobacco is also banned. The marketing of beer in Norway is less than competitive. Under political pressure, the brewers drew up a voluntary cartel scheme in the 1930s.

This ensures that brewers concentrate on their own hinterlands, and do not engage in sales wars with their neighbours. Sales out-side the brewery's immediate territory are arranged by quotas which are worked out to two decimal places. If a brewer sells too much in a competitor's territory, he may have to pay a compensatory levy.

There are 15 brewery companies, owning 18 plants. None is widely known outside of Norway, though Ringnes, of Oslo, has some export trade to the United States. The capital has another two breweries, Frydenlund and Schou, which are owned by a single com-pany. Breweries in Oslo, Trondheim and Stavanger produce Tuborg under licence at a density of 10.5 Plato (Tax Class II). In Bergen and Arendal, Heineken is brewed under licence. In the smaller towns, brewer-ies are tiny and very local indeed; the brewery at Sandefjord is not even in the trade organization. The local brewery in Tromsø is the Northernmost in the world.

The biggest-selling beer-style is the *Pilsener*-type, which has an alcohol percentage by volume of 2.5–4.75 per cent (Tax Class II). In the same Tax Class is the *Baier* (Bavarian) style, which is a dark copper-brown, and has a malty palate. A stronger *lager* is marketed as Export beer, with an alcohol content of 5.4 per cent volume (Tax Class III). The strongest styles are the very dark, strong-tasting, rich *bokk* and the *Jule* Christmas beer, which is full-bodied malty and sweetish. Both styles have an alcohol content of 6.3, and fit into Tax Class III.

The laws concerning drink in Norway and some of its neighbouring countries are sub-ject to change, and they do not always evolve in a liberal direction, as has happened elsewhere. In Norway the Right-leaning populist Christian Democrat party takes a strong moral stand. Temperance is by no means a dead issue, notwithstanding the nation's brewing heritage.

Sweden

LIVING TOGETHER on the one peninsula, and having in the past been unified politically, Norway and Sweden inevitably share many traditions. Rural customs have, however, better survived in Norway, which is even more thinly populated than Sweden, and considerably less industrialized. Home-brewing nonetheless enjoyed a revival in Sweden during the 1970s, though this was a curious mix of urban chic and rural tradition.

In the earlier years of the 20th century, a maltless beverage was brewed in many parts of Sweden, again with the use of juniper. The drink was "marvellously good," according to the Swedish author Harry Martinson. He recalled the brew having been commonly drunk in his home around 1915, usually served in wooden drinking vessels. One problem was the uneven ripening of the juniper berries. "When all the berries of the juniper bush ripen at the same time, the Day of Judgment is drawing nigh," wrote Martinson. So popular was the juniper beer that it was marketed commercially in the 1960s by a small local brewery at Vimmerby, about 250 kilometres South of Stockholm. A beer with angelica flavouring, and a honey mead (in Swedish, *mjöd*) are a couple of comparable specialities devised by the local brewery in Östersund, a town which might claim to stand at the middle of Sweden.

Sweden also has *svagdricka*, a dark and sweet brew with added yeast and a low alcohol content (usually 1·8 per cent by weight; Tax Class I). There are breweries which produce only *svagdricka* (as there are firms in Denmark which produce only low-alcohol beers), but it is also marketed by most conventional brewers. *Svagdricka* is especially popular among older people, and in rural areas, so its future may be in some doubt.

The more conventional style in Class I is *lattöl* (small beer). Like most Swedish beers, this is a mildly-hopped, light-coloured *lager*. Its name indicates nothing other than the modesty of its alcoholic intentions. Class II was until 1977 split into "A" and "B" classes, the first with an alcohol content of 2·8 per cent by weight, the second with 3·6. In that year, legislation was introduced to combine the two categories, but to do so at the lower limit. In effect, Class IIB was abolished. Until then, the higher *Mellanöl* category had enjoyed 65 per cent of all Swedish beer sales.

The abolition of Sweden's most popular beer-category followed much noisy debate among the public, in the Press, and in Parliament. In pubs and cafes, the question was asked out aloud, with a mock-Shakespearian gravity more suited to matters Danish: "IIB

Among today's Swedish beers, Three Towns has a literary ring, though the name refers simply to Gothenburg, Stockholm and Malmö, all major Pripps' territories. The sailor is a Northerner from Norrlands. Sadly, Åbro no longer produces a juniper ale.

or not IIB?" When the decision was finally made, drinkers hoped that it might at some date in the future be reversed, but hopes were dashed soon afterwards when the moderate-Left Social Democrat party was defeated at a General Election. The Social Democrats, and the moderate Right, are generally sympathetic towards the beer-drinker, but the Centrists and the rural Populists include many temperance supporters among their ranks.

Already, Sweden's mild *porter* was brewed at a meagre 2·8 per cent, and the new law threatened the country's *mörkt* (dark) beers, a 3·6 per cent, bottom-fermented approximation of the English *pale ale*. (A more malty "Bavarian-style" beer can also sometimes be found). These *mörkt* beers had been very much the choice of the regular, dedicated beer-drinker. There is a more respectable 4·5 per cent category (Class III), but sales of this allegedly "strong" beer are restricted to the 300 State-controlled alcohol shops.

Public drinking-places in Sweden manifest themselves under a variety of names. The traditional *öl café* is dying out. It is a male preserve, and increasingly one for old men. Unlike the English pub, it has not managed to retain its essential character while simultaneously attracting new generations of drinkers. Even in Stockholm, there are only half a dozen *öl cafés* in the original style, though mock-English pubs have become a recognized drinking-place in Sweden. Beer is also drunk extensively in cafes where music (often jazz) is performed, and at discos and restaurants. The law requires meals to be served with drink, but this rule is no longer enforced except in small, temperance-minded communities. Aperitifs, whisky and brandy are also usually available without a meal, but it is less easy to obtain drinks of the schnapps and vodka type, including Swedish *aquavits* and the local pure spirit commonly known as *renat*. In common with home-brewing, there is also a custom of (illegal) home-distilling.

The country's biggest brewing company was formed by a merger in 1963. The partners in the merger were two major concerns, the Stockholm Brewery Company, and the Gothenburg firm of Pripps. The Stockholm name was dropped, because its metropolitan connotations were not necessarily helpful in provincial markets. In 1975, the Swedish Government took a 60 per cent share in the merged company, which continues to be known simply as Pripps. The original Pripps was founded in 1828, in Gothenburg, and today's semi-State company still has one of its main breweries there, as well as the Stockholm brewery and another major plant in Malmö. Pripps has half a dozen smaller breweries elsewhere in Sweden, and has bought others for conversion into distribution depots. It has 50 depots, one of which is 100 kilometres North of the Arctic Circle.

The second largest beer-producer is a private corporation, Falken, of Falkenberg, on the West Coast. Falken has been controlled by the same family for three generations. Close behind, and larger if non-beer interests like soft drinks are taken into account, comes the Wårby co-operative. This concern, in a suburb of Stockholm, is a consumers' co-operative, selling its products through its own shops and outlets. There is also a consumers' co-operative in Sollefteå, about 450 kilometres to the North, and a substantial producers' co-operative at Skruv, in the South-East.

In all, the country has 15 brewing companies. Apart from Pripps, although some firms have a couple of breweries, most have only one. Among the smallest are Åbro, in Vimmerby; Appeltofftska and Östra, both in Halmstad; Nässjö, in the town of the same name, between Stockholm and Gothenburg; and Kopparberg, in the town of the same name, West of Stockholm. Kopparberg is outside of the Swedish Brewers' Association.

Until 1976, Swedish brewers were permitted to use adjuncts or sugar to the extent of 20 per cent. Some use less, and few of them use more, despite a change in the law. In 1976, the permissible percentage was increased to 35 per cent, though this level is generally found only in beers from other parts of Europe which are brewed under licence.

Finland

THE CUSTOM OF BREWING was brought from Asia to Northern Europe by the first tribes to cross the Gulf of Finland, in about A.D. 100 or 200. They even had a god of beer and barley, called *Pekko*. To what extent these same peoples may have introduced brewing to Central Europe during their migration is not clear, but beer remained a central part of their folk-culture long after the introduction of Christianity in 1150.

Hops, too, were introduced to Finland at a very early stage. In 1442, King Christopher acted to stop the import of the costly cone, by decreeing that every farmer should have a hop-garden of at least 40 poles. By the late 1800s, when Finland was part of the Tsarist Empire, the country had (along with Poland) the most advanced brewing industry in all the Russias. One of its most famous breweries was an early bottom-fermenting plant at Viborg, capital of Karelia. This town is in the lands which were subsequently taken over by the Soviet Union, though there is still a brewery in Karelia at Lappeenranta, on the Finnish side of the border.

The restrictions on alcohol which spread through the whole of the North in the early part of the 20th century were, ironically, toughest of all in Finland, with its deeply-rooted beer culture. Finland was the only European country to introduce total Prohibition, which lasted from 1919 to 1932/3.

The glacial purity of
the Finlandia brew gets
a helping hand in the
lagering tanks at
Mallasjuoma (below).
Tampere's brewery goes
to war with Admirals
of all nations. The
maritime beer has a
conventional density of
12·5 degrees Balling.

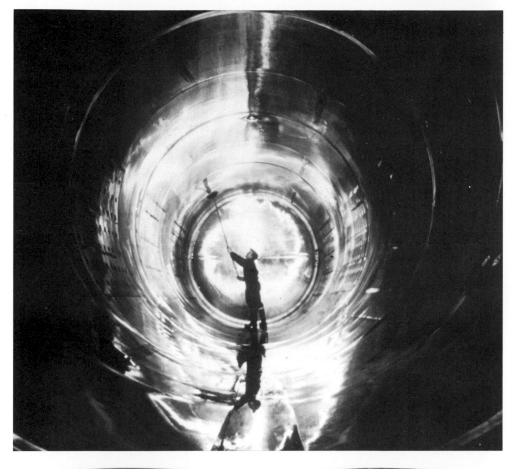

While this thirsty legislation has long gone, a
law which favours the drinker remains in
force. No grains other than barley may be
used in the brewing of beer, though this law
does permit the use of sugar. This pure-beer
edict cannot, of course, be imposed in the
case of home-brewing, which has a distinctive
flavour of its own in Finland.

A unique beverage called *sahti* is produced
by the home-brewers of Finland. It is made
with a mix of barley and rye malts. Hops are
used, but they work along with juniper
berries and branches, and straw. Apart from
contributing to the flavour, the juniper
branches and straw act as a filter. In true ale-
wife tradition, it is the women who brew the
sahti, and their conscientious care in this
matter has been celebrated since Olaus Mag-
nus wrote his history of the Scandinavian
peoples during the time of the Vasa dynasty.
In particular, he praised the cleanliness of the
women brewers; if the wrong micro-organisms get into the brew, it can easily be spoiled.
The preparation of *sahti* is a long day's work,
and fermentation takes a week, usually in
milk churns. In many country households,
the sauna is considered to be a suitable
building in which to brew, and a relaxing
place in which to drink the end-product.

The magic of *sahti* was described in the
following terms by a Finnish magazine: "It
is a deceptive drink, just as Champagne is.

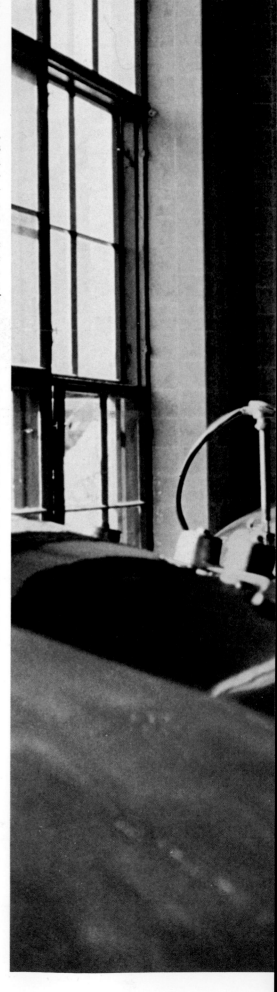

You drink, relax, talk . . . and then, when you try to get up, your legs won't hold you . . . you're wonderfully sleepy." The writer argued that *sahti*, if properly made, will not cause a bad hangover. It can, nonetheless, be very strong, sometimes containing as much as ten per cent alcohol by weight.

It is rather easier for the State to control the strengths of beer produced in commercial breweries. These are all light-coloured *lagers*, with a medium-to-heavy hopping rate. The term *bock* is used, though hardly with its German significance, and there is a lone, full-bodied, sweetish 5·5 per cent *stout*, brewed by Sinebrychoff, of Helsinki. This *stout* is available only at alcohol stores, and not in bars or restaurants. Sinebrychoff is one of three major brewing companies which share 85 per cent of the market.

The biggest is Mallasjuoma, with breweries in Lahti, Heinola and Oulu. Mallasjuoma attributes the quality of its Finlandia beer to, "a 10,000-year-old phenomenon of the glacial age." The brewery says that its water is of a particularly fine quality because it "springs forth from fountains formed inside the gravel eskars during the glacial epoch." An eskar is a ridge of post-glacial gravel in a river valley. The brewery adds that gravel is "the finest filter known." For good measure, it adds: "Scientists have also proved that the light summer nights of Finland and the bright, clear sunshine especially contribute to the development of such a full-flavoured malt barley."

The other major brewing company is Hartwall, with breweries in Turku and Vaasa, as well as the one in Karelia. There are also four very small brewing companies: Olvi, of Iisalmi; Lapin, of Tornio (which produces only Class III beer); Ranin, of Kuopio (which also produces alcohol-free beer); and Pyynikki, a family firm in Tampere. The latter produces a Class AIV beer called Admiral, labelled with a whole series of great mariners, from Horatio Nelson to Alfred von Tirpitz.

The breweries are strictly controlled by the State Alcohol Monopoly; in effect, they are franchised by this body, which also has its own liquor stores and distils its own Finnish vodka. The most widely available beer is of 2·25 per cent alcohol by weight (Class I). Although they have a right to produce a Class II beer (2·25–3·0 per cent), the breweries feel there is no market for half-measures, and decline to take up this option. Therefore the next category is Class III (3·0–3·7 per cent). Since 1955, a fourth class has existed. These Class IV (or "A"-Class) beers have an alcohol content of 4·0–4·5 per cent. *Stout* is a special case.

The serving of alcoholic drinks is generally permitted only in connection with a catering business, but the drinker is not compelled to eat. Some cafés and restaurants are not permitted to serve spirits, and they are all categorized according to the classes of beer which they may provide. Any slackening of Finland's tight drink laws has been vigorously opposed by the Christian League. Local veto rights exist, and 40 out of Finland's 500 communities have voted to keep out Class III and IV beers. Temperance pressure also led to the establishment of a long-term Parliamentary Committee to review drink laws.

Karelia is celebrated by Hartwall, while the Olvi brewery remembers two war heroes, Johan August Sandels and Georg Carl von Döbeln. Both fought in the Russo–Finnish war of 1808–1809.

Belgium

The kingdom of beer ... where The Netherlands, Belgium and France stand side by side across Flanders fields. Where man's industry and his destructiveness have made history, his thirst must be slaked. The life and lifestyle of the Low Countries go on in the heart of Belgian Flanders (left). Bike, beer and frites ... café in Tielt.

IF EUROPE's King of Beer were alive today, he would be a Belgian. He would be happy to return to his native land, and take up residence in the towering, gabled and gilded *Maison des Brasseurs*, in Brussels, the only one of the guild-halls in the Grand' Place which is still used for its original purpose (as well as housing a small beer-museum). He would be suffused with joy at the zeal and devotion which his present-day subjects bring to the pursuit of his interests, challenging the world in both the size of their thirsts and the exotic range of their brews.

The monarchy of beer in Europe was bestowed by legend upon the 13th-century Duke Jean I of Brabant, Louvain and Antwerp in honour of his bibulous deeds, still celebrated by the Belgian brewers' *Chevalerie de Fourquet*. The Duke, known in Flemish as Jan Primus and all over Europe by the corruption "Cambrinus," is credited, among his other attainments, with having introduced the toast as a social custom.

A glass might also be raised, with sac-ramental reverence, to Saint Arnoldus the Strong, of Oudenaarde. He performed a miracle, which has made him a patron saint of brewers ever since. He successfully invoked God to create more beer when an abbey brewery had collapsed in Flanders during the 11th century. Several abbeys in Belgium still brew their own beer, and they produce some very distinguished ales.

Oudenaarde remains a famous brewing town, though it may be better known outside Belgium for its Gobelin associations, or as the site of a famous victory by John Churchill, 1st Duke of Marlborough, against the French, in 1708.

Saint Arnoldus of Oudenaarde is also said to have reconciled the two ethnic groups between whom Belgium is divided, and whose monumental appetite for beer is one of few shared attitudes. Even such thirsty corners of the world as Bavaria and the parched Northern Territories of Australia are rivalled in their beer-consumption by the Dutch-speaking segment of Belgium: the provinces

Almost every town in Belgium has its own brewery, and there is a whole range of local "speciality" beers, the popularity of each extending around its own home district. Pilsener-type beers are brewed, and drunk, everywhere but most especially in the triangle between the cities of Brussels, Louvain and Mechelen.

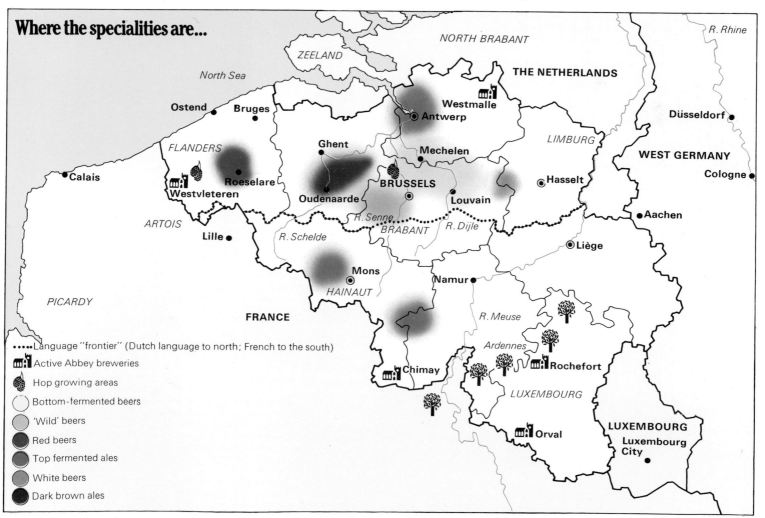

Where the specialities are...

- ●●●● Language "frontier" (Dutch language to north; French to the south)
- Active Abbey breweries
- Hop growing areas
- Bottom-fermented beers
- 'Wild' beers
- Red beers
- Top fermented ales
- White beers
- Dark brown ales

The Grand' Place of Brussels is swathed in small streets named after the historic industries and trades of the city. A moment's walk from the brewers' street is their palatial guild-house and museum, headquarters for the Knights of the Mashing Fork.

of Flanders (with their dark beers); Antwerp (with its top-fermented draught ale); Limburg (with a classic Pilsener); and bi-lingual Brabant (with its bizarre cherry beers and wheat brews). Nor is the staggering national average seriously diminished by what passes for moderation in French-speaking Hainaut, Namur or Liège. Even beyond the Ardennes, in the Belgian province of Luxembourg (French-speaking) and the sovereign Grand Duchy of the same name, they take considerable amounts of beer with their wine.

Wine-production in Belgium is of minimal proportions. Fine grapes are grown near Brussels, in the area of Hoeilaart and Overijse, but the local people of that district are equally likely to wash down their favourite dark bread and butter with a draught of beer. Acres of vineyards in the Ardennes were destroyed in the First World War, and Belgians have since contented themselves with their neighbours' wines, especially those of the Grand Duchy. The whole of Belgium produces only 13 thousand hectolitres a year, compared with 122 thousand in the Grand Duchy, six million hectolitres in Germany, and 50 million in France.

Despite the French cultural influence, and the Belgians' well-deserved reputation as gourmands, the Belgians are only modest wine-drinkers. They drink more wine than they grow, but they must be a slight disappointment to Bacchus. The Flemings readily wash down mountains of Zeeland mussels, and icy spreads of oysters, with beer. They even cook their national *carbonade* in beer, so they can hardly be expected to accompany it with any other drink. Even though the people of the Walloon (French speaking) provinces sample the grape more often, the national average consumption of wine per head each year is a mere 15 litres, compared with about 140 litres of beer. In the volume of their beer-drinking, the Belgians have on occasion headed the world's league-table, and are always among the top three countries (along with West Germany and Czechoslovakia).

Almost half of Belgium's beer-consumption is in the home, yet the country's ten million people support 60,000 cafés, as many as there are pubs in England, a country with five times the population. Since these cafés are crowded into a country which is no bigger than Wales, and smaller than Bavaria or Ohio, they appear at every street-corner, and often next door to each other, three or four at a time, especially in the towns and cities of Flanders.

Café Sport vies for attention with *Café Stadhuis*, *Chez Theo* with *Chez Michel*. No

R.S.C. ANDERLECHT '75-'76

licence is required in order to open a café; there are no laws demanding that the establishment close at any time, save that it should not have loud music after 11.00. Most of the drinkers are men, and women are usually accompanied. There are the larger, rather stately, cafés, and there are the little places — where pinball machines clatter, table-football spins, and bar-billiards pursues its leisurely pace. On the walls, markers bearing the names of city football teams may be slotted neatly into leagues, reflecting the fortunes of Anderlecht (Brussels) or Standard (Liège) and lesser *équipes* in their various divisions. There'll be little to eat, beyond the odd sausage, but no shortage of beer.

The serving of spirits in cafés was forbidden by law in 1919, at a time when the United States was introducing Prohibition and the British their own restrictive laws concerning drinking hours. The national spirit of the Low Countries, *jenever* (juniper gin), has continued to be available "under the counter," while the law has had the effect of sustaining a whole range of very strong beers as an alternative form of short, potent drink.

Café Sport . . . one of the most distinguished soccer teams in Europe are Anderlecht, of Brussels. They are sponsored by the local Belle-Vue brewery. The smaller Timmerman's brewery backs a cycling team (top picture).

The distillation and fermentation of berries, fruits, spices and herbs, the manufacture of both spirits and flavoured beers, date back to the time when Bruges was a great Burgundian trading port. Belgian drinkers still occasionally add a drop of grenadine to their wheat beers – a practice which may have given birth to the odd British custom of topping up "lager" (Pilsener beer) with lime. The Burgundian connection is also subconsciously evoked when a fine brew is discussed. Good beers are often described by devotees as "the Burgundy of Belgium."

Like Frenchmen drinking wine, Belgians are inclined to order *le ballon*. Belgium's *ballon* will vary in shape depending upon the beer which it is meant to hold. Each brewer has his own style . . . delicate glasses which might suit a fine brandy; chunky goblets; tall-stemmed bowls worthy of medieval castles. Fastidious drinkers might equally request *la flûte* (the tall type of Champagne glass), *la chope* (a mug), *la pint*, or some other shape of glass which is kept by their favourite café. Even the regular Pilsener beer, the *pils*, the everyday "café" drink, may on occasion be served in a distinguished-looking glass, but it is the great array of local specials which demand such presentation as a matter of right. Many local brewers also have their own individualistic bottles, often corked, including shapes which in other countries might be thought more fitting to a Burgundy, or even a Champagne.

The most unassuming of Belgian brews would pass as acceptable beers in many countries. Some of the better "household beers,"

Glasses fit for the Burgundy of Belgium

An imposing, classic ballon is usually chosen for the serving of a distinguished abbey beer. Each brew has its own variation on the theme.

The distinctive shape is that of the thistle, Scotland's national emblem. In Belgium, this unusual symbolic glass is used for Gordon's Scotch Ale.

A dark beer with a dense "head" can best display its creamy quality in a wide glass . . . another ballon variation

The Germanic peoples of Northern Europe are beer-drinkers, while the Romantic nations of Southern Europe prefer wine. The cultural line between the two groups runs right through Belgium, but the national drink is unquestionably beer.

What the Europeans drink

Figures per head per year in litres

	West Germany	Belgium	France	Italy	The Netherlands	Britain	Denmark	Ireland
Beer	147	143	45	16	73	112	128	126
Wine	19	15	106	101	8	4	10	2

dismissed as being "for the kids," may still have potencies of around 3·0 Belgian degrees. Although this figure is based on original gravity, it does give a very rough indication of alcoholic percentage by volume. (Belgian degrees are used by the excise authorities. The Plato system is also used in Belgium, notably in laws concerning the labelling of foodstuffs.)

All the beers of the Benelux countries are labelled according to the same standard categories. The lesser household beers, other-

For a golden triple, a lofty glass . . . all the better to display its glittering clarity.

The shaped Chimay glass contrives to retain the fragrant aroma of this rich, full-bodied beer.

Even the most conventional bottom-fermented beer can be given a touch of elegance in a stemmed, tall glass.

DEDIÈ AUX BRASSEURS, NÈ

FARO REGALE SES AMIS À L'OCCASION

Notez Bien, Ces bières jusqu'a la première Separation sont de Bruxelles Gand et les

A. Père Faro. B. Susse Lambic. C. Jef Half en half D. Lieve

Liere   Hoegaerde   Termonde

I. Janneken Kavesse. K. Pié Hoegaerds. Pauwel Kwak . L. M

The individualistic brewmasters of Belgium produced endless local specialities in the early 1800s, when the drawing on the right was produced by the caricaturist De Loose. Most of the brews which he personified are long forgotten. Even Faro, father of all Belgian beer types, is little more than a shadow.

wise known as "table beers," are labelled as "Cat III." Those around the 3·0–4·0 degree level (formerly known in Belgium as "Bock," and "Export," though these descriptions mean different things in different countries) are rated as "Cat II." The regular café beers are usually around 4·6–4·8, and are rated "Cat I." Stronger beers fit into "Cat S" ("Superieur"); terms like "De Luxe" are meaningless. Most Belgian versions of English ales, and the better-quality brown beers, have ratings in the 5·0–7·0 range. A Belgian drinker might regard these beers as being of "medium" strength. Abbey beers and Belgium's popular "Scotch" ales are usually in the 7·0–10·0 range, along with several strong and brown ales.

In the range of their beers, if not quite the extent of their thirsts, the Belgians can match their mighty neighbours to the East, across the German border. To the immediate North, Dutch beer-fanciers congregate in those provinces which interlock with the Belgian border (sharing the same historic names, like Brabant and Limburg – though the eponymous cheese-town confuses geography further by lying 100 miles across the German frontier). To the immediate South, French Flanders, the French Ardennes and the Alsace-Lorraine are the greatest homelands of the Gallic beer-drinker. Across the water to the West lies the English county of Kent, where Britain's hop-growing industry was implanted by Flemish immigrants, and whence fine bitter ales have come ever since.

Belgium has always been a crossroads; Brussels is the political capital of Western Europe; but the country's role as a beer kingdom may owe less to politics or geography than it does to geology. In a country where horses are still used to pull the plough, it takes the sudden headstocks of coalmines around Mons and Liège to recall what was in the 1700s and 1800s Europe's Industrial Revolution. From Dover under the English Channel to Pas de Calais, from the Somme to the Ruhr, lies the remains of a single great coalfield. This region was industrialised by the British, Belgians, French and Germans; it has been fought over by the soldiers of each country; and the tastes of each nation are apparent in the beers drunk there.

The memorials of past struggles – of blood, sweat and tears – may not coincide precisely with the manifestations of thirst, but the relationship is close. The region once known as the Austrasian coalfield might also be regarded as the heartland of beer-drinking in Western Europe.

It is a heartland to match that of Bavaria and Bohemia in the East.

...CIANTS DE BIÈRE, CABARETIERS ET À TOUT LE MONDE.

FARO HOUDT FEEST TER GELEGENHEYD VAN DEN VREDE.

A PAIX
E. Karel
n-Brnynen.
Depose

Drydraed. F. Tonne Leuvens G. Lamme Peeterman. H. Luppe Diesters.

M. Signor Geersten-bier N. Colas brune. O. Bruynen Bacchus. & &

Veteran drinkers in Belgium may regret the passing of many fine brews, the victims of mergers and closures, but the present-day café still stocks a range of drinks which is the envy of visiting beermen from other countries. Most cafés adopt the formality of displaying in their windows a menu-card which identifies the drinks on offer within. The list will be dominated by different types of beer: no spirits, perhaps an aperitif or wine towards the end of the card with the coffee, tea and bouillon. The regular café brew is a Belgian Pilsener-style beer. The *pils* may be by Stella Artois, Jupiler, Maes, Lamot or one of the many smaller brewers. There may also be a Belgian premium *pils* with a mock-Czech name, and there will certainly be an imported *pils*, probably from Denmark. There may also be an abbreviated local imitation Dortmunder beer, perhaps even a Münchener. Then comes the serious beer-drinking. There will be a gueuze, the wild, wheat brew of the Brussels area, and possibly some more fanciful derivative of this type. The greatest variety of all is among the top-fermented ales. Indigenous Belgian ales, strong ales, dark brown beers, ales brewed in the Trappist manner, beers brewed in England specially for the Belgian market, "Scotch" ales which are unique to Belgium, a variety of stouts, Belgian, English and Irish . . . the top-fermented brews beloved of Belgium's beer connoisseurs cover a whole range of colours and densities. Their strengths are categorised in their labelling, but distinctions between their styles can be only arbitrary. Every brewer of a top-fermented beer is inclined to regard his product as a unique speciality, to be ordered by its brand-name. Belgian drinkers tend to agree or, in the brewer's locality, perhaps to ask for a *"spéciale"*. Such *spéciales* are many :–

Red beers

IF THE HUNGARIANS had not thought to call one of their full red wines *Bull's Blood*, the name might have been applied instead to the beer brewed in West Flanders by Rodenbach, of Roeselare. This dark beer, known simply by its maker's name, qualifies better for the

Individualistic . . . a taste to acquire

epithet "red" than any of the copper-coloured English brews which are sometimes similarly described in Continental Europe.

Not only the colour and fruity bouquet of Rodenbach, but also its alchemy, qualify it as a one-off among Belgium's colourful beer styles. A regular top-fermented brew is blended with a beer which has been aged for at least 18 months in oak. Barley, maize grits, semi-dark Vienna malts and caramel go into the brew, the latter two ingredients creating the colour. The formation of lactic acid in the brewing process imparts a flavour which is tingling-sharp and acid-sour.

Rodenbach is very much an acquired taste, and one which some drinkers might be happy to live without. Other drinkers are equally positive in their devotion to this unusual, refreshing, medium-strong beer. As a one-brewery speciality, Rodenbach is among the many individualistic Belgium beers which are vulnerable to any harsh economic wind that might blow round their neighbourhood. There is no substitute for Rodenbach, but its devotees might also enjoy *Oud Piro*, a brew produced not far away by Bevernagie, of Lichtervelde, West Flanders.

White beers

LIKE THE GERMANS, with their *Berliner Weisse*, the Belgians have traditionally brewed a "white" wheat beer. The Belgian variety has been associated with the town of Louvain. Since the town is Flemish, and lies at a point of some linguistic confusion, these beers are less properly referred to as *Blanche de Louvain* than as *Leuwense Wit*.

An altogether easier solution was the use for many years of the brand-name *Peeterman's*

Refreshing . . . for a cloudy summer's day

to describe the town's favourite local special. The people of Leuven are known in Belgium as Peetermen after the town's church of St Peter.

In the mid 1970s, production of *Peeterman's* was run-down by the Artois company, which owned the brewery. The *Peeterman's* bottle, one of the few with the old-fashioned white pot stopper, slowly vanished from the shelves of local cafés. White beer, so called because of its cloudy colouring, had been something of a seasonal hot-weather re-

fresher. It was a low-density beer, but it had its devotees. Now, it was left in the hands of any local small brewer who caught the summer mood.

One brewer has keenly persisted with his own stronger, clearer version of white beer in the town of Hoegaarden, about 20 miles to the east of Leuven. The local brewery there closed in the 1950s, after 500 years, but a local man restarted production of *Hoegaardse*

Wit in the 1960s. Appropriately, this brewer of white beer was formerly in the milk-bottling business.

The Hoegaarden brewery also produces a strong "Triple," called *Grand Cru*. Some of the equipment from the original Hoegaarden brewery can now be seen not far away in the huge open-air museum of Belgian country life at Bokrijk, near Hasselt, in the province of Limburg.

Keeping the Grand Cru tradition

Revivalist brewer . . . tending the mash tun in Hoegaarden. The white beer of Hoegaarden and its companion Grand Cru are full-flavoured, extremely dry and thirst-quenching.

As featured on the beer's label . . . the traditional Hoegaarden jug, which is kept closed to retain the natural effervescence of the brew. This example belongs to the owner of the Hoegaardse brewery.

Wild beers

IT IS BECAUSE they "rebel" against the orthodoxies of brewing, by fermenting without the addition of yeast, that the wheat beers of the Bruegel country have on occasion been termed "wild". These spontaneously-fermenting beers are produced by traditional methods in only a very limited area, which coincides roughly with the Belgian National Tourist Board's "Bruegel route." The area is called Payottenland, and its atmosphere is held to contain micro-organisms which promote the fermentation of beer without the assistance of the brewer.

Payottenland is on the Senne, Brussels'

river, to the west of the capital's Anderlecht district. From his home in the Marolles, the Flemish "Old Town," Bruegel could soon have been in the Senne valley. Perhaps it was there that he captured such beery scenes as *The Peasant Dance*.

Because Payottenland is on the edge of the capital, the Bruxellois regard its beers as their own local speciality. The basic "wild" wheat beer is known as *lambic*, but in Bruegel's day, a weaker version called *faro* was the everyday beer of Brussels. Although the Vanderlinden brewery still uses the name *faro* for one of its lesser *lambic* beers, the term is almost extinct.

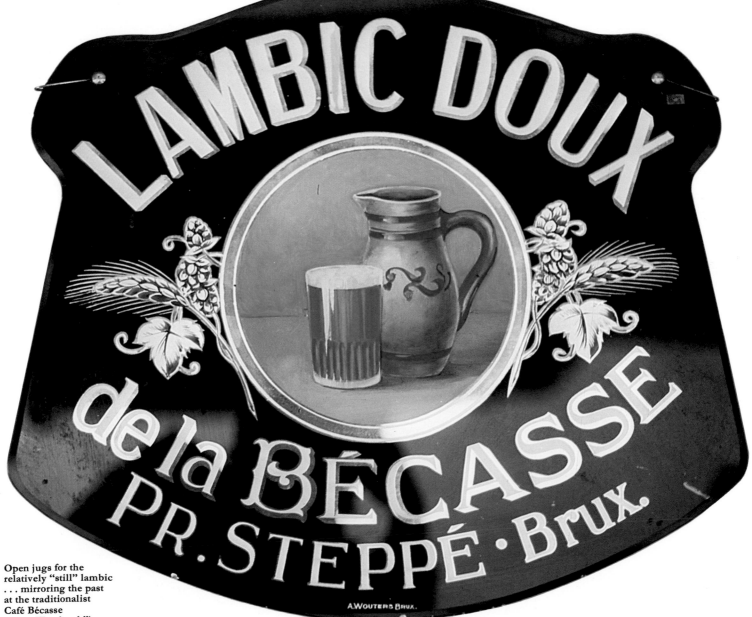

Open jugs for the relatively "still" lambic ... mirroring the past at the traditionalist Café Bécasse ("The Woodcock").

117

Bruegel was living in Brussels, close to the countryside of Payottenland, when he painted "The Peasant Dance." As his festive Flemish rustics celebrated their saint's day, were they drinking lambic from those stoneware jugs?

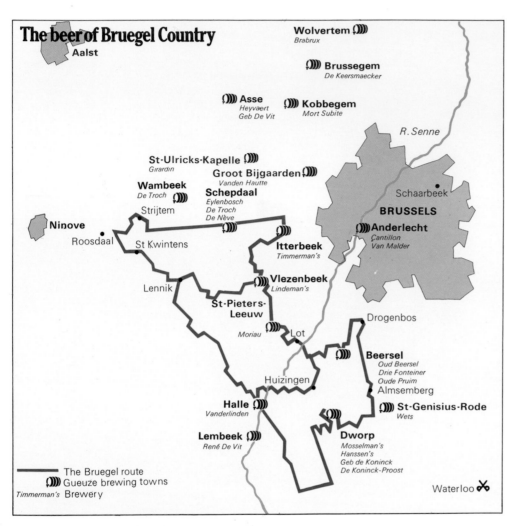

The beer of Bruegel Country

Aalst

Wolvertem 〰
Brabrux

〰 **Brussegem**
De Keersmaecker

〰 **Asse**
Heyvaert
Geb De Vit

〰 **Kobbegem**
Mort Subite

R. Senne

St-Ulricks-Kapelle 〰
Girardin

Groot Bijgaarden 〰
Vanden Hautte

Wambeek 〰
De Troch
Strijtem

Schepdaal
Eylenbosch
De Troch
De Nève

Schaarbeek

BRUSSELS

Ninove
Roosdaal
St Kwintens

〰

Itterbeek
Timmerman's

〰 **Anderlecht**
Cantillon
Van Malder

〰 **Vlezenbeek**
Lindeman's

Lennik

St-Pieters-Leeuw

〰 Lot
Moriau

Drogenbos

〰 **Beersel**
Oud Beersel
Drie Fonteiner
Oude Pruim
Almsemberg

Huizingen

〰 **Halle**
Vanderlinden

〰 **St-Genisius-Rode**
Wets

Lembeek 〰
René De Vit

〰 **Dworp**
Mosselman's
Hanssen's
Geb de Koninck
De Koninck-Proost

Waterloo ✂

—— The Bruegel route
〰 Gueuze brewing towns
Timmerman's Brewery

Bruegel's wanderings in Payottenland merged in his mind, providing a backcloth for graphic scenes of Flemish life. Visitors to Payottenland can follow his meanderings, and sample en route many fine and characteristically-local gueuze-lambic beers.

Vanderlinden's *faro* is a speciality of the Café Sainte Catherine, in the street and quarter of the same name, in the Old Town. *Lambic* itself is a speciality of the Café Bécasse, a popular rendezvous for young beer-drinkers, not far from Brussels' Grand' Place, off the Rue des Fripiers. At the Bécasse, *lambic* is served from the barrel, in blue-grey stoneware jugs.

Apart from such specialist cafés, the villages of Payottenland are the best place in which to sample pure *lambic*. Some cafés buy their *lambic* still fermenting in the barrel, when it is a mere three months old, slightly cloudy, and very sour. In other cafés, it may be three or four years old, clearer, with a vinous bitter-sweet flavour. Young *lambic* has no froth whatever, and it gains only a slight "head" in the process of ageing. The expert drinkers of Payottenland know where to find the *lambic* of their preference; visitors have to discover this by trial and error. Some cafés have both young and old *lambic*, but these are very few.

The beer is "young" until its first birthday, and "old" after not less than "two summers."

A surviving art

The art of the gueuze brewer lies in his ability to judge the maturity of his basic lambic brews, to blend them with sensitivity, to ferment the melange for just the right length of time. The brewing of a true gueuze defies the wisdoms of modern business. The beer has to be fermented for several years, tying up valuable space and capital. Even after it has been bottled, it is still racked for further conditioning (right). Belgian drinkers far from Payottenland cherish the foil-topped bottle (1), but it might well explode if the fermentable solids were not first filtered out. The labels of the regular filtered (2) and unfiltered (3) bottles differ slightly in design as well as text. Local drinkers in the neighbourhood of the brewery like their gueuze still to bear the mark of its maker (4).

Maturing *lambic* at the Timmerman's brewery, in Itterbeek, lies in gallery after gallery of wooden barrels. Some of the barrels, which are 75 years old, stand eight feet high, and contain 6,000 litres. The galleries are dark, cool, and cobwebbed, providing an amenable home for the magical micro-organisms of Payottenland. It is said that successful *lambic* brewers dare not change anything in their breweries for fear of disturbing these micro-organisms, and research at the Flemish University of Leuven has yet to solve wholly the puzzle of spontaneous fermentation.

Most *lambic* is blended to make a fruity beer called *gueuze*. This contains one-third old beer and two-thirds young, and the melange is then fermented for a further year in the bottle before being distributed to cafés. At Timmerman's, those galleries not bulging with barrels are stacked from ground to ceiling with litre bottles of maturing *gueuze*. When the bottles are laid down, the upper side is marked with whitewash. When they have to be moved, the same side is left upwards, so that the brew is not disturbed.

Local drinkers in Payottenland favour the traditional litre bottle, stopped with a cork rather than a metal cap. For wider distribution, Timmerman's uses the more conven-

A God and a Devil among the gueuze pantheon of beers. The Devil is a native of Payottenland; the God is an outsider.

tional modern method of bottling. The brewery's naturally-conditioned *gueuze* is clearly labelled *refermentation naturelle en bouteille/met natuurlijke bergisting in de fles*. Timmerman's also produces a filtered *gueuze* – which does not, of course, carry this mark. Filtered *gueuze* is less likely to cause an explosion in the bottle during transportation, but lacks quite the "bite" of "live" beer. The time taken to produce the traditional *gueuze* hardly matches up to the criteria of modern industry. Brewers who pursue the traditional

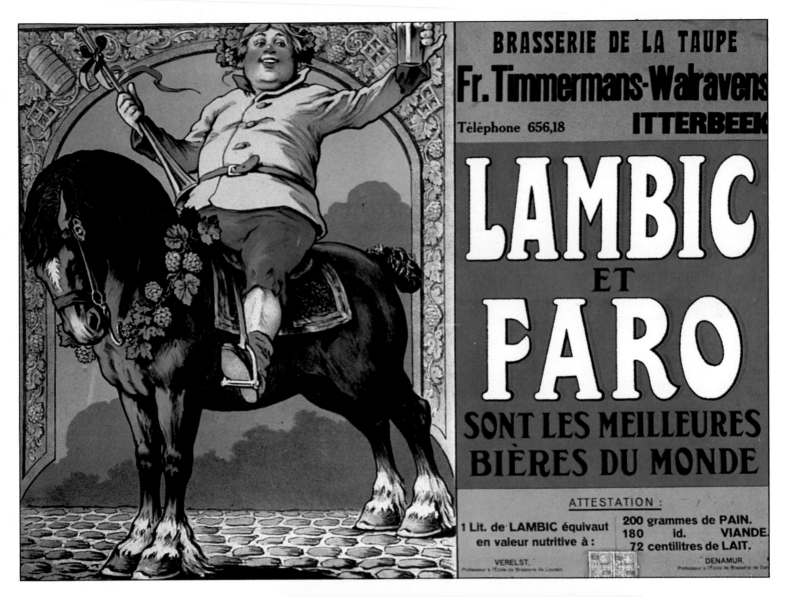

method are always at risk of being taken over by a more cost-conscious concern. A good *gueuze* will have a strength of not less than 5·2 Belgian degrees.

Drinkers who appreciate Timmerman's will probably enjoy the equally-traditional De Troch brew. The Bruxellois swear by *Mort Subite* ("Sudden Death"). A local joke would make a fine slogan for this brew: "from *bière* to *bière*." People who successfully seek Sudden Death may then find themselves confronted with Devil's Beer (*Duivelsbier*), a dark *gueuze* type of beer brewed by Vanderlinden.

Other brewers in Payottenland include Girardin, Lindeman's and Eylenbosch. The De Neve brewery has continued to use traditional methods despite having been taken over by the manufacturers of *Belle-Vue*, a mass-marketed *gueuze*-type beer which is sometimes served *en pression*.

The triumphs of lambic may be limited today, faro may be barely visible, but the beer family which they both represented is still going strong. The above poster, from a generic campaign on behalf of the lambic brewers, was produced in the 1920s. The Timmerman's legend is still proclaimed in the brewery's home village of Itterbeek.

Cherry beers

BRUEGEL COUNTRY is also the home of the authentic cherry beer. Originally, this brew was made with local cherries from the Schaarbeek district, now part of the Brussels urban area. Fruit from the northern part of Belgium is still used, and the cherries are of the dark, bitter variety. Red cherries are known in Dutch as *kersen*, but the black variety are called *krieken*. Cherry beer is properly known as *krieken-lambic*, since it is made with the said wheat brew.

The cherries are harvested in late July or early August, and 50 kilos of the fruit are added to every 250 litres of beer to make a full-bodied *krieken-lambic* worthy of the name. The cherries, complete with skin and pips, are macerated in young *lambic* for between four and eight months. The flesh of the fruit ferments in the brew, and the resultant beer can be drawn off, leaving the pips behind. *Krieken-lambic* is stored the whole year round, and blended to achieve a delicate balance of taste. The blending of *kriek* and *lambic* of various ages is a brewer's skill which rests more on judgment and instinct than on any more scientific formula. Although the brew's bouquet should betray its origins, the fruity tang should counterpoint with a refreshing acid sharpness. Nor is *krieken-lambic* a weak brew. Although it improves with age, a *kriek* of more than five years becomes enormously alcoholic, while at the same time losing its cherry flavour. A quality *krieken-lambic* like Timmerman's may have an alcoholic content per volume of five or six per cent.

Timmerman's, whose brewery disgorges a sea of cherry-stones, was specially commended when the consumer journal *Test Achats* reported on ten well-known brands of *kriek* beers. The journal revealed that Timmerman's did not use artificial colouring, a common sin. Nor, the magazine reported, did De Koninck (a small *lambic* brewer, not to be confused with the bigger Antwerp company of the same name). De Koninck was reprimanded for using saccharin, but chosen as best buy on the grounds of its lower price. The magazine pointed out that brands calling themselves *kriekenbier* were sometimes brewed outside the Payottenland district, without the use of *lambic*.

In Flanders, there is still a tradition of kriek-brewing at home. Sometimes cherries are macerated in café-bought beers.

One unusual *kriek* which cannot be disqualified, despite its geography, is the brand made at Oudenaarde by Liefman's. This is a strong *kriek*, of more than seven per cent alcohol per volume, based on the characteristic local brown ale. The beer has a primary and secondary fermentation before being macerated. A beer brewed one year will be infused with cherries the next year and bottled the year after that. Even then, it will spend several months in the brewer's *caves*, "ripening" in the bottle before being sold.

Madame Rose's mighty brew

Belgium acquired its only woman brewer when Madame Rose Blanquaert-Merckx succeeded to the job at Liefman's, of Oudenaarde. Madame Rose took over when times were difficult in the industry, especially for producers of specialist beers, but she brought her own fighting spirit to both brewing and marketing at Liefman's. The firm dates back to at least 1679, according to tax documents (below). Its products include an unusual variation on Belgian cherry beer, and a famous Oudenaarde brown. The brown is intended to be put by as a "Provision" for special moments. Both beers appear in an astonishing range of giant-sized bottles, wrapped in tissue.

Brown beers

TOWNS ALL OVER BELGIUM produce their own top-fermented specialities, ranging in colour from amber to black, but the district of Oudenaarde is synonymous throughout the country with dark brown beers. The local water of Oudenaarde is not dissimilar from that of Munich, with a high carbonate content, and was well suited to the production of brown beers in the days before such matters could easily be adjusted by brewers. In those days, there were more than 20 brewers in Oudenaarde; today, the whole administrative district surrounding the town has only three or four.

A highly characteristic Oudenaarde brown is produced right in the town itself by the Liefman brewery, which dates back to 1679. In more recent times, this brewery gained the additional distinction of being run by a woman. Madame Rose Blanquaert-Merckx succeeded to the position of head brewer, pursuing production with a particularly keen eye to sparkling copper kettles and well-racked cellars.

The brewery is surrounded by fields, in which cows graze, and where a spring provides water for the production of Liefman's *Gouden Band* (Golden Band) beers. *Gouden Band "Special"* is a medium-strength brown ale, with a dry palate and a slightly sweet aftertaste. There is also a *Gouden Band "Provisie,"* which is matured for between eight months and a year, and is bottled at a stage when it has not quite fermented out. It is further "ripened" in the *caves* before being sold, and has a rating of more than 6·0.

Madame Blanquaert bottles her beers in litres and Jeroboams, corked, and wrapped in tissue paper. She intends that they be laid down until such an evening when the household requires a leisurely and luxurious drink. They will, she pledges, retain their condition for a good many years.

In the nearby village of Mater, no less than three *Oudenaarde bruin* beers, and several other dark ales, are produced by the Roman brewery. Although the brewery's name might suggest that it dates from the time of Asterix, the company is quite content to trace its history back to 1545. In all, Roman produces a dozen or more brews, including a well-hopped Pilsener of some quality. The brewery also imports beers from Germany, Denmark and Britain, bottling some of them in Mater. The main brown, again with a dry palate and a sweet aftertaste, is called "Mater." This has a rating in Belgian degrees of something less than five per cent, while "Special Mater" has around 5·5, and "Double Brown" about 7·0. The brewery's range of dark ales includes brown table beers, and

Brown town

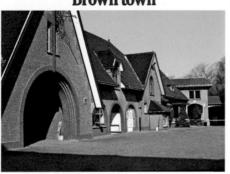

The famous local brown ales of Oudenaarde include a whole selection, each of a different density, made by the Roman brewery (above). Despite its devotion to the regional speciality, this brewery is also well-known for its pils.

Among the strongest ... Roman's double brown

The special ... a very substantial beer

Mater ... regular brown, named after the village

Brunor ... a brown ale to serve at the table

To beermen, Oudenaarde may be a city of proud brews. Historically, it belonged to Gobelin; to Flemish weavers, whose pride was reflected in their civic buildings (above); to armies in many battles ... right, George II leads his squadron into action during the War of Spanish Succession.

strong "Scotch" and "Christmas" ales.

Not far from Oudenaarde, closer to Ghent, a dark brown ale is among the top-fermented beers produced by the Crombé brewery, of Zottegem. These brews, which also include a pale ale, are sold in Champagne-style bottles. The brewery uses the brand-name *Oud-Zottegem*.

Several brewers produce *Münchener*-style brown beers, but one has become a Belgian speciality in its own right. This is *Gildenbier*, brewed at Diest, between Brussels and the Limburg provincial capital of Hasselt. *Gildenbier* is matured for at least nine months, and is very strong. There are two versions, one having an alcohol content in the region of seven per cent by volume, the other nine per cent.

There are also several very sweet brown ales, of a fairly low strength. A typical example is Van Lubbeek, something of a favourite in the Leuven district. Some Leuvense folk favour a *half om half* mixture of Van Lubbeek *bruin* and *pils*. The lower-density browns, like those in other countries, are favoured by an aging group of drinkers. The future of these beers may thus be in doubt.

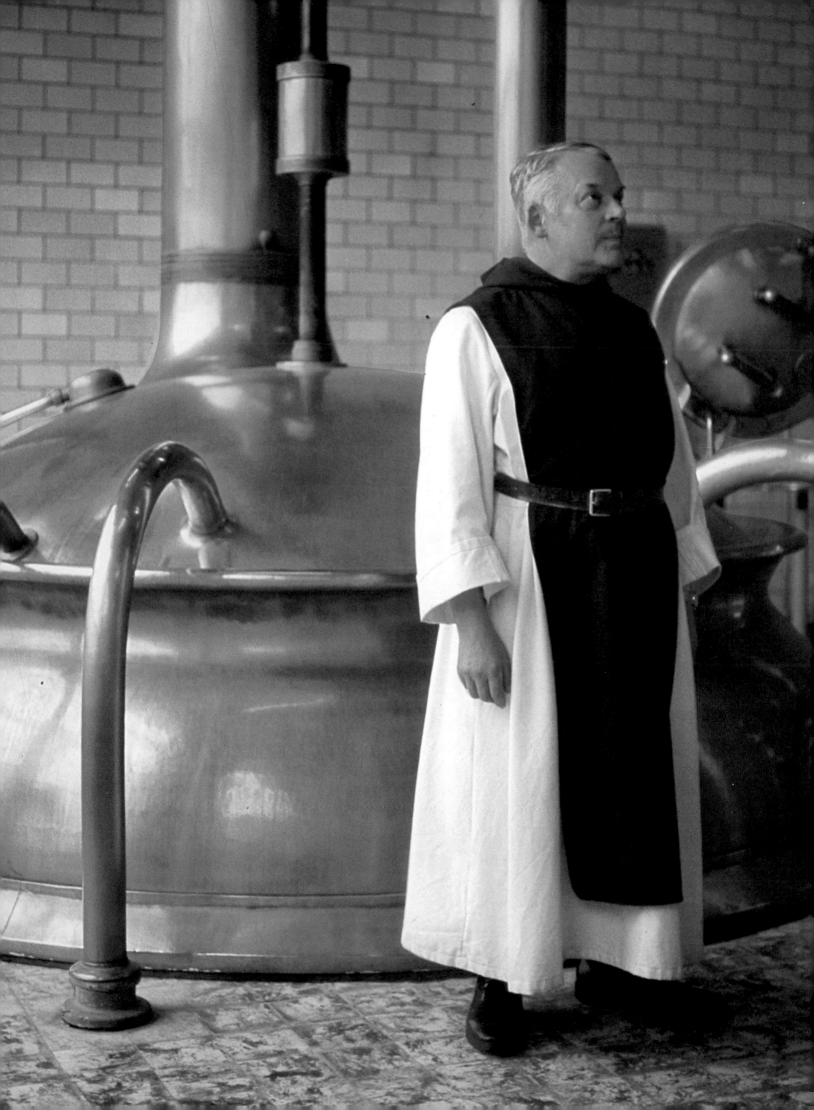

Abbey beers

They brew exceptional beer, and make fine cheese, at the abbey of Chimay (left). Blue-top is the strongest, then white, then red. Five abbeys still brew, but many beers proclaim their ecclesiastical links, even some whose precise antecedence is lost to history.

HOLY ORDERS in France may prefer to earn their daily bread by making Montélimar nougat or Benedictine liqueur, but in beer-loving Belgium there can be no doubt as to which path they should follow.

Cistercian monks have brewed in this part of the world since the Middle Ages, and their beers have been sold to an appreciative public for more than 100 years. Cistercian Trappist abbeys like the one at Westmalle, in the province of Antwerp, brewed originally for their own use, and then for the local community, before selling their beers more widely. Now, profits from the beers pay not only for the upkeep of the monastery, but also for philanthropic work.

Westmalle's "Triple" Trappist beer is an unusually golden colour, superbly full-bodied, dry with a good hop bouquet. It has an alcoholic content of about eight per cent by volume, while Westmalle "Double" is darker, with a strength of about six per cent.

Another Flemish monastery, St Sixtus, has a selection of excellent dark ales, ranging in alcoholic content from four to twelve per cent by volume. St Sixtus is in West Flanders, at Westvleteren, near Poperinge.

The first abbey to sell its beer on a commer-cial basis, and one with a deserved reputation for very fine brews, was founded by monks from Flanders who went south to the French-speaking provinces. This abbey is in wooded countryside close to the French frontier, and the borders of Hainaut and Namur, at Scourmont, Chimay.

In common with all the Trappist beers, those of Chimay are top-fermented, and a little yeast is added at the bottling stage to promote a secondary conditioning. Like Westmalle's Triple, Chimay's *Capsule Bleu* (Blue Top) is a beer of outstanding quality and character. It has a deep, copper colour, a creamy, dense head, and a fairly fragrant aroma. It is very well hopped, but carefully balanced, with a rich, full flavour. *Capsule Bleu* has about eight per cent alcohol by volume, and the similar *Capsule Rouge* something in excess of six. Between the two is the seven per cent *Capsule Blanche*, a rather different beer, lighter in colour, with a pronounced bitterness reminiscent of a high-density pale ale.

A similar beer, with an even more emphatically bitter palate, is produced not far away by the Trappist fathers at Villers-devant-Orval. In its skittle-shaped bottle, the distinctive and vigorously-hopped Orval

The Fathers...and the Brewers

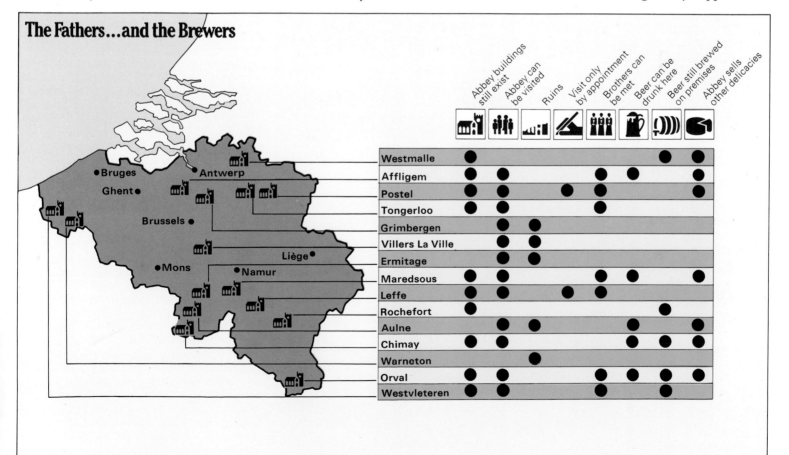

	Abbey buildings still exist	Abbey can be visited	Ruins	Visit only by appointment	Brothers can be met	Beer can be drunk here	Beer still brewed on premises	Abbey sells other delicacies
Westmalle	●						●	●
Affligem	●	●			●	●		●
Postel	●	●		●	●			●
Tongerloo	●	●			●			
Grimbergen		●		●				
Villers La Ville		●		●				
Ermitage		●		●				
Maredsous	●	●			●	●		●
Leffe	●	●			●			
Rochefort	●						●	
Aulne	●			●			●	
Chimay	●	●			●		●	●
Warneton				●				
Orval	●	●			●	●	●	●
Westvleteren	●	●			●		●	

Although they are available throughout Belgium, three of the genuine Trappist brews might best be enjoyed in the Ardennes (below). In addition to Chimay, Orval and Rochefort, the region gave "Spa water" and "Bouillon" to the gourmet vocabulary.

Fermented on High

The five monastic beers which are still brewed in the abbey are exclusively entitled to bear the inscription "Trappist" on their labels. They are (above, from left): Orval; St Sixtus, of Westvleteren; Westmalle; Chimay; and Rochefort. St Sixtus brews beer solely for the use of the brothers, and for sale at the abbey. There is on more general sale a beer produced according to the St Sixtus method by a nearby brewery at Watou. Coincidentally, that brewery is named after another saint, St Bernardus. Several abbeys of other orders have in the past made similar licensing agreements. The names of other abbey beers have more tenuous origins. Some are named after long-gone abbeys. Most of them are high-quality top-fermented ales, though the mysteriously-named Jacobins is a gueuze. Pater Lieven is named after a local patron saint. Thélème was named after the Rabelaisian symbol of good eating and drinking.

beer is another of Belgium's classics. Yet a third Trappist brew is produced in this same part of French-speaking Belgium – all three abbeys are in rustic, rolling countryside, amid the foothills of the Ardennes. The third brewery is at Rochefort, not far from Dinant. Rochefort produces a copper-coloured brew, not dissimilar from Chimay's *bleu* and *rouge* types, of six, eight and ten Belgian degrees.

The Trappist abbeys are the only Belgian monasteries which still produce their own beer on the premises. They are the sole abbeys permitted by law to use the term "Trappiste" in their labelling. However, many cafés offer "Trappiste" beers on their lists of available drinks when they are, in fact, referring to abbey brews made elsewhere.

At least a dozen more abbeys, of other Orders, have a brewing tradition. Although none of them continue to brew within the abbey, they have made arrangements with outside brewers to produce their beers, in return for a royalty on sales. While perhaps lacking the aura of the Trappist brews, some of these "abbey" beers are nonetheless very good. The pale and extremely bitter Floreffe abbey beer, conditioned in the bottle, is produced in the historic brewing town of Malines (known in more modern times by its Flemish name of Mechelen). Floreffe is made by the Anker (Anchor) brewery, which has an excellent reputation for strong ales. The ruby and amber beers associated with the Maredsous abbey are produced by the respected Moortgat brewery. Nor is the golden beer bearing the name Abbaye de Leffe Triple necessarily unworthy of its considerable reputation simply because it is brewed by a

Strong ales

ALTHOUGH CHARLEMAGNE was Holy Roman Emperor, a beer named after his golden coinage presumably counts as being a secular brew. The Gouden Carolus strong ale of Mechelen is, in any case, ambivalent about its origins. The later Emperor Charles V, who was born in Flanders, grew up in Mechelen. Gouden Carolus, brewed by Anker, is one of three or four highly-individualistic strong ales in Belgium. It is dark in colour, a very deep copper-brown, with a rich, malty palate. Both its bouquet and its flavour suggest an extremely strong beer, though 19 degrees indicated on the bottle are measured in the Balling scale, meaning something closer to eight per cent in terms of alcohol by volume.

A counterpart light-coloured strong ale, again highly individualistic, is Duvel. This

The right bottle, the right glass . . .

bright, golden beer is brewed in the same part of Belgium, at Breendonk, by Moortgat. It has a smooth and deceptively light palate, with a strong hop bite, and a density of more than seven per cent. It is labelled as being, "a natural beer, brewed with the best malts and hops, rich in vitamins, and without chemical additives." In fact, the hops are Czech, the malts Danish, and the rest of the description equally credible in a country where such matters are not taken lightly. Duvel is

understandably popular among discerning drinkers in Belgium. The beer is matured in the bottle for two or three months before leaving the brewery. The 25-centilitre Duvel is

Southern brew, especially potent . . .

filtered, but the 33-centilitre size is conditioned in the bottle. Duvel is usually served in a glass which has been kept in the freezer, so that the condensation promotes a "frosted" appearance.

There are several other local strong ales. In Brussels, Wielemans (brewers of Wiel's *pils*)

Gallic ale, from Marbaix . . .

have a pale, strong ale called Coronation. Further south, near Tournai, the Dubuisson brewery has an unusually-strong (10 per cent) copper-coloured brew called Bush Beer. Not far away at Marbaix, near Charleroi, a similar ale is brewed under the curious name of Gauloise, with a strength of eight degrees.

subsidiary of the huge Artois brewery company. (De Leffe also has a couple of excellent companion dark ales.) Perhaps other abbey brews are less than heavenly, their ecclesiastical connections rather tenuous, but most of them provide an acceptable strong ale.

The Trappist abbeys, and one or two of the others, maintain taverns at which their beers may be enjoyed, and in some cases cheeses made by the Order may also be bought. Although these *auberges* are not usually of any great historic or ecclesiastical interest in themselves, Belgian families (and people from across the borders in France, Germany and The Netherlands) find them a pleasant venue for a weekend drive.

Several beers which make less direct claims to holy status affect rather solemn names. The best-known of these is probably Cuvée de l'Ermitage, a well-regarded strong, amber ale, with a sweet palate, of about eight degrees. This is produced by the Union brewery, in Hainaut, which has two or three good top-fermented beers. Cuvée St Amands is a dark, strong ale, of medium palate, brewed in Bavikhove, West Flanders; Special d'Avignon is a dark, sweetish ale, produced not very far from Chimay, in Nismes.

St Feuillion is a golden, abbey beer from Roeulx, to the north of Mons, and the Marcel Contreras brewery at Gavere, in East Flanders, produces a fine golden-coloured abbey-style beer of medium strength.

All of these beers' names are allusions to either abbeys, beguinages, chapels, or figures in the monastic movement which left such a pronounced mark on the culture and countryside of Belgium.

The strong ale of Emperor Charles V is brewed in the former capital of the Austrian Netherlands, the city once known as Malines, and now as Mechelen. The town has two more breweries . . . and a fine Aldermen's House.

Belgian ales

Only Antwerp has a top-fermented beer as its regular café brew, but every region has at least one ale. Bruxellois look out for Speciale Aerts (below), while several Southern towns retain the tradition of the regional "saison" ales.

THERE ARE GOOD REASONS in plenty for visiting Antwerp; it was the city of Rubens, and has plenty of his paintings to prove it; like Amsterdam, it is a centre of the diamond-cutting trade, and several workshops can be visited; it is the world's third-largest port, with the bars and life of the waterfront; and it is a town of very considerable architectural worth. Drinkers who need excuses could quote any of these, or merely say they wish to see the *Brouwershuis*, whence water was once pumped from the canal to 24 local brewers. Today Antwerp has only one brewery within the city limits, but the beer produced there makes the whole trip worthwhile before a single sight has been seen.

When the Belgian brewing industry began to switch en masse to bottom-fermentation, after World War One, the Antwerp firm of De Koninck found itself in conservative mood. It felt lacking in either the capital or the expertise to re-equip, and therefore continued to ferment on top. Today, the name of Koninck appears on the fascias of cafés with the legend *hoge gisten*. Belgian drinkers are sophisticated enough to respond when they see that a beer is top-fermented.

While there are innumerable small Belgian brewers producing top-fermented beers of one sort or another, "specials," browns, "Trappisten" and the like, De Koninck is the regular everyday brand in many of Antwerp's cafés. It is much the same price as Belgium's Pilsener-type "café" beers, and much the same strength – but it is a rich, reflective, copper-coloured brew, vigorously full-bodied, with a palate which is all its own. It is creamy, yet translucent; malty, yet very well hopped.

In the Antwerp area, De Koninck is widely available on draught, and it is most definitely at its best in that form. It is filtered, but not pasteurised, and should be served under very gentle pressure. The bottled version is pasteurised, and carefully carbonated with

gases recovered from the fermenting vessels.

Although no other large city has a top-fermented beer as its main local brew, several take pride in indigenous ales. Not far from Antwerp, Brasschaat has a bottle-conditioned

Southern season, bottle-conditioned . . .

top-fermented beer, light in colour, called Witkap Pater. Bruxellois, on the other hand, swear by Special Aerts, traditionally sold in Burgundy bottles. In the South of the country, top-fermented beers are sometimes called *saisons*. An excellent example, in Mar-

baix, is Saison Regal. This is conditioned in the bottle, while Dinant's pleasant local Copère brew regrettably isn't.

There are also several brands which are to varying extents "national": Op Ale; Palm Ale (the latter brewery produces two or three different beers); Ginder Ale; and Vieux Temps. Many Belgian ales are true originals; others are a response to the popularity in the country of a few high-quality English top-fermented beers. The Belgian brews usually taste yeastier than English ale (or German *alt*). This may be because the Belgian brewers tend to be faithful to a single yeast culture, whereas the British use blends of yeasts. The Belgian ales are often aromatic in their flavour and bouquet. In the case of the true local speciality, this may owe much to the craft of the brewer; in the case of the imitation-English ale, it may owe more to his craftiness.

Belgium's second city is Antwerp (left), a Flemish cultural capital, with its huge cathedral and dockland riverscape . . . it is a city for feasts of eels in green sauce, Zeeland mussels and oysters . . . and De Koninck's top-fermented ales.

Le pale ale

FEW ENGLISHMEN have ever heard of John Martin's Pale Ale, but many a Belgian beer-drinker might believe it to be as British as Tommy Atkins.

Despite the English spelling of the name, John Martin is a Belgian, who imports beer to Antwerp, and bottles it there. He gets his pale ale from England, where it is known as Courage's Bulldog. Not that Courage's Bulldog is a particularly well-known brand in England, either; being of a very high gravity, it is very much a speciality beer.

Courage's have a whole range of pale beers (including a regular light ale, and their "John Courage" premium brand), but few of them would be strong enough for Belgian tastes. Some English pale ales have densities which in Belgian degrees would amount to about 3·1; a regular brand of English bottled pale, draught bitter, or "keg" might have a rating in the region of 3·5–4·5, though probably closer to the lower figure; "John Martin's" has a rating well in excess of 6·0.

Thus the Belgians are given a somewhat flattering impression of English beers, while the visiting Britisher is provided with a whole series of pleasant surprises. The bottled brand of Bass, an English pale ale of some distinction, is sold in Britain at an equivalent density of about 4·2 Belgian degrees. The version brewed for Belgium is about 5·4. The Belgian Bass is probably even a shade stronger than England's much-loved Worthington White Shield, though regrettably none of the imported pale beers are bottle-conditioned like that brew.

Bass has been imported to Belgium for a century and a half, perhaps deriving its original market from the presence of many British during the country's early industrial development. The red label used in Belgium is reminiscent of those which can be seen in Manet's *The Bar at the Folies Bergères* (painted in 1882), while the British counterpart has long since vanished. Bass also owns the Lamot brewery in Belgium, which produces a top-fermented beer of just under 5·0, with the brand-name of "Burton." True to the spirit of Tommy Atkins, this beer was originally brewed for British troops in their NAAFI canteens after the Liberation of Belgium.

Whitbread's excellent Pale Ale, and their rather sweeter Brewmaster, are both available in Belgian versions. They are imported from Britain, though Whitbread do have a brewery in Belgium, which is largely used to service other European countries. (One popular wisdom peddled among drinkers is that Brussels likes Bass, while Antwerp prefers Whitbread.) Watney's brew English-style beers at Châtelet, in the South of Belgium.

Belgium has "British" beer brands which are quite unknown across the English Channel. Winston is a wholly Belgian beer, from the same fine brewery which produces Saison Regal, in Marbaix. John Martin is an Antwerp firm. Even the famous Bass pale ale is brewed specially to suit Belgian tastes.

Scotch ales, Christmas ales and stout

Belgian "Scotch": Gordon's, McEwan's and Younger's all originate from Scottish and Newcastle Breweries; Campbell's is by Whitbread. "Scotch" ales are produced at breweries in Belgium by Watney's and Young's.

Christmas ales are linked with "Scotch" in unholy wedlock. Several Belgian brewers produce Christmas beers (always spelling the word in English). The Roman brewery (far left) even adds a Christmas Bell.

THE FACT THAT THE SCOTS do not celebrate Christmas (preferring to save their serious drinking for New Year's Eve) might surprise Belgians. In Belgium, "Scotch" is not a whisky, but a very dark and creamy beer of winter strength. "Christmas Ale" is its close companion, sold in the appropriate season, at a higher price and usually a slightly higher density.

Just as the Belgians have John Martin's Pale Ale, which is unknown in England, so they have Scotch Ales – with clannish names like "Gordon's" and "Campbell's" – which are unknown in Scotland. Furthermore, when "Gordon's Scotch" slips south of the border into France, it has to be known as "Douglas Scotch" (thus changing clans). In France, "Gordon's" means English gin.

Such Eurocomplications can be blamed, once again, on the importers and bottlers, Martin's of Antwerp. They started to import Scottish beers during the 1920s and 1930s, since when these brews have established themselves as an important part of the Belgian drinker's repertoire. In the meantime, the term "Scotch Ale" has sunk into somewhat limited and erratic use in Britain, where it no longer has a very clear definition. Similarly, Belgian "Scotch" has remained a strong ale, while Britain's fiscal policies and social habits have depressed the strength of beers in both Scotland and England.

A "Scotch" or "Christmas" ale may have a density of eight, nine or ten Belgian degrees. Such brews may thus on occasion surpass the strength of Belgian "specials" or "Trappisten," while also offering a slightly different palate (being maltier, and usually longer fermented).

Scottish and Newcastle Breweries produce several slightly different "Scotch" and "Christmas" brews for the Belgian market: These include Gordon's (marketed by Martin's of Antwerp), McEwans (marketed by Bass-Lamot), and Younger's (marketed by Whitbread). The latter brewery has a further brand of its own (Campbell's), while Watney's, Young's and one or two Belgian breweries also have their "Scotch" and "Christmas" beers.

Belgium enjoys additional privileges in respect of stout. This heavy beer, with the roasted barley flavour, is available to Belgians in several brews which are unfamiliar to the drinkers of the British Isles.

A bitter stout is sold under the Whitbread name in the Belgian market; a beer of milder palate comes from Lamot under the name of Bass Imperial Stout; and Watney's Stout is a medium sweet brew produced in Châtelet. All three are stronger than British or Irish stouts.

Bottom-fermented beers

Bergen Bier owes its name not to a Nordic mountain, but to the lesser peaks of Mons. Bergen means "mountains" in Flemish, though the townspeople are more likely to speak French. There are local pils (bottom) in the most surprising places . . .

HOSANNAS AND HIGH PRAISES are, naturally enough, accorded to the top-fermented specialities of Belgium, and to the wheat brews; they provide all the rich colour and variety of the nation's beer. When it comes to everyday drinking, though, the bottom-fermented beers sweep all before them.

Pilsener beers alone, the ubiquitous *pils*, have more than 70 per cent of the market. One *pils* brand, Stella Artois, has more than a third of all beer sales in Belgium. It is also the only Belgian brand to have achieved any great level of awareness among drinkers beyond the country's immediate border areas, though its export efforts are small compared with those of similar Dutch and Danish beers. The company was named not in honour of the neighbouring region of France, but after one of its early principals, Sebastian Artois. Its several brewhouses crowd the town of Leuven, where Artois also owns the local Leopold *pils* brand.

The Belgians being such great beer-drinkers, and *pils* being their everyday drink, there are dozens of brands. In a highly

competitive market, drinkers evince considerable brand loyalties, but these are highly subjective. When *Test Achats* magazine carried out a sampling of unidentified *pils* beers, including a score of Belgian and popular imported brands, no brew was recognised consistently by the majority of tasters.

Both the weakest and the strongest beers tested were imported brands, with the Belgian *pils* flowing right down the middle. The weakest appeared to be the Dutch Amstel beer, though its companion brew Heineken came into the middle stream, with a more favourable flavour-rating than its reputation in Belgium would suggest. The strongest were the French (or Alsatian?) Kronenbourg, with 5·5 per cent alcohol, and Danish Tuborg (5·7). The latter beer is said to be popular in Antwerp, and its compatriot Carlsberg (which has a marginally lower density) in Brussels, much as similar comparisons are made regarding imported English beers. Imports of Danish beer overtook those of English ale in 1970, though local production of British brands helps keep the Union Jack flying high.

German beers, which are of slightly different types, are usually "purer" and somewhat stronger than those elsewhere in Western Europe. They might be expected to sell well in Belgium, but their market slot has been damaged by the mixed reputation of local imitation Dortmunders. Belgian "Dort" usually has a density of more than 5·0, and is

NSMO. BRUX. TÉL 3798.19

Belgium's beer balance

Figures in hectolitres

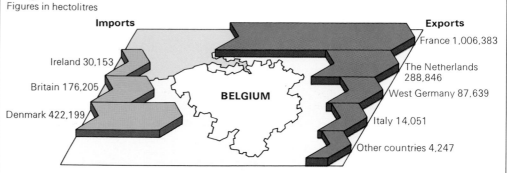

Imports

Ireland 30,153
Britain 176,205
Denmark 422,199

BELGIUM

Exports

France 1,006,383
The Netherlands 288,846
West Germany 87,639
Italy 14,051
Other countries 4,247

therefore a little stronger than the average *pils*. It is less hopped, and made without the use of maize to augment the barley malt. Brand-names reminiscent of the original Czech Urquell are also used by Belgian brewers for their premium *pils*, which are again in the range of 5·0-plus.

Only the glamour of something "foreign" can explain the popularity in Belgium of imported *pils*-type beers. Belgium's pilseners are at least as good as those of some neighbouring countries, and could provide tough competition in the export trade if they were not so busy with their insatiable home market. The Belgians still don't pasteurise many of their *pression* beers for home-market consumption,

Three major pils brands . . .

and such excesses as continuous fermentation have not yet arrived.

Belgian *pils* often has a rather mild palate. The *Test Achats* tasting, for example, found one big brand (Haacht) to be only "slightly" bitter. Lamot is another major *pils* with a less than aggressive palate and a very smooth taste. Lamot has a certain *chic*, perhaps because the brewery has pursued rather selective distribution policies in order to ensure that the beer is served in good condition, rather than relying wholly on additives to preserve shelf-life. A very well balanced *pils* which enjoys huge sales is Jupiler, brewed near Liège but marketed nationally. Maes is a well-hopped *pils*, while Romy, Safir and Kruger are smaller brands of a similar palate.

One Belgian *pils*, however, stands out among them all. This is Cristal Alken, brewed

in Limburg but enjoying a fairly national distribution. Cristal Alken is unusually well-hopped, very pure, with a distinctive and clean taste. It is a fine beer, which deserves a reputation beyond its own shores (connoisseurs of

. . . all hoppy, clean-tasting

Pilsener might also enjoy the local brew of Eupen, in Belgium's tiny German-speaking region).

If similar tributes could be paid to a good many Belgian beers, that is surely because the country's brewers owe more to craftsmanship than to chemistry. A majority of Belgium's breweries are still family concerns. (The ten million people of Belgium can choose from the products of more than 150 breweries, while the 200 million Americans make do with 60 or so). As small businesses, Belgium's craft

and very well balanced . . .

brewers have proven to be commercially vulnerable, but as their numbers diminish, so the survivors are increasingly appreciated.

In Belgium, as elsewhere, the bigger firms' attempts to "rationalize" drinkers' tastes may ultimately achieve the opposite effect.

PRODUCT LAMOT LTD

The Netherlands

THE MOST POPULAR imported beer in many parts of the world is Dutch. The brand concerned is Heineken, and it has greater sales outside of its own local market than any other beer. Whether its loyal consumers are always sure of its precise "nationality" is another question. The name "Heineken" trips easily from the tongue and sounds very credibly Northern European, as the names of good beers should. It is not a name which instantly suggests any particular nationality, but Heineken is most definitely Dutch, and beer runs *jenever* a close second as the national drink of The Netherlands. Heineken had its origins in 16th-century Amsterdam, and its headquarters is still there. The company also has breweries elsewhere in The Netherlands, in the provinces of South Holland and North Brabant. Heineken bought its home-town rival Amstel in 1968, and brewing continues there. Amstel remains a famous beer in many parts of the world.

The Netherlands has two giant brewing companies, and ten or a dozen small ones, mainly in the South.

The second giant is Skol. Like some notably successful enterprises in other fields, Skol is Anglo-Dutch. It was conceived in 1964 as an "international brand," with brewers in several countries (notably Canada and Sweden) sharing in its ownership. To-

day, it is 90 per cent owned by the British group Allied Breweries, whose main overseas subsidiary is in The Netherlands. In some respects, Skol is less British than Dutch, for all that it is brewed in more than a dozen other countries under licensing and franchising agreements. In Britain, Skol is just one among several big *lager* brands, which together hold less than 20 per cent of the market. Outside of Scotland, the big *lager* brands do not have any regional loyalties within Britain. In The Netherlands, Skol is the country's second biggest brewer, with major markets in Rotterdam and North Brabant. Dutch Skol is produced at the *Oranjeboom* brewery, in Rotterdam, and the *Drie Hoefijzers* (Three Horseshoes) brewery, in the important provincial town of Breda, North Brabant. Both breweries enjoyed some international reputation before they were bought by Allied, and *Drie Hoefijzers* still has links in Africa and Asia, notably in Indonesia. The names *Oranjeboom* and *Breda/Drie Hoefijzers* continue to be used in The Netherlands, though on a limited scale.

No discerning Dutchman would let the drinkers of the world ignore the fact that Grolsch beer comes from The Netherlands. Grolsch was customarily served in the White House when Gerald Ford was President – his home State of Michigan is, after all,

Dutchmen value their small breweries, while the world is more familiar with the international brands which originate from The Netherlands. "De Sleutel" was a small brewery, but the name survives only as a local Heineken bock brand.

On the canals of Amsterdam

When this consignment of hops was delivered in the late 1800s, Heineken and Amstel were deadly rivals. The two breweries, about a mile apart on the same canal in Amsterdam, merged in 1968. Heineken brews a "pils," a brown beer and a bock. Amstel has a parallel range, including a big-selling "pils."

It is on the Meuse, in historic Southern cities like Maastricht (below) that the pre-Lenten Carnival reaches its beeriest proportions. The South also has most of the small breweries, though the Eastern firm of Grolsche (bottom) has a special reputation.

nearly as Dutch as The Netherlands – but the beer's true claims to fame are closer to home. Grolsche (the brewery is spelled with a final "e," but the beer isn't) has a special place in the heart of the Dutch drinker. It is no giant, but it is more than a midget. Grolsche is the only independent brewery to have anything like national distribution in The Netherlands, and in a country dominated by the two giants, it is a conspicuously traditionalist company. This conservatism is demonstrated not only in such outward gestures as its adherence to the characteristic pot-stoppered bottle, now something of a Grolsch symbol, but in the more important matter of its brewing methods. Unlike its giant rivals, Grolsche does not pasteurize. It uses the whole hop, rather than an extract, and it uses fewer adjuncts than its competitors. Grolsche claims that its beer undergoes no less than 12 days of primary fermentation, and an astonishing three months of con-

ditioning. By whatever means it is achieved, the end-result is a light and clean-tasting beer of notable delicacy. The Grolsche company believes that its foundation may pre-date the oldest extant records, which were written by the master of the local brewers' guild in the mid-1600s. In those days, the brewery's home-town, in the Eastern part of The Netherlands, was called Grolle (hence Grolsche); today, the town is called Groenlo. The company now has an additional brewery, also in the East, at Enschede.

The only other beer to be produced in the East comes from yet another famous brewer, Artois, of Belgium. Artois bought the old-established local brewery at Hengelo in 1974. The name "Hengelo Pilsener" is still used. The Belgian company also owns a brewery in the South at Valkensward, near Eindhoven, North Brabant, producing Stella Artois "Special Dutch." This "special" beer has a fractionally lower density than the Belgian

Stella, which is also available in The Netherlands. Yet a third Artois operation in The Netherlands is run in conjunction with the Trappist fathers at Our Lady of Koningshoven, near Tilburg, also in North Brabant. The fathers have the only abbey brewery in The Netherlands, the *Schaapskooi* (the sheeppen). They have a *Pilsener*-type beer and a top-fermented, bottle-conditioned *Trappiste*, of about 6·5 per cent alcohol by volume. That the fathers should have chosen North Brabant in which to found their monastery and brewery is no accident. A Dutchman would not expect to find it anywhere else, unless it were in the neighbouring province of Limburg. It is all a question of social history.

For a country so tiny, and so united in its dealings with the rest of the world, The Netherlands accommodates a breathtakingly wide range of social and moral stances, which naturally affect attitudes towards drink. The

behaviour of the Dutchman, if stereotypes are to be believed, varies from province to province, city to city. At one end of the country, the Frisians still feel a degree of isolation, guarding a language and culture which once spanned the whole coastline of Northern Europe. They have no breweries; the Frisian national drink may be called *Beerenburg*, but it is a herbal bitters. Friesland also has an excellent *jenever*, called Bokma, which is now owned by Heineken. Then there are the more common stereotypes: the Northern *boer*, with his deep-rooted Protestant ethic; the earnest, socially-responsible lawmaker in The Hague; the conscientious Dutch working-man, in Rotterdam; and the libertarian raver in Amsterdam. The lore of the land types the Amsterdammer as the only Northerner who ever lets his hair down. In the Catholic South, it is a different matter. The people down South are the true drinkers of The Netherlands, and this is especially

true where the beverage concerned is beer.

The Netherlands has 11 provinces and 13 brewing companies. Nine of the brewing companies are very small local firms clustered together in two provinces: North Brabant and Limburg.

The tiny brewery at Budel, in North Brabant, is a good example. It employs only 15 people, and has passed through four generations of the same family since it was founded in 1870. None of the *Budelse* beers are pasteurized. The range of beers is typical of that produced by almost all Dutch brewers: a *Pilsener*-style beer of about 12·5 degrees Plato, 4·0 per cent alcohol by weight, 5·0 by volume; a sweet *oud bruin* (old brown) of 3·5 per cent by volume; and a seasonal *bok* of 6·5 per cent by volume.

Oud bruin is, for long-forgotten reasons, sometimes ordered in the Netherlands as "*lager*." The *bok*, available in October, November and early December, is a reddish-

137

The Trappist fathers at the only monastery brewery within The Netherlands have a regular Pilsener-style beer as well as a stronger top-fermented product more typical of abbey brewing in the Low Countries. The abbey's brewery is commercially operated in association with the Belgian Artois group.

black colour, with a malty palate. Some brewers also produce a beer similar in style to the *pils* but of a higher density, as a premium line. An almost identical range is produced by another firm of a similar size in North Brabant, the *De Kroon* (Crown) brewery, of Oirschot. *De Kroon* beers are pasteurized, and the *pils* and *oud bruin* have won prizes in the past. The Bavaria brewery, of Lieshout, North Brabant, varies the range by including a 5·0 per cent *Dortmunder*.

Beers which have a fine reputation well beyond their native Limburg are produced at Brand's brewery, in Wijlre. The brewery still possesses documents dating from 1340, and its history is believed to go back well beyond that. It was bought by the Brand family in 1871, and remains in their hands. In 1971, it was granted the title *Koninklijke* (Royal) by the Queen of The Netherlands. The Royal Brand's brewery uses no adjuncts, and does not pasteurize. It produces a *pils* with a good bitter palate and a well-hopped beer of the same density with the silly name of Brand Up '52. Close by is the Gulpen brewery, another private company, which was established in 1825. Its continued existence as the one company makes *Gulpener* the oldest brewing firm in Limburg. Gulpen's beers are not pasteurized. The company produces a hoppy *pils*, a 6·0 per cent *Dort*, and *oud bruin* and a *bok*. Unpasteurized beers are also brewed in Limburg at Neer, by the tiny firm of Lindeboom. At Valkenburg, it is possible to stand on a hill and see three countries (hills are very scarce in The Netherlands, and they confer a certain distinction on

the places which they grace with their presence). It is also possible, and perhaps more sensible, to come down from the hill and drink *De Leeuw* beer, a much respected brew. Unable to put their finger on anything else, connoisseurs say it must be the water that makes *De Leeuw* (The Lion) so good. The strongest beer in The Netherlands is the 7·5 per cent Super Dortmunder brewed by Alfa at Schinnen, in Limburg. A 6·0 per cent *Dortmunder* by the curious name of Maltezer is produced at a brewery called *De Ridder* (The Knight), in Maastricht, Limburg's provincial capital.

The history of brewing in the region of Brabant and Limburg goes back at least to the days of Charlemagne, whose capital was at Aix-la-Chapelle (now better known as Aachen, and today sitting right on the Dutch frontier with Germany). Charlemagne is reputed to have taken a considerable interest in brewing, and he may have learned about the use of hops from King Pepin. It is possible that the Southern Netherlanders were making hopped beer while the Northerners of Amsterdam were still importing it from the great brewing centre of Hamburg. In 1376, there were said to be 126 Hamburg brewers producing beer for the Amsterdam market. They were apparently known as *braxatores de Almstelredamme*. At the same time, the Bishop of Utrecht (the historic city which stands right at the middle of the present-day Kingdom) noted that his people were in the habit of making hopped beer. History is, however, confused on this point, since it is also argued that a trade in beer *en route* from Hamburg to

Flanders made a substantial contribution towards the growth of Amsterdam as a commercial centre.

When The Netherlands and Belgium split on religious lines in 1830, the Protestants of the Northern Kingdom nonetheless retained large swaths of Roman Catholic Brabant and Limburg (today, despite the nation's Protestant history, more than 40 per cent of the population of The Netherlands are Catholic). The border lands which the Dutch held manifested much the same social and cultural attitudes as those across the frontier, and to an extent they still do. Limburg extends Southwards like an isthmus between Belgium and Germany, taking in what was in those days a rich coalfield, and reaching out for the historically important city of Maastricht. It is easy to understand why these are beer-drinking territories, and a degree of cultural and physical isolation has helped them retain their traditions.

This is most graphically illustrated at the time of the pre-Lenten Carnival, when the beer-drinking lasts for three days, with barely an interruption for sleep. One important Carnival town is Breda, which may also have been the birthplace of Bruegel, who created so many scenes of demonic revelry. There are several theories about Bruegel's origins, but he was certainly born somewhere in the Brabant–Limburg region, and grew up there before going to Antwerp and Brussels. Bruegel's more grotesque fantasies were clearly influenced by the work of Hieronymous Bosch, who lived in Brabant. Hieronymous took his name from the town of Den Bosch, where he worked, though his family name of van Aken would suggest that they originated from Aachen. Den Bosch, more formally known as 's-Hertogenbosch (The Duke's Wood), or Bois-le-Duc, is the provincial capital of North Brabant. For most of the year, it drowses in the shade of its Burgundian past and its magnificent Gothic cathedral, but at Carnival time, the streets are alive with the sound of music. Brass bands march, almost everyone wears fancy dress, a Carnival Prince is elected, and the beer-drinking proceeds round the clock. So it is all along the river Maas (Meuse).

While the Northerners drink 70–80 litres of beer per head each year, the Southerners drink well over a hundred, and the average is probably much higher in the Carnival country. During Carnival, a single small bar has been known to sell about 40,000 glasses of beer. When a member of the Brand brewing family was asked about Southern attitudes, he replied simply: "In the South, we enjoy our pleasures better."

The breweries of The Netherlands

GOING LOCAL...

Both Oranjeboom and Breda are names known to beer-drinkers beyond The Netherlands. Despite this, they are regional brands within their home country. Oranjeboom (Orange Tree) belongs to the Rotterdam area. Breda is brewed in the town of the same name, in North Brabant. Both beers' availability has become more localized since the two breweries were taken over by the British group which has the controlling share in the international Skol brand. "International" or not, Skol is a local brand in the Southern part of The Netherlands.

The Artois company has its own brewery in The Netherlands, and owns the Hengelo company. There remain nine small independents. All of them are in the two Southern provinces. Despite its name, the Bavaria brewery is in Brabant. Nor, German though it may sound, is Edel Pils brewed beyond the borders of Dutch Limburg.

Dutch drinking styles

In common with many other countries, The Netherlands underwent a period of considerable temperance activity during the early part of this century. The poster below appeared relatively late, in 1935. It was designed by Aart van Dobbenburgh.

PUBLIC DRINKING is a serious business in The Netherlands. The Dutch, after all, are a serious people. First, there is the question of the barman's competence. Every bar-owner in The Netherlands must have a certificate to show that he took classes in his trade for six months.

Just to keep barmen on their toes, the Dutch brewers' organization has for 25 years run an annual beer-tapping "Olympics," awarding medals to the winners. Local heats proceed for the best part of three months, then there is a grand final before a ten-man jury of bar-keepers and brewery nominees. Owners of one-man bars can compete alone, but teams of two can enter from larger bars. At the starting signal, two glasses of draught are tapped, and a bottled beer is taken from an ice-box and opened. They are then carried to the jury, where the bottle is poured.

The outside of the glasses must be dry, and the tray spotless, but the critical area is the froth. The beer, including the froth, should fill the glass. Unlike drinkers in some other countries, the Dutchman regards the *schuim manchet* (froth cuff) as an integral part of the drink. He may occasionally be seen gauging its depth to see whether it is the requisite "two fingers" deep, which will amount to about one-fifth the content of a normal Dutch beer-glass. The judges, marking their score-cards at the Tapping "Olympics," will also expect the collar to be "tight." A dense froth acts as a "lid," retaining the liveliness of the beer right to

the last swallow. The beer is served cool.

The sizes of beer glasses which are in common use in The Netherlands provide some measure of the renowned Dutch tolerance. Some very popular bars have a 50cl glass, but a 30cl size is usually regarded as *groot* (large). A 25cl glass is *gewoon* (normal) and a smaller vessel is described as a *kleintje*

(a diminutive of small – perhaps a "baby.") The *kleintje* is sometimes served in a Dutch cola glass. In that case, it is called a *colatje*. Just to complicate things further, some bars regard the 30cl as normal, and the 25cl as small. One bar's *groot* can be another's *gewoon*.

Every city in The Netherlands has a wide range of restaurants, bars and pavement cafés (with heated canopies for the cold, rainy winter of the Low Countries), but the most Dutch of drinking places is the *kroegje*. This street-corner local is a hybrid between the English pub and cafe. In turn, the most Dutch of *kroegjen* is the Brown Café, so called because of its dark-wood panelling and nicotine-stained walls. There are hundreds of Brown Cafés, most of them comfortably unpretentious, but a few have become trendy "in" places. The best-known example, in Amsterdam, is the café called Hoppe, in the Spui. The nearby Koningshut even goes as far as to scatter sawdust on the floor, but also offers the more tangible advantage of Brand's beer, which is not widely available in Amsterdam. Off the Spui is another café for the beer-drinker, the Gollem Bar, in an alley called Raamsteeg. Sixty different beers are stocked, including several Belgian *Trappisten*, Irish Guinness and Newcastle Brown, from the North of England.

The city of Utrecht has a similarly-blessed beer-bar called Jan Primus, in appropriate deference to the Prince of Ales. Amsterdam is, though, undeniably the best town for the

The beer-tapping Olympics

... the beer should be drawn in one movement, with a dense, creamy head ... excess froth should be removed with a moist skimmer ... the head should not exceed two fingers in depth ... and Contestant Number One seems to be in trouble ...

... there still appears to be too much froth as the hypercritical panel examines a freshly-drawn glass. The glasses bear the emblem of the Dutch brewers' association, which organizes the contest. The object is to promote sales by maintaining high standards in the serving of beer. In each heat, the judges include bar-owners from "neutral" towns.

The oldest bar in Amsterdam is the Papeneiland (Papists' Island), on the Prinsengracht (Prince's Canal). Legend says that in times of religious strife it was linked by a passage under the canal to a nearby monastery.

bar-browser. The old inner city has a bar at every canal-bridge, and more. West of the Damrak (Amsterdam's main thoroughfare), the canal-bridges lead to the *Jordaan*. The name is a corruption of *Jardin*, and the district was once populated by Huguenot refugees. For years it retained the immigrant ambience of London's East End or New York's Lower East Side, until the Swinging Sixties applied an overlay of Greenwich Village. The mixture makes for some interesting drinking. On the opposite side of the Damrak, the red-light district provides a special quality of bar, getting brasher as it approaches the Zeedijk, the main street of Amsterdam's seaport nightlife quarter.

Predictably enough, a Dutchman is apt to use his beer as a chaser for a *jenever*. If a drinker in a café suddenly adopts an exaggerated stoop, he is not engaging in some act of deference, he is bending down to take the first sip from a brimful glass of *jenever*. It is an old custom to fill the glass so full that it cannot be picked up. There are about 100 distilleries in The Netherlands, with Bols by far the best-known. Famous names like Bokma, Coebergh and Meder are owned by Heineken; Warninks is owned by Allied Breweries. De Kuyper is independent. *Jenever* also comes flavoured with lemon (*citroen*) and blackcurrant (*bessen*), and the same companies produce other Dutch drinks, like *advocaat*. The origin of this name is something of a puzzle. One theory insists that Dutch sailors in the West Indies saw rum being drunk out of avocados, and tried to imitate the mixture. A more flippant explanation suggests that the stuff makes drinkers talk like advocates. Dutch liqueurs are especially famous, most of them flavoured with the fruits of the nation's colonial history. Cocoa liqueurs are a typical example; so is Curaçao, made with the oranges from the island of the same name in the Dutch West Indies.

A country with little dry land and much coast must inevitably become a nation of mariners. It was in the golden age of Dutch sea-trade that the port of Schiedam became the distillery town of the Northern Netherlands. Raw materials were imported, and the finished drinks exported, or distributed throughout The Netherlands by canal. Yet, despite all the exotic potions which were produced, nothing more fanciful than juniper was to prove the favourite. Before the hop, juniper had been a popular flavouring agent in Dutch beer. Now, juniper gave birth to *jenever*, and the name was corrupted a second time by the English to make *gin*. The British also had another name for it: they called it "Dutch courage."

WORLDWIDE CORPORATIONS can be family firms, too. The Dutch brewery which is today an international giant has always been in the hands of the Heineken family. Gerard Adriaan Heineken was only 22 when he bought a declining Amsterdam brewery in 1864. It seems he had a little money to spare, and no job. The brewery, which was already nearly 300 years old, was called "The Haystack." The building no longer stands but the site, in the heart of Amsterdam, now accommodates an hotel and tourist restaurant called Die Port van Cleve. Heineken moved his brewery to its present site, only marginally less central, in 1868. Around that time, beer was first exported to the colonies.

A second Heineken brewery, in Rotterdam, was opened in 1874 (this has now been replaced by another plant in the same province, a new "Haystack," at Zoeterwoude). As early as 1886, pure-yeast propagation was introduced. Until refrigeration was developed, the canals provided a handy source of ice to cool the lagering cellars.

Immediately after the repeal of Prohibition, the first shipment of Heineken was sent to the United States aboard S. S. Statendam. The first Heineken salesman in the United States was a former assistant baggage master with the Holland–America shipping line, Leo van Munching. He was in the habit of loudly demanding Heineken in bars which did not serve it. Shortly afterwards, by apparent coincidence, a Heineken representative would present himself at the bar, seeking an order. Van Munching or a friend would

The haystack that grew

then follow up by calling again, noisily buying rounds of Heineken for as many customers as possible. Van Munching became a millionaire. He still has the contract to import Heineken, and it is renewable in the name of his son. Heineken Pils and a dark, bottom-fermented beer of the same density are imported. Heineken is not produced under licence.

Heineken opened a third brewery in The Netherlands, at Den Bosch, North Brabant, in 1958. Also in the 1950s, the oldest brewery in The Netherlands was bought, *De Sleutel* (The Key), at Dordrecht, South Holland. *De Sleutel*, founded in 1433, no longer brews,

but the name is used locally on the group's *bokbier*. In 1968, the Amstel brewing company, of Amsterdam, was bought. Amstel Pils is the second biggest-selling beer in The Netherlands and the name Amstel Gold is used for the group's premium brand, with an alcoholic content of 6·5 per cent by volume. Amstel is also brewed by affiliates in Greece, several Middle East countries, and South Africa, among other places. In Curaçao, it is made with sea-water which has been treated at a desalination plant. Drinkers say this gives the beer an especially sharp taste.

A majority interest was taken in the French Albra group in 1972. This group's brands include Mützig, Ancre, Perle, Old Lager and Colmar. In 1974, Heineken and Whitbread, of London, jointly acquired a majority interest in the Italian Dreher brewery group. Heineken has affiliate companies in at least 20 countries, notably in the Caribbean, West and Central Africa, the Middle East, Asia (Malaysia, Singapore, Indonesia), and Australasia (New Zealand, New Caledonia, Papua). In many cases, Heineken has a substantial or majority stake, and it always provides technical advice. The affiliate companies normally market Heineken plus their own brands.

Heineken is a quoted company on several major stock exchanges, but the controlling interest remains firmly in the family. The chairman, Alfred ("Freddy") Heineken, is the grandson of the founder. Some haystack . . .

The original Mr Heineken (top) went into business in 1864, in Amsterdam, and opened a second brewery in Rotterdam ten years later. The Heineken "beer-brewery company" started to produce a bottom-fermented beer in the "Bavarian" style which was sweeping Europe and North America.

Luxembourg

THE DRINKER, not to mention the gourmet, could choose worse places to live than the Grand Duchy of Luxembourg, the smallest State in the European Community. He would find himself sandwiched happily between the Ardennes and the Moselle; between a great brewing nation (Belgium), a great wine-growing nation (France), and a nation which excels in the production of both beverages (Germany). The Luxembourgers have fruitful relationships with all of their neighbours. Culturally, the Grand Duchy is dovetailed with the Belgian province of the same name; economically, with Belgium and, to a lesser extent, with The Netherlands (in the Benelux group of countries); industrially, with the Saar and Lorraine regions of Germany and France. There are only 350,000 Luxembourgeois, and they are among Europe's most prosperous citizens. The importance of their State as a financial centre in the European Community gilds the gingerbread.

They spend a lot of their money on drink.

Luxembourg stands fourth in the world league-table of spirit-drinkers, sixth among beer-drinkers (with a consumption of 129 litres per head per year), and seventh among wine-drinkers. Although Luxembourg is hardly world-famous for its wines, it produces some very drinkable light whites, usually extremely dry and crisp. The beer-drinker can enjoy himself, too. With beers from the Rhineland and Saar readily available, the brewers of Luxembourg are accustomed to meeting high standards. Their beers are usually well-matured, sometimes for as long as three months, and those brews which are purely-local are not pasteurized. Furthermore, the people of this minuscule State can choose from the products of no less than six brewers.

The biggest, and best known outside Luxembourg, is Diekirch, in the town of the same name. Brasserie Nationale was formed in 1974 by the merger of the Bofferding and Funck–Bricher breweries. Stella Artois has

a very small stake in the Mousel et Clausen brewery, a concern which traces its origins back into the mists of Luxembourg's history. The other three breweries are smaller: Henri Funck, in Luxembourg–Neudorf; Battin, in the coal-and-steel town of Esch; and Simon, in Wiltz.

Although six brewers is a good tally in such a small country, the range of beers available is less impressive. Each brewer produces only three or four brands: usually a basic, *Pilsener*-style beer; a brew of slightly higher density, sometimes in the *Dortmunder* style; and perhaps a stronger beer, possibly with *bock* aspirations. Some of the strong beers are seasonal. A good range of excellent beers is produced by the family-owned Simon brewery: Pils, at 11·3 degrees Balling; Regal, at 12·4; and Extra, with quite a bitter palate, at 16·6. At a slightly higher density than the Extra, Brasserie Simon produces a Christmas beer. This is a strong-tasting dark beer of which the brewery is very proud.

Steam-brewing, European style

Brewer Albert Mousel proudly presents his products (above). At the time, brewers took great pride in their use of steam power. "Steam brewery" did not have the same meaning in Europe as it did across the Atlantic. It was a big moment when a new boiler was delivered to the brewery. M. Mousel was succeeded by his son (far right).

The labels of Luxembourg . . . Brasserie Nationale's Meisterbock and Christmas beer are both pale lagers. Mousel has a premium brew called Royal Altmunster and a dark Luxator, both at about thirteen degrees.

Brasserie Simon Wiltz Luxembourg bière blonde du type pilsen

Britain and Ireland

The British way of drinking (left). It must be a top-fermented ale or stout; it must come in a pint glass; and it mustn't be too cold . . . but "Continental-style" lagers gained popularity (see chart below) during the warm summers of the mid 1970s.

BRITISH BEER IS DIFFERENT. Britain and the Republic of Ireland are the only countries where all the principal home-grown beers are brewed by top-fermentation. Being brewed in this way, they best express their flavours at cellar temperature or thereabouts, and are therefore rarely chilled. This causes consternation among foreign visitors, but the excessive chilling of a good British or Irish beer is likely to provoke even greater outrage among regular customers.

What the rest of the world gains in the thirst-quenching "edge" of cold beers, the British especially gain in the richly varied palates of their brews. British beer is an acquired taste, but so are oysters, steak tartare, or marron glacé. Before British beer can be enjoyed, experience is required, but the same could be said for sex. In both cases, mistakes are inevitably made, but the triumphs make the disasters worthwhile.

For the visitor to Britain, the difficulty is compounded by the wide range of beer types. They may predominantly be top-fermented, in colours ranging from copper to black, but Britain's beers manifest themselves in at least ten styles. Even the British drinker is often unsure about the precise meanings of these different designations.

In other countries, the selection of beers available varies according to regional custom, but all British pubs stock a wide range of the nation's brewing styles. Because the majority of pubs are tied to brewers, many of the beers in any one house will come from a single source, but their type will vary no less for that. Even a small pub will stock upwards of a dozen different beers, including the odd one or two which are classical examples of their type, and others which are quite dismal. The trick lies in knowing which type is which – and which brewers excel in that particular type.

The range is likely to include at least one "*keg*" beer (hardly a favourite with the knowing drinker); a couple of draught *bitters* and at least one *mild* (if it is a good house); bottled *light*, *pale* and "*export*" beers; one or more *brown ales*, possibly of different gravities; a *strong* or *old ale*, or a *barley wine*; a *sweet stout*; a bitter Irish *stout* (invariably Guinness) and perhaps a draught Guinness, too (the two are different beers); one or more British-brewed *lagers* (in Britain, this means a beer very vaguely approximating to *Pilsener*); and at least one imported *lager* from Northern Europe. This is to set aside a variety of fringe designations, not to mention the odd import from Australia, the United States or some other country.

All types of draught beer – "*keg*", *bitter*, *mild*, *stout* and *lager* – are commonly drunk by the pint. Half-pints are regarded by serious beer-drinkers as being rather effete, and suitable only for women. The half-pint is the smallest vessel used for draught beers. There has been no suggestion of a move towards smaller measures, like some of those used in Continental Europe, and the British

The styles...and their shares of the national thirsts

All lager beers 20%

Draught bitter ales 40%

Draught mild ales 13%

Bottled and canned pale and light ales, etc 10%

Bottled brown ales 4%

Bottled extra-strong ales 1%

All bitter stout 8%

All sweet stout 4%

Lager-brewing vessels were imported from the United States at the turn of the century, and taken to Burton by train. A contemporary report (below) was sceptical about the new Bavarian-style beer. "The very name spells 'Continental.'"

300 MILES FOR A GLASS OF BRITISH LAGER.

Three hundred miles for a glass of Lager beer. It sounds absurd when you can go round to the corner house and get a glass of bitter. Nevertheless a number of experts on beer went three hundred miles instead of going round the corner.

To put it plainly, Messrs. Samuel Allsopp and Co. organised on Wednesday last an excursion—a most delightful excursion—to Burton-on-Trent, in order to show to the United Kingdom and to the World that the great little town in the valley of the Trent is worthy of its fame, and equal to the production of beer in all its stages of superiority of quality—competent to compete with Continental rivals.

It wasn't so much the thirst that affected us early on the morn of the 17th instant, as the invitation from the directors of Messrs. Allsopp and Co., Limited, to catch a train leaving Euston at 9.55 that made us search our wardrobe for waterproofs, mufflers, thick boots, and rugs. It looked like being an awful day.

Regardless of consequences we ran the gauntlet of chill and fog that holds us with a damp and uncomfortable wreath, so much identified with London in October, and cabbed it to Euston. All was damp until we entered the "special" provided for us to taste this one glass of Lager beer—the first that has ever been produced in the British Isles. A glass of Lager, perhaps, might never be very magnetic, because the very name spells Continental. But the fact that we were offered the glass from Burton-on-the-Trent Metropolis ...... made us ....

CONSIGNMENT OF THE PFAUDLER VACUUM COMPANY'S CYLINDERS FROM NEW YORK FOR BRITISH LAGER BEER.

from the necks of bottles. There was no fog then, only ...tion of the Pfaudler Vacuum system of fermenting... ...right ....inting ...... "...ere a ...llow" leaves... ...are perfectly fermented...... to six ...

drinker does not have to concern himself with maintaining a fresh chill on his beer. A pint of beer must, by law, be poured brimful – into a glass which bears the stamp of the Weights and Measures Department. If there is to be a "head," this should stand above the top of the glass (or the "Plimsoll Line," if the glass is marked in this way).

Attitudes towards froth vary from region to region. In many parts of Britain, drinkers prefer their beer to look slightly "flat." In other parts, the worth of the froth is judged by its ability to stick to the side of the glass, marking a ring to commemorate each magnificent swallow. Guinness is a special case, and was judged as such by a court sitting in Bristol in 1964. The court held that, in the case of Guinness, the froth was "an integral part" of the beer. The Guinness company regards three-eighths of an inch (about one centimetre) as the optimum head, at an ideal temperature of 58°F (14·4°C).

The protocol and etiquette of British beer-drinking is infinitely complex. Not only are the size and density of head a matter of great local importance, so is the style of drinking vessel. Glasses with handles are thought in some places, and especially by the Northern English, to be notably lacking in the appropriate machismo. Personalized pewter mugs can seem irredeemably suburban unless they hang in a truly rural pub. All that is cherished beyond doubt is the pint.

In Britain, when people go for a drink, they go "for a pint." The drink, and the place, are identified by the quantity. The words "go for a pint" extend, and are universally understood, to mean a visit to a pub, where several large glasses of beer will be consumed. The pint was derived from an ancient measure used for corn, and centuries of peaceful English life have proven it the perfect quantity for beer. A pint is just the right amount to tickle the palate for an expectant moment, rush headlong at the thirst, and demand a courteous amount of time for drinking before the next round falls due.

Like the pint, the round system makes for drinking in quantity. If two Englishmen meet together in a pub, each has to buy the other a drink. The same applies to Scots and Welsh, whatever the English may say about their alleged meanness. Two men means two drinks. These drinks have to be paid for as they are served, so such debts of courtesy cannot be buried, Continental-style, in the sheaves of bills which are boozily totted-up at the end of the evening. A drinker who misses his round is noticed, and avoided in future. Three men means three drinks. Four men means four drinks. The haste to buy a round is fuelled by honour, machismo, and Britain's beat-the-clock licensing laws – a restriction which grew out of the First World War, and which refuses to die.

Such expansive drinking customs may help explain why so many British beers are of unassuming gravities, though the depressing activities of the taxman and the avarice of the brewers must also be held accountable. Although Britain's best have the kick of a vigorous *bock*, the everyday beers are of a markedly lower gravity than many elsewhere in Europe. The strongest regular draught beer in Britain has the very respectable gravity of 1054·5, and 5·79 per cent alcohol by volume, but the average brew is around 1036, with about 3·5 per cent alcohol. There are even regular draught beers which dip below the 1030 mark. Continental European *lager* beers which are marketed

• Independent brewers referred to in text
■ Home breweries and other very small breweries
● Other independent brewers
○ Important brewing town

Breweries trading under the corporate names of the "Big Seven" are identified solely by symbols, as follows. Breweries indicated in italic type are subsidiaries or associates of "Big Seven" companies, and are accompanied by the symbol representing their parent group.

▲ *Bass Charrington*

◖ *Watney*

🐓 *Courage*

✋ *Allied Breweries*

▯ *Whitbread*

★ *Scottish and Newcastle*

⬥ *Guinness*

Beamish and Crawford
Murphy
Cork ●

CHANNEL ISLANDS

The Guernsey Brewery Co.
Bobby Ales
St Peter Port

Boxer Ales
Ann St Brewery
St Helier

Skol
Maclay
Alloa

Belhaven
Dunbar

Tennent
Glasgow

Traquair House
Innerleithen

Lorimer
Dryborough
Younger
McEwan
Harp
Tennent
Edinburgh

Scottish and Newcastle
Northern Clubs
Newcastle

Theakston
Carlisle

Vaux
Sunderland

Jennings
Cockermouth

**Cumbrian Brewers
(Matthew Brown)**
Workington

Castle Eden

Cameron
Hartlepool

Castletown
Castletown

Okell
Douglas

ISLE OF MAN

Hartley
Ulverston

**Mitchell's
Yates and Jackson**
Lancaster

**Samuel
Smith**
Tadcaster
John Smith

**Timothy
Taylor**
Keighley

Theakston
Masham

Webster
Halifax

Selby
Selby

North Country
Hull

Macardle
Harp
Dundalk

Harp Manchester
Whitbread Salford
Wilsons Manchester
Boddington Manchester
Holt Cheetham
Lees Middleton
Pollard Stockport
Robinson Stockport

Heineken
Samlesbury

**Matthew
Brown
Thwaites**
Blackburn

Tetley
Leeds

REPUBLIC OF
IRELAND

Dublin

Higsons'
Liverpool

Oldham
Oldham

Darley Doncaster

Stones
Ward
Sheffield

**Hardy's
and Hanson's
Home
Shipstone**
Nottingham

Bateman
Skegness

*Carling
Black Label*
Runcorn

**Burtonwood
Greenall Whitley**
Tetley
Warrington

Mansfield
Mansfield

Fighting Cocks
Grantham

Border
Skol
Wrexham

**Everard
Marston**
Burton
Worthington

Smithwick's/Perry
Kilkenny

All Nations
Madeley

Banks
Wolverhampton

Hoskins
Leicester

Ruddle
Oakham

Elgood
Wisbech

Norwich
Norwich

Mitchells and Butlers
▲ Birmingham
▲ Wolverhampton
▲ Walsall
Ansell's
Birmingham

**Simpkiss
Batham**
Brierley Hill

Davenport's
Birmingham

Carlsberg
Northampton

Greene King
Bury St Edmund's

Adnams
Southwold

**Hanson
Holden
Old Swan**
Dudley

Litchborough
Litchborough

Wells
Bedford

Paine
St Neots

Tolly Cobbold
Ipswich

Three Tuns
Bishop's Castle

Cherry/Phoenix
Waterford

Donnington
Stow-on-the-Wold

Flowers
Cheltenham

**Hook
Norton**
Banbury

Greene King
Biggleswade

Heineken
Luton

**Rayment
(Greene King)**
Furneux Pelham

McMullen
Hertford

Ridley
Chelmsford

**Buckley
Felinfoel**
Llanelli

Rhymney

Mason's Arms
Witney

Morrell
Oxford

Wethereds
Marlow

Romford

Truman

**South Wales
Clubs**
Pontyclun

Brain
Cardiff

Arkell
Swindon

Morland
Abingdon

Brakspear
Henley

London

Young
Wandsworth

Fremlins
Faversham

*Welsh
Brewers*

**Miners'
Arms**
Priddy

Wadworth
Devizes

Reading

Fuller
Chiswick

**Shepherd
Neame**

Flowers
Tiverton

Usher
Trowbridge

Gibbs Mew
Salisbury

Romsey

Harp
Alton

Gale
Portsmouth

**Harvey/
Beard**
Lewes

Wateringbury

Palmer
Bridport

Burt
Ventnor

King and Barnes
Horsham

Devenish
Redruth

Eldridge Pope
Dorchester

Hall and Woodhouse
Blandford Forum

Blue Anchor
Helston

St Austell
St Austell
Plymouth

Devenish
Weymouth

The oldfangled English . . . the Harbour Inn, at Southwold, Suffolk, has a rural stoicism and Adnams' magnificent ales. Being on the North Sea coast, it is flooded on occasion by high tides from the direction of Continental Europe.

in Britain (and often brewed locally) usually cost more than the indigenous ales, but may be even weaker. A European beer which is marketed in its home country at 12·0 degrees Plato, and with an alcohol content in excess of four per cent, might appear in Britain with a gravity of less than 10·0 degrees and an alcohol content closer to three per cent.

British chauvinism apart, it is surprising that such feeble brews managed even to achieve their 20 per cent share of the market during the hot summers of the mid-1970s, and this after almost 100 years of trying. The first *lager* brewery in Britain was established in 1882, at a time when brewers all over Europe were switching to bottom-fermentation, but that was a period when the island race was in no mood to take lessons from foreigners.

The British have never been very happy about newfangled ideas. They took much the same attitude when the Flemings introduced hopped beer to England during the 15th century. The new beer first arrived by cask as an import, then Flemish settlers in the South-East of England started cultivating hops there for the purpose of brewing. The Flemings called their drink *biere*, and it was for a time regarded as a beverage quite separate from good old English *ale*, although the terms are today synonymous.

"*Bere* is the naturall drynke for a Dutche man," commented the 16th-century writer Andrew Boorde. "It is used in England to the detryment of many Englisshe people; specyally it killeth them the which be troubled with the colyke, and the stone and the strangulion. The drink doth make a man fat, and doth inflate the bely, as it doth appere by the Dutche men's faces and belyes."

The "wicked and pernicious weed hops" was at one point banned by authorities in Shrewsbury. Henry VIII's brewer was warned not to add hops or brimstone to ale. The Brewers' Company of the City of London petitioned the Lord Mayor that "hoppes, herbs or other like things" be kept out of ale, which should be made only from "licour (water), malt and yeste."

Hops neatly counterpointed the insularity and the tolerance which are equally famous in the English character. Henry VI commanded the Sheriffs of the City of London in uncompromising terms: "Certain malevolent persons, attempting out of great hatred cunningly to oppress those brewing the drink called *biere*, have sown grievous murmurings and discords so that people turn against the drink, wherefore the brewers do not dare brew the said drink of *biere*, to the damage and hardships of very many of our

Gin came from Holland, and caused degradation. "Gin Street" (top) was one of the "moral subjects" depicted in engravings by the great English artist William Hogarth. By contrast, his "Beer Street" (above) was a place of robust good cheer.

subjects who relish that drink and prefer to drink it as a notable, healthy and temperate drink. You shall cause it to be proclaimed that all such brewers of *biere* shall boldly make, sell and exercise as they were wont, forbidding our lieges that none of them molest or hinder those brewers of beer whereby they may not freely brew as hitherto, or use intimidation or threat to the same, under the peril that befalls."

Biere came to stay. So did the Flemings and their hops. Where they settled, a thousand hops still bloom. Charles Dickens has Mr Jingle saying, in *Pickwick Papers*: "Kent, sir? Everybody knows Kent – apples, cherries, hops and women." The garden countryside of Kent is still given its own character by the silhouetted cowls of oast-houses, where hops are dried, though the buildings' traditional design has become less common with modernization. Some traditional oast-houses have even been converted into weekend homes for London business-men, as if they were barns in the Dordogne. Siegfried Sassoon described oast-houses in Kent as "a wonderful sight . . . I felt that almost anything might happen in a world which could show me twenty hop kilns neatly arranged in a field."

Between the White Cliffs of Dover and the dormitory towns of London, there are 20,000 acres of hop-gardens in Kent and Sussex. There are another 15,000 acres in the West Midland counties of Herefordshire and Worcestershire, where they are known by custom as hop "yards." Hop-picking once provided a "working holiday" for thousands of poor families from London and West Midlands. A hundred thousand "holiday-makers" were recorded as having worked in the South-East in 1908, and there were still 30,000 aboard the 61 special trains which ran from London Bridge station in 1945. The last, lone train ran in 1960. Prosperity and mechanization had together eliminated the need for such arduous holidays. Now, they are remembered with nostalgia by once-poor Londoners who have fallen upon soft times, like the distinguished journalist Louis Heren (in his book, *Growing-up Poor in London*) and the comedy-writer Johnny Speight (*It Stands to Reason*).

Nostalgia might also be appropriate in the case of Mr Fuggles and Mr Golding. These two Englishmen gave their names to famous varieties of hops, which are now being superseded by more resilient but less rustic-sounding, strains. Sex is an issue, too. In Continental Europe, male plants are excluded from the gardens with an almost vindictive zeal, so that the hops may be seedless. The seeds are of no use to the brewer, and can get in his way, but the British still prefer their hops seeded.

Beer is, without rival, England's national drink. Bohemian beers have to share their cellar with Moravian wines; German beers have a similar experience; Denmark has aquavit as well as beer. England has beer. England has gin, too, but that is what comes of getting involved with the Low Countries. Gin was one of several mixed blessings which came across the sea in the 17th century. "London Gin" and "Plymouth Gin" might find their forbears in, say, Schiedam or Ghent. At a time when beer was being sub-stantially taxed to pay for William of Orange's campaigns in Ireland, cheap gin flooded London, causing acute social prob-lems. The misery caused by gin, and the robust content brought about by beer, were contrasted in two famous engravings by Hogarth. Whisky is from Scotland, unless it is spelled with a penultimate "e," which makes it Irish. Hibernian whiskey attacked the English market in the 19th century, followed soon afterwards by Caledonian whisky. Irish arrived first, but Scotch lasted better.

English beer is more than just English, but rather less than wholly British. Despite the considerable cultural and social differences between the two countries, the English style of beer has been accepted most of all by the Welsh among the other British nations. The beers brewed in Cardiff by a company called Brains ("It's Brains You Want," says their slogan) are among several fine examples. Wales has slightly more restrictive licensing laws than England, especially on Sundays, but it is not without joys for the beer-drinker. Scotland, on the other hand, has its own brewing tradition, differences in ter-minology, and its devotion to whisky. Things are different again, though some-times for the best, in Ireland both sides of the border. The Isle of Man and the Channel Islands are self-governing, and are not part of the United Kingdom. The Isle of Man has unpasteurized beers of the British type, protected by its own historic Purity Law (which permits sugar, but not adjuncts). The Channel Islands also have some excellent and interesting English-style beers, at lower prices than in Britain, and more liberal licensing laws.

Such complications aside, the Englishman at least would agree with the Reverend Sydney Smith, who asked in the 18th cen-tury: "What two ideas are more inseparable than beer and Britannia?" A rhetorical question, of course.

The English Pub

"Pub" is as English as a word can be. It is a familiarization to describe the most familiar place in the neighbourhood, all 70,000 of them. Yet "pub" is a surprisingly recent expression. "Public house" did not become a recognized term until the latter half of the 19th century. This was the pub's brassiest age . . . turn-of-the-century pomp in Liverpool, 1890s swank in the West End of London, solid Victoriana in Manchester. Etched glass and mahogany partitions provided privacy for the drinker, while mirrors reinstated the light, and reflected the new electric bulbs. Like the Music Halls which they begat, the pubs of the 1800s were a focal point, a place of entertainment and sociability for an English people newly wrenched by the Industrial Revolution from the order and ritual of rural life. In the rapidly-growing cities, these establishments touted their alcoholic attractions with such brass neck that they were dubbed "gin-palaces," even though the insidious spirit had already done its worst in the 1700s.

Little more than a century earlier than that, the courtyards of inns had given birth to the Shakespearian theatre. Strolling players for travelling men . . .

Before them, the *King's Head* (England's most popular pub name) had been the *Pope's Head* of pre-Reformation times. Was the *Cat and Fiddle* a name derived from the more godly *Catherine Fidelis*? Did the curious *Goat and Compasses* have more comprehensible origins in a pilgrims' resting-place, an abbey inn called the *God Encompasseth Us*? The *Angel and Royal*, at Grantham, Lincolnshire, has probably been an inn since 1213. The *Trip to Jerusalem*, in Nottingham, is believed to have been a church hospice in 1070. It is one of several claimants to the title of England's oldest pub. There are probably thatched pubs in the countryside which stand on the site of Saxon ale-houses.

The Romans recorded that the Britons were "accustomed to gathering in their ale-houses to govern and adjudicate." Little has changed . . .

This page : Northern English pomp and Edwardiana. Decorative caryatids at the Sawyers' Arms, Manchester (1), the Philharmonic, Liverpool (2) and the Vines, in the same city (3). Windows at the Lord Clyde, Manchester (4), the Vines (5), the Bridge Hotel, Salford (6) and Whitelock's, Leeds (7). Gaslight at the Vines (8). *Following page :* Rose and Crown, Bradford Abbas, Dorset.

BAR PARLOUR

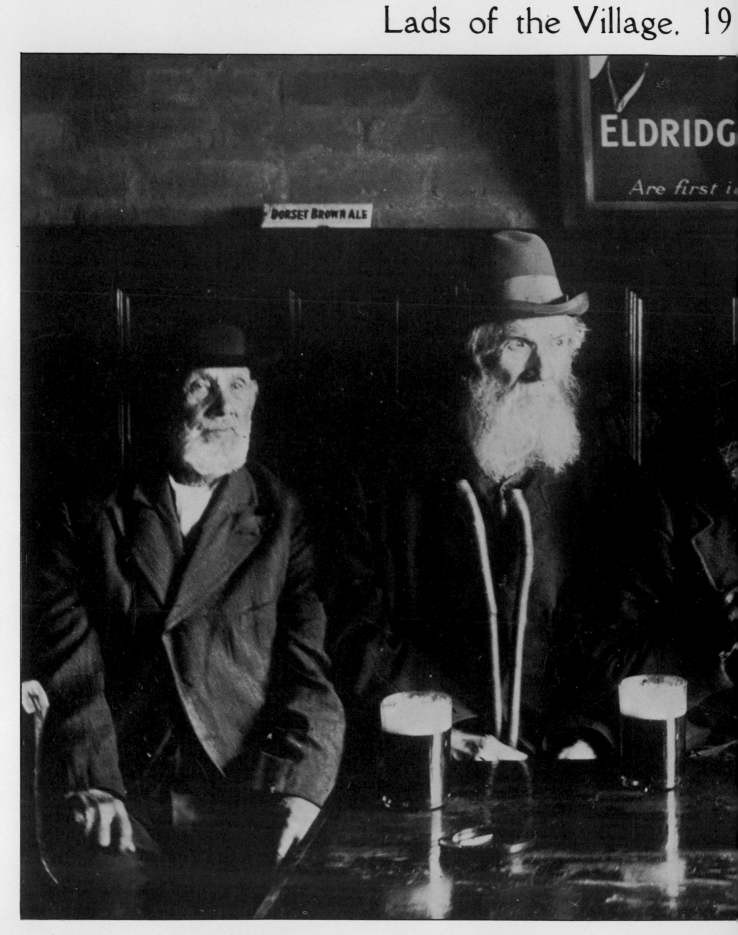

DORSET BROWN ALE

ELDRIDG

Are first i

GEORGE CHAINEY, 87.   JAMES HIGGINS, 87.   SAMUEL

TOTAL

Bradford Abbas, Dorset.

NG. 90.   THOMAS COOMBS. 89.   SIDNEY PARSONS. 81.

434 YEARS.

Porter and bitter stout

FADED SIGNS outside a few English pubs still promise a glass or two of *porter* upon entrance. Beers described as *porter* are still brewed in Czechoslovakia, California, Canada, and a variety of other places. The most famous beer to issue from the British Isles today is a direct descendant of *porter*, though it is better known simply as "Guinness." Neither the British nor the Irish brew *porter* any more. They brew *stout* instead. *Porter* is a lost, though not forgotten, beer.

Porter was first brewed in 1722, in Shoreditch, London. It was last brewed in the British Isles in Dublin, in 1973. The last draughts of the brew were consumed, in true Irish style, at a wake for *porter* which was held in a country pub near Belfast in May of that year. The mourners wore black bowlers, downed the *porter*, and consigned its container in a coffin draped in "Guinness black."

Porter was the first nationally popular beer-type in Britain. Until it was created, brewing styles were strongly localized. London and the surrounding towns had their own styles, which have long vanished. The Midlands of England, Yorkshire and Lancashire had brewing reputations which endure to this day. The far North of England and the South of Scotland enjoyed a good name which has faded somewhat.

In London, drinkers would order a combination from two or three different casks to be mixed in their glass (or pewter, or pot). Then a brewer called Harwood developed a beer which was said to combine the merits of the entire range. This he called "*Entire*," but it gradually became known as "*porter*." The most popular explanation for this name is the popularity of the drink among porters in the London markets. Another suggestion is that Harwood's delivery man was in the habit of shouting "Porter!" to announce his own arrival at his customers' houses. The name stuck.

Whitbread and Charrington are just two of today's major British brewers whose success was built on *porter*, even though the ascendancy of the style lasted only a hundred years. In his study, *The Brewing Industry in England* (Cambridge University Press, 1959), Peter Mathias compares the development of *porter* with the introduction of mule-spun muslin in the textile industry, or "pressedware" pottery. Like so many pioneers, Harwood himself made no fortune from his invention. *Porter* was a notably bitter beer, probably brewed with roasted malt, well fermented, dark and thick, and eminently suited to the process of brewing with London's water. "All nations know that

London is the place where *porter* was invented," wrote John Bickerdyke, in *The Curiosities of Ale and Beer*. "Jews, Turks, Germans, Negroes, Persians, Chinese, New Zealanders, Esquimaux, copper Indians, Yankees and Spanish Americans are united in one feeling of respect for the native city of the most universally favourite liquor the world has ever known."

It was the luck of the Irish that *porter* took longer to establish itself in their country. In Ireland, communications were bad, the country people inherently conservative, and the brewers had to compete with a strong tradition of distilling. The fashion for *porter* was slow to take hold there but its successor in England, *pale ale*, still hasn't. *Porter* became the national drink, passing into Irish literature and legend.

Donleavy is one of the countless Irish writers who have had a word on the subject: "When I die, I want to decompose in a barrel of *porter* and have it served in all the pubs in Dublin. I wonder, would they know me?" An Irish–American in the legendary brew might be more appropriate than the Negro whom early mythology had as the prime ingredient. That was in the days before Britain was a multi-racial country.

Guinness, founded in 1759, switched entirely to *porter* production forty years later. Guinness "Plain Porter" became the beer of the Irish working man, until the higher-gravity "Extra Stout" version of the drink gradually took its place. The bottled type of Guinness is still known as "Extra Stout." The word "stout" originally referred to the strength of beer, but its significance gradually seems to have shifted towards body and colour. The expression pre-dates Guinness. Before they started brewing, Swift wrote:

> "*Should but the Muse descending drop*
> *A slice of bread and mutton chop*
> *Or kindly when his credit's out,*
> *Surprise him with a pint of stout.*"

Disraeli, Thackeray and Robert Louis Stevenson all mentioned Guinness in their writings, giving some indication of the extent to which the Irish brew quickly established itself in the British market. Dickens also makes several mentions of the beer. In the original edition of *Pickwick Papers*, a drawing of Sam Weller by the famous illustrator Phiz includes a placard advertising Guinness. The beer's name was mis-spelled with only one "n," but that did not inhibit Guinness when the company belatedly started advertising. The Phiz illustration appeared in one of the first newspaper advertisements, in 1929. After Phiz's unintended contribution, Rex Whistler and

The beer that travelled well

First there was "entire," then there was "porter," and still there is "stout." This evolving family of dark-brown and black top-fermented beers has been characterized by thorough mashing, the blending of several worts, the use of roasted (and sometimes unmalted) barley, and an extremely high hopping rate. Like some of the other classic styles, these beers are the subject of much mythology, often muddled and contradictory. "Entire" is said to have been born in the early 1700s in Shoreditch, a cosmopolitan neighbourhood even in those days, at the Eastern edge of London's "City" district. A century later, the style still had pride of place (top) in the area of its birthplace, and was sold throughout England, but its popularity had reached its peak. English brewers still customarily offered "ales and porter" in the early part of the twentieth century, but the style itself had emigrated. Guinness porter became the national drink of Ireland, and was even bottled and marketed for the Dublin firm by rival brewers. Porter survived until the 1970s (right) in the North of Ireland, but had long been overtaken in popularity by stout, a different blend, with a slightly higher density. The Hungarian and Russian porters (far right) are bottom-fermented, but San Francisco's Anchor brand has a closer relationship with the original.

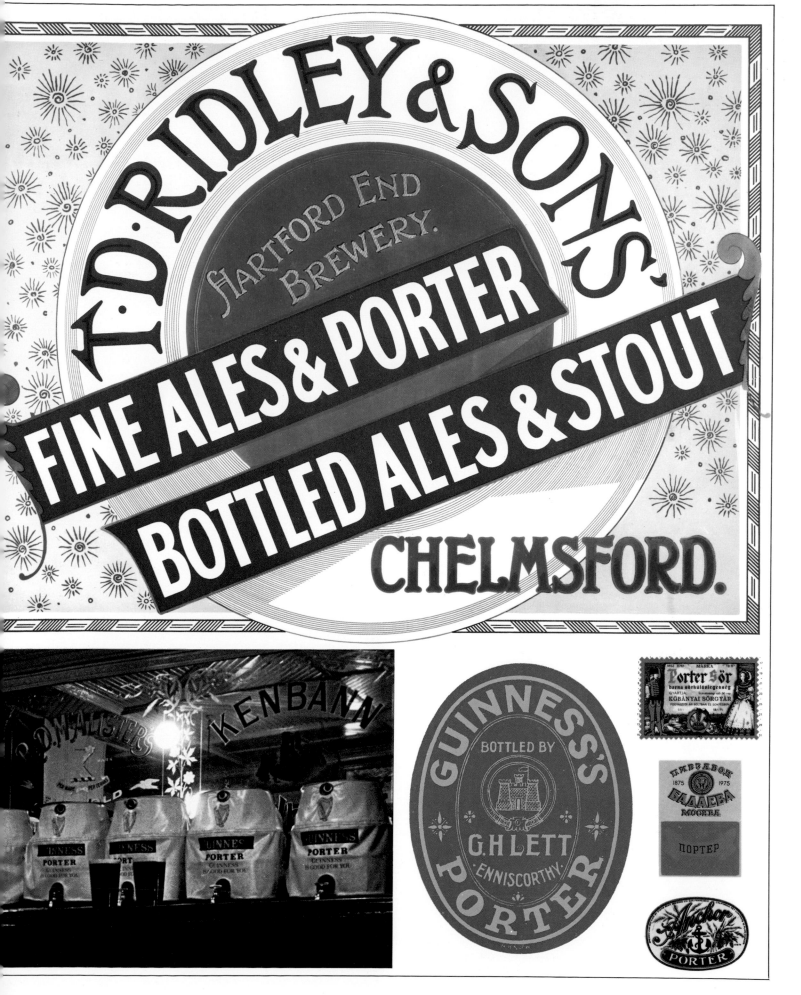

Guinness posters (Top row) 1934   1935   1936   (Middle row) 1937   1938   1939   (Bottom row) 1940   1949   1953 (*Coronation Year*)

In the British Isles, even the most experienced barman would be baffled by a request for a "bitter stout." People ask for "Guinness" because it is the only one. The Irish brew has a unique palate, although there are rivals in other countries.

H. M. Bateman were commissioned to provide illustrations for Guinness advertisements, and later artists ranged from Erté to the famous political cartoonist Vicky. Among the copywriters who worked on Guinness was Dorothy L. Sayers, creator of the English detective Lord Peter Wimsey. The beer's best-remembered slogan, *Guinness is Good for You*, turns out to have been the product of some very early attitudinal research. Almost as well known is *My Goodness, My Guinness*, which introduced a series of adventures involving a zoo-keeper and his animals. The animals were so strongly associated with the product that they could confidently be used without any mention of Guinness when the company prepared a poster to celebrate Queen Elizabeth's coronation. The creations of illustrator John Gilroy and the staff of the Benson advertising agency, which held the account for an astonishing 40 years, established a tradition of allusive and exclamatory publicity which has never been rivalled in Britain. Guinness caught the public imagination again when its neon signs and Festival of Britain novelty clocks became popular places at which to make a rendezvous.

Guinness achieved as much recognition for its advertising as it did for its fine brew. People who disliked beer, or didn't even drink, still knew that Guinness was some type of long, black alcoholic beverage. The product's progress can hardly have been hindered by the waves of Irish immigrants who left their impoverished homeland to do thirsty work in Britain, but its success also owed something to inspired marketing. While all the other British brewers had chains of "tied houses" which served as their outlets, Guinness was in the unique and apparently disadvantageous position of owning no pubs. (The brewery is the lessee of the *Castle*, amid hop fields on the Kent and Sussex border at Bodiam, but that is a whimsical exception). This lack of pubs should have been a critical handicap, second only to the supposed unfashionability of *porter*-type beers. In both cases, these drawbacks were turned to neat advantage. The other brewers were persuaded that, publess and porterful, Guinness offered no direct competition. Paradoxically, the decline of *porter*-brewing in Britain had left a gap which Guinness Extra Stout gratefully filled. The Dublin brewery became the biggest in the world, and continues to supply much of Britain, but the Southern half of England has since 1936 been serviced by another large Guinness brewery on the edge of London.

In Britain, a drinker who fancies a glass of *bitter stout* will not order it by that description. He will simply ask for a "Guinness". The brewer's trademark is so well known that there is no need to identify the type of beer being requested. Nor will any other brewer's product be offered, since there has never been any successful rival to Guinness stout in the British market. A few local breweries produce a dryish stout, sometimes with oatmeal, but not a truly bitter one. The British drinker is offered two different forms of Guinness.

Guinness Extra Stout, an unpasteurized beer which is conditioned in the bottle, is available in every British pub. It has a gravity of between 1042 and 1045, being brewed at the heavier end of this scale during winter. Draught Guinness is a slightly different brew, with a very creamy consistency, and a gravity of about 1040. It is widely, though by no means universally, available in Britain. For the British market, it is pasteurized, and served by the company's own restrained pressure system. In Ireland, where it is available at all bars and consumed at a ferocious pace, pasteurization is not thought necessary, though the same system of dispensing is used. All Guinness is brewed with roasted malts, and some roasted unmalted barley, providing the dark colour and full body which accompanies the characteristically bitter and well-hopped palate. It is of a higher gravity than *porter* was, but it is still sometimes described by the old term in Ireland. Oddly enough, *porter* – after having been created to replace a complicated blend of beers – ended its life by being mixed in the bar from two separate casks. Some drinkers still mix Guinness with *bitter* to produce a drink which is known as a "Black and Tan," but the military connotations of this mixture's name are properly dangerous in the light of the recurrent Anglo-Irish Troubles. A safer mix is Guinness with Champagne. This is known as "Black Velvet."

The advertising is as much of a legend as the beer. The famous Guinness toucan was one of several advertising characters reproduced in Carlton Ware pottery. "Flights" of toucans in different sizes were hung on pub walls. This example was made in 1955.

Pale ale

THE BAR AT THE FOLIES-BERGÈRES, as depicted by Manet in 1882, must have been a splendid place at which to drink. Displayed quite clearly among the Champagne on the bar are two bottles bearing red triangles. This symbol was not intended to communicate that danger lay within; on the contrary. The red triangle has been the famous trademark of two quite different beverages: Apollinaris mineral-water, and Bass beer. Manet's bottles, on closer inspection of the labels, clearly contained the superb *pale ale* brewed by Bass in the town of Burton on Trent, England. This small town in the Midlands remains world famous in the brewing industry, and it still produces the definitive example of *pale ale*, the classic English beer-style. The description *amber ale* is occasionally used with more accuracy to describe beers of this type, but the Burton brews were considered to be pale in comparison with the black *porters* and *stouts* which were their London rivals. Such are the quirks of history and geography that *pale ale* is now England's classic, and *bitter stout* Ireland's.

The *Folies-Bergères* bar staff had a proper sense of perspective about drinks. They must have at least partially agreed with Bickerdyke when he called *pale ale*, "that splendid liquid which, when bottled, vies with Champagne in its excellence and delicacy of flavour, and beats it altogether out of the field when we take into consideration its sustaining and restorative powers." The fame of Burton on Trent was celebrated in a rather debatable fashion by the rhyme:

"*Ne'er tell me of liquors from Spain or from*
France,
They may get in your heels and inspire you to
dance,
But the ale of Old Burton if mellow and right
Will get in your head and inspire you to fight."

The first famous *pale ale* was brewed by a largely forgotten London brewer called Hodgson in the mid 1750s, yet it was Burton which became famous for the style. Today, the town might be bracketed with Pilsen, Munich, Dortmund and Dublin as one of Europe's key brewing centres. Even in the 1750s, the brewers of the Trent valley had already been famous for at least 100 years, and had been mentioned in the writings of Defoe, but the emergence of *pale ale* as a new style gave them their chance to sparkle. The water of Burton has a high gypsum content which makes it well suited to the production of pale, sparkling beers, while London's water at the time favoured the brewing of dark styles. Even today, brewers in other parts of the world treat their water

with a process known as "Burtonization."

Bass was to become Burton's most famous brewery. It was once described as "the greatest *pale ale* brewery in the world." The company was started during the reign of George III, in 1777, by William Bass. He also owned a carrying company, but the brewery was so successful that he sold his other interest to the Pickford concern. Today, Pickfords, owned by the State, is Britain's most famous removal company. It

Like Queen and Empire,
this label is long gone,
but the style survives

was the enterprise of the Burton brewers which made them world-famous. The cutting of a canal linking the Trent with the North Sea port of Hull opened the way for a huge trade via the Baltic to Russia during the 1700s, and later to the British East Indies. The term "India Pale Ale" is still widely used today. When French conquests and Russian hostility closed the Baltic to British trade in the early 1800s, the Burton brewers had quickly to find new markets. They looked closer to home, and started seeking new British markets, including London.

The impact on the London market of Burton *pale ales* was such that companies from the Southern brewing town of Romford opened breweries on the Trent in order to share in the benefits of the local water. The Romford brewery of Ind Coope moved into Burton in 1853, and years later took over the great Allsopp company. The Allsopps had been involved in brewing locally since the Crusades. Hugh de Allsopp had fought in the Holy Land under Coeur de Lion, while his family at home were learning the brewing trade from monks in Burton. A later Allsopp

was brewer to Charles II. The merged companies of Ind Coope and Allsopp are today a principal component of Allied Breweries. Another Romford brewery which set up in Burton was the long-established concern of Truman, Hanbury and Buxton, which is today linked with Watneys.

Bass itself became linked with another great brewing company, Worthington (founded in 1744), and much later with the London firm of Charrington. Bass's famous red triangle was certified to be the symbol of the *pale ale* in 1876, and subsequent documents suggest that it may have been England's first registered trade-mark. A rather tenuous explanation of the symbol has been offered in times past: that it was originally intended to represent a pyramid. Apparently the pyramid-builders of Ancient Egypt worshipped a god called Bassareus, the son of the goddess Ops. Bass and hops have always enjoyed a close relationship, but so have the drinking of beer and the telling of tall stories. The triangle was probably a shipping mark, but little is known beyond that. It is nonetheless a matter for sentimental regret that the company's most famous *pale ale* is no longer marketed under that label. Today, their classic *pale ale* is called Worthington "White Shield."

Worthington White Shield is often available in pubs which are not tied to the Bass Charrington group, and is usually sought out by drinkers who do not fancy the beer of the house. Unlike other Worthington bottled beers, White Shield is not pasteurized, and is conditioned in the bottle. The yeasty sediment thrown by a bottle-conditioned beer is particularly visible in a brew which is very light in colour, and the manner in which a barman pours this renowned beer is some measure of his professional pride. Even barmen shell-shocked by hangovers have struggled manfully to maintain a gentle pouring action, thus preventing the sediment from falling into the glass. Some drinkers actually prefer the beer with the yeast in the glass, but this is apt to cause confusion and dismay in a proud pub.

White Shield has a gravity of about 1053, and a dry, slightly fruity palate. It is fermented with the aid of a magnificent arrangement called the Burton Union System, which is unique to the brewers of this town. This is a traditional process of circulatory fermentation in yeastily-foaming rows of wooden casks. "Beers brewed by this system have a particular quality of flavour which is much appreciated," wrote E. J. Jeffery in *Brewing Theory and Practice*, in 1936. The beer is in prime condition about four

The Bass at the Folies-Bergères

The label so carefully observed by Manet was still in use when the bottles below were sold, probably in the 1930s. Their bottler added the legend, "East India Pale Ale."

Registered Trademark Number One . . . Bass is one of the most famous names in the brewing industry. On one occasion, a French brewer faked Bass labels and applied them to his own lesser product. Other brewers have devised brand-names with a curious resemblance to Bass. The firm was started by William Bass, who built his first small brewhouse in 1777. The engraving above shows the brewery in 1834, with the owner's house in the foreground.

Bass

161

The pride of Burton

In Britain, the name of Bass has become primarily associated with draught beer, while the original Pale Ale is now known as Worthington "White Shield." The two breweries merged in 1926. Beers under both names are fermented in the famous Burton Union System, shown here as it was in the 1870s, and as it is today.

weeks after bottling. A numeral in the middle of the label, and a number of nicks on the right-hand edge of the label, indicate respectively in which week of which quarter the beer was bottled. Many brewers have similar marking systems, but their significance is rather greater in a sedimented beer of such delicacy. White Shield can stay in condition for up to nine months, after which it may develop an unpleasant flavour, though after about 15 months it sometimes reaches a new and very drinkable condition.

White Shield is the classic English pale ale in bottle-conditioned form, but there are hundreds of light-coloured pasteurized beers. Every brewery produces at least one such brew, and often several. These are known by a variety of designations, the most usual of which are *light ale, pale ale, IPA* (*India pale ale*) and *export*. A brewer producing just one pale beer may use any one of these names. A brewer producing several such brews would probably regard the names listed here as indicating an ascending order of gravity.

Among the large breweries, Courage's is a typical example. Its range includes a *light ale*, a popular *pale ale* called John Courage, and an excellent high-gravity beer called Bulldog Pale. This latter beer is also marketed in Belgium as Martin's Pale. It is unusually strong for a *pale ale*, with a gravity in the upper 1060s. Whitbread's range includes a pleasant *light ale*, which has a drier palate than the slightly higher-gravity *pale*. Some drinkers prefer the lower-gravity, and cheaper, beer. Whitbread's Brewmaster, acquired in the takeover of Flower's brewery, has a loyal following, though it is considerably sweeter and softer-tasting than the typical English *pale ale*. Whitbread also produce a diabetic beer which, like most diet beers, is delightfully dry. You don't have to be a diabetic to enjoy this beautiful beer, which is of a high gravity, and very well fermented. Whitbread's label is "English Ale," but it is better known as the "Gold Top" beer of the old Fremlin brewery, in Faversham, Kent.

Any small local brewery which is popular with beer-drinkers is likely to produce a good *pale ale*. Young's, in London, is a fine example, with a very bitter *light ale*, a stronger Ramrod, and an unusually strong Export. Ruddles produce an unusually and superbly dry Light Ale and a maltier and higher-gravity County Ale, both available beyond their home territory in the East Midlands. Off the beaten track, Randall's, of Jersey, produce a well-hopped and thoroughly-fermented Boxer Pale Ale.

Bitter

Tall handles made from mahogany and brass (below) are characteristic features of the English pub. Unless they are "fakes," left there for the purpose of decoration, the beer-pump handles indicate the presence of a cask-conditioned bitter.

THE SPLENDOUR OF ENGLAND's pale beers flowers more freely in their draught form. On draught, although terms like *pale ale* and *IPA* are still sometimes used, these beers are best known simply as "*bitter*." While many British drinkers find the bottled light beers rather gassy, the true *bitter* is inscrutably calm. The singularity of the bottle-conditioned *pale* contrasts with the multiplicity of cask-conditioned *bitters*. These unpasteurized draught beers must be sought out by the drinker who wants to experience *bitter* in its traditional form. It is an acquired taste, but one worth acquiring.

Unlike any other beer in the world, the true *bitter* is delivered to the pub in an unready condition. It undergoes its secondary fermentation in the cask, reaching perfection in the cellar of the pub. It has then to be sold quickly, before it loses its condition. When the landlord taps beer in his cellar, he has to carry out careful rituals of "soft-pegging" and "hard-pegging," in which timing is critical. Finings made from the sturgeon's swim-bladder are added to settle the beer.

Purists like to see the beer served by thumb-taps from a cask behind the bar, but few pubs have room for this. Nor does it always provide the beer at quite the right temperature. This simple gravity method is still sometimes used in country pubs, but manifestations of such rustic practice in the town should be viewed warily. Fake casks, all polished and painted, are sometimes displayed to hide CO_2-pressure pumps. Unless handled with great care, gas pressure gives a disagreeable "bite" to *bitter*. Far worse, its use is often accompanied by pasteurization, which kills stone-dead all the life and character of the real English *bitter*. The classical method of serving *bitter* is a manual pump, operated by tall ebony-and-brass handles on the bar. This "beer engine" requires a slight effort on the part of the barperson, and a gentle pumping action produces half a pint per stroke. If a pump is not operated in this fashion, it may actuate a more questionable mechanism. Many pubs display the pumps purely for show, relying on CO_2 pressure to draw pasteurized beer. Such pubs are not for beer-drinkers.

The minefield which confronts the serious *bitter*-drinker was laid in the 1960s, by corporate strategists far from the field. Small breweries were absorbed, and "national brands" created, their arrival announced by brightly-coloured plastic devices which suddenly paraded themselves hideously on the honest wooden and pewter bars of England. The new brews were called "*keg*" beers, though the description hardly fitted a pre-processed product delivered in a huge sealed can. These "*keg*" beers were filtered, pasteurized, often artificially carbonated and chilled until they surrendered. "*Keg*" beers lack subtlety of flavour, palate, bouquet. They are also a great deal sweeter than many of the traditional beers – not in itself a complaint until the original beers are taken

163

Pulling a pint

In England, beer was drawn straight from the cask until the development of the hand-pump (far right) in the 1770s. The new method meant that casks could be kept in a cool cellar while the beer was drawn in the bar at ground level. Although the system is known as a "beer engine," the pumping action is purely manual. The system was in common use by the mid 1800s (near right) and so it remains today (centre right), along with various other serving methods. In the 1960s, electric pumps and CO_2 pressure were widely introduced. The latter method, which is almost universal in other countries, met with some disfavour among British ale-drinkers. This was partly because CO_2-pressure often went hand-in-hand with pasteurization and artificial carbonation, but drinkers also disliked the effect of the gas on the palate of the beer. Devotees of bitter ale do not like their drink to be highly carbonated. The 1970s saw a swing back to traditional serving methods. During this time, many pubs installed pumps with decorated handles like those shown below. These examples were hand-painted at a pottery in the Midlands of England. Some of them were designed exclusively for brewers which have since vanished.

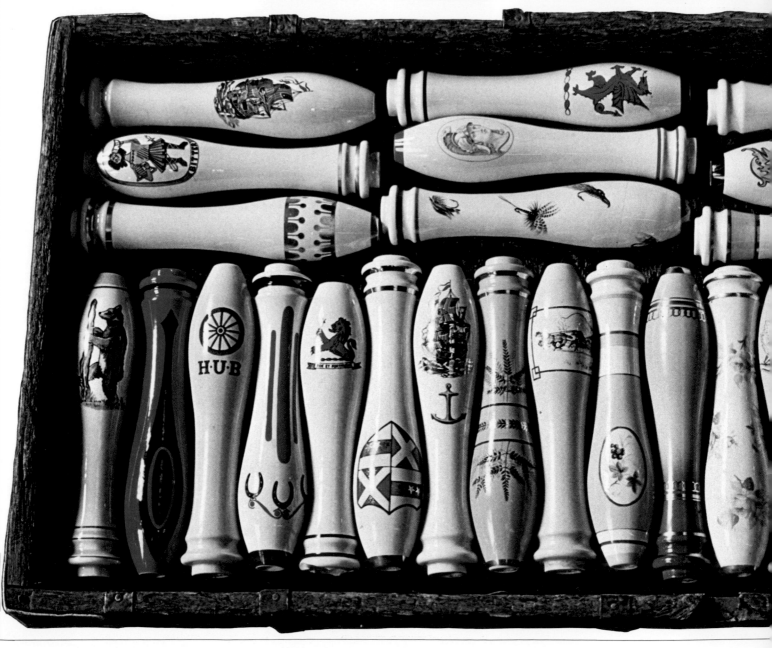

Among England's
traditionalist brewers,
the firm of Young's
brings a touch of the
countryside to the
heart of inner London.
Young's keeps not only
dray-horses but also
a ram (its mascot)
and some geese for
good measure.

off the market, or themselves rendered sweeter to meet a "public taste" which has more to do with supply than demand. Such beers were intended to widen the brewers' market to include womenfolk and the young; to have a long "shelf-life" with a minimum of care on the part of bar staff; to provide economies of scale; to suit the needs of nationally-networked television advertising; to be marketed at "premium" prices. "National brands" were the worst thing since sliced bread. No copywriter described these much-advertised brews with quite the colour and accuracy of the disgruntled drinker who said that they were "all piss and wind, like a barber's cat."

The fate which had overtaken so many of life's pleasures seemed set to overtake beer, and to do so irreversibly. The distinctive was being wiped out by the bland. A new generation of drinkers was growing up having known nothing other than "national brands", and suspicious of anything with taste.

The consumers revolted in the early 1970s. The Campaign for Real Ale was started almost in fun by a group of young beer-drinkers. It has since been described as the most successful consumer movement in Europe. The Dunkirk Spirit, a necessary precondition to any energetic action on the part of the English people, could be invoked once it was established that a national institution – traditional *bitter* – was in danger. Friends began to exchange details of pubs which served unpasteurized beer on hand-pumps. Such secrets were imparted conspiratorially, as if in recognition of the fact that this was a resistance movement. The Campaign for Real Ale (CAMRA) started to produce an annual guide to pubs fit for beer-drinkers. The *Good Beer Guide*, a modestly-priced paperback publication, became essential equipment for the discerning beer-drinker.

At first, the brewing giants were able to dismiss the Campaign for Real Ale without even bothering to disguise their contempt, but soon they were falling over one another to declare their devotion to traditional *bitter*. Even the group most reviled by beer-buffs, Watneys, made the tiniest of token gestures in this direction. Having banished "Real Ale" from their houses in favour of pasteurized and pressurized beers, Watneys reintroduced it on a very limited scale in the form of a brew which they called Fined Bitter (a well-balanced malty *bitter* with a gravity of 1044). In the North of England, the Wilson subsidiary is less grudging with its supplies of "Real Ale."

Another national group, Allied Breweries, launched a naturally-conditioned beer called Burton Ale in some of the pubs owned by their Ind Coope subsidiary. In the North, Allied own Tetley, whose popular beers are sometimes available in a naturally-conditioned state. The Courage group responded to the "Real Ale" movement by giving a new lease of life to their superb Directors' Bitter (1047). Bass have always served their renowned draught *bitter* (1040), custodian of the red triangle, in its natural state in many of their pubs. The Charrington half of the group is rather less considerate in the matter of naturally-conditioned beers. Whitbread continues to vary dramatically from district to district. In London, most Whitbread pubs serve only pressurized beers, but a handful of houses sell the splendid *bitter* from the old Wethered brewery in Marlow. Only the CAMRA *Guide* can tell.

There are vast and unhappy swaths of Britain where no "Real" draught exists, but something approaching half of the country's pubs still serve acceptable *bitter*. Of the 150 or so operating breweries, owned by about 100 firms and dominated by the Big Six (Watney, Allied, Courage, Bass Charrington, Whitbread, Scottish and Newcastle), almost all produce at least some cask-conditioned *bitters*. In some cases, Real Ale represents only a tiny part of the output; in other cases, it is the principal product.

In London, the relatively small Young's brewery serves naturally-conditioned *bitter* in every one of its houses. Young's (not to be confused with Younger's) has only a handful of pubs in the middle of town, but they are worth finding. One of the most central is the

Beers fermented in the
Yorkshire Stone Square
system by Sam Smith's
have a limited national
availability. So do the
Burton brews produced
by Marston's, though
the historic Cheshire
Cheese pub, off Fleet
Street, offers a rare
London outlet.

Guinea, in Bruton Place, off Berkeley Square. This is a typical basic English pub, despite a clientele laced with bright young chaps from the advertising industry, and an expensive adjoining restaurant. Most of Young's houses are utterly unpretentious London locals, on the South and West sides of town. The only other small local brewery in London is Fuller's, which brews Britain's strongest draught *bitter*. Fuller's Extra Special has an original gravity of 1054·5, and is available in Central London at the *Star Tavern*, Belgrave Mews. Fuller's has a rather eccentric selection of houses, mainly in West London. The *Dove*, on the Thames at Hammersmith, is a delightful and historic Fuller's pub, again with a rather breathless young clientele. There are two more pubs near the brewery, on the road to the airport, at Chiswick. Many provincial brewers send small supplies of their beers to London. From the brewing town of Burton on Trent, the Marston company supplies beer to just one London tied-house, the celebrated *Cheshire Cheese*, off Fleet Street.

Nottingham, also on the river Trent, is one of the provincial cities best blessed with *bitter*. There are three brewers of naturally-conditioned draught beer in the Nottingham area, among which Shipstone's produces a beautiful dry-hopped *bitter*. Wolverhampton is another city for the beer-drinker. At least half a dozen naturally-conditioned *bitters* are available in the area between Wolverhampton and Birmingham. The Northern capital, Manchester, is every bit as rich in traditionalist brewers. Among a clutch of well-regarded breweries, Boddington's and Holts are especially notable for their very hoppy, bitter beers.

Rural drinking can be a delight in England,

though some of the best brewers have only a handful of pubs, all in their own immediate areas. To the West of London, Brakspear's Henley Brewery has some picturesque pubs in the Thames Valley. Further West, in the Wiltshire countryside, Wadworth's brews some fine fruity *bitters*. In Hampshire, Gales offers a range of distinctive traditional beers. An especially well-hopped *bitter* is brewed by King and Barnes in mid-Sussex. Kent has Shepherd Neame, and Essex has Ridley's. Some devotees argue that Adnams' beer, in Suffolk, is Britain's best. Ruddles of Rutland (once, this was England's smallest county, but it is now officially a part of Leicestershire), also has a particular reputation among serious

beer-drinkers. "Good Honest Ales" are produced by Bateman's, in Lincolnshire.

Yorkshire has its own beer-town, Tadcaster, and its own brewing system. The "Yorkshire Stone Square System" makes for a very full-bodied beer, as exemplified by those of Samuel Smith. A slow-fermenting yeast is used, and the characteristic vessel is a stone or slate trough. Across the border in Lancaster, Yates and Jackson produce a truly dry *bitter*. Not far away, and on the edge of the Lake District, Hartley's of Ulverston brews a superbly full-bodied and malty *bitter*. The Lake District and Cumbrian Coast are a happy hunting-ground for the determined *bitter*-drinker. As Hartley's beer is malty, so Jennings', brewed in Cockermouth, is hoppy. All tastes are catered for.

As if such rustic riches were insufficient, there are also a number of home-brew pubs, most of them long-established, a few of them revivalists. Two of these are in Shropshire (or, as the civil servants will have it, Salop). These are the *Three Tuns*, at Bishop's Castle, and the *All Nations*, at Madeley, near Telford. Not far away, in the West Midlands, is the *Old Swan*, at Dudley. The West Country has an historic home-brew house called the *Blue Anchor*, in Helston, Cornwall.

Many of the most famous *bitters* taste as their name suggests they should, and a detail of English life would be obliterated if they ceased to be available, but it is equally true that a good number of respected brews have a sweet palate. There is no such thing as a definitive British beer taste. A scientist who attempted what he described as a "sensory analysis of beer flavours" in Britain, in order to produce a "standard vocabulary of tastes," found that his respondents used more than 250 terms to describe the beers they drank. These ranged from "toffee-like" and "buttery" to "nutty," "earthy" and "cabbagy."

"Real beer makes no concessions to immature taste buds," wrote the essayist Alan Brien, in the London *Sunday Times*. His reveries continued, "soon you forget you had to force yourself to swallow it . . . there were nights when six or seven pints coursed down as if served in magic thimbles . . . nothing can equal a good local brew after a long walk . . . faintly cloudy, just on the cool side of tepid . . . it wraps round you like a sticky horse-blanket and cuddles you to sleep."

Graham Greene, like many a young Englishman, forced down his first pint to prove his manliness. He records that, some days later, "I drank *bitter* for the second time and enjoyed the taste with a pleasure that has never failed me since."

Mild

A rare pale mild on sale in Outer London is A.K. (below), brewed by McMullen's, of Hertford. Further North, many brewers produce both pale and sweeter dark milds. Examples in the Manchester area include Hydes, Boddington's and Lees.

Brown ale

STANDING SIDE BY SIDE, upright and proud, the hand-pumps dispensing *mild* and *bitter* beers were inseparable Good Companions in the Public Bars of post-War England. Like the Public Bar itself, *mild* ale was a product of the social segmentation of pubs during the 19th century. It retained about 40 per cent of the draught beer market until the 1960s, then began to suffer a severe decline. The brewers wished to abolish "the Public," so that Saloon Bar prices could be charged throughout their houses. In many pubs, especially those of Central London, *mild* ale was banished in the same assault. *Mild* is an old beer. It is a cloth-capped beer for the working man. It is a cheap beer. Its characteristics do not endear it to marketing men and accountants.

As its name suggests, it is milder than *bitter*. Usually, it is of a lower gravity than *bitter*. Often, though by no means always, it is dark, malty and caramel-sweet. At its best, it can be a delightful change from *bitter*.

Mild has pulled its cap down tight, tied its muffler round its collar, and confronted the cold winds of time and tide. The stronghold of *dark mild* is the West Midlands, where every brewery produces the style. Mitchell and Butler is a famous name, especially notable for the Highgate Mild (1034·6) from its Walsall brewery. Among the smaller brewers, all producing well-liked *Milds*, Batham's (1036) is a fine example. In the East Midlands, all three Nottingham breweries have *dark milds*. So popular is *mild* in the Greater Manchester and Mersey area that most brewers there produce both dark and light varieties.

JOHN BROWN, BOB BROWN and Danny Brown are beers. So are innumerable Nutbrowns, not to mention Cobnut, Forest Brown and Sussex Wealdman. The basic British *brown ale* is the bottled version of *dark mild*. It was once a Public Bar habit to mix *brown* and *mild*, in another throwback to the pre-*porter* days. This blend produced a very sweet and malty beverage which was a little more lively than the pure *mild*.

Brown ale was typed as a South London drink by the satirist and jazz singer George Melly, in his book *Owning Up*. He described Londoners from South of the river Thames as being Transpontine people who drink *brown ale* and deal in used cars. Many a young man remembers *brown ale*, with rather more affection, as his gentle introduction to beer-drinking, and many an old man returns to it

Brown ales from three rural breweries. Badger ales are from Dorset, in the West; Bateman's from Lincolnshire, in the East; Hartley's from Cumbria, in the North, close to Lakeland. All three are local in their distribution.

Milk stout

The reproduction mirror testifies to the nationwide legend of Newcastle Brown, even if the beer's name is something of a misnomer. Double Maxim is a similar beer brewed a few miles away, but less widely available.

in his later years. Surprisingly, while the popularity of *brown ale* has declined with that of *mild*, it continues to be universally produced. Almost every British brewer produces at least one *brown*, and often several, some of which will be drier or stronger than the norm.

The only nationally-famous *brown ale* comes from the far North of England, and is misnamed. "Newcastle Brown" might be described as a Vienna-type beer if such a creature were known in Britain. While the typical *brown ale* is dark and opaque, the Newcastle version is a translucent reddish-copper colour. Not only is it far less brown than the typical examples of the style, it is also less sweet. Furthermore, it is considerably stronger than most *browns*, with a gravity of 1047. This, however, hardly justifies the mythology which has grown around the potency of the brew. The legend, which arose in the days when Newcastle Brown was less widely available, probably derives from the area's reputation as the home of hard-drinking shipbuilders and miners. The city's local brewery, owned by the Scottish and Newcastle group, also produces an unusual paler beer called Amber Ale. Both Brown and Amber are available in distinctive clear-glass pint bottles. A few miles away in Sunderland, the smaller Vaux brewery produces a strong beer, similar to Newcastle Brown, called Double Maxim. Although Newcastle Brown and Amber, and Vaux Double Maxim, do not belong to any recognized style, they represent a mode which is unique to their home county.

THE KENT FARMER who sought the right of way for his cows to pass through the Mackeson brewery yard on their way to milking did the company an inadvertent service. Visitors to the brewery were always impressed, the story goes, to see the cows wandering by. For Mackeson is the most famous example of a beer-style which was then known as *milk stout*. A less romantic explanation for the name is that it derives from the lactose used in the brewing of this sweet type of *stout*. The term milk stout is still used by the Guernsey Brewing Company, in the Channel Islands, but it has vanished in Britain since the introduction of tighter laws on trade descriptions. Names like Farm Stout, Meadowsweet Stout, Nourishing Stout, Barley Cream and Cream Label did, however, stay in use after the legislation.

While *bitter stout* is available only from Guinness, a great many regional and local breweries produce *sweet* or "*medium*" *stouts*, but always in the bottle. The nearest thing to a "national" *sweet stout* is Mackeson, now produced by Whitbread, but Courage's Velvet Stout and Bass Charrington's Jubilee

are also widely available examples of the style.

The rich, roasted-barley palate of Guinness is also apparent in the *sweet stouts*, but there the similarity ends. Guinness is very bitter indeed; the *sweet stouts* enthusiastically live up to their sugary name. The two styles are quite distinct and different. Like *mild* and *brown ales*, the *sweet stouts* have declined in popularity, but they resolutely refuse to die.

In *The Curiosities of Ale and Beer*, Bicker-dyke casts light on a possible explanation for the evolution of *sweet stout*. He recalls: "Macklin, the actor, who lived to be a centenarian, was accustomed to drink considerable quantities of *stout* sweetened with sugar, at the *Antelope*, in White Hart Yard, Covent Garden." Such eccentric behaviour was probably rendered unnecessary during the 19th century by political pressures to use sugar from Britain's Caribbean possessions in the brewing of *porter*. Eventually, *bitter* and *sweet* styles seem to have emerged as separate drinks.

A sweet drink sometimes called "Sheffield Stout" is made in South Yorkshire by mixing a malt-extract "Black Beer" which is brewed locally, with lemonade.

on Draught per Pint - 8d.
..O.S. in Bottle - per Half-pint 5½d. | Public Bar Prices
..M.S. in Bottle - per Pint - 7d. |

Y BRITISH STOUT

Made at HERTFORD BREWERY from the BEST BARLEY MALT made at McMULLEN'S Maltings, HERTFORD,

CHAMPION PRIZE HOPS

Grown by

Irish stout is bitter, British is sweet. Mackeson is the most widely available brand. In Dorset, Eldridge Pope used to produce a "Milk Stout" and another brand which was brewed with a portion of malted oats.

Old ales

Bière de garde

... a beer worth keeping. Thomas Hardy's Ale is bottle-conditioned. Right: dry-hopping at the brewery in the 1930s.

FAR FROM THE madding crowd, in Dorset, the poet and novelist Thomas Hardy clearly enjoyed the local Eldridge Pope ales. He produced a fable for the entertainment of the brewer, and wrote an introduction to the Pope family history. He also permitted the brewery to use in its publicity the following passage from *The Trumpet Major*, describing the beer of Casterbridge (in reality, Dorchester, home of Eldridge Pope):

"It was the most beautiful colour that the eye of an artist in beer could desire; full in body, yet brisk as a volcano; piquant, yet without a twang; luminous as an autumn sunset; free from streakiness of taste; but, finally, rather heady. The masses worshipped it, the minor gentry loved it more than wine, and by the most illustrious country families it was not despised. Anybody brought up for being drunk and disorderly in the streets of its natal borough had only to prove that he was a stranger to the place and its liquor to be honourably dismissed by the magistrates as one overtaken in a fault that no man could guard against who entered the town unawares."

By chance, in the 1960s Eldridge Pope stumbled upon 2,000 Victorian bottles, empty, and wondered how best to fill them. Fortuitously, a Thomas Hardy Festival was being planned in Dorchester, and it seemed appropriate to produce a special brew in recognition of the writer's deeds. The Festival was so successful that it was decided to repeat the event every ten years, and the beer was so much appreciated that another brew has been produced every two or three years since. Thomas Hardy's Ale comes in numbered bottles, each brew a "limited edition." It is unpasteurized, and the brewery recommends that it should be kept for not less than three years, and preferably four or five, before drinking. As if this were not a difficult enough request with which to comply, a note is attached to the bottle pointing out that it will improve if kept for 25 years, at 55°F. The 1968 brew was listed in the *Guinness Book of Records* as the world's strongest beer at that time, with 10·5 per cent alcohol by weight, and 12·58 by volume.

This type of beer, usually dark, malty but just slightly less rich or heavy than *barley wine*, and rather drier, might best be described as an *old ale*. There are many examples. Another superb and individualistic brew is Gale's Prize Old Ale, also produced on the South Coast, at Portsmouth. This is one of the few English beers still closed with a cork. It has a reddish colour, and an almost herbal palate. It is, of course, unpasteurized. Prize Old Ale has a gravity of more than 1090, and about 10·7 alcohol by volume. Burton on Trent has Owd Roger (1080), brewed by Marston and occasionally found on draught;

Old Peculier is known far beyond Yorkshire, and Old Timer beyond Wiltshire. Old Tom and Lees Strong Ale are from Greater Manchester. Little John is, of course, from Nottingham.

the North West has Robinson's Old Tom (1079), also available on draught; and North Yorkshire has its famous Old Peculier (*sic*), which has an original gravity of 1060. Although Old Peculier is among the lesser *old ales*, Yorkshire's thirsty drinking habits can render such a brew lethal. Legend has it that locals in Masham, where it is brewed, called the beer "lunatic broth."

Russian stout and barley wines

DEVOTEES OF STRONG BEER have much for which to thank Catherine the Great. The Empress of all the Russias is said to have developed a particular taste for a very high-gravity beer brewed in Britain, and her patronage is believed to have helped it achieve a popularity which it retains to this day. The brewery's records show that "Imperial Russian" was shipped to the Baltic from at least the 1780s, and the trade continued until the First World War. The exporters also set up a joint-stock brewery in Estonia, which was gutted in the First World War, and later nationalized by the USSR. Compensation of £240,000 was finally paid out in 1971.

"Imperial Russian" is widely available in Britain, at pubs owned by the Courage group. It has an original gravity of 1101·8 and an alcohol content of about 10·5 per cent by volume. The standard 17cl "nip" bottle contains more alcohol than two pub-measures of a regular Scotch whisky. "Imperial Russian" has the added distinction of being conditioned in the bottle. The brew is matured for two months in the cask and a further year in the bottle before leaving the brewery, unpasteurized. It will then keep for a good five years.

The original home of "Imperial Russian" was the Anchor brewery, on the river Thames at Southwark, London. Dr Samuel Johnson, the writer and lexicographer, became involved in the sale of this brewery to Barclay and Perkins (to become, in more recent times, part of Courage). He said of the transaction, "we are not here to sell a parcel

of boilers and vats, but the potentiality of growing rich beyond the dreams of avarice."

Although the brewery has moved a few miles down the Thames from its original site, little else about "Imperial Russian" has changed. It is described on the label as a *stout*, but it has only a passing resemblance to other beers bearing this designation. Its roasted-malt flavour hints at *stout*, but its high gravity (originally intended to preserve it during the long journey, and to warm hearts during the Russian winter) produces a quite different style of beer. Not only is it far stronger than modern bitter or sweet *stouts*, it also has a palate which fits into neither category. It is an extremely rich beer, with a powerful bouquet, and a barley taste which is almost fruity. Such fruity, strong beers are normally known in Britain as *barley wines*, even though they are stronger, volume for volume, than many grape wines.

Barley wines are usually dark, but there is the occasional pale version. In this and other respects, they bear some resemblance to the German *doppelbock* beers. A particularly fine pale *barley wine* is available in Whitbread pubs. This is the Gold Label produced at Whitbread's Sheffield brewery. Gold Label is less fruity than Imperial Russian, has an original gravity of 1098·6, and is very well attenuated. These two beers are the strongest regular brews in Britain, but there are a great many more *barley wines* available. Young's has one devilishly called Old Nick, while Ridley's prefers Bishop Ale, and Whitbread's Blackburn brewery has the zealously-named Oh Be Joyful!

The wreck of the Oliva

Russian Stout may well have been brewed by Barclay Perkins (now Courage) from the outset, but it was subsequently produced to the specification of the bottlers, A. Le Coq, who marketed it in St Petersburg and elsewhere during the 1800s. A shipment of beer from London was aboard the steamer Oliva when she sank in the Baltic in 1869. Bottles (below) were recovered in the area in 1974. In the early 20th century, increased import duties had persuaded Le Coq to buy a brewery within the Russian Empire, at Tartu, Estonia. The bottom picture shows the brewery's founder, Oscar Hyde Sillem (left) with the President of Estonia and the British ambassador.

Gold Label

Strong as a double scotch Less than half the price.

Among the beers of the barley wine type, Imperial Russian and Whitbread Gold Label are the strongest and most widely available. Many local brewers have their own barley wines, often with colourful names.

IMPERIAL EXTRA DOUBLE STOUT
A·LE COQ.
ANALYSES AND MEDICAL REPORTS.

АНАЛИЗЫ И ОТЗЫВЫ ОБЪ
АНГЛІЙСКОМЪ ПОРТЕРЬ
А·ЛЕ КОКЪ.

The shipping of stout to Russia was hindered not only by defensive tariffs but also by the production of imitations by the growing local brewing industry. Some even falsely bore the name of Le Coq embossed on the bottle.

Le Coq, founded by a Belgian but bought by a Briton in the mid 1800s, promoted its product with great flair. A publicity booklet (left) contained professorial testimonials to its properties. A gift of 5,000 bottles to hospitals (right) was rewarded with a warrant to supply the Court. The brewery (below, right) proclaimed its wares at local fetes (below, left).

The fortified beer

The inner gates of Traquair Castle are open to visitors between May and September, and guests may taste a naturally-conditioned version of the powerful brew produced there (right) by the Laird, Peter Maxwell Stuart. It is as good a Scotch Ale as can be found in its native country. Several gallons of beer were part of the payment for the workers who built a further set of gates at the perimeter of the castle grounds. These outer gates have been securely locked and bolted since this Border Country castle provided rest and shelter for Bonnie Prince Charlie (Charles Edward Stuart) during his campaign to seize the Crown from the Hanoverian George II in 1745. After taking Edinburgh, crossing the border and successfully invading a large part of England, the Prince was forced to withdraw. He ended his life in drunkenness and debauchery as a refugee. Today's brewer-Laird is a member of the main branch of the Stuart family, which pledged not to open the main gates of the castle until one of their offspring was back on the throne. Despite this, the Laird joined other brewers in producing a jubilee beer during 1977 to commemorate the twenty-fifth anniversary of the accession to the throne of Queen Elizabeth I of Scotland (better known elsewhere as Elizabeth II of England). The kings of Scotland originally used Traquair as a hunting lodge, but it later became an important border defence. The castle dates back to 1107. The main part of today's building dates from the 1500s.

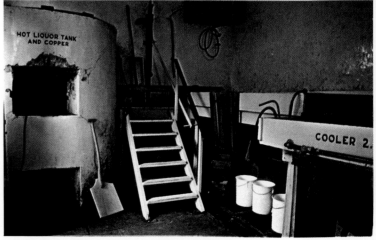

Scotland

Battles past are recalled
in the windows of
the Cottar's Howff, a
popular bar in the
Scottish capital. The
bar is in Rose Street,
which is famous for its
pubs. This beery
thoroughfare runs behind
the stately facades of
Princes Street.

A LORD OF THE MANOR is a "Laird" in Scotland. Peter Maxwell Stuart is the 20th Laird of Traquair, about 20 miles South of Edinburgh, and he is the brewer of an exceptional Scottish beer. The Laird lives, and brews, in Scotland's oldest inhabited castle. His beery career started when he made a discovery while clearing out the stable block, in 1965. He found a collection of brewing equipment, and subsequently discovered that it dated back at least to the early 1700s. Clearly, his ancestors had brewed at the castle, and the Laird was immediately anxious to restore this honourable family tradition. The product of his efforts is a near-black, well attenuated, malty brew, with an original gravity of 1080.

The Laird is making his own small con-tribution not only to the restoration of a family tradition, but also the reputation once enjoyed by Edinburgh and the surrounding area as one of Europe's great brewing dis-tricts. In order that the ancient wooden scutcheons and the 1739 copper might be brought back to the land of the living, the Laird sought the assistance of the excellent Belhaven brewery, on the coast not far from Edinburgh. Belhaven also produces its own "Wee Heavy" strong ale (1070), a rich "Eighty Shilling" *bitter* (1042), a beautifully balanced "Seventy Shilling Heavy" (1036), and a dark fruity "Sixty Shilling Light" (1031). The Scottish shilling-ratings, which date back to the days when a whole cask cost that much, have come back into fashion with the "Real Ale" revival in cask-conditioned,

Not far from the taverns of Rose Street is the Café Royal (below), where a frieze in the public bar celebrates great inventors. The Waverley is in St Mary's Street, just off the Royal Mile, which leads to the palace of Holyrood house.

draught beers. They indicate whether a beer is a luxury brew, a regular brew, or a cheaper brew. *Heavy* and *light* are Scotland's approximate counterparts to England's *bitter* and *mild*. Thus a *light* can be dark.

The beer town of Alloa, in Central Scotland, has the country's only other independent brewery, Maclay's. This company produces some pleasant beers, which are available on a very limited scale in Edinburgh. Alloa also has a Skol *lager* brewery. Edinburgh has two breweries in the Scottish and Newcastle group, which produce cask-conditioned beers on a very limited scale under the McEwan and Younger names. A further two Edinburgh breweries are owned by Vaux, of Sunderland, and they produce a well-liked draught beer under the Lorimer (formerly Usher) name. Edinburgh also has Dryborough, part of the Watney group, producing "*keg*" beers only. Both Edinburgh and Glasgow have Bass Charrington breweries under the Tennent name, both mainly producing British versions of *lager*-type beers. *Lager* enjoys considerably more popularity in Scotland than it does in England.

Opening hours are becoming more liberal, and the tide of pasteurization has been turned very slightly, but Scotland has a long way to go before it reaches the beery glories of its past. Nor will drinkers who have enjoyed *Scotch ales* in Belgium and elsewhere find anything quite comparable in Scotland, though they might appreciate Younger's Double Century.

A haven for the drinker

"Bavaria cannot produce the like," said the Emperor of Austria. "Belhaven beer is the Burgundy of Scotland . . ." "The best small beer I ever had," said Boswell, the biographer of Johnson. The brewery, in the tiny seaport and resort of Dunbar, has its origins in a fourteenth-century monastery. It has been a commercial brewery since 1719. Belhaven's full-flavoured and well-conditioned beers are in great demand.

Ireland

IRELAND IS A SMALL COUNTRY, with a population of only 4·5 million, but its influence on the worlds of literature and politics has long been felt by larger nations across the seas. It follows that a country concerned with such fundamental aspects of life would hardly neglect the matter of beer.

The Republic of Ireland runs level with Denmark as the biggest exporter of beer within the European Economic Community. Almost all of this beer is Guinness *stout*, and a great deal of it is exported to Britain (despite the existence of a very large Guinness brewery in London). About 40 per cent of the beer brewed in the Republic is exported, compared with less than 30 per cent of Denmark's output. Despite the boozy image of the Irish, their consumption per head is slightly lower than that of the Danes.

The rumour that Guinness tastes better in Ireland is well-founded. It has, however, nothing to do with the water of Dublin's river Liffey. Contrary to myth, neither Liffey Water nor Holy Water make Irish Guinness great, though the clear lakes and streams of the nearby Wicklow Mountains may have something to do with it. A more likely explanation is simply that Irish Guinness, in both draught and bottled forms, is unpasteurized. Dublin has only Guinness as its local *stout*, but the Republic's individualistic second city, Cork, has two such black brews. One of them is produced by Murphy's, a company which is now owned by a consortium of hoteliers and bar-owners. Murphy's *stout* has a rather softer palate than Guinness. Beamish and Crawford, Ireland's oldest brewing company, is owned by Carling O'Keefe, the Hibernian-sounding Canadian brewing giant. Beamish produces an excellent *stout*, similar to Guinness, but very slightly lighter in colour, and with a whiter head. Both of Cork's *stouts* are pasteurized, as are all the *ales* and *lagers* produced in Ireland.

Stouts, draught and bottled, have gravities of around the 1039/40 mark in Ireland. *Ales* are all about 1036. Although *stout* has more than 60 per cent of the market in the 26-county Republic, *ale* is growing in popularity. Guinness has the controlling share in no less than five *ales*, with a minority stake

A stout threesome

The Guinness brewery in Dublin was the biggest in the world when the engraving above was made in about 1890. The size of the mash-tuns, and their mechanical operation, bears witness to the sophistication of the brewery at that time. Guinness, founded in 1759, became a joint-stock company in 1886. The other two stout-brewers which still survive (right) in Ireland were established in 1792 and 1883 respectively.

held by Allied Breweries, the large British group. These include: Smithwick's, a sweetish *ale*, mainly served on draught but also bottled, widely available, brewed in the town and county of Kilkenny; Macardle's, drier, hoppier and darker, mainly bottled but also available on draught, traditionally an East Coast beer, but gaining a wider popularity, brewed near the border in Dundalk; Phoenix, very bitter, available only in the bottle, and concentrated near the former Cherry's brewery in Waterford; Perry's, much the same type of beer as

Smithwick's, on draught only, available only in a tiny traditional market around Rathdowney, County Laois; Double Diamond, brewed in Dublin and nationally available.

Visitors to Ireland who remember an *ale* with the rather terminal name of "Time" will not be surprised to hear that it has vanished. Nor is *ale* any longer produced in Enniscorthy, County Wexford, by Lett's, though the company was shrewd enough to keep up to date its brewing licence. Enniscorthy-style beer can thus still be produced under licence in France with a vestige of

Ireland is a country in which to drink bitter stout, rather than ale, though the traditional black brew enjoys less of a monopoly than it once had. Irish ales make an occasional change, and have their own distinctive palates.

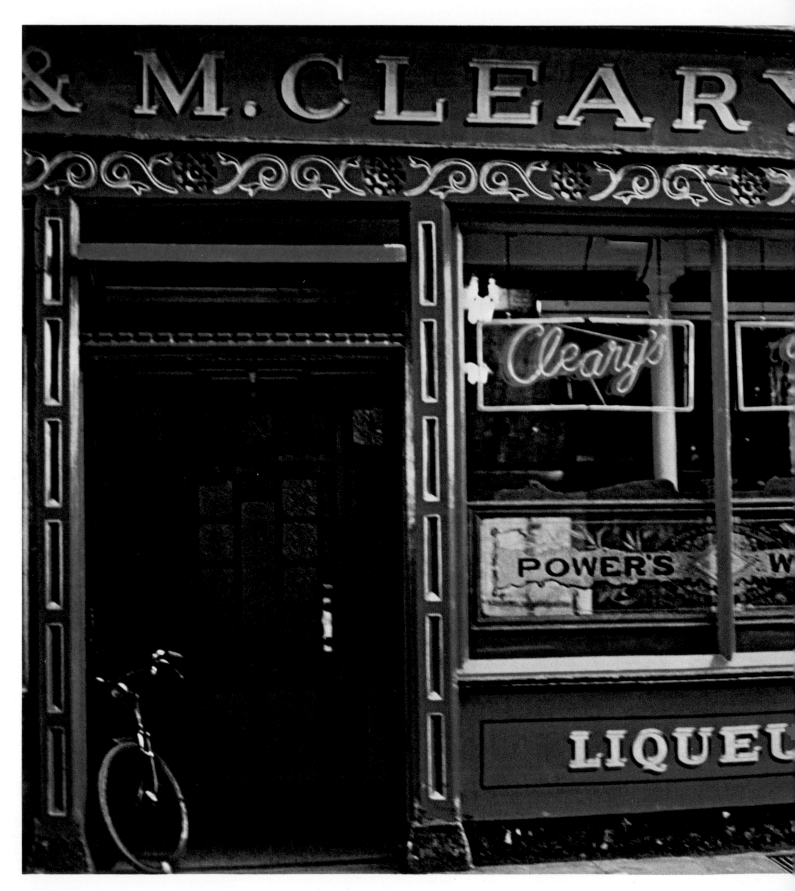

Whether it doubles as a grocery shop or a liquor store, the tiny, family-owned bar is a focus of rural Irish life from Donegal to Kerry. In addition to stout, such establishments do a predictably good trade in whiskey.

Gallic integrity. Murphy's has a pale and not very hoppy *ale* called Schooner, while Beamish and Crawford produce a rather sweet and reddish-coloured *ale* under the Bass name.

Guinness invented Harp Lager, which is marketed in Britain by Courage, Scottish and Newcastle, and Greene King. In Ireland, only the Dundalk-brewed premium version of Harp (1041) is sold. Beamish and Crawford, as might be expected in the light of their ownership, brew *lagers* under the Carling (1039) and Carlsberg (1042) labels.

In the Six Counties of the North-East which remain linked with Britain, the Scottish ethnic background of a large proportion of the population seems to have affected their tastes in beer as much as it has their religious and political attitudes. Although *stout* has traditionally enjoyed a large share of the market, *Scottish ales* and *lagers* are very much in evidence.

Dublin's drinking places have a character of their own, a unique hybrid between the Irish bar and the English pub. Belfast has pubs, bars and clubs. In country areas, things are different. Rural bars often serve simultaneously as grocery shops. Sometimes, the premises have a dividing wall, but often the drinking is done between counters which are stacked with tea, or hung with sides of bacon. Like some Scottish bars, these places have no name in the pub sense. They are known simply as "O'Connor's," "Rafferty's," "Maclean's," or whoever's. On both sides of the border, drinking places are open from 10.0 in the morning until 11.0 or 11.30 at night. Dublin's pubs and bars close for an hour between 2.30 and 3.30. This is known as the "Holy Hour," perhaps because it is a gesture to more temperate ways.

The Dubliners have another explanation. They say that the parish priest likes to have a beer in peace.

The brewery on Friary Hill

The last small independent brewery in Ireland ceased to produce its popular ales in 1956, but still retains its beery connections. The firm of Lett's, at Enniscorthy, County Wexford, not only licenses its Ruby Ale to Pelforth (right), but also distributes other brewers' products locally. The waterwheel provided power until 1952. A doorway in the brewery dates back to 1456, when there was also an abbey on the site, which is still known as Friary Hill. Relics from the brewery can be seen at Enniscorthy's town museum, which is in a Norman castle.

France

A weighty heritage . . . in the **Region du Nord**, craft-brewing survives, and there are one or two superb top-fermented speciality beers. The one produced by the Duyck family brewery (left) is an excellent example. The brewery is near Valenciennes.

THE WORLD'S GREATEST wine-growing nation also has a weighty heritage of beer-drinking. The one reputation has in modern times obscured the other, but in some small ways this position is now shifting. When provoked, the French will even assert that the Ancient Gauls invented beer, though such a claim does not run unchallenged elsewhere in the world. Tacitus talked of "drinking orgies which continue for a full day and night, and are in no way considered as shameful." Even today, the legendary cartoon-character *Asterix* still likes a drop of *cervoise* with his roasted whole boar. For that matter, weren't Charlemagne and King Pepin likely pioneers of hopped beer? Even William the Conqueror was the son of a brewer.

Modern brewing is another question altogether. The godfather of modern brewing is indubitably a great Frenchman, Louis Pasteur. His guiding hand led the innovative brewers of the 19th century to a whole new understanding of the fermentation process, and he involved himself directly in the problems of the industry. One of Pasteur's greatest disciples, and himself a central figure in the furtherance of brewing technology, was another Frenchman, the Marseilles brewer Eugene Velten. A century later, each of them might be a little surprised to see how traditionalist are the tastes of today's *cognoscenti*.

Pasteur, who once made a problem-solving visit to the Whitbread brewery in London, would probably be astonished to note the *chic* which attends unpasteurized beers in Britain today. For reasons of time, travel and multinational marketing, unpasteurized beers are not among the *snob* British brews which are most readily available in Paris, but Pasteur might be equally amazed at the way in which top-fermentation has survived and returned to fashion.

Ales and *stouts* from the British Isles, and Belgian beers in the *haute tradition* were much in evidence when the suave magazine *Réalités* delved into the specialist beer-bars of Paris. Such places are vulnerable to the vicissitudes of fashion but *Réalités*, which has an eye for

Many Frenchmen have made important contributions to the art of brewing, and none more than Louis Pasteur, who was the godfather of modern brewing.

Most brewing countries have witnessed a concentration of their brewing industry. During one decade, more than fifty breweries were concentrated into six major groupings.

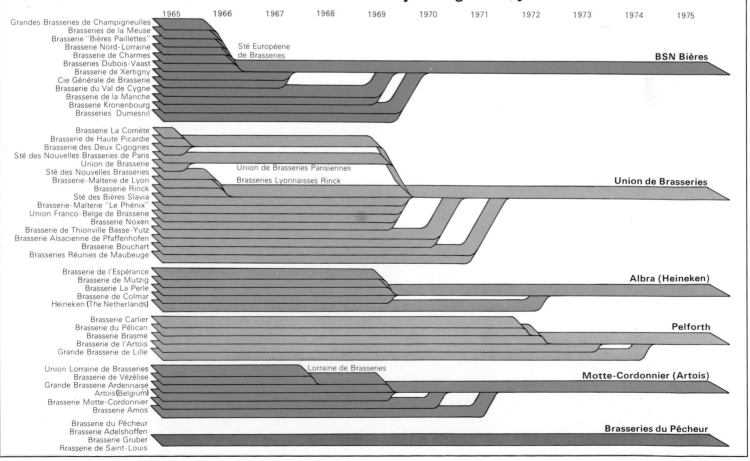

How the small brewers were swallowed by the Big Six...in just one decade

179

Small beer-festivals take place in many Northerly parts of France during the summer, often sponsored by brewers. The one opposite was in Alsace. The same region's Pêcheur group (bottom) is also known as Fischer.

Keeping the haute tradition

The historic Rimaux brewery is typical of the tiny family firms which still survive on both sides of the Belgian border. Its ancient equipment was put out of commission in 1976, while the brewery had an overhaul, but there is little chance of mass-production taking over at Rimaux.

such matters, reported on the following establishments: Académie de la Bière, 88 bis, Boulevard du Port-Royal; La Bonne Bière, 23 Faubourg du Temple; Le Général Lafayette, 52 Rue Lafayette; and Le Bar Belge, 75 Avenue de Saint-Ouen.

The British *ales* available in France tend to be those produced by the big and ambitious corporations, but the smaller craft-brewers of Belgium, nearer neighbours spiritually – if not always geographically – win more acclaim from the knowing French beer-drinker. This shows good judgement on his part, though it remains less than fair to some of France's native brews. Precisely because cultural influences straddle the frontier, French Flanders and the Région du Nord in general have their own excellent indigenous beers. Just in case anyone misses the point, the little Ricour family brewery of St Sylvestre Cappel brands its beer with a drawing of a windmill, plus the legend, "une bière des Flandres!" The exclamation-mark is theirs. The beer is called *du Moulin,* not *van de Molen,* despite the Flemish spellings common in this area. The real attractions of the border country have less to do with language than with yeast. The North still has a handful of top-fermenting brewers. Years of "rationalization" have taken their toll but, where they can still be located, such brewers are at last being appreciated.

Between the Belgian border and the town of Valenciennes, there was once an abbey brewery, dating back to 1714, at Crespin. It survives today in the form of the Brasserie Rimaux, producing a full-bodied and fruity *haute tradition* beer called Réserve Saint Landelin. Just South of Valenciennes, at Jenlain, on the Route Nationale, a superb *haute tradition* beer is brewed by Brasserie Duyck, a small family business. Jenlain Bière de Luxe is presented in a bottle of the type used for wine, wired at the top, Champagne-style. It bears the following haughty assurances: "Garde Fermentation Haute; Garantie Sans Colorants." Monsieur Duyck's beer is a smooth, medium-dry full-bodied brew, of 20 degrees Balling, with a deep bronze colour. It has eight days' primary fermentation and one month of maturation, and is filtered but not pasteurized. Locally, it can be found on draught and the bottled version finds its way to selected outlets as far away as Clermont-Ferrand and St Etienne. A similar brew is produced in the Département Nord, at Monceau St Waast, by the Brasserie Descamps.

A far larger producer of top-fermented beers is Pelforth, one of France's "Small Three" brewery groupings. Pelforth's Peli-

can brewery is near Lille, the capital of the beer-drinking North. Pelforth Brune is a dark, reddish, slightly sweet and very malty brew. There is also Pelforth Pale. The company's name additionally appears on the "Russet Ale" which is produced by a process described as "Irish Top Brewing," under licence from George Killian Lett, of Enniscorthy, County Wexford. This is a full-bodied, copper-coloured *ale,* malty without being unduly sweet, and with a strong, smooth taste. Discretion demands that it be regarded as an indigenous French speciality (in much the same way that "Russian Stout" is an English speciality), since it is much too agreeable a beer to be branded as a fake. Although Mr Lett wisely kept his brewing licence up to date, and therefore has the right to franchise it, he has not produced any beer for nigh on 20 years. It is a Gallic-Gaelic conspiracy worthy of Wolfe Tone. Irish legend has also been harnessed in the marketing of the beer. The publicity of Bière Rousse records that the first king of Ireland was riding his horse one day when he was enveloped in a magic cloud, within which he met a Celtic god. With the god was a beautiful young girl, symbolizing the sovereignty of Ireland, and to honour their encounter she handed him a glass of foaming Red Ale.

Not only is the Pelforth group blessed by the gods, it also has Government money in the shape of a minority shareholding taken by the Department of Industrial Development in 1972. The remaining shares are in French hands, and the group has about eight per cent of national beer-sales. It is notable for its high level of door-to-door selling, this being an important means of marketing beer in the North. Between 1972 and 1974, Pelforth took over several smaller brewers in the North, including one called de l'Artois, from Roeux, in Pas-de-Calais. This brewery took its name from the region, unlike the far larger Artois group in Belgium, which was named after one of its early principals.

Coincidentally, a second Lille-based member of the "Small Three" is now owned by Artois of Belgium. This group, based on the Motte Cordonnier brewery also includes

The cosmopolitan beer-bars of Paris (top) serve brews from Lorraine, Bavaria, and the Republic of Ireland, Burton ales from England, Dutch lagers and much else besides. Such distractions are not required by a steadfast local drinker at Champigneulles (above). His home village was the scene of a beery miracle.

several companies in Lorraine and Alsace, including such well-known names as Vézelise/Sedan and Amos.

While the Région du Nord is the area for top-fermented beers, Lorraine and Alsace produce France's finest bottom-fermented brews. Just as the North has its Franco–Flemish cultural blend, so Alsace–Lorraine has its Germanic influence. France's smallest brewery group, in Schiltigheim, bilingually styles itself Bières Fischer/Pêcheur, and its Belle Strasbourgeoise beer is labelled with an allusion to the German *Reinheitsgebot*. Fischer does its own malting, uses hops rather than extract, and claims to mature its beers for ten weeks. The latter claim exceeds even those made by some German brewers. In keeping with this Teutonic tone, the group also produces an excellent full-bodied beer called Rheingold, which originates from its Adelshoffen brewery.

The geography of brewing in France is very tightly defined. More than half of the nation's 80-odd breweries are in the Région du Nord, but they produce less than a quarter of the nation's beer. This figure reflects the extent to which small plants still survive in the region. Elsewhere, the picture is very different. There are four breweries in Lorraine, and a dozen in Alsace, yet the latter region produces well over a third of the nation's beer, and its share is rising fast. There are a further five breweries in the Paris and Ile de France region. Taken as a national average, beer-consumption is only 45 litres per head per year, and France stands at number 23 in the world league-table, but this is only part of the story. With a population of 51·5 million, it requires enough beer to place it at number seven in the table of gross output, with an impressively-large production of 21 million hecto-litres. The first figure makes life almost impossible for small breweries, unless they happen to be in the thirsty North, while the second figure makes high-volume production for national distribution eminently worthwhile. Most of the groupings still have a strong regional bias, but there has been a continuing and immense concentration of the industry since the war.

In 1969, four important breweries in Alsace merged under the name of Albra, and in 1972/3 they were taken over by Heineken. This grouping uses primarily the Ancre and Mutzig brand-names, and has a market share of more than nine per cent. It is thus the biggest of the "Small Three." Heineken, with its considerable resources and expertise, could conceivably start chasing the "Big Two."

The smaller of the "Big Two" is Union de Brasseries, the former Brasseries et Gla-cières de l'Indochine, once famous throughout the French Empire for its "33" beer. Slavia is one of its best-known domestic brands. The group is controlled by the insurance company La Paternelle, and has taken over 16 breweries in as many years. It now has six plants and 15 per cent of the market. With a colonial history but no geographical base, Union de Brasseries has its biggest plant near Paris, at Drancy.

Among its well-known brands is Porter 39, a dark, *stout*-type beer, with a slightly bitter aftertaste. Porter 39 originates from a brewery in the North, at Maubeuge, where a sizable local beer-festival is held for several days in mid-July each year.

At least a dozen brewing companies, including some of the biggest, went through a three-pronged series of mergers in the 1960s, only to be bitten off the fork and swallowed whole by BSN, France's biggest bottle-maker. The resultant grouping, BSN Bières, now holds half of the national market. BSN Bières has 17 breweries throughout the country, with major plants near Paris and Strasbourg. It is highly unlikely that all 17 breweries will remain in operation, and half a dozen might ultimately be thought sufficient. The grouping has two principal components, which operate as autonomous subsidiaries. One is Société Européen de Brasseries, based on such famous names as La Meuse; the other is Kronenbourg. After "33", "Kronenbourg" is probably the French beer-name best known elsewhere in the world. The company was founded in 1664 by the Hatt family, who continue to manage it, and the best-known brand is simply called "Kronenbourg." Another well-known brand is Tiger Scotch; beers with this designation presume to emulate their Belgian counterparts. Kronenbourg's original brewery, greatly expanded, is still in use. It is outside Strasbourg, and a second brewery was opened not far from the city in 1969.

The brewers of the Alsace have notably concentrated on *de luxe* beers. This category, which indicates a minimum alcohol content of five per cent by volume, represents 75 per cent of sales. In 1955, it had less than half of the market. There has been a corresponding decline in the so-called *bock* beers, which have an alcohol content of 3·5–4·0 per cent by volume.

France's impressive position in the world beer-brewing league is improving all the time. In two decades, production has increased by 80 per cent. More than half of the beer brewed is drunk by women, and the 16-to-24 age group accounts for more than a quarter of consumption. These figures would no doubt be even higher were not beer the everyday drink for all age-groups in the North. Nationally, it is the young who have acquired the taste, while the middle-aged and elderly stick to wine, as they always have done. Nor is beer a drink of the manual workers; middle-managers and white-collar staff are significant among the beer-drinking groups, while agricultural labourers consume less than two per cent of the total, presumably preferring local domestic wines, scrumpy, and moonshine.

The archetypal Frenchman could yet be pictured holding a glass of beer. Once before, it was so. Just as the Belgians had their St Arnoldus, so the French had a saint of the same name some centuries earlier. There is some documentary evidence of the existence of both saints, and each of them has passed into folklore as a patron of beer. The French saint, who was the Bishop of Metz, performed a miracle after his death. His remains were being carried in a casket from one village to another in the Vosges on a hot day in 642. At the village of Champigneulles, the bearers were wilting in the heat, and faint with thirst. They stopped for a rest, and wanted to refresh themselves, but only one person among the hundreds of mourners had as much as a mug of beer. While they contemplated with some resignation the prospect of continuing their journey, a foaming tankard suddenly materialized in the hand of each and every mourner. The tankards contained beer, of course. So much for Biblical tradition, not to mention France's reputation as a wine-loving nation.

There may be fewer breweries than there once were, but a bewildering array of beer-brands still exist. Kronenbourg is now internationally known, and few Frenchmen can be unaware of Pelforth. La Meuse is an historic French beer-brand, and Champigneulles rightly has its own brew. In France, names like Sedan and Adelshoffen mean beer . . .

The breweries of Switzerland

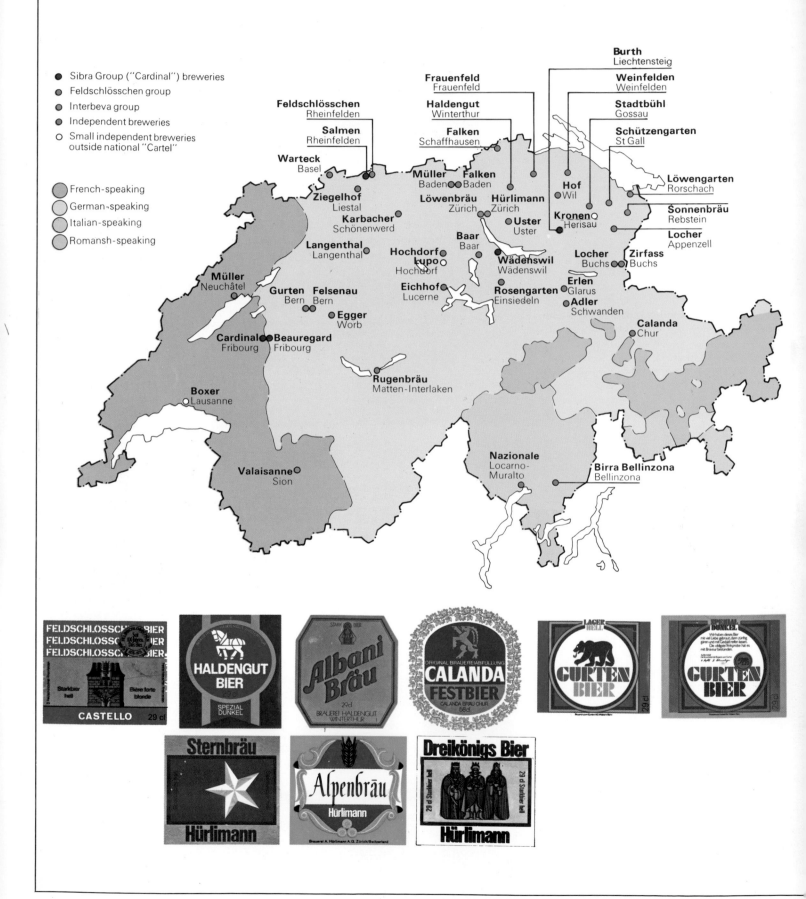

- ● Sibra Group ("Cardinal") breweries
- ● Feldschlösschen group
- ● Interbeva group
- ● Independent breweries
- ○ Small independent breweries outside national "Cartel"

- French-speaking
- German-speaking
- Italian-speaking
- Romansh-speaking

Burth
Liechtensteig

Weinfelden
Weinfelden

Stadtbühl
Gossau

Schützengarten
St Gall

Frauenfeld
Frauenfeld

Haldengut
Winterthur

Löwengarten
Rorschach

Feldschlösschen
Rheinfelden

Falken
Schaffhausen

Sonnenbräu
Rebstein

Salmen
Rheinfelden

Müller
Baden

Falken
Baden

Hof
Wil

Locher
Appenzell

Warteck
Basel

Löwenbräu
Zürich

Hürlimann
Zürich

Kronen
Herisau

Ziegelhof
Liestal

Karbacher
Schönenwerd

Uster
Uster

Locher
Buchs

Zirfass
Buchs

Langenthal
Langenthal

Baar
Baar

Erlen
Glarus

Müller
Neuchâtel

Hochdorf
Hochdorf

Lupo

Wädenswil
Wädenswil

Gurten
Bern

Felsenau
Bern

Eichhof
Lucerne

Rosengarten
Einsiedeln

Adler
Schwanden

Egger
Worb

Calanda
Chur

Cardinal
Fribourg

Beauregard
Fribourg

Boxer
Lausanne

Rugenbräu
Matten-Interlaken

Valaisanne
Sion

Nazionale
Locarno-Muralto

Birra Bellinzona
Bellinzona

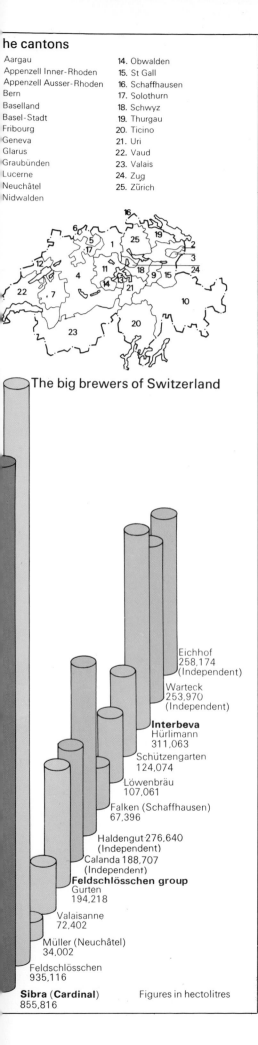

The big brewers of Switzerland

Eichhof
258,174
(Independent)

Warteck
253,970
(Independent)

Interbeva
Hürlimann
311,063

Schützengarten
124,074

Löwenbräu
107,061

Falken (Schaffhausen)
67,396

Haldengut 276,640
(Independent)

Calanda 188,707
(Independent)

Feldschlösschen group
Gurten
194,218

Valaisanne
72,402

Müller (Neuchâtel)
34,002

Feldschlösschen
935,116

Sibra (Cardinal)
855,816

Figures in hectolitres

Switzerland

Brewers of an earlier epoch live on (below) at the Cardinal brewery, in Fribourg. Cardinal is one of Switzerland's giants, as shown by the output chart (below, left). Only a selection of labels is shown, but the map includes all of the country's breweries.

CIVILIZED MEN, wherever they are to be found, enjoy beer. When missionaries from Ireland took classical learning and traditions back to the European mainland after the Barbarian invasions, they naturally brought beer with them. Saint Gall, a Benedictine priest from Ireland, was a good example. When he built an abbey South of Lake Constance in the seventh century, he incorporated not one brewhouse but several. Three types of beer were subsequently produced there: a regular brew for the monks; a weaker variety for beggars; and a "special" for high-ranking clergy and noblemen passing through on pilgrimages. To keep the beer in good order, the brewery had a cooling room, based on the principles first used by the Ancient Romans. Thus, a thousand years before von Linde or Kelvin, the need for such facilities was recognized by the brewers of St Gallen. The ruins of this sophisticated brewery can still be seen, close to one of Europe's outstanding baroque cathedrals and the fine medieval library of St Gallen.

When brewing rights passed from monks to powerful trade guilds, it is recorded that the burghers of St Gallen were less than tolerant of bad beer. Witches were blamed if the beer turned sour. The last "beer witch"

was burned at the stake in 1581. Such supernatural hazards were not the only threat to beer. Switzerland is an intensely wine-conscious nation, with an insatiable thirst for the grape. In good harvest years, wine was cheaper to produce, and brewers had to play second fiddle. Only with the great technical advances of the mid-19th century did Switzerland gain a strong national brewing industry. For this reason, all Swiss beers are bottom-fermented, and the influences are strongly those of the lands to the immediate North and immediate East. There are no national traditions in brewing, but the drinker can nonetheless enjoy beers which are produced according to the *Reinheitsgebot*, and are hardly ever pasteurized.

Switzerland has 42 breweries, in 22 cantons, and eight of the breweries are in canton St Gallen. Since the Swiss speak different languages in different parts of the country, it follows that they also have different cultural patterns. Beer-drinking is popular throughout the German-speaking Northern cantons, but especially in St Gallen and neighbouring cantons of Thurgau, Appenzall and Glarus. Only among the ski resorts is more beer drunk. Holiday makers at their energetic leisure in St Moritz, Davos, Klosters and the like are reckoned to inflate drinking statistics

in the canton of Graubünden, which lies a little further to the East. This canton is primarily German-speaking, though Italian is spoken in two or three valleys, and four dialects of Romansh. In the Italian-speaking South and the French-speaking West, less beer is drunk. Nationally, the Swiss stand fifteenth in the world league-table of beer-drinkers, with a consumption of 71·8 litres per head per year. In gross volume of production, Switzerland appears at number twenty-nine, sandwiched between Venezuela and Argentina. The Swiss brewing industry concentrated considerably during the 1970s, and a variety of different trading agreements led to the emergence of "national" brands.

Probably the most widely-known beer-brand is Cardinal, which originates from the university town of Fribourg. Although Fribourg is in the West, and not in a heart-land of beer-drinking, this location has its advantages. Demand for beer may be modest in the French cantons, but a market still exists. Precisely because there is no vigorous tradition of brewing, Cardinal has little competition in this market. Fribourg also has the strategic advantage that it stands on the border of French-speaking and German-speaking Switzerland, offering a gateway to the beery North. The original brewery was founded near Fribourg's Bernese Gate in 1788, and the present name was assumed in 1890, when the town's archbishop became a Cardinal. The brand-name gained national proportions when the Cardinal company, Sibra, took over three other brewers in 1973. Cardinal beer is now marketed by each of these breweries. One of them, Brasserie Beauregard, is also in Fribourg. The others are in the North, not far from Basel, at the

brewing town of Rheinfelden; and in the canton of Zürich, at Wädenswil.

The other "national" brewing group is Feldschlösschen, of Rheinfelden. Feldschlösschen owns Müller, of Neuchatel; Gurten, in Bern; and the local brewery in Valais, at Sion. These breweries continue to use their own names. The big regional brewer Haldengut, in Winterthur, also co-operates with this group. So does Calanda, from the Graubünden town of Chur.

A third grouping, called Interbeva, brings together eight breweries, most of them in the East. These are independent firms which work together in the buying of raw materials, marketing and promotion. They include the large and well-known brewing company of Hürlimann, in Zürich; Schützengarten, in St Gallen; Löwenbräu, in Zürich; Falken, in Schaffhausen.

Other sizable regional breweries include Eichhof, in Lucerne; Warteck, in Basel; and H. Müller, in Baden. The remaining 20-odd breweries supply very local markets. All but three of them are closely associated by means of the Swiss Brewers' Society, popularly known as the "cartel," not least because of its influence on pricing policies. The influence of the cartel has been challenged on occasion, but hearings on the question have always ruled that any disadvantages to the consumer are outweighed by its usefulness in the protection of a relatively small and vulnerable brewing industry. The three "mavericks" are Boxer, an individualistic brewer in Lausanne; Lupo, in Hochdorf, Lucerne; and Kronen, in Herisau, South of St Gallen.

All of the brewers produce similar ranges of beers, and variations in palate are subtle. French-speaking Switzerland, with a tradi-

tion of white wines, likes its drinks served cold. Beer there is usually chilled, and is often light and dry – like the wines. In the Italian-speaking region, which has rather harsh red wines, with a pronounced after-taste, beers may be a trifle heavier, with plenty of hop bitterness. A similar point is made about the acidic *rosé* wines of the Black Forest and the slightly vinous beer across the frontier in the tiny German-speaking canton of Schaffhausen. Elsewhere in German-speaking Switzerland – by far the largest of the nation's linguistic divisions – beer tends to be sweeter, with a lower hopping rate. Often, it is served only lightly chilled, or even at room-temperature. This is particularly noticeable in the Easternmost canton of Graubünden, where red wines are very popular, though they are not grown locally. Only Graubünden's skiers, of course, go as far as to mull their beer. As in all matters, and especially those concerning taste, the Swiss are apt to be cautious about their drinks. Even today, many health-conscious Swiss take their soft-drinks at room temperature for fear of liver complaints. They were never a people for reckless habits.

With commendable principle, the brewers of the cartel do not use the term *Pilsener,* on the grounds that it is misleading. Pilsen is not in Switzerland, it is in Czechoslovakia; and that is that. Notwithstanding such honesty, the drinker may still have difficulty is sorting out what is what. The terms used are less than clear-cut. The everyday beer of Switzerland is usually looked upon simply as a *lager,* with no further qualification. In French, the cumbersome description *bière de fermentation basse* spells it out; in Italian, *birra invecciata*. It is brewed at about 11·5 degrees Balling, and is available on draught. Several other styles of beer are produced in Switzerland, but all within the range of 13·5–14·0 degrees Balling. The designations used, depending upon language, include: *speziell/special/speciale; luxusbier/bière de luxe/birra di lusso; festbier/bière festive/birra festiva;* and the like. Beers designated as *bock* in German are simply called *forte* in French and, curiously, *birra di marzo* in Italian. To confuse matters further, some beers are simply designated as being "strong," and are therefore labelled *stark* in German, and *forte* in French and Italian. The *stark/forte* classification does, however, appear to be in decline.

"Special" is the term commonly used for the higher-density draught beers, which are gradually increasing their market share. "De luxe" beers are intended to have snob-appeal, and are usually packaged in a fanciful and sometimes feminine manner. One brand

Transports of delight

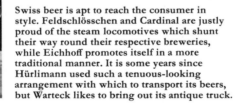

Swiss beer is apt to reach the consumer in style. Feldschlösschen and Cardinal are justly proud of the steam locomotives which shunt their way round their respective breweries, while Eichhoff promotes itself in a more traditional manner. It is some years since Hürlimann used such a tenuous-looking arrangement with which to transport its beers, but Warteck likes to bring out its antique truck.

is actually called "Chic." Despite the Gallic name, this brand emanates not from French-speaking Switzerland, but from Birra Bellinzona, of Ticino. "High Life," which catches a similar mood, has nothing to do with the famous beer from Miller's of Milwaukee; it is brewed by Schützengarten, of St Gallen. For Lake Michigan, read Lake Constance. "Top," nothing to do with hats, is brewed by Cardinal. At a more secular level, the "President" label is used jointly by Feldschlösschen and Haldengut. "Five Star" is the de luxe beer from Hürlimann. The latter is one of the few Swiss breweries to persist vigorously with the promotion of dark (*dunkel/brune/scura*) beers. A good example is Hürlimann's ruby-coloured Hexenbock, which has a rich, full palate. This is promoted as a "witches' brew." True to the Swiss–German habit of coining abusive diminutives, the smaller bottle is known as a *Häxli*, or "little witch." A similar *bock* is brewed by Warteck, in Basel. Both pale and dark *bock* beers are available, though they hardly measure up to German standards of potency. Much the same applies to "festival" beers, which are produced at Easter and Christmas. Despite the connotations of its name, Hürlimann's "Dreikönigsbier" is available all year round, in both pale and dark styles. The kings in this instance were originally the civic emblem of Enge, a district of Zürich which was once on a pilgrim route. Dreikönigsbier is classified as a *starkbier*. Strong beers are at the top of the Swiss alcohol-range, but they still contain no more than 5·5 per cent by volume. Haldengut's Albanibräu is an agreeable example, a beer with a distinctive bouquet, promoted as a good nightcap. This is not an unreasonable claim: a short, strong beer at bedtime certainly makes for a good night's sleep. Well-liked *starkbier* brands are also produced by Gurten, in Bern, and the two Baden breweries: H. Müller and Falken (the latter is a small firm not connected with Falken of Schaffhausen).

The enterprising Hürlimann brewery also produces a *Berliner*-style wheat beer called Schneider Weisse, but this has only a limited sale, primarily in Zürich. Let the Germans make a cult of beer, but the Swiss are altogether more serious. Their only truly indigenous styles are the diet-beers and near-beers made by locally-developed processes. The Swiss take a serious view of health, and of drunken driving. Their near-beers, like Hürlimann's Birell and Feldschlösschen's Ex-Bier, are already well-known in other European countries. Others may mock, but others buy.

The hub of an empire

The famous Vienna colour may be less prevalent than it was, but the brewery at Klein Schwechat never was a haven of conservatism. Sadly, the name of Anton Dreher (right) no longer appears on today's beers. In the early years of this century, his Klein Schwechat brewery (right) was the hub of the world's greatest brewing empire. Within the grounds of the brewery is a pavilion which dates back to the period of Maria Theresa, the eighteenth-century ruler of Austro-Hungary. The pavilion (far right) was built at a time when the grounds still belonged to an extensive hunting area.

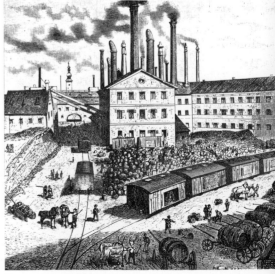

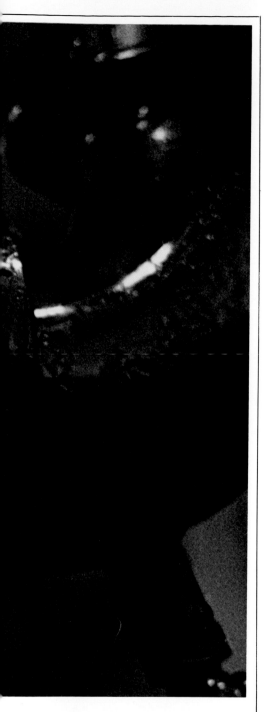

Austria

FEW CITIES HAVE A DRINK which they can call their own, but Vienna has three. It has been famous for its coffee-houses since Imperial times and before; coffee was left behind by the Turks during the Ottoman siege of 1683, and thus the drink was introduced to the West. Vienna has a special relationship with the grape, too. In the *World Atlas of Wine,* Hugh Johnson puts it this way: "There is no capital city which is so identified with wine as Vienna. New wine seems to be its life-blood. Vineyards hold their ground within the heart of residential districts and surge up the side of the surrounding hills into the Vienna woods." Today, wine-growing villages like Grinzing are within the city of Vienna, ready at hand to provide citizens and tourists alike with the young *heurigen* wines. Then there is beer. Historically, Vienna was one of the great brewing cities of the world, with two quite separate claims to attention. It was probably from Bohemia that the beer-drinking tradition arrived in Lower Austria during the early 1300s, but Vienna's great renown as a brewing centre came with the rise of the Dreher family. One account says that the Drehers were already brewers in the early 1600s. This may be true though it also seems that the original brewery, near Vienna, at Klein Schwechat, was founded in 1632 by an aristocrat and subsequently bought by the Drehers in 1796. However it started, their great success was due to the work of Anton Dreher in the mid-1800s.

Among the great breweries of the Austro–Hungarian Empire, only that at Pilsen, in Bohemia, was bigger than Dreher's establishment near Vienna. Dreher also had his own brewery in Bohemia, at Michelob – a name which may have a familiar ring for American beer-drinkers. More important, Dreher had substantial breweries in Budapest and Trieste. "The Dreher breweries now represent the largest business conducted under one management in continental Europe," wrote an awed journalist in a brewing-trade magazine at the turn of the century. The Trieste brewery gave rise to Dreher of Italy, and the name survives there today, though that branch of the original business is now owned by Heineken and Whitbread.

Dreher had studied with the leading brewers in Germany, and was a friend of the great Munich brewer Gabriel Sedlmayr. The two collaborated, and it seems that the first of the revolutionary new bottom-fermented beers brewed in the middle of the last century was produced at Dreher's Vienna plant in 1841. In later years, the time and place of this brewing breakthrough became a

matter of contention between Vienna and Munich. The confusion was furthered in the layman's mind by the reputation of Pilsen, though there is no doubt that the Bohemians switched to bottom-fermentation in 1842. A century later, the argument between Vienna and Munich exercised the mind of none other than Adolf Hitler. An article in the German wartime propaganda magazine *Signal,* demonstrating proprietorial pride towards the Pilsen brewery, clearly credits Munich with having provided the expertise there. The personal feelings of Hitler in this matter are not known, though they must surely have been mixed. He was sufficiently concerned to order a commission of inquiry, and had he confined himself to such fascinating exercises, the world might have been a happier place.

In 1942, the commission ruled that Dreher had produced the first modern *lager* beer.

Traditionally, coppers
using direct fire were
built with brick jackets
like this one at the
small Noppinger
brewery, at Oberndorf,
not far from Salzburg.
The Noppinger
brewery, founded in
1630, produces a well-
liked range of beers.

range of beers, among which Kaiser Bier, a basic *lager,* is the biggest-selling. Kaiser Bier, like the rest of this company's products, is widely stocked by supermarkets. The company also has a very pale and well-hopped Kaiser Pils.

Following at some distance behind the "Big Two" is a third major brewing company, in Styria. A light, well-hopped Steirisch Pils and a slightly darker and heavier Spezial are among the well-liked beers from the Gösser brewery, nestling in the foothills of the Alps, at Leoben. This company's headquarters are adjacent to a Renaissance Benedictine abbey, in which is housed a beer museum. Although the historic relationship between the brewery and the abbey is less than clearly defined, Gösser sponsors the museum. The brewery also produces a popular "abbey brew," called Stiftsbräu, a thirteen-degree beer of reddish colour.

Colour is Austria's second claim to fame in the brewing business. When *Münchener* beers were still dark brown, and the golden brightness of the *Pilsener* style a novelty, *Wiener* beers offered a characteristic amber colour. Today, golden-coloured beers dominate in almost every part of the world but for Britain and Ireland, with their copper *ales* and black *stouts*. Austria still has its amber beers, notably in the *spezial* category, but they no longer enjoy their former ascendancy. The amber Vienna beer added character to the world's range of beers, and its decline as a distinct style is to be regretted. How odd that the drinker must cross the border to Bavaria to find a *Märzenbier* in the traditional Vienna colour. Even Mexico still celebrates the colour of a beer-style which it calls *Vienna*, and the city is remembered by brewers all over the world when they wish to produce a reddish beer. They use what they term "Vienna malts."

In Austria, maltsters still have to know their business, since brewers are not permitted to use artificial colourings. This is forbidden in a law derived from the Codex Alimentarius of the Hapsburg period. The law lays down that beer be made from water, hops and cereals, but does not specify which cereals. Those few beers which are nationally-marketed are sometimes pasteurized, but the overwhelming majority of Austria's 60-odd operating breweries sell their beers locally, and without pasteurization. A number are small craft-brewers, and there are monastic breweries at Schlägl, in Upper Austria, and at Salzburg.

Hardly surprisingly in the light of its history, Austria is a nation of bottom-fermenting brewers, but it does have the very

Austria had in the meantime gone through several traumatic upheavals, and more were to come before it emerged in its shrunken post-war condition. Before the First World War, the great Dreher concern had already been acquired, through a series of mergers, by the old Austrian brewing family of Mautner–Markhof. They lost control at the time of the Second World War, but retained an involvement, and regained their position as recently as 1976. In the post-war period, the company has taken over at least a couple of dozen smaller breweries.

Today, under the name of Schwechat, the brewery produces half a dozen different beers. The everyday beer of Austria is a golden-coloured brew of 12·0 degrees Plato, known simply as *lager.* This category is also sometimes confusingly known as *Märzenbier* though it bears no similarity to the stronger beers bearing this designation elsewhere in the world. In addition to its basic *lager,* Schwechat also produces a 12·5 golden-coloured beer, with a dry palate, called Krone. At slightly less than 13·0 degrees, Schwechat brews a Skol Pils. It seems ironic that a brewery so close to Bohemia should be

using a mock-Scandinavian brand-name originating from Britain. Then comes the largest-selling draught beer in Austria, Steffl Export, which is also available in the bottle. This is a "medium blond" beer, said to be conditioned for three months. In general, Austrian brewers quote long conditioning periods for their beers, and wooden *lagering* casks can still be found. Another thirteen-degree beer, called Hopfenperle, is brewed by Schwechat. This is slightly darker, full-bodied and less well-attenuated, with a good bouquet and a high degree of carbonation. A dark-brown, sweet, thirteen-degree beer is called Schwarzquell Spezial. Finally, Schwechat produces pale and amber *bocks* for Easter and Christmas at 16·0 and 19·0 degrees. These are said to be conditioned for more than four months.

Although the basic Austrian beer-designations are *lager, spezial* and *bock,* the range brewed by Schwechat is typical, especially among the larger brewers. Schwechat is the second largest, outdistanced only by Österreichische Bräu, which is based in Linz but has seven breweries in different parts of Austria. Österreichische Bräu has a similar

The Seven Sigls

The brewery at Obertrum, also near Salzburg, boasts a top-fermented weizenbier and a history going back to 1601. Since 1775, seven generations of the Sigl family have been involved in the brewery. The illustration on the left shows the brewery in 1910. The group photograph of the staff was taken in 1930.

occasional *weiss* or *weizen* beer, which can reliably be found in the Salzburg region. The local brewery at Obertrum produces a *Weizengold* which is commonly drunk with a dash of lemon juice.

Salzburg and Styria are the great beer-drinking regions of Austria, and both have beer-halls not unlike those across the frontier in Munich. The city of Salzburg has, among others, the Stieglbräu, the Sternbräu and the Zipfer Bierhaus. In Styria, the provincial capital, Graz, has the Steinerhof, the Gösser Bräu, the Puntigam and the Winterbierhaus. These two provinces have a per-capita consumption in the region of 146 litres a year, compared with a national average of about 100. Having a population of only 7·4 million, Austria has a brewing industry of commensurately modest size. Its output is twenty-first in the world league-table, but the country's drinkers stand eleventh in the table of per-capita consumption. Aside from any considerations of history and culture, price can only help the popularity of beer. The Government controls the prices of goods, and Austria's beers are among the cheapest in Europe.

Austria has far fewer clearly-defined beer-styles than Germany, but its sixty or more operating breweries produce a wide range.

The Mediterranean

"IT WAS NECESSARY to give people in the South a taste for beer who were hitherto accustomed to wine-drinking. This was truly a desperate undertaking; but, to a reformer like Dreher, this was no impediment."

Such unflinching dedication to duty . . . it sounded almost foolhardy. In its own incredulous way, a business journal of the time was discussing the decision of Anton Dreher, the famous Viennese brewer, to move into the city of Trieste in 1868. "The general opinion at the time was that it was an impossibility to produce good beer in Trieste." The climate and the water "were pronounced to be such as to prevent successful brewing." Undaunted, Dreher pressed on. When his draught beer went on sale in Trieste, one establishment sold 120 casks in a single day. "The people were not a little anxious to try the new barley wine . . . and it must have suited their tastes pretty well," the journal reported. "Like a bold conqueror, he pushed his beverage further South," and soon his beer-shops were to be seen all the way down the Adriatic to the Mediterranean and beyond.

Italy continues to have the lowest beer-consumption per head in Western Europe, though the figure has increased four-fold in the last 20 years. Dreher still brews in Trieste, and in five other Italian cities, though it is no longer owned by the Austrian company of the same name. Since 1974, Heineken and Whitbread have held the majority stake in Dreher of Italy, which now has headquarters in Milan. Dreher is one of Italy's Big Four brewery groups. The biggest of the four is the Italian-owned Peroni group, with eight breweries. The Wuhrer group, also locally-owned, has four breweries. So does Prinz Brau, owned by the German Oetker group. Poretti and Moretti have two breweries each, and there are a further half-dozen smaller firms, including a Henninger associate. All Italian beers are bottom-fermented, usually in the range of 10·0–12·0 degrees Plato, and pasteurized. There are a handful of dark, bottom-fermented beers, sometimes bearing saints' names.

Among Dreher's receptive markets in those pioneering days were Istria and Dalmatia, and those regions still consume a respectable quantity of beer. Modern Yugoslavia has about 20 breweries, as well as being a substantial producer of hops. The hop-gardens are primarily in Slovenia, which is also the region where most beer is drunk. The biggest-selling beer, Union, is produced in Slovenia, at Ljubljana. Beer was not widely popular outside Slovenia until the 1960s, but then its fashionability began to grow. Yugoslav beers are bottom-fermented, and usually

The names of Hellenic Breweries (left) and Fix are familiar to thousands of tourists, while Cyprus offers Keo Beer. In Yugoslavia, the best-known brew is Union, produced in the Slovenian city of Ljubljana. Despite the goat, Zlatoroc is a twelve-degree pale lager. It is also brewed in Slovenia, at Laško. Neither Yugoslavia nor Italy (bottom four labels) offers a wide range of styles.

pale, though the odd dark brew is also available. Most of the country's beers are hoppy and dry, but palates vary and brands tend to be available on a very localized basis. Two well-liked brands are brewed in Croatia: Osijek, from North of Zagreb, and Karlovac, from South of the same city. A popular, full-bodied beer is brewed at Nikšić, in Montenegro, and bears the town's name. In many parts of the country, especially on the coast and in the South, beer faces powerful competition from local wines, and occasionally from more exotic drinks like the Turkish-style *boza*, a non-alcoholic brew made from corn. Among the big cities, Zagreb has the most *pivare* – taverns which are specifically intended for the drinking of beer. Belgrade has few, though Serbian and Slavonian music can be heard at the *Pivnica* in the street called *Cirila i Metohija*. Establishments identified by the word *restaurant* usually serve beer, and it is not obligatory to order a meal, but a *kafana* is

definitely an eating place. So is a *poslasticarnica*, though more in the vein of a French *patisserie* or Greek *kafenion*.

Elsewhere in the Balkans, thousands of tourists are familiar with Fix beer and several similar brands, in Greece, along with the Athens-brewed Amstel (11·6 Plato). Henninger is also in Greece, with a brewery on Crete. European Turkey has its Tekel and Efes breweries, the latter producing a conventional *Pilsener* and a dark beer which, curiously, has the same name. The drinker is guided by the different colours of the labels. The dark beer, with a hoppy palate, has a density of 13·4 Plato. Cyprus has Carlsberg and Keo, a very agreeable *Pilsener* produced by a local public company.

There is an inexplicable law of beer-drinking which says that interesting things happen on islands. This is borne out by places as far apart as the Isle of Man and the Seychelles; both have pleasant surprises for the beer-

drinker who calls by. For all that it is a drinkable beer, there is nothing unusual about the Keo of Cyprus, but another island – Malta – has what are surely the only top-fermented beers in the Mediterranean.

These mementoes of the British military presence are produced by the tiny island's only brewery, Farsons (an Anglo-abbreviation of Farrugia). They include a darkish draught *mild* called Blue Label (original gravity, 1040); a light but hoppy *bitter* (1052); a mellow *pale ale* (1040), called Hop Leaf; and a *sweet stout*. The draught beers are unpasteurized.

The top-fermented beers are Farsons' best-sellers, though a pale *lager* (1043) is also brewed, under the name of Cisk. There was until 1947 a rival brewery on the island called Cisk. Farsons also absorbed a beer-importing business established in Malta by Simonds, the British brewery which is now part of the Courage group.

The ale island

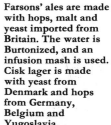

Farsons' ales are made with hops, malt and yeast imported from Britain. The water is Burtonized, and an infusion mash is used. Cisk lager is made with yeast from Denmark and hops from Germany, Belgium and Yugoslavia.

Iberia

SAN MIGUEL IS ONE of the international beers, though to the people of Spain it is the principal local brew. To Spain's annual tide of visitors, it is as Spanish as *sangria* or *paella*, and no less agreeable. When the magazine *Business Week* carried out a survey of drinking habits in the executive suites of the United States, one respondent, a banker, described San Miguel beer as "the best in the world." Such an unqualified assessment calls into question the judgment of the men who manage our money, but it is some indication of San Miguel's following. The beer itself might better be described as a distinctively light and fairly dry *Pilsener*-style brew of 13·0 degrees Balling, 4·3 alcohol by weight and 5·4 by volume. San Miguel is virtually a one-brand company in Spain, though a luxury beer called Selecta XV was launched in the mid-1970s. The Roman numeral is a reference to the beer's density of 15·0 degrees, which produces an alcoholic content of 5·1 by weight and 6·4 by volume.

San Miguel brews at Burgos, in the North; Lérida, in the North-East; and Málaga, in the South. Elaborate comparative tests are carried out to ensure that all three breweries produce the same quality of beer. San Miguel does not follow the practice of those other Spanish breweries which produce a *Münchener*-style *cerveza negra*. For that matter, and despite its name, San Miguel is not truly Spanish. In the light of its sales, it is surprising to note that San Miguel was not brewed in Spain until 1957. Today it may have become the national beer of Spain, but it originates from a former Spanish colony, The Philippines, where it has been brewed since 1890. In Asia, San Miguel is a huge, multi-product conglomerate and commodity-trading company.

Despite its short history in Spain, or perhaps because of that, San Miguel has far outstripped other local brands. There are a couple of dozen other breweries in Spain, the Baleares and Canaries, but these have increasingly been concentrated into groupings. The largest of these is Damm, based in Barcelona, which was assembled with the backing of Oetker, the German group. Damm's products include a pleasant *Märzen*-style beer which has a powerful, malty bouquet and a dry palate.

A wide variety of national influences have flowed through the breweries of neighbouring Portugal, producing an interesting mix of palates. Brewing has a long history in the country, and documents from the 1600s refer to a *Patio da Serveja*, in Lisbon. Commercial brewing on a substantial scale started during the early 1800s, and there were eventually six firms competing furiously in Lisbon, and a further seven in Oporto. Beer was also imported from Britain in exchange for port. The first two commercial breweries in Lisbon were started by Frenchmen, and no sooner had a Portuguese brewer established himself than his business passed into the hands of a Dane, J. H. Jansen. The Portuguese got their own back in 1881, when two of Jansen's employees formed their own company, which was the precursor of today's principal brewery group. The company was at first called *Leâo* ("The Lion") after the adjoining restaurant; later it became known as the *Germania* brewery, but this name was changed to *Portugalia* at the time of the First World War. Finally, the economic crisis of the 1930s precipitated a concentration of Lisbon's breweries around *Portugalia* to form a grouping now known as Sociedade Central de Cervejas (S.C.C., for short).

This company has 68 per cent of the market, with a *Dortmunder*-style beer called Sagres (12·0 degrees Plato; 3·65 per cent alcohol by weight) and a *Preta* (a *Münchener*-style dark beer). The main plant is at Vialonga, near Lisbon, and there is another at Coimbra, in the centre of Portugal. The Oporto breweries also eventually merged, and they survive as Companhia União Fabril Portuense (C.U.F.P.), producing a *Pilsener*-type beer called Cristal. In the 1970s, a new brewing company was established at Belas, producing beers under the Cergal brand-name. This brewery has a *Pilsener*-type beer of 11·8 degrees Balling, available unpasteurized on draught, and a *Münchener*-type dark beer. A brewery on Madeira produces a *lager* at 11·5, a *sweet stout* at 12·5 and a bottom-fermented sweet black brew called Tonica. There is also a brewery in the Azores.

Spain has San Miguel, among many others, with the likes of Tropical (left) and C.C.C. in the Canaries. The latter produces a dark beer. Portugal has Cergal and others, while Madeira has its Coral.

The road to Vialonga

The cheery countenance of the Dane John Henri Jansen greets the beer-drinkers of Portugal. He brewed in Lisbon in the late 1800s.

After the French and the Danes came the Germania Brewery. In this case, the name had less to do with ownership than with brewing style. The name was adopted in 1910, and dropped six years later. Today, the beer is called Sagres.

Eastern Europe

EAST GERMANY AND CZECHOSLOVAKIA are special cases, but they are not the only brewing nations of Eastern Europe. Beer from Poland is widely exported to the West; Hungary has a lively brewing industry; and the Soviet Union stands third or fourth in the world's league-table of gross beer-production, though it is nearer twentieth place in per-capita consumption.

When the Polish Pope Klemens was on his deathbed, he made an urgent utterance which sounded like, "O, Santa Piva di Polonia!" The people at his bedside thought for a moment that he had created a new saint, called Piva, then it was realized that he wanted a beer. "Piwo" means "beer" in Polish. Brewed drinks go back as far as Polish history, though hops were introduced from Bavaria in the 1200s. Even a people as ethnically-individualistic as the Poles are not immune to influences from elsewhere.

One of the most important brewing areas in Poland is Silesia, which has had its share of German influence, and where coal-mining helps sharpen thirsts. The great Silesian city of Wroclaw, formerly Breslau, has no less than three breweries. Just a little further East, near Katowice, Tychy has two breweries, including the biggest in Poland. Galicia is also an important brewing area, though such excuses are hardly necessary for a visit to Cracow, one of Europe's most beautiful and least spoiled historic cities. The dry, light beers of Galicia make a splendid aperitif before the sort of meal which begins with carp-in-aspic, or *bigos*, and progresses to even more substantial delights. Galician beers owe a lot to the influence of the Austrian Empire, in which Cracow was an important provincial capital. The Austrians also brought delightful coffee-shops, *Sacher torte* and all. Then there is vodka as a *digestif*.

Galicia's most famous brewery is in Zywiec, a small town to the South of Cracow. Water for the brewery tumbles from the Tatras in a stream called the Leśnianka before flowing into the Sola river. Zywiec and Krakus beers are exported not only to other European countries but also to North America. A fourth significant brewing town is Okocim, also in the Cracow hinterland.

In all, Poland has 92 brewhouses, organized into 20 groups, and producing several beer-styles. *Slodowe* is a low-alcohol, dark, sweet brew; *jasne* is a low-alcohol (1·8–2·6 per cent by weight), amber-coloured bitter *lager*; *pelne* or *full-light* (the English words are often used) indicates a dry, well-hopped pale *lager*, the Polish equivalent of *Pilsener*, with an alcohol content of 3·5–4·0 per cent by weight; *porter* has a medium palate, and is heavy and strong,

with about 6·0 per cent alcohol by weight.

Austrian influence also explains the brewing tradition of Hungary, which might otherwise be regarded predominantly as a wine-growing country, along with other Eastern nations like Rumania and Bulgaria. The *lager* revolution of Vienna, Munich and Pilsen boosted the popularity of beer throughout much of Austro-Hungary. By happy coincidence, the quarrying of stone to build Buda's twin town of Pest had left enormous rock caverns where beer could be *lagered*. This gave rise in 1854 to the Köbánya brewery, in what is now part of Budapest. German and Austrian brewers came to Köbánya, bringing their knowledge of the new technique, and the brewery still produces some of Hungary's best-known beers. Today, Hungary has five breweries, and 44 bottling plants. At the turn of the century, breweries were built at Pécs, in the South-West, and Sopron, in the North-West. In the post-War period, production started at Nagykanizsa, in the South-West. Then, in 1972, a new brewery was opened at Borsod, near Miskolc, in the North-East.

Apart from a malt-extract type of beer called Nektar, the weakest brews are the *Világos*, everyday pale *lagers*, with a mild palate and a density of 10·5 Balling (about 3·0 per cent alcohol by weight). These are consumed in large volume, and are generally unpasteurized. The other styles are usually pasteurized, and draught beer is rare. All breweries produce a *Világos*, and a twelve-degree *Kiniszi* (about 3·5 per cent by weight).

A more distinguished twelve-degree beer called *Rocky Cellar*, with a full flavour and a good hop bouquet, is brewed by Köbánya. The Pécs brewery produces a very light thirteen-degree beer, but Köbánya and Nagykanizsa have beers in the same category with a drier palate and a stronger hop bouquet. Two strong pale beers are produced, both with a density of 18 degrees and 6·0 per cent alcohol by weight. These are *Sirály*, from Nagykanizsa, and *Hungária*, from Köbánya. The latter is similar to the *Zsiráf* (Giraffe) export brand which was once marketed in Africa. Today, home demand is growing so fast that exports have ceased. All breweries produce a malty dark beer called *Barna*, which usually has a density of 14·0 degrees (4·0 per cent by weight), but there are also stronger dark beers. These range from 18 to 22 degrees, though they are not as well attenuated as the pale beers. A sweetish, eighteen-degree *Porter* is produced by Köbánya, and a stronger-tasting dark beer called *Bak*, while the Pécs and Nagykanizsa breweries also have some interesting examples.

Russia has, in a sense, one of the world's

All the wine-producing nations of the Eastern Bloc also have beer, but Hungary takes a special pride in its brewing industry. "Rocky Cellar" evokes the ghost of Anton Dreher.

oldest brewing techniques. The traditional Russian *kvass*, a low-alcohol sweet drink, is made by the fermentation of bread in much the way that the Ancient Egyptians carried out their brewing. Modern brewing on a large scale came to Russia in the 1800s. Early in the century, beer imports from Britain were so great that at least one English *porter*-brewer set up his own plant in St Petersburg, and at the end of the century bottom-fermentation arrived. By 1913, there were more than 1,000 breweries and the number has not fallen substantially.

Western visitors often criticize the quality of Russian beers, and lack of variety in palates. Similar questions are aired publicly from time to time by Russian drinkers. Like their counterparts elsewhere, they decline to be easily pleased. A reader's letter in *Moskovsky Komsomoletz*, a Young Communist newspaper, took up the point, first of all criticizing the beer-halls: "An unimaginable number of people manage to crowd into a very small area and, while you drink the sour and foamy liquid which they call beer, you have only one care – to keep your teeth safe. In a crowd like that, it's not hard to knock them out with a

In Poland, cafes like the one below serve their beer on draught, but they are by no means universal. In restaurants, bottled beer is more usual, and it thus has a certain snob-appeal. Brewers cannot keep up with demand for bottled beer.

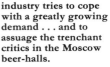

Russian beers . . . the industry tries to cope with a greatly growing demand . . . and to assuage the trenchant critics in the Moscow beer-halls.

glass of beer." The writer also complained about the mess left after people ate the customary fish snacks with beer, and the number of signs – "everything is either 'forbidden' or 'strictly forbidden.'" The newspaper elicited comments from officials who promised more and better drinking establishments, and an improvement in the beer supply. Moscow has 79 beer-halls, 45 beer-bars, and 31 beer-stalls.

The programme of brewery-building is impressive. In the last 20 years, 142 breweries have been re-fitted and 86 new ones built, 66 of them since the beginning of the 1970s. The Dutch organization which monitors alcohol statistics reported in 1977 that the Soviet Union was producing fifty-four million hectolitres of beer per year, but the news-agency Novosti estimated that the figure had by then reached seventy-two million. This would place the Soviet Union third in the world league, ahead of Britain. Novosti candidly suggested that consumer-demand would not be fully met until 1990, and that per-capita consumption would by then be 150 litres per year in major cities of the North. Beer-drinking is encouraged in the Soviet Union as

a counter to hard liquor, though vodka-and-chasers are popular, and a dash of the national spirit is sometimes added to the brew. Although per-capita consumption in those Northern cities may reach German levels, in Eastern and Southern parts of the Soviet Union beer is challenged by excellent local wines, tea and *koumyss* (the fermented milk of the mare or camel).

Because of the Soviet Union's great land-area and relatively thin spread of population, distribution costs can defeat the economies of centralization, and brewing remains relatively local. Even the biggest of the new breweries have a capacity of only 1·5 million hectolitres, which places them on a par with those in many big Western cities, but not with the national or multi-national giants. Among the newest generation of breweries are 15 plants which were bought "off-the-peg" from Czechoslovakia. An example is the Yantar (Amber) brewery, at Nikolayev, on the North coast of the Black Sea. This produces 720,000 hectolitres a year, in six different styles. The range includes Russia's everyday beer-brand, the light (11·0 degrees Balling) "Zhiguli," which is named after the region where the

barley is grown. In the brewing of "Zhiguli," unmalted barley and corn-flour are used as adjuncts. Then come "Riga," a *Pilsener*-style brand of 12·0 per cent; the heavily-hopped "Slavyanskoye," also 12·0 degrees; "Moscow," a thirteen-degree beer which uses rice rather than corn as an adjunct; a thirteen-degree, dark "Ukrainian" beer; and a nineteen-degree "Amber," which is matured for not less than 82 days. "Amber" has a pronounced hop bouquet and vinous aftertaste. Like most beers which require such a long period of maturation, it is produced on a fairly small scale. Most of these beers are also produced elsewhere in the Soviet Union, though there are 62 brands in all.

In the Nikolayev area, home-made clay beer-mugs are occasionally used, and in the North, wooden drinking vessels can sometimes be seen. Beer-drinking in the Soviet Union still has its folksy moments. Two Englishmen reported to the British beer-buffs' newspaper *What's Brewing* that they found a "well-hopped strong bitter *ale*, dispensed by water-pump from wooden barrels" at a cafe on the military road connecting Ordzhonikidze with Tbilisi.

Canada

The Canada Temperance Act of 1878 gave local authorities the option to go "dry." Ontario had Prohibition between 1916 and 1927, and the haul shown below was seized during the 1920s. About 160 casks were dumped in Elk Lake.

WHEN HE WAS BUSTING the bootleggers on late-night television, the celluloid detective Eliot Ness used to study the impounded liquor bottles and say knowingly: "Looks like a Canadian job." In those days, liquor was more readily available North of the Great Lakes, even though Canada had its own rather haphazard version of Prohibition. The irony is that, while alcohol restrictions in Canada were applied with less consistency, they lasted much longer. Until the 1950s, it was necessary for Canadians to buy an annual permit before they could purchase drinks, and temperance patterns in the Far North of the American continent are remarkably similar to those in the Far North of Europe. This cannot be attributed simply to the preponderance of Scots in much of Canada, since the restrictions on alcohol are more reminiscent of those in Norway, Sweden and Finland.

Canada has large "dry" areas, notably in Saskatchewan, and in most cases liquor stores are run by a Government monopoly. People living in remote areas can, however, buy beer by mail-order. Most drinking is done at home. In Quebec, taverns are for men only. In Alberta, "beverage rooms" are sometimes divided to cater for "men only," "women only" and "women with escorts." In most places it is difficult to buy a beer on Sunday, though there are no restrictions in the Yukon. Newfoundland, which became a part of Canada in 1950, has fewer restrictions than the other Provinces and Territories, though it has no draught beer. Nor has Prince Edward Island, the only Province to be without a brewery. Nationwide, draught beer represents only about 12 per cent of the market.

Drink prices are controlled by the Government of each Province or Territory, and advertising is rigidly restricted. Beer may not be advertised at all in Saskatchewan, and television or radio commercials are forbidden in British Columbia. In those places where tv advertising is permitted, the drink must not touch the actors' lips. Only sponsorship of cultural events, and more especially of sport, remains relatively unfettered.

Nonetheless, drinkers in the United States still sometimes look to Canada for their supplies. In the Northernmost parts of upstate New York and Vermont, Americans favour Molson's bottled beers, from Montreal. Although beer crosses the frontier in the opposite direction, too, it is not received with quite the same enthusiasm. The view persists that Canadian brews are stronger. This may well be the case if strengths on each side of the frontier are averaged out, though it is equally true that Canadian beers are limited in law to a maximum alcohol content of 5·5 per cent by volume. This limitation applies to *lagers, ales, porters*, and the heavier *stouts* which are also available in Canada. *Porters* and *stouts*, which sometimes contain malted oats, have a tiny share of the market, and their future is in some doubt. The alcohol limit does not apply to those stronger beers which are designated as *malt liquors*, but this style of brew has failed to establish itself in the Canadian market. Molson's produces a curious example called India Pale Ale Malt Liquor, which is marketed in Newfoundland.

Molson's is one of Canada's Big Three brewing groups, between them owning 36 breweries, some of which still operate under their old names. (There is also a Small Three, owning seven breweries). Although Molson's is not widely known outside North America, this pioneer conglomerate owned

The first tycoon

The men who built the Canadian brewing industry, and whose companies dominate it today, were powerful pioneering characters. Each of them left his mark on the nation. None more so than the first of them, John Molson (left). He set out from the county of Lincolnshire, in England, in 1782, to sail for the New World. He arrived in Quebec nearly two months later, and walked to Montreal. Within four years, he had opened a brewery. The drays which he used in those early days were still plying the streets of Montreal 50 years later (right). Molson built Canada's first railway (below) in 1836, and opened his bank in 1855. Though neither of the other two brewing groups can match these feats, each is in its own way heavily diversified. Labatt's diversification is in the twentieth-century style. Carling belongs to worldwide brewing-and-tobacco group.

The "Streamliner" was a truck specially designed for Labatt by Count Alexis de Sakhnoffsky. It was described as "one of the two most beautiful things in Canada," the other being Lake Louise. The first Streamliner appeared in 1936.

The name of John Labatt lives on in Canada's best-selling beers. In 1971, Labatt also bought Oland's breweries. Despite this, the Oland family remains in the industry by way of the Moosehead breweries.

Canada's first steamship, Quebec's first railroad, and the Molson Bank, which is now part of the Bank of Montreal. Molson's was founded by an English immigrant in 1786.

A better-known brewing name elsewhere in the world is Labatt, founded in London, Ontario, in 1853. John Labatt was an Irishman, and he would no doubt be pleased to know that his brewery now produces Guinness under contract. The ads for Guinness suggest that it should be served chilled, and it is very popular among Toronto's considerable Black population. Labatt, a founder member of the Skol consortium, also has brewing interests in Brazil, Zambia and Israel. It is the market-leader in Canada, where it has also diversified heavily into foods and confectionery.

Best-known of all the Canadian beer names is Carling, which also has breweries in the United States. Carling is a major beer-brand in Britain, where it is licensed to Bass Charrington; as if in exchange, the British group licenses its Toby Ale to Carling in Canada. The Toronto company, part of the Rothman tobacco group, is properly known

as Carling O'Keefe. The name derives from Eugene O'Keefe, who arrived from Ireland in 1832. O'Keefe set up as a brewer of *ale* and *porter*, the latter being his national style. Considering the present plight of *porter*, perhaps it would have been better had this Irish company not subsequently introduced bottom-fermented *lager* beers to Canada. As if to make amends, some years ago the firm acquired the Beamish *stout* brewery in O'Keefe's native County Cork.

Among the Small Three, Moosehead Breweries, of New Brunswick and Nova Scotia, is notable for its characterful beers, including *ales* and *porters*. Moosehead was founded by a colourful family of Anglo-Swedish adventurers called Oland, who also ran breweries under their own name. The family is still involved in Moosehead, but the breweries under the Oland name were sold to Labatt. Another colourful member of the Small Three was a giant of a man called Ben Ginter, a former bulldozer-driver who started a brewery group in British Columbia. "Uncle Ben" had his picture printed on all the labels of his products. Then, in 1976, Uncle Ben's

Tartan Breweries ran into troubles, and new owners took over. The smallest of the Small Three, and the youngest, was founded in 1973 in Hamilton, Ontario. This is Henninger, a Canadian company set up in association with the famous German brewery. Henninger of Canada produces its own distinctive products under supervision from Frankfurt.

Canada's six brewers produce more than 100 brands, though the number is being eroded by the tide of "rationalization." National brands have been established, but different Provinces and Territories cling to their favourites. Newfoundland is particularly proud of its full-bodied local beers, which tend to be darker, heavier and more bitter than many elsewhere, though the much-vaunted Dominion Ale is, in fact, bottom-fermented. *Ale* is popular in the Maritimes, especially Nova Scotia, but the real devotees are in Quebec, where the top-fermented brew has more than 95 per cent of the market. Although *ale* has slipped in Ontario, it still holds more than 56 per cent of the market. Canadian *ales* are very pale in colour, less copper than golden, and they are becoming lighter and less bitter in palate. The national brewers insist that the Canadians want a light beer, but the truth is that the choice is being removed.

In Nova Scotia and New Brunswick, Moosehead Premium Ale is more bitter and full-bodied than most, and in Ontario, O'Keefe's Blended Ale enjoys some popularity. One of the more bitter national *ale* brands is Charrington Toby, and Labatt's Extra Stock is a very agreeable firm *ale* with a slightly bitter finish. Molson's Export Ale has a characteristic aroma and a light, soft taste, and Carling O'Keefe's Red Cap is well-liked.

Even among *lagers*, the well-hopped bitterness found in local beers like Moosehead Alpine is giving way to a lighter palate. The "Canadian" character is giving way to the "American." When the *Financial Post* magazine, of Toronto, carried out a blindfold test, the panellists were hopelessly incapable of identifying their favourite brands. The locally-brewed Carlsberg, from Carling O'Keefe, was chosen as the best Canadian brand. The same group's sweetish Old Vienna, a pale *lager* despite its name, came second. Carling Black Label came third. This seems a little hard on Labatt's Blue, another sweetish pale *lager* which is well-liked. Labatt's lightest brand, Cool Spring (3·9 per cent) was not included in the test. The overall winner, ahead of all local brands, was imported Kronenbourg. It comes from the Alsace, but to the Canadians it is surely French?

The original Carling

Carling Black Label is a worldwide beer-brand, licensed to brewers in several different countries. The Carling Brewing and Malting Company was started in Ontario in 1840. Its founder was

Thomas Carling, who passed the business on to his son Sir John (top). Eugene O'Keefe started his brewery (above) in 1862. The two firms had already merged when the post-Prohibition boom took place.

The United States

THE UNITED STATES produces a greater volume of beer than any other country. Its annual output approaches 200,000,000 hectolitres, which is more than West Germany and Britain together produce. There are single breweries in the United States which produce as much beer as entire European countries. The Anheuser-Busch group, the biggest brewing company in the world, produces almost as much beer as the Soviet Union. At one brewery, Coors has an output approaching that of Belgium. The United States is, in that sense, the world's greatest brewing nation.

Biggest can also mean fewest. For all its great output, the United States has little more than 50 brewing companies, owning less than 100 breweries. Some of these breweries use a great many labels, but few of them produce more than three or four beers. Nor is biggest necessarily best. In the matter of beer, the citizens of America accept this caveat almost too readily. They drink only about 80 litres (21 gallons) per capita each year, which places them well outside of the top ten beer-drinking nations. A people usually anxious to proclaim the virtues of things American are uncharacteristically self-deprecating about their nation's beers, despite a great brewing tradition. Perhaps this is due to a proper sense of awe towards the European lands which fathered (or grandfathered) the brewers of America. A new Bohemia or Bavaria will never be built in Pennsylvania, Missouri, or Wisconsin, but such ambitions are hardly relevant to modern America. If the mist of mythology can be penetrated, there remains much about American brewing which deserves a better appreciation.

Because the national giants are so very big, it is easy to overlook some of the interesting smaller breweries, whether they are regional corporations serving five or six States, or tiny local firms. Likewise, because the big brewers have put such energy into the creation of national brands, each designed to win the widest possible acceptance, the true differences between these beers are lost in the commotion. Popularity may owe something to fashion, but the distinctions between beers are not entirely a matter for subjective judgment.

This holds true even among the everyday beers of the United States, which are all highly-carbonated, lightly-hopped, pale *lagers*, sometimes affecting the description *Pilsener*, though hardly deserving it. The differences between American beers might be better appreciated if, instead of being frozen into tastelessness, they were served at a civilized temperature. If a *lager* is worth drinking, it should not be served at less than 45 degrees Fahrenheit (7°C). At that temperature, it will be perfectly quenching, while still retaining its flavour. Only if the flavour is execrable should it be frozen out. The least that can be said for most American beers is that, because of their lightness, they are good thirst-quenchers. That is one of their particular merits. *Ales*, however, should not be regarded in this way. Even in freezer-happy America, *ales* should not be served at less than

The indigenous American style . . . at the turn of the century, "steam beer" was brewed not only in its native San Francisco Bay area, but also in places as far away as Milwaukee, better known today for the typically light American lager.

203

55°F (12°C). *Ale* is a different kind of beer. It is meant to be savoured for its full, well-hopped palate, not bolted like a soft-drink.

The United States has a good many *ales*, and drinkers should take care of them. They are more than a part of Colonial history; they add a much-needed variety to the drinking scene, and there is no reason why products of specialist appeal should be extinguished in the name of popular taste. *Ales* are a persecuted minority. The danger is that their contribution will not be fully appreciated until the tumbrels are inexorably on the move. A great musician or artist may be enjoyed long after his own lifetime; a movie actor may become the subject of a posthumous cult; but you cannot drink a beer which you once enjoyed if the brewery has gone out of business. It may be less easy to enlist support for a vulnerable beer than it is for a threatened building, though the palate deserves as much consideration as the eye. Perhaps architecture is more important than alcohol, but both go through the same cycle of superficial fashion. First, comes the "new, revolutionary" phase; then the "outmoded, obsolescent" phase; then the "worthy of preservation" phase. The difficulty lies in surviving the "outmoded" stage for long enough to become "worthy of preservation." Unfortunately, people who take destructive and irreversible decisions based upon "public taste" are usually ten years behind everyone else in their appreciation of whatever is at stake. People who quote "taste" to support their argument usually have no taste and no argument.

While most American *ales* are a little stronger than the nation's *lagers*, the same goes for seasonal *bock* beers, several of which still survive in the United States. Brewers of both styles may well be encouraged by the revival of the West Coast *steam beer*, a splendid indigenous speciality. Nor should it be forgotten that, while the United States has introduced some questionable habits to the business of brewing, it has also nurtured some commendable practices. In the past, American brewers were especially fond of *krausening* their beers, and several claim that they still do this. *Krausening* means the addition of a little young beer to the *lagering* brew in order to create a secondary fermentation and a new carbonation.

For the health of the brewing industry, as well as the benefit of the consumer, such flashes of individualism should be maintained. A visit to a single beer-garden in Germany, or just one English pub, might provide more variety of palates than a coast-to-coast tasting trip across the United States, but the last journey would most emphatically be worth-

while. Nor would it be without surprises.

The States which cling to the Great Lakes might well provide the axis for such a trip. The nation's strongest regular beer, Maximus Super, is produced in upstate New York by the West End Brewing Company, at Utica. Maximus Super is brewed like a conventional bottom-fermented beer, but with a density of 16·0 degrees Balling. It is then fermented for many weeks until it is very well attenuated, producing an alcohol content of 7·5 per cent by volume. The brewery points out that it does not introduce enzymes to further the fermentation process (this method is frequently used to boost the alcohol content of the so-called *malt liquors* which are produced in the United States). The West End Brewing Company produces an interesting range of *krausened* products which would probably have won the recognition they deserve even if they hadn't been promoted by some of New York's most inventive advertising agencies. Utica Club Cream Ale is top-fermented and well-hopped, with a density of 11·8; Matt's Premium is an all-malt *lager*, brewed with imported hops (11·6); and Utica Club Pilsener is light and dry, with a density of 11·5.

The name Utica Club was originally applied to a range of soft-drinks which were marketed when Prohibition curbed the primary role of the West End Brewing Company. During this time, breweries switched to the production of mineral-waters, fruit-juices, ice-cream, dairy products and the like, but many did not survive. Prohibition probably dampened beer-strengths for all time, and left behind a patchwork of restrictions which vary from State to State and town to town. In some places, beer is still limited to 3·2 per cent alcohol by weight, though 4·0–4·5 per cent is a more common strength. *Ales* are usually 5·0–5·5 alcohol by weight, and *malt liquors* may be 5·5–6·0, though not necessarily with a high density.

Prohibition harshly accelerated the "rationalization" and "modernization" of the industry, and put out of business countless craft-brewers. Some, though, were especially resilient. The West End Brewing Company was founded in 1888 by F. X. Matt, who learned his trade at the Duke of Baden's brewery (now the Baden State Brewery), at Rothaus, in the Black Forest. In America, Matt was a noted consumer of his own products, and this is alleged to have been the cause of his longevity. He died at the age of 99, in 1958, leaving a son as president, with yet a third generation of his family in senior management. The year of the company's foundation is celebrated in an 1888 Tavern, where tourists get a drink, and the trip round

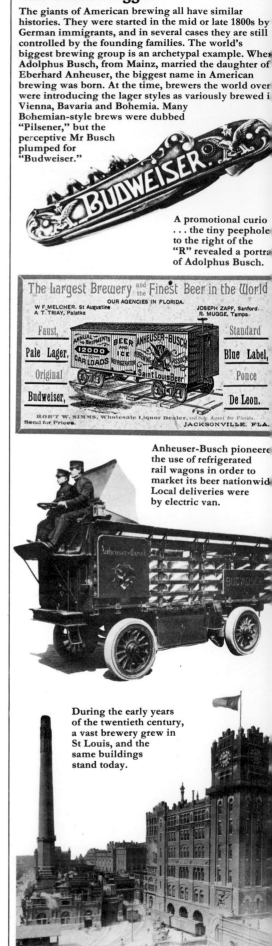

The world's biggest

The giants of American brewing all have similar histories. They were started in the mid or late 1800s by German immigrants, and in several cases they are still controlled by the founding families. The world's biggest brewing group is an archetypal example. When Adolphus Busch, from Mainz, married the daughter of Eberhard Anheuser, the biggest name in American brewing was born. At the time, brewers the world over were introducing the lager styles as variously brewed in Vienna, Bavaria and Bohemia. Many Bohemian-style brews were dubbed "Pilsener," but the perceptive Mr Busch plumped for "Budweiser."

A promotional curio ... the tiny peephole to the right of the "R" revealed a portrait of Adolphus Busch.

Anheuser-Busch pioneered the use of refrigerated rail wagons in order to market its beer nationwide. Local deliveries were by electric van.

During the early years of the twentieth century, a vast brewery grew in St Louis, and the same buildings stand today.

The breweries of the United States

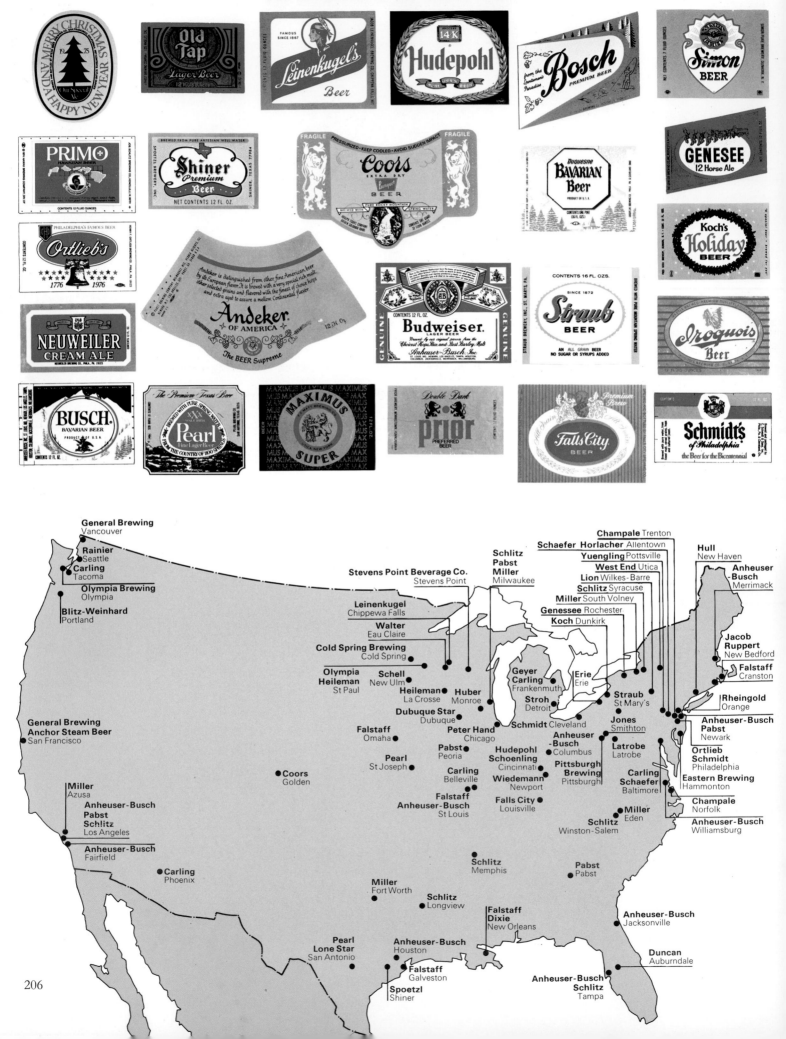

206

The first brewers of Manhattan were Dutch, and the Netherlanders established a thriving industry which left a great impression on the city. Nonetheless, today the custodians of beery tradition in New York proclaim their Irishness.

the brewery is made easier with the aid of a Victorian trolley-car.

Not far away in Rochester, New York, two *ales* and a *bock* are among the beers produced by the Genesee Brewing Company. The full-bodied, malty Genesee beers are also *krausened*, and the company has its own maltings. To the South of Buffalo, in Dunkirk, New York, the family-owned Fred Koch brewery produces a wide range of *lagers* (11·0–11·8) and *ales* (12·5). The latter include the well-liked Black Horse Ale, which is also produced by Champale, the *malt-liquor* specialists, in Trenton, New Jersey.

The Eastern seaboard having been settled first, it has a brewing tradition rooted deeply in the old ways, and strongly influenced by the British and Dutch, as well as the early Bohemian and German settlers. Two centuries later, a fresh infusion of brewing skills came from Germany during the political upheavals which followed the Hungry 1840s in Europe. By then, *lager* was set to become the world's principal beer-style. Although *lager* was developed in Europe, its introduction in many nations was brought about by American engineering. In the late 1800s and early 1900s brewers all over the world bought bottom-fermenting vessels from Pfaudler, of Rochester, New York.

New York City itself is no longer a brewing centre. It lost its last three breweries, all in Brooklyn, amid the crises of the early 1970s.

Happily, their beers are still available. Nostalgic New Yorkers were particularly sad to lose Rheingold, though it moved only as far as Orange, New Jersey. For 20 years, until the early 1960s, this brewery was associated with the Miss Rheingold beauty contests, which always caused great debate in the bars and delicatessens of the city. In a more relevant competition, Rheingold was the American brew most highly rated by the tasting team of *New York* magazine when they held their first Underground Beer Olympics.

Rheingold has for decades also provided the own-label *ale* and *porter* specially brewed for McSorley's bar, in East 7th Street. McSorley's serves only *ale, porter* and imported *stout*. Until 1970, it didn't serve women, either. It was "liberated" in that respect by a

successful lawsuit on behalf of the National Organization for Women. Even after that, the celebrated establishment declined to instal a ladies' cloakroom. There are those who would argue that women were fortunate to be barred from a place like McSorley's, yet others would accord the place great respect. The distinguished and demanding critic Craig Claiborne, who eats out for the *New York Times*, has said that McSorley's should be declared a national monument. He has prescribed the same treatment for P. J. Clarke's, at 915 Third Avenue.

The other two brewers in New York merged. Schaefer took over Piels, and then moved the short distance to Allentown, Pennsylvania. The same town has the small Horlacher Brewing Company, which produces a strongish (5·57 per cent) sweet beer called Brew II. Pennsylvania as a whole has a dozen breweries, which is more than can be counted by any other State. Some of them are very small, and held in some affection. Typical is the local brewery at St Mary's, owned by the Straub family, who have been brewers in Pennsylvania since the 1830s. Their beer contains no sugar or syrups. Stegmaier Gold Medal still has some local following, though the brewery has now merged with its home-town rival in Wilkes-Barre.

Among the much-loved small breweries of Pennsylvania is the oldest brewing company

The oldest brewers in the United States

North America owes its ales and porters to the early British settlers. Thus these styles are most usually found in old colonies like Pennsylvania, home of Pottsville Porter.

The top-fermented specialities of Pottsville survive despite the fact that the brewery has always been owned by German-Americans. By the turn of the century, Germans dominated the industry.

The first American brewers

When Christopher Columbus landed on the shores of the New World, he observed that the American Indians were in the habit of brewing. Their method: to throw a handful of maize (what the Americans now know as corn) into an earthen jug, pour in a dollop of sap from the black birch tree, then fill the jug with water. Natural fermentation did the rest.

The earliest record of non-Indian brewing in America dates from 1587. English explorer Richard Hakluyt quoted his colleague Thomas Heriot as saying of the corn in Virginia: "We made of the same in the country some mault, whereof was brewed as good ale as was to be desired." The Pilgrim Fathers had intended to sail to Virginia, but they ended their journey prematurely, at the point which we now know as Plymouth Rock. A diarist aboard the Mayflower had a simple explanation for this history-making decision: "Our victuals are being much spent, especially our beere."

The first commercial brewery was opened by the Dutch West India Company in Lower Manhattan, in 1632. William Penn operated the first brewery in the State which was named after him. He would no doubt be proud to see that Pennsylvania today

supports more breweries than any other State in the Union. George Washington maintained a private brewhouse on his estate at Mount Vernon. His handwritten recipe for beer – said by his peers to be superb – is still on display at the New York City Public Library. During the Revolutionary War, American troops were supposed to receive a daily quart of beer each. On one occasion, General Washington wrote to Congress complaining that the supply had run short. Both Samuel Adams and Revolutionary War General Israel Putnam were professional brewers at some point in their lives. In 1789, future-President Madison persuaded the House of Representatives to limit the tax on beer to eight cents a barrel (it is nine dollars today), because "this low rate will be such an encouragement as to induce the manufacture of beer in every State of the Union."

In 1861, America's first privately-endowed college for women opened its doors. The college was founded by Matthew Vassar, a brewer.

America's oldest trade organization is the United States Brewers' Association, founded in 1862, and still going strong.

Brewing Company, was once a producer of *weissbier*. Among today's products from Ortlieb is Neuweiler's Cream Ale, beloved of Philadelphians.

Philadelphia's other surviving brewer, the largest in the State, is C. Schmidt and Sons, founded in 1860, and still privately owned. Its brands include two *ales*, a dark *lager*, and several more conventional beers. Its flagship brand is known simply as Schmidt's Beer. In a "blindfold" test conducted by the food editor of the *Philadelphia Inquirer*, the panel chose the clean-tasting Schmidt's as the best of ten brands. European brews like Heineken and, astonishingly, Becks, were among the also-rans. So were fashionable American beers like Coors and Rolling Rock. The latter brand is also produced in Pennsylvania, at Latrobe, once the home of a monastery brewhouse.

In another panel test, carried out under more scientific conditions by a professor at a local college, a similar result emerged. In this case, both Schmidt's and the same brewery's cheaper Valley Forge brand beat Michelob, Coors, Budweiser and Rolling Rock. Schmidt's delightedly publicized the test results in Press and television advertising.

The most popular beer in Western Pennsylvania is Iron City, from Pittsburgh. The same brewery also produces a concoction called Hop'n'Gator, which is a beer flavoured with lime. Hop'n'Gator was launched in 1970, along with Lone Star's Lime Lager and National Brewing's Malt Duck (a strongish beer flavoured with grape concentrate). Anxious because the student generation seemed to favour sweet wines over beers, the brewers devised these bizarre drinks as an alternative. Apparently, the tactic worked.

National Brewing, of Baltimore, Maryland, was bought by Carling in 1975. Carling is the North American arm of the Rothman group's brewing interests. Its traditional market is Canada, but it is also very active in the United States, where it had been losing ground until the consolidation with National. The merger left the new corporation with no less than 20 brands, ranging from Carling and Tuborg to Colt 45. In a captious critique of American beers, Hugh Hefner's *Oui* magazine gave notably sympathetic attention to two National brands. National Bohemian was rated as "clean and pleasant, but not innocuous . . . generally placed high on taste tests . . . by discriminating judges . . . against stiff opposition . . . does not let down the good family name." National Premium did even better: "For some time, we were convinced that this beer was the best in America . . . it not only scored well against all pre-

in the United States, D. G. Yuengling and Son, of Pottsville. David G. Yuengling was born in Germany in 1806, and started his firm in 1829. Like many of the early American breweries, Yuengling's was built into a mountain-side, so that caves could be dug into the rock to act as lagering cellars. The brewery also has its own private mountain spring as a water supply. Malt was originally hauled from Philadelphia by way of the Schuylkill Canal. In the early days, Yuengling trained many young brewers who later became distinguished practitioners of the art. The brewery is still owned by the family, and the current head of the firm is the founder's great-grandson. Yuengling produces a colourful range of brews, among which are a

lively, sweetish and well-hopped, top-fermented *ale* called Lord Chesterfield (11·0 degrees Balling) and a *porter* (11·2), again with a sweetish palate. The "Celebrated Pottsville Porter," to give the brew its full title, is accorded cult status by followers in three States and the District of Columbia. Yuengling also brews a *bock* and two regular *lagers*, called Premium Beer and Old German. Both *lagers* have a density of 10·7, and the Old German is intended to be the more mellow of the two.

Pennsylvania's greatest city used to be an unrivalled brewing centre. In 1879, Philadelphia had 94 breweries, more than any other city in the United States. Today, it has two. The smaller of the two, the Henry F. Ortlieb

COMPLIMENTS OF
Adolph Coors, Golden Brewery,
Golden,
Colo.
ADOLPH COORS
GOLDEN, COLORADO
...ver Depot, "WEWATTA"
bet. 21st & 22nd Sts.
TELEPHONE 862

Neither the wheelbarrow nor the drayhorse could survive for long in Detroit, and the local brewery outgrew them both, but it clings steadfastly to its technique of "fire-brewing." The brew-kettles of Detroit get a good "rolling boil."

miums, but held its own in blindfold tests against the best European labels ... Premium seemed to offer the best aspects of both European and American beer...dry, pleasurable to contemplate ... distinctive bitterness ... clean and light."

In the end, *Oui* gave its best mark to Royal Amber, brewed by Wiedemann, in Newport, Kentucky. Once again, the American tasters rated their native beer more highly than European brands. It is not clear whether this was due to underdeveloped taste-buds or stale imports and questionable licensing arrangements. According to *Oui*: "Five out of six blindfold tasters preferred Royal Amber to Carlsberg, Löwenbräu and Heineken, calling it dry, crispy, tangy, smooth ... light foretaste, bittersweet afterbite ... a few other American beers hold up when the chill wears off, but this one actually gets better." Royal Amber was again highly rated, and commended for its "nutty" flavour, in *Esquire* magazine's "first ever American regional beer survey," carried out by Nathaniel Benchley. Kentucky also has a beer called Drummond Brothers, but this turns out to originate from the Falls City Brewing Company, of Louisville. The name "Drummond Brothers" was devised by an advertising agency because it allegedly had a nostalgic sound which would appeal to the young market. Grown-up drinkers might prefer the regular Falls City brand, which has a higher hopping rate.

Next door to Kentucky, and almost swallowing Newport, is thirsty Ohio, with a large German population in Cincinnati. The citizens of "Cincy" have two breweries at their disposal, Hudepohl (also brewing the Burger, Hofbrau and Tap brands) and Schoenling (also brewing Top Hat). Although the Teutonic Mid-West is the heartland of American brewing, it has suffered

grievously from mergers along with the rest of the nation.

In Detroit, Stroh's brewery and Goebels used to confront each other across a main road. Now, the two are one. Stroh's remains fiercely proud of its history, and makes a particular point of its "fire-brewing" technique. It is the only American brewery to heat its kettles by direct flame instead of steam, and claims that this imparts a uniquely smooth flavour to its beers. The method had at one stage been abandoned, but was actually reintroduced in 1912 after a member of the Stroh family had become convinced of its superiority while on a brewery-visiting trip to Europe. The Strohs originate from Kirn, in the Rhineland Palatinate, and their home town records a brewing tradition dating back to the 1500s. At least as early as the 1700s, a Stroh was a local innkeeper and brewer there. His grandson Bernard Stroh arrived in Detroit in 1850, and shortly afterwards pioneered the Bohemian (i.e. *Pilsener*) style of *lager* brewing there. Until then, Detroit had been accustomed to English-style *ales*. Bernard Stroh delivered his beer in small casks on a wheelbarrow. The original culture for today's yeast was brought from Germany in 1911, and the brewery is still in the hands of the Stroh family. Visitors are invited to have a drink in either the "Strohhaus" or the "Rathskeller." Apart from its two regular beers, Stroh's Bohemian and the fractionally lower-density Goebel, the brewery also produces an all-malt *bock*. The brewery takes a positive interest in the *bock*, claiming it as the best American example of the style, and noting that sales are rising.

Chicago would seem ethnically ideal as a brewer's market, yet it almost became brewery-less in the early 1970s. Happily, the Peter Hand Brewing Company, a name dating

back to 1890, was given an infusion of new management and it survives as Chicago's sole brewery. Peter Hand produces six brands, among which Van Merritt is the most noteworthy. Beer-writer Norman Jackson describes it as "an articulate American answer to Heineken." When the well-known journalist Mike Royko carried out a blindfold test of more than 20 beers for the Chicago *Daily News*, his panel chose Würzburger, from Germany as the best beer available in the city (*New York's* panel came to the same conclusion); then Bass, from Britain; Point Special, from Wisconsin; and Heineken.

So fast has been the conglomeration of American brewers that neither the industry nor the consumers can keep track. The much-loved and nationally-marketed Ballantine *ale* brands (including an *I.P.A.*) had barely been acquired by Falstaff, of St Louis, when that corporation was swallowed by General Brewing, of San Francisco. The latter company was at the time best known for its supermarket brands. The takeover left the great beer city of St Louis as a one-company town, though brewing companies don't come any bigger than Anheuser-Busch.

The world's biggest brewery started life falteringly, in 1852, under the name of Georg Schneider. After twice facing collapse, it was bought by a creditor, Eberhard Anheuser, in 1860. His daughter subsequently married a brewer's supplier, Adolphus Busch, who had emigrated to the United States from Mainz. Adolphus Busch became President of the company, and the father of modern American brewing. Like one or two of his contemporaries, he made a tour of Europe in the 1800s, studying the great changes which were taking place in brewing methods there. He saw the success of Bohemian *lager* beers, a notable example of which was the one brewed at Budweis. Among those American brewers who brought home the *lager* message, Busch was its greatest champion. The *Budweiser* beer first produced in St Louis in 1876 was advertised as "the very highest point known to the art of modern brewing." Busch wanted to produce a beer which would transcend regional tastes, and he clearly succeeded. Budweiser became the first nationally-marketed beer in America, and then the best-selling brand in the world.

As the fame of the St Louis beer spread, confusion arose in territories where the original Budweis brew was marketed. It seems that in time some agreement was reached, though the Americans and Czechs give differing accounts of this.

Nominally, the everyday beer from the St Louis giant is Busch "Bavarian," a lighter

During Prohibition, brewers adopted some odd expedients. Coors made a malted milk which became a popular product. When Prohibition ended, brewers presented celebratory cases of beer to public figures who had supported repeal of the law.

and cheaper brand. Budweiser is described as a "premium" beer. This description was originally applied to all nationally-distributed beers. Theoretically, the consumer was getting something rather grander than his local brew, and had to pay a little extra to have it transported to him. The idea may have made some sense in the earlier part of this century, but it hardly does today. Nationally-distributed beers are now commonplace, and the biggest brewers usually have plants all over the country (Anheuser-Busch has nine). Thus "premium" has been rendered a meaningless term, and is dying out, but Budweiser can still make a legitimate claim to be a cut above the average big-selling beer.

The most publicized of Budweiser's selling points might be viewed with a raised eyebrow in other countries. American brewers are refreshingly frank about their use of adjuncts, notably corn, and Budweiser proudly proclaims a preference for rice. It is pointed out that rice is generally more expensive than

corn, and the brewery claims that it "contributes to the snappy taste, clarity, and brilliance of the beverage." Anheuser-Busch also claims to use more malt per barrel than any other U.S. brewer, though it is difficult to see how this can be proved. Surprisingly, Anheuser-Busch makes little of the fact that it uses hops, rather than hop-extract. Perhaps this is because "Bud" is a rather lightly hopped beer. Indeed, its lightness of palate is the characteristic which has been most widely emulated by other American brewers. Anheuser-Busch says that Budweiser is *kraeusened* (the company spells it with the additional "e"), and clarified with the help of porous beechwood chips. An especially forthright claim is made regarding fermentation times. Anheuser-Busch says that Budweiser is *lagered* for 32 to 40 days (a very respectable period by anyone's standards), while "the company's leading rival takes only about 14 days, using the 'agitated batch-fermentation process.'"

The same claims are made, naturally

enough, for the Anheuser-Busch "super-premium" beer, Michelob. Super-premium brands like Michelob (and Andeker, another good example, from the Pabst Brewing Company) are full-bodied beers, usually with fewer adjuncts, comparable in style and price with some of the European imports. The name Michelob was adopted in 1896 by the ever-enterprising Adolphus Busch, and he would no doubt be pleased to see it being used in this way by the fourth generation of his family.

The three greatest rivals to Anheuser-Busch are all based in Milwaukee, Wisconsin, which is the unchallenged brewing capital of the United States. Pabst is one of the three. Its origins were in a brewery founded in 1844 by an immigrant called Jacob Best, from Rheinhessen. Frederick Pabst subsequently married into the family. The Pabsts came from Antwerp, but had settled in Leipzig before emigrating to the United States. Pabst's principal brand is the sweetish Blue

The beers that made Milwaukee famous

Joseph Schlitz (left) died when the liner S.S. Friedrich Schiller sank after hitting a rock near Land's End, England. The brewery was taken over by the Uihlein family, who had been involved since the early days. Schlitz was the biggest brewing group in the United States during the early 1950s.

Frederick Miller's brewery had a slower growth, but it became famous in modern times for its nationally-marketed High Life beer. The company then entered a state of some decline, which was dramatically reversed when it was taken over by the Philip Morris tobacco group.

Ribbon. It has a cheaper brand called Red, White and Blue, the super-premium Andeker, one of the better dark *lagers*, and a nationally-distributed *ale* called Old Tankard.

A second famous name also owes its origins to the Best family. Two Best brothers started a brewery which was taken over in 1855 by a man called Frederick Miller. His name survives by way of Miller's High Life, another national brand. High Life is a conventional American beer, perhaps slightly more well-hopped in comparison with its competitors, but still mild by European standards. For years, it was the only product of the Miller Brewing Company, but all this changed when the corporation was taken over by Philip Morris Inc. Miller began to experiment with additional brands, adopted more sophistica-

ted marketing techniques, and achieved considerable growth. Miller's acceleration was hitched to the popularity of the so-called "light" beers, which turned out to be a surprise success with weight-conscious Americans. These are weak and watery brews, in no way comparable with the genuine diet beers brewed in Germany, Britain and some other countries. The American "light" beer was pioneered by Rheingold's Gablinger brand, but it was Miller's *Lite* which proved to be the great national success.

The growth of Miller's threatened the long-standing position of Schlitz as America's second-biggest brewer. Producing a beer similar in style to Miller's High Life, Schlitz is also traditionally a one-brand company, but its product is undoubtedly the most

famous beer to emanate from the "Cream City." It is, in Schlitz's own oft-repeated words, the beer that made Milwaukee famous. The company has its beginnings in the August Krug brewery, founded in 1849. When Krug died in 1856, Joseph Schlitz took over the business. Schlitz, who originated from Mainz, was drowned in 1875, on a trip to his homeland. The company passed to the Uihlein family, which remains in control.

The giants apart, Wisconsin is also noted for small breweries, like Leinenkugel's, at Chippewa Falls. The brew simply labelled "Leinenkugel's" (with a density of 11·80) is a fine example of a mild-tasting regular American beer at its most characterful and delicate. The company also produces a "light" beer (11·20) called Chippewa Pride, a dark lager

Philip Best (right) was one of a brewing family in Milwaukee. His brewery (below) subsequently passed to Frederick Pabst (bottom), also a member of the family. Pabst, once a cabin-boy on a Great Lakes steamer, became a noted businessman.

(12·05) ·and a seasonal *bock*. The original Leinenkugel, who arrived from Cologne with his wife and five sons in 1845, founded a brewery in Sauk City, Wisconsin. One of his sons, Jacob, started the brewery at Chippewa Falls in 1867, to cater for the thirsts of the lumberjacks there. Not far away, at Eau Claire, the Walter Brewing Company produces another fine Wisconsin brew, of delightful delicacy.

Probably the most successful regional brewer in the United States is the fast-growing Heileman, of La Crosse, Wisconsin, which has Blatz as its most widely-distributed brand. Heileman's *krausened* beers sell briskly wherever they are available: Special Export in Milwaukee, Old Style in Chicago, and Schmidt (not to be confused with its Eastern

namesake) in the State of Minnesota. The company also owns Wiedemann, in Kentucky, brewer of the excellent Royal Amber.

For all that the Mid-West is the traditional heartland of American brewing, it has encountered a singly powerful challenger from the Mountain States. The cult of Coors' beer, brewed in Colorado, has derived largely from the limited availability of the product. There is some irony in this question of scarcity value, since Coors' brewery, in scenic mountain country at Golden, is the biggest in the world. Coors is the market-leader in a good many States of the West, and its total sales ensure that it stands among the nation's Big Five brewers, yet in the East it retains the cachet of a regional speciality. This reputation was enhanced when Easterners started

to "bootleg" Coors to their home cities, a fashion which was followed by several stars of stage, screen and State Department. Coors has indicated that it does not rule out eventual national distribution, and it is an open question whether such a move would damage its appeal. Certainly the celebrity of the beer was narrowed by Coors' diversification into a strongly Right-wing television news syndication service in 1973. A diversification of broader appeal was the switch to Coors Malted Milk during the Prohibition years. The malted milk was also used in the production of candy bars like Mars and Milky Way.

In 1975, the company offered non-voting shares to the public, but control remains in the hands of the Coors family. Adolph Coors was born in Rittershausen, in Rhineland, and

came to Colorado in 1872. He founded his brewery a year later, in partnership with Jacob Schueler, whom he subsequently bought-out. The Coors family takes a strong line on socio-political issues. The firm has made a particular point of environmental responsibility, and pioneered the use of aluminium cans (which can be recycled), later adding non-detachable opening tabs (which are not, therefore, thrown away as litter). Coors issues a "company profile" which ends with the words: "The free enterprise system has developed over the years, beyond any doubt, into the greatest economic system on the face of the earth. All Americans must stop taking it for granted, and must fight with every effort to preserve it for all time."

An article in *Business Week*, in 1976, noted that, "Coors has not advanced much further than the Adam Smith school of marketing. William Coors himself jokes about his company's paltry advertising expenditures, which are half the industry's average. And while other brewers are bringing out new products, Coors still insists that one product is enough to grow on." That product is labelled as Coors Extra-Dry Banquet Beer, "Brewed With Pure Rocky Mountain Spring Water," but drinkers know it simply by its maker's name. In theory, it is a *Pilsener*-style beer, and it has the sparkle to justify this claim, though not quite the hoppiness. Coors is so clean-tasting, so delicate, that one critic jokingly complains, "it tastes more like Rocky Mountain Spring Water than beer." The company has its own strain of barley, developed in Europe, and supplies seed to Western farmers. Coors also has its own maltings, uses rice as an adjunct, and gives its beer a lengthy conditioning period. The real key to its palate, though, is so obvious that it does not seem to be appreciated by many drinkers. Coors, whether on draught, in the bottle, or canned, is not pasteurized. The beer is transported by fast (350 hp) refrigerated trucks and by insulated rail-wagons. The further the distribution stretches, the greater the difficulty in maintaining Coors fresh taste. Another brewery could be built, but the East does not have Rocky Mountain Spring Water. Therein lies Coors' happy dilemma.

Coors' is a unique success story, but there are lesser regional brewers which entertain national ambitions. A fast-growing brewer further West is Olympia, in Washington State. Olympia is the company's home-town as well as being the name of its principal brand. It is a clean-tasting beer, brewed with water from Artesian springs at the nearby Tumwater Falls. Olympia has speeded its growth by acquisition. In 1975, it bought

If small is beautiful, then the brewery run by Fritz Maytag (left) is America's finest. Maytag has saved one beer-style from extinction, and offers the drinker further choices which are increasingly hard to find elsewhere.

Hamm's, another brewery noted for its clean-tasting beer, in St Paul, Minnesota. Then, in 1976, Olympia went South to buy Lone Star, of San Antonio, Texas, which also has a considerable popular following.

Lone Star has to face tough competition from the Pearl Brewing Company, also in San Antonio. Pearl has, if anything, an even more dedicated clientele for its fresh-tasting beers. The company also produces a brand called Near Beer, one of three such survivors from Prohibition days (the others are Malta, from Schaefer, and Metbrew, from Champale). Not far from San Antonio, the German and Czech inhabitants of a town called Shiner for years supported a rare example of true *Münchener*-style brewing. Their local brewmaster, Kosmas Spoetzl, was a Bavarian who arrived in Shiner in 1915. His daughter, "Miss Celie," took over the ownership of the brewery when he died in 1950. The brewery is now owned by eight stockholders, and beers of a lighter weight are produced. Nonetheless, the Spoetzl Brewery still produces as its draught Premium a full-bodied and dark brew with a character all of its own.

No beers in the United States are more idiosyncratic than those produced by the Anchor Steam Brewing Company, of San Francisco. It was more than Western prejudice which persuaded columnist Charles McCabe, of the *San Francisco Chronicle*, that the only two American beers worth drinking were the *ale* brewed by the Rainier company, in Seattle, and Anchor Steam Beer.

The colourfully-named *steam beer* is produced by the only brewing method invented in the United States. It is, in that respect, the nation's sole indigenous beer-style. *Steam-beer* was developed in the West during the Gold Rush, and there were dozens of breweries producing this style in the San Francisco Bay area during the late 1800s. While brewers in New York, Philadelphia, Michigan and Wisconsin could find plentiful natural ice during the winter to cool their *lagering* tanks, those in temperate States like California couldn't. Until refrigeration became widely available in the West, *steam*-brewing was a compromise. That is why, in body and palate, the amber *steam beer* resembles a slightly eccentric *ale*. It is fermented at *ale* temperatures (60–70 degrees Fahrenheit; 15–20°C), but with bottom-fermenting yeast. This difficult trick is made possible by the use of long, shallow pan-like fermenting vessels called clarifiers. The beer is then conditioned at the relatively warm temperature of 50–55°F (10–12°C), and *krausened*. The end-product has a lively head, and the pressure released when the casks were tapped was dubbed "steam."

A rare Western ale

According to a writer in the San Francisco Chronicle, the only two American brews worth drinking are Anchor Steam Beer and Rainier Ale. Nathaniel Benchley described Rainier as being "nutty, woody, smoky . . . a mixture of all three." The Seattle firm was founded in 1878, and later bought by a European immigrant. The group picture was taken in 1910.

Hence the name for the process, which has nothing whatever to do with steam power.

The Anchor Steam Brewing Company, in San Francisco, is the last surviving establishment to produce beer in this way. It was about to close in 1965 when it was rescued by Fritz Maytag, a wealthy young scion of the washing-machine family. Maytag, who was then 27, had an affection for the idea of *steam beer*, and thought he might be able to help out financially. In the end, he became the proprietor. His *steam beer* is very highly hopped, and has a density of 12·3 degrees Balling. Not satisfied with having saved this unique brew from extinction, Maytag and his staff of six produce several other highly individualistic beers, using whole hops and solely barley-malt in every case. There is a bottom-fermented *porter* with the very high density (by American standards) of 17·0 degrees Balling. This is sweeter than Guinness, but still very well hopped. Then there is a top-fermented *ale*, dry-hopped, and carbona-

ted solely by bunging before fermentation ceases. This has a respectable density of 14·0–15·0 Balling, is full-bodied, and has a powerful hop bouquet, though it is not quite as bitter as some British *ales*. Experiments have also been carried out with a very strong (more than 25·0 Balling) top-fermented *ale* similar in style to the best of British *barley wines*. The resultant brew is very rich, with a strong bouquet, sweet, but slightly vinous.

The purchase of the Steam Brewing Company may have seemed at the time to be a dilettante gesture, but it has been followed through with both dedication and inventiveness. *The Wall Street Journal* reported: "This tiny operation has climbed back into the black . . . it is outgrowing its premises as demand outpaces capacity. That just isn't supposed to happen to a small, independent brewer . . ."

The smallest brewery in the United States has added a whole new dimension to American brewing.

The Caribbean

AS MIGHT BE SUGGESTED by the international reputation which attends Red Stripe Lager, "the Beer of Jamaica," there are some very acceptable brews to be drunk in the Caribbean. Nor is there any shortage of places in which to drink them. The two million citizens of Jamaica can choose from no less than 12,000 outlets for beer, including bars, rum shops and cold-supper shops. On a warm West Indian day, a beer goes down very well with some bread and cheese, or fish, at a cold-supper shop. In Jamaica, places which sell drink do not require licences, and the informality extends to the customers; usually, the beer is drunk straight from the bottle.

Red Stripe itself is a conventional pale, mellow *lager*, with an original gravity of 1048, and 4·6 per cent alcohol by volume. There is nothing special about the way in which it is brewed – corn is used as an adjunct, and the beer is pasteurized – but its quality is nonetheless most distinctive. Its reputation owes a lot to the vivacious manner in which the Jamaican people promote their country and culture, but it has taken more than that to make Red Stripe such a widely-known name. In the Black neighbourhoods of some British cities, a bottle of Red Stripe is a cherished memory of home. In the United States, where it is more easily, but expensively, found, the beer was given an "excellent" rating in the *New York* magazine First Underground Gourmet Beer Olympics. From Chicago, *Oui* magazine commented, in its own consumer-test: "Superlight . . . so smooth, so clear, so clean that it is a better means of rehydration than water . . . rather remarkable."

The first Red Stripe was an *ale*-style brew, produced in 1927; the *lager* took over in 1934. The brewery, Desnoes and Geddes, of Kingston, also produces a strong sweetish *stout* (1070), called Dragon. Its seemingly innocent slogan, "Dragon Puts It Back," is commonly taken to have sexual connotations. Mackeson "Milk Stout," from Britain, and Heineken beer, are produced under franchise. Heineken has extensive involvements in the Caribbean, with associate companies in Trinidad, Martinique, Curaçao, and on the South American mainland in Surinam. In addition to Heineken, these companies produce their own brands.

Guinness is also in the West Indies, with one of the world's most unusual and distinguished beers, its "Foreign Extra Stout." This brew has a gravity of 1073, far higher than regular Guinness. It has the characteristically full body and dry, roasted-malt palate, but also has a sharp, quenching acidity. This difficult trick is achieved by the introduction of some older Guinness into the brew in order to create lactic acid by fermentation. Once the requisite palate has been achieved, the beer is pasteurized, and therefore stabilized. It is the quenching quality which makes "F.E.S." so well suited to the tropical countries in which it is marketed. In part, Foreign Extra Stout has its origins in the West Indies. Beers from the British Isles have been sold in the Caribbean since the late 1600s, and Guinness had a product called West Indies Porter in the early 1800s. In his book *Guinness's Brewery in the Irish Economy*, Patrick Lynch writes: "It was a commonplace to brew with a certain proportion of hops three or four years old, possibly because of very big seasonal variations in price. It was desirable, therefore, to hold larger stocks when hops were cheap. But West Indies Porter seems always to have been brewed with the newest hops available." West Indies Porter gave rise to a beer called Foreign Double Stout, which in turn spawned today's F.E.S.

The Guinness brewery in Jamaica is at Spanish Town, the former capital. It is run by a public company in Jamaica, in which Guinness holds the controlling share. The company also produces a beer called Mac-Ewan's Strong Ale (1086), in association with Scottish and Newcastle Breweries. In some export markets, the name McEwan is given the extra "a" in order to make it more pronounceable.

Guinness F.E.S. is also brewed in Trinidad, along with a sweet *stout* called Royal (1054) by the Carib company. Carib produces one of the distinctive *lagers* which are characteristic of the West Indies. Carib Lager (1049) is the biggest-selling beer in the Republic of Trinidad and Tobago. Two more *lagers*, Skol and Allsopps (both 1046) are brewed by Carib under licence from the British group Allied Breweries.

Caribbean *lager* beers are usually rather lightly hopped, in the American style, but almost end-fermented. The low hopping-rate and the high degree of attenuation together produce a beer which is crisp and quenching without being too dry. A higher gravity would produce a less quenching beer, but the end-fermentation creates as high an alcoholic content as is possible. Being traditionally rum-drinkers, the West Indians are not keen on weak-tasting beers.

An excellent example of a Caribbean *lager* is Banks' Beer, produced by the enterprising brewery of the same name, in Barbados. Banks' Beer, which has an alcoholic content of five per cent by volume, has won several prizes. The company also produces a strong (nine per cent) dark *lager* called Ebony. This unusual beer keeps company with another

two offbeat products at the lower end of the alcohol scale. Banks produces a diet *lager* of 3·5 per cent, which is flavoured with lime (perhaps a more justifiable gimmick in the West Indies than it might be elsewhere) and a remarkable patented creation called an "action drink." This looks like beer, even to the extent of having a "head," but it is a brewed restorative drink containing no alcohol. The "action drink," which has the brand-name Plus, is rich in glucose, fructose, amino acids and vitamin C. It has a make-up similar to that of honey, and is very quickly digested. It is a popular "energizer" among sportsmen (similar, in this respect, to the German *malzbier*), and allegedly a hangover cure.

Many Caribbean breweries produce a *malz*-type drink, generically known as *malta*. There are breweries on a good many islands, including Grenada and St Kitts, and on the Caribbean mainland, in Honduras (Belize has its Belican beer) and the Hispanic countries.

Action must wait for the cool of night . . . in the heat of the day, a cool, crisp Caribbean beer is provided by Banks of Barbados (above), Red Stripe, the beer of Jamaica (far left), Carib of Trinidad, and some potent stouts. Stout is enjoyed for its potency, but it can also be a surprisingly quenching drink when it is chilled.

Latin America

THE BIG-LEAGUE of brewing nations was joined in the early 1970s by Mexico. Shortly after entering the top ten, Mexico climbed higher in the league by overtaking Canada and East Germany. Not far behind, though not yet in the big-league, lies Brazil, where a family of German origin controls one of the world's biggest brewery groups. Another sizable group, called "Bavaria," helps make Colombia a substantial brewing nation. Venezuela, Argentina and Peru also have brewing industries of a respectable proportion, and there are local beers in every nation of South America.

In some of these countries, cut-throat business practices and varying political pressures bring occasional changes to the colour and shape of the brewing industry, but it survives and thrives. Social change has made brewing a growth industry in Latin America. The more prosperous and fashion-conscious sections of youth, where such social groups exist, see beer as a modish international drink. More important, in comparison with some of the more potent local liquors, beer is often regarded as being less of an intoxicant than a thirst-quencher. This distinction is significant, and it has a long historical perspective.

Talking of a local liquor, one Aztec emperor made an outstandingly eloquent condemnation of the evils of alcohol: "That drink which is called *octli* is the root and the origin of all evil and of all perdition; for *octli* and drunkenness are the cause of all discords and of all dissensions, of all revolt and of all troubles in cities and realms. It is like the whirlwind that destroys and tears down everything. It is like a malignant storm that brings all evil with it. Before adultery, rape, debauching of girls, incest, theft, crime, cursing, bearing false witness, murmuring, calumny, riots and brawling, there is always drunkenness. All those things are caused by *octli* and by drunkenness." *Octli* was made from a desert plant. Its descendants are *pulque*, *mezcal* and *tequila*, which worry today's authorities just as much. Ever since the conquest, Mexico has been plagued by alcoholism.

Beer, of course, is a more wholesome beverage altogether. The Aztecs and Mayas knew this, and they had their own precursors of beer. Mexican historian Manuel Orozco y Berra compares *sendecho* with the beers of the "ancient Germans," explaining that maize was used instead of barley. *Sendecho* was flavoured with a vegetable called *tepozán,* which was highly regarded as a restorative. An amber beverage called *tesguino* was, according to Spanish chroniclers, "beaten with a hand-mill before drinking, in order to raise a great froth."

Mexico had the first commercial brewery in the New World, set up under the auspices of the King of Spain in the mid-1500s, during the period of Cortés. By the 19th century, when Mexico gained independence, the number of breweries was growing, and several German and Swiss settlers were active in the business. A German brewmaster introduced a Bohemian-style beer at the new Cuauhtémoc brewery, in Monterrey, in 1890, and top-fermentation eventually vanished from Mexico. Today, pale *lagers* are usually characterized simply as being *clara* (clear). Mexico is one of the few countries to retain Vienna-style beers, which are described as being *semi-oscura.* There are also *Münchener*-style (*oscura*) brews.

Cuauhtémoc, named after an Indian hero who was murdered while a prisoner of Cortés, still exists. Its "Bohemian" brand is famous, and the company is one of Mexico's Big Three brewers, which have in recent years absorbed more than a dozen smaller firms. Cuauhtémoc also has a one-third holding in the only "independent" brewery, Yucateca, in the South-East. Yucateca produces the pale Montejo and a superb, well-hopped dark brew called Leon Negra. Another splendid dark beer is produced seasonally by Moctezuma, in Veracruz. This is called *Nochebuena* (Christmas Eve). Moctezuma also brews the Vienna-style Dos Equis which has become popular in the United States. The remaining member of the Big Three is Modelo, in Mexico City, which produces the highly-carbonated Victoria, a *clara* which is probably the country's biggest-selling beer and a favourite of the working man.

On the quenching-drink principle, the consumption of beer is actually encouraged by the Government, which mounts publicity campaigns to this effect. Under a law introduced in 1931, beer is not classified as an intoxicant, because its alcoholic strength is kept within a limit of five per cent by volume. Brewers may thus label their product, *la bebida de moderacion.*

Surprisingly, the quenching quality of Mexican beers does not seem to be harmed when they are ordered *al tiempo* (at room temperature) rather than *frio* or *helado* (chilled). The thirsty Mexican adds a flourish by dressing his can of beer with a slice of lemon and a little salt. The mood of moderation is, however, shattered by those drinkers who prefer a *calichal,* a lethal 4-to-1 combination of *pulque* and beer, or a *submarino,* a glass of *tequila* submerged inside a glass of beer. Jokers say that a *tequila* won't keel-ya, but a few *submarinos* certainly will.

What *tequila* is to the Mexicans, *cachaca* is to the Brazilians. This spirit, also known as *pinga,* is made from cane sugar. There are about 20,000 registered *cachaca* distilleries, but a further 40,000 are believed to be in operation illegally. Brazil also has its own wine, grown in the South of the country and sold at extremely low prices. The same is true of locally-distilled whiskies, usually with Scottish (or, incongruously, English) names. New brands are constantly being introduced. Despite all of this, beer production increased by 50 per cent in the five years between 1968 and 1973.

Almost 90 per cent of the beer market is in

¡¡¡ Beber Cerveza de Toluca- ó no beber !!!

the hands of two groups. The biggest is Brahma, which has since 1906 been controlled by the Kunnings, a family of German descent. Brahma is based in Rio, but has breweries all over the country. Its Brahma Chopp "*Pilsener*-type" beer is exported elsewhere in Latin America, and to the United States and Britain. Although *Chopp* means "draught," this brand is sold in cans. Brazil does also have draught beer on tap, very occasionally still supplied in wooden casks. This is served by CO_2-pressure, but cooled by being passed through a coiled tube inside a box of ice. Brahma is not a true *Pilsener* either, though the same might be said for beers all over the world which affect this designation without offering the requisite hoppy dryness. Brazilian brewers have something of an excuse, since the national taste in all types of drink is decidedly sweet. Again on the quenching-drink principle, Brazilians seem to prefer their everyday beers to have unassuming gravities. "Premium" beers have been introduced by well-known brewers without success, and Brahma Chopp runs at an original gravity of 1048. There are occasional surprises, though. Bitter *porters*, with original gravities in the 1070s, are a popular speciality drink, sometimes served by the nip. Brahma's

is the most bitter, as well as being unpasteurized.

The second-largest brewery group is Antarctica Paulista. The name has nothing to do with Paulaner, the Munich beer, or even Hamburg's St Pauli brewery. On the contrary, it is derived from São Paolo, the world's fastest-growing city and the second biggest in all the Americas. São Paolo may be a coffee city, but it is a beer city, too. It may, in ethnic make-up, be an Italian city, but it is a German city, too. At several times in their history, the Germans have taken to Brazil, and their presence has hardly hindered the progress of the brewing industry. Their influence is evident, too, in the use of names like *bock* and *München*.

A third sizable brewing group, Skol-Caracu, has about eight per cent of the market. This grouping is linked with Labatt, of Canada.

In recent years, five or six small independents have scrabbled for the remaining two or three per cent of the market. They have enjoyed better fortunes in the far-flung regions than in the Southern coastal hinterland of Rio and São Paolo, but everywhere the tide of "rationalization" has been hard to resist.

The brews of Mexico . . . and (far left) a bear of moderation. Toluca was founded by a Swiss brewer in 1865, to produce top-fermented beers. It is now part of Cuauhtémoc.

Australia

WHEN THEY CLAIM to be the world's biggest beer-drinkers, the more machismo-minded Australians have the full backing of their national stereotype. For every embarrassed Australian who might wish to erase this legend, there seems to be another who is set upon consolidating it. Rumour has it that, in the early days, the water in the cities was so foul that the population drank nothing but beer, which they imported. This may be so, but it can hardly be an adequate explanation for the Australians' obsession with beer.

In his delightful book *Beer, Glorious Beer*, Cyril Pearl says: "Beer is a religion in Australia. In the sound judgment of newspaper editors, it is more important than conventional religions. Beer makes front-page news. A threatened strike of brewery workers, a threatened shortage of beer, a threatened price rise, has much more reader-interest than a decision (of the Church) on divorce, or a Papal encyclical on birth control." Pearl cites the case of the Courage brewery which opened in Melbourne in 1968. This new brewery made the whole of the front page of the Sydney *Daily Mirror*, despite the fact that the

beer was not to be available in the paper's home State.

A threepenny rise in the price of beer caused a rebellion in the Northern Territory at the end of the First World War. The most peaceable aspect of this rebellion was in itself incredible – a boycott of beer, which lasted for three months, "an act of self-denial to be appreciated only by one who has lived in Darwin through the hot and humid summer," says Pearl. The less ascetic aspect of this uprising involved rowdy demonstrations, the virtual imprisonment of the Territory's Administrator in Government House, and eventually his forced removal from office. A second Administrator was hounded out of town by the thirsty citizens before order was restored.

Darwin prides itself on being the beer-drinking capital of Australia, and a local tourist souvenir is a 2·25-litre bottle of Northern Territory Draught. This half-gallon giant is produced in the city by a brewery which is jointly owned by C.U.B., of Melbourne, and Swan, of Perth. The mighty container is known as the "Darwin Stubby,"

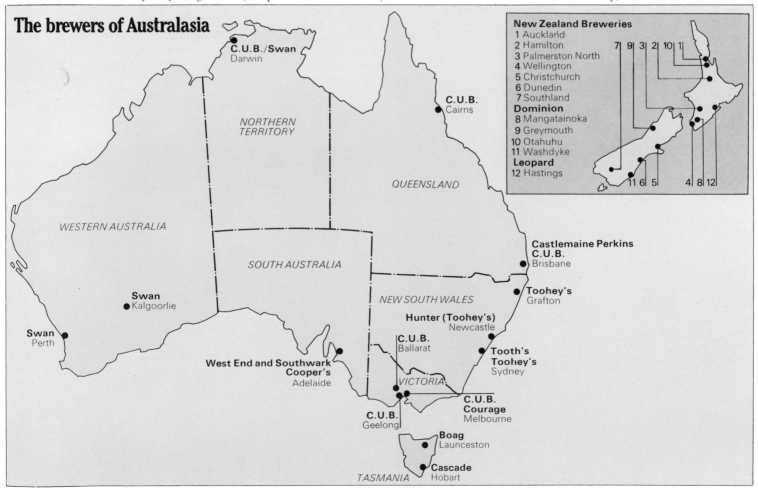

The brewers of Australasia

C.U.B./Swan
Darwin

NORTHERN
TERRITORY

C.U.B.
Cairns

WESTERN AUSTRALIA

QUEENSLAND

SOUTH AUSTRALIA

Swan
Kalgoorlie

Castlemaine Perkins
C.U.B.
Brisbane

NEW SOUTH WALES

Toohey's
Grafton

Swan
Perth

Hunter (Toohey's)
Newcastle

C.U.B.
Ballarat

Tooth's
Toohey's
Sydney

West End and Southwark
Cooper's
Adelaide

VICTORIA

C.U.B.
Geelong

C.U.B.
Courage
Melbourne

Boag
Launceston

Cascade
Hobart

TASMANIA

New Zealand Breweries
1 Auckland
2 Hamilton
3 Palmerston North
4 Wellington
5 Christchurch
6 Dunedin
7 Southland
Dominion
8 Mangatainoka
9 Greymouth
10 Otahuhu
11 Washdyke
Leopard
12 Hastings

7 9 3 2 10 1

11 6 5   4 8 12

the latter being the colloquial name throughout Australia for a small (37cl) bottle. The "Darwin Stubby" is produced for its novelty value, but the smaller bottle has the practical advantage that it is easier to keep refrigerated in these tropical climes. Large bottles or small, Darwin almost certainly consumes more beer than any other city in the world. Its citizens are said to have put back something like 230 litres of beer per head in a thirsty year, a figure which would surely shame even Munich or Prague if comparable statistics were available.

As a nation, the Australians can't quite keep up with the citizens of Darwin, but they can try. Suggestions that Australia leads the world in national beer-drinking may merit a snort of disbelief, but the average consumption does seem to increase year by year. Australia has, with some authority, been rated at least once as the world's third greatest beer-drinking nation, with a tally of nearly 145 litres per head. It is always among the top five, along with Czechoslovakia, West Germany, Belgium and Luxembourg.

High-speed drinking has been rendered unnecessary since licensing laws were relaxed during the 1950s and 1960s, but the long-distance beerman has come into his own. In some States, drinkers used to line up their schooners for the last, frantic "Six O'Clock Swill," but now bars in most parts of Australia are open from 10.0 in the morning until 10.0 in the evening or later, with the odd local variation.

The enthusiasm with which the beer-drinking Australians press their claims to the world title is matched only by their chauvinism about their nation's brews. "Best beer in the world," says a confident barman in the John O'Grady novel *Gone Troppo*, and Cyril Pearl cites this as a typical attitude. He also notes that the novel mentions beer 43 times in about 200 pages. Second to national chauvinism comes inter-State xenophobia. Pearl has the Melbourne drinker insisting on his favourite local beer . . . "Can't stand this Sydney piss." He says that such State rivalries are "the source of endless disputation," and he is scathing about their lack of foundation. It is, he argues, a myth that the average Australian drinker can even tell one beer from another, and he recommends that tiresome xenophobes should be silenced by means of a blindfold test. Pearl is confident that such a sampling would expose them for the poseurs which he believes they are.

Just such a blindfold test was carried out by the *Sydney Sun*, using an experienced wine-taster, a journalist (said to have displayed "a lifelong dedication to beer-drinking") and a "celebrity" actor. The trio sampled beers from several Australian States, and from other countries, which are available at the *Menzies Hotel*, in Sydney. The beer which emerged as favourite was Löwenbräu. Next came Carlsberg, tying with the local Resch's Dinner Ale. Then the panel named Heineken, tying with Resch's *Pilsener*. Only after these brews did three beers from the State of Victoria feature in the list. Sydney's best-selling beer, Resch's KB, came next to last. The panel, perhaps rightly, wondered whether they had had an unusually bad sample of KB, which is normally quite an agreeable beer. Nor was the test entirely fair in that it ignored the other Sydney brewery, Tooth's.

The Australian brews which are available in the United States, Britain and Asia, and which enjoy some popularity in those parts of the world, present a misleadingly narrow range of palates. Australia has nine brewing companies, which operate a couple of dozen breweries and produce more than 70 brands. Australian drinkers have no *Reinheitsgebot* to protect them, and the brewers have no craft tradition on the European scale, but the traces of German influence have not entirely vanished. Not that all the beers are bottom-fermented, despite the Australian's devotion to his *lager*. There are one or two interesting top-fermented brews, which deserve more favourable attention than they get from Australia's alleged connoisseurs.

Once, the boot was on the other foot. At the turn of the century, the principal beers of Australia were top-fermented *ales* and *stouts*, well-attenuated and strong. "There can be no two opinions as to which is to have supremacy in Australia," pronounced Alfred Ross, a brewer from New South Wales, in 1903. "The *Colonial* is a taste acquired by these colonies, and is just as distinctive and peculiar to the country as British beer, *bock* or *lager* is to those countries whose tastes have been educated and developed in the varieties named. Under present conditions, therefore, it would be a useless waste of time, energy and money to attempt to undermine the allegiance of our countrymen to a beverage that is as natural to them as *lager* is to the average citizen of the United States."

The early settlers in Australia took with them the British maritime habit of rum-drinking, and that was the first national tipple. "Like the British Navy," recounts Pearl, "New South Wales was built on rum and the lash." The first attempt to brew was made by a free settler, John Boston, soon after he arrived in Sydney in 1794. He made his malt from maize, which he described as

"Indian corn," and flavoured his brew with the leaves and stalks of the Cape gooseberry, which he mistakenly referred to as the "love apple" (an early name for the tomato).

Hops were first successfully grown in Australia by a convict called James Squire, who had been transported. When he became a free man, he set himself up as a brewer and publican, at Kissing Point (now Ryde), on the Parramatta River, not far from Sydney. When he died in 1822, the *Sydney Gazette* said that "The Patriarch of Kissing Point" had been the first man in the colony to brew beer of an excellent quality. In 1827, a brewery was established on the site where Toohey's Standard Brewery now stands. Eight years later, Tooth's first brewery was established in the city. At the turn of the century, the peak of the breweries' proliferation, there were 21 in Sydney. The Carlton brewery, in Melbourne, opened in 1864, and took over four or five other local firms just after the turn of the century. Today, Carlton and United (C.U.B.) is the biggest brewing group in Australia, with further interests in Fiji.

Lager was first brewed in Australia by two Germans, who founded the Gambrinus brewery in Melbourne in 1885. Soon afterwards, the Foster brothers, from New York, started a second *lager* brewery, giving birth to Australia's most famous beer-brand. Castlemaine, of Brisbane, started brewing *lager* in 1889.

Today, 60 per cent of Australian hops come from Tasmania, and 40 per cent from Victoria, where they are grown in the Ovens and King Valley areas. Several states grow malt-

The glass·structure

ing barley, though Tasmania is again a major producer. The island also has the brewing company with the longest unbroken history of operation in Australia: the Cascade Brewery. Streams which cascade down Mount Wellington originally supplied not only the water for brewing, but also the power for the plant. They also provided a name for the district of Hobart where the brewery is to be found. The Cascade Brewery was built in 1824, and nearly a century later the company bought Boag's Brewery, in Launceston, at the other end of the island.

Both breweries produce bottom-fermented beers which have a characteristic pale-amber colour. Cascade's Red and Blue Label brands are dry beers, with an alcohol content by weight of 3·92 per cent. The Green Label brand is stronger and more bitter, at 4·56. Cascade's malty *stout* has an alcohol percentage of 5·60, while Boag's has 4·36. Boag's has a dry Red Label beer (4·11) and a more bitter Blue Label (4.18). In common with some of their competitors, the two Tasmanian breweries pasteurize only their bottled and canned beers.

Most Australian brewers produce a wide range of brands, though it is quite true that the differences between a company's various beers may be rather subtle. The country's brewers also play astonishingly fast and loose with terminology. "*Ale*" may occasionally mean a top-fermented beer, as the name suggests, but it far more often means a *lager*. A "*bitter*" is also most likely to be a *lager*, though one with an ostensibly high hopping rate. "*Draught*" may be a brew which was originally served on tap only, but which is now also available in the can or bottle.

A stream which cascades down Mount Wellington, on the island of Tasmania, also decorates the local Blue Label beer. Tasmania provides a relatively small local market for its two breweries, but it does offer them fine hops and barley close at hand. Between them, they use most of the island's malting barley.

The sizes of glasses in which beer can legally be served vary bewilderingly in Australia. So do the names by which they are known. Although fashions change, and idiosyncrasies vanish, drinkers still "shout" some odd-sounding orders, and the terminology is even more confusing when State-lines are crossed:—

Queensland: The most popular measures are a Small Beer (five ounces) or simply a Beer (eight ounces). A Pot is ten ounces.
New South Wales: There exist small measures like the Pony (five ounces) or the Glass (seven), but the businessman's Middy (ten) and the working man's Schooner (15) are more popular. The State also has a Pint (20).
Victoria: The Small Glass, or Pony, has four ounces in this State, but a Glass (seven) or a Pot (ten) are more widely ordered.
Tasmania: Glasses are known simply by their size, in ounces. Tasmania has a Four, a Six, an Eight, and a Ten.
South Australia: A six-ounce glass is known as a Butcher, and the Schooner in this State has nine ounces. There is also a rare measure called the Reputed Pint, which has 15.
Western Australia: The Pony is four

ounces, but more popular measures are the Glass (five) and Middy (seven). The Pot can be 10, 15 or 20.

In some places, glasses are also known by their shapes: "Ridged," "Super," "Tavern," and the charming "Lady's Waist," for example. New South Wales pioneered, by legislation, the practice of sterilizing glasses after use. In practice, this means that the drinker cannot have his glass topped up. He must have a fresh glass.

In bars, pubs and clubs, beer is frequently served at ferociously cold temperatures, often as low as 36°F (2·2°C). This is much too cold if the taste of the beer is to be appreciated, but it might be safer not to argue with an Australian pub-keeper. Cyril Pearl was surely succumbing to hyperbole when he damned all pub-keepers as being surly and contemptuous of their customers, but Australian barmaids can certainly be tough characters, as their job demands of them. Australian brewers usually recommend that their beers should be served at 42°F (5·6°C), but Pearl is sceptical as to whether the customers appreciate this.

If a beer were served at a more flavoursome temperature, he frets, an Australian would probably shave in it.

South Australia

THE TRUE BEER enthusiast will brook no argument as to which is Australia's most interesting brewery. This accolade goes, beyond doubt, to the Adelaide firm of Cooper and Sons.

Cooper's is the only family-run company left in Australian brewing, but its real claim to fame is its naturally-conditioned, top-fermented Sparkling Ale. Only the beer's name is inappropriate, since its heavily yeasty sediment gives it a cloudy appearance. Connoisseurs like their Cooper's to look yeasty, though this characteristic has alienated many less discerning Australian drinkers, weaned on bright *lagers*. Cooper's Sparkling Ale is fermented and conditioned in wooden casks, has a good hop character, and an alcoholic content of 4·25 by weight. It is available only in the bottle – unpasteurized, of course – with its characteristic red label. A lower gravity (3·80) Light Dinner Ale is brewed in the same way, and identified by its green label. A third naturally-conditioned beer produced by the same process is Cooper's sweetish Extra Stout, with the substantial alcohol content of 5·50 per cent by weight. The brewery points out in its advertising that some Australian drinkers enjoy a "Black and Tan," or add a little less beer in order to make a "Black Dash." *Stout* with lemonade is known as a "Porter Gaff," and Cooper's suggests that its dark brew makes a fine "Black Velvet."

Cooper's adds some welcome colour to Australia's brewing industry, and does so in several different ways. Another delightful Cooper habit is the annual *Schützenfest* beer, produced for the annual carnival held by the German Club of South Australia. Each year, a different style of brew is produced for the shooting festival, and a successful *Schützenfest* may be left in production. It is a charming way in which to experiment with a new brand, though it might not meet with the approval of slide-ruled marketing men. The 1974 *Schützenfest* beer was Big Barrel Lager, a sweetish, copper-coloured brew which is now in regular production. Big Barrel, the drier Gold Crown, and DB (Diet Beer) are all bottom-fermented and pasteurized brews of 3·80 per cent alcohol by weight. Not only does Cooper's win praise for its top-fermented *ales*, its Gold Crown has also been described as Australia's best bottom-fermented brew.

Yorkshireman Thomas Cooper founded the firm after emigrating to Australia in 1862, and it is still managed by his family. In its centenary year, a 25 per cent stake was bought by the South Australian Brewing Company, and in 1965 Cooper's was incorporated as a public company. The South Australian Brewing Company, also publicly quoted, is Adelaide's only other brewer. It has plants in the Southwark and West End districts of the city, brews pasteurized bottom-fermented beers, and uses both local names for some of its brands. The Southwark beer is slightly more bitter than the West End brew; Premium is a pleasant appetizer, with an alcohol percentage of 3·45; *Pilsener*, with the unusually low alcohol content of 2·50, is regarded as a dinner beer; and a darker Export is made for the market formerly served by the now-defunct Broken Hill brewery.

The yeasty swell of a top-fermented ale in the wooden cask. Cooper's (left) is the brewery that time left behind, producing misunderstood glories in a nation which barely remembers its pre-lager traditions. Cooper's shares its market with the West End and Southwark breweries.

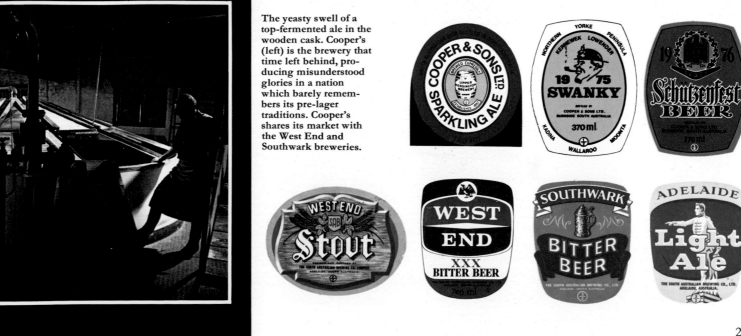

Victoria

THE CLICHÉ of the perpetually-thirsty Australian is completed by his endless quest for one particular beer . . . "an ice-cold Fosters." This is probably the Australian beer which is best known elsewhere in the world. Fosters is just one brand among about ten *lager*-type beers which are produced in Victoria by C.U.B., in breweries at Carlton, East Melbourne, Abbotsford, Geelong and Ballarat.

Five of the brands share the same alcoholic strength, 3·90 per cent by weight, and are sometimes supposed to be identical. This is not the case, though the differences are subtle. Foster's is characterized by its malty full body, sweetish taste, and uncompromisingly pale colour. Carlton Crown Lager is very similar, but Abbots Lager (named after Abbotsford, where it is brewed) has a more evenly-balanced palate. Despite its name, Victoria Bitter is a *lager* beer, rather light in flavour, and fractionally darker in colour. Melbourne Bitter is also a *lager*, but its palate is slightly truer to its name.

The C.U.B. range in Victoria also includes three *lager* beers with more pronounced

Bertie's bitter experience

Ballarat Bertie first appeared on the labels of his local beer in 1926. Even after the Ballarat Brewery was taken over by C.U.B. in 1958, he stayed put. Then, in 1972, Bertie was removed as part of a corporate-image exercise. Such was the outcry that he was sneaked back within two months . . .

differences in their palates. There is a very full-bodied and full-flavoured Malt Ale (3·82); an agreeably dry diet beer (Dietale); and a crisp, hoppy, highly-carbonated *Pilsener*. Running right down the middle of the range is the group's basic beer, Carlton Draught (3·97), which is low on malt, well-fermented, with a medium bitterness, and a slightly fuller colour than the rest. Double and Invalid Stouts are also listed among the company's products, though they are barely promoted.

Only two new brewing companies have started business in Victoria during this century, and one of them failed. The second, which appears to be succeeding, is Courage Australia. This company is partly owned by the British brewers of the same name, but another major stake is held by Australian Allied Manufacturing and Trading Industries Limited, and about 25 per cent of the shares are quoted on the stock exchange. Courage Australia was launched in 1966, after exten-

Six Clydesdale horses are still kept by C.U.B. in the brewery's own stables. The horses have names like "Vic" (Victoria) and "Foster," after the company's beers. During the summer, a team can be seen once a week drawing a dray through the streets of Melbourne. Thus they maintain a tradition, and promote the beer, but their prime job is to appear at ceremonial events. The team above was pulling a float at Melbourne's annual "Moomba" procession, held on Labour Day weekend. The picture on the right was probably taken in the 1930s.

sive surveys of the market. Brewing started, near Melbourne, in 1968.

Some interesting beers are produced by Australia's newest brewing company, as well they might be, considering the weight of the long-established competition. One of Courage's brews tries to emulate the original *Colonial* style, though it is produced by bottom-fermentation. Old Colonial has the reddish colour of some English *pale ales*. It is full-bodied and well matured, with a palate rather on the sweet side, though this is mitigated somewhat by Australian serving temperatures. The drier and slightly fruity Courage Draught allegedly aims at a *Dortmunder* palate, though the folk of that German city might find this a puzzling claim to be made on behalf of such a beer. Likewise the aspirations of Crest Lager to a *Pilsener* palate are rather undermined by its modest hopping rate. For all the terminological inexactitudes, these are agreeable beers, all with an alcohol content of 3·90 by weight. A higher gravity (4·40) *lager*, fairly dry and even slightly sharp, has the confusingly English-sounding name of Tankard Bitter.

Miner Sam Griffin used to walk into an hotel at Walsh's Creek, Victoria, every day at 11.00 a.m., and demand a glass of Carlton. A young artist painted him, and the brewery later bought the portrait for use on posters. In Australia at least, Courage can offer no such traditions . . . despite its "Tankard" and its 1770 ale.

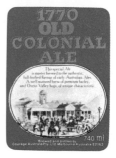

New South Wales

COAL-MINERS ALWAYS were reputed to have a hearty taste in beers, and the local colliers are credited with having maintained the popularity of the deep-brown, top-fermented *ale* produced at the Hunter brewery in Newcastle, New South Wales. Hunter Ale, a well-attenuated but fruity beer with an alcohol content of 3·41 per cent by weight, also appears as Toohey's Old. The Hunter brewery is owned by Toohey's, of Sydney, who have a further plant at Grafton, New South Wales. Another dark beer, closer to bronze in colour, is produced by Toohey's under the name of Flag Ale (3·54). The flag concerned fluttered above the original Standard Brewery in Sydney.

In addition to these dark beers, Toohey's brews no less than three *stouts*. These include a relatively hoppy *sweet stout* under the Miller's label (Miller's was acquired in 1967), a medium Oatmeal Stout, and Guinness.

Toohey's produces a golden-coloured sweetish *lager*-type beer under the name New Special Draught (3·48), and a sweet-but-hoppy *Pilsener* (3·53). The group's premium product is the full-bodied Stag Lager (3·92). There are also a series of malty-but-dry *lagers* under the Miller's label, including a diabetic beer called Hi-Lo. These all have an alcohol content in the region of 3·65 per cent by weight.

"*Old ale*" is said to have been so designated by the drinking public when the new bottom-fermentation beers began to gain popularity. The "old" beer produced by Tooth's, the other Sydney brewing company, is better known as XXX ("Three-'x'"). This has an alcohol content by weight of 3·84 per cent. Tooth's also produces a bitter Sheaf Stout and a pale, hoppy *lager* of about 3·90 per cent which is known as D.A. (Dinner Ale). The company has a *lager*-type Special New on

draught at 3·69 per cent, and its regular *lager* on draught has an alcohol content of 3·94 per cent.

Tooth's has owned the Resch's brand since 1929, and produces some very agreeable hoppy *lagers* under this name. The most popular brand, KB (alcohol content 3·76 per cent), is named after the company's Kent Brewery. The firm's founder, John Tooth, came from the English hop-growing county of Kent in the 1830s. The Kentish White Horse emblem is still used as a symbol by the company. Tooth's is a very tradition-conscious company, and its literature still recalls that the White Horse of Kent was derived from the battle standard of two Saxon Chiefs, Hengist (stallion) and Horsa (horse), who invaded Britain more than 1400 years ago. The White Horse has to share its Australian home with a rather Scottish-looking Red Lion, the original symbol of Resch's beers.

Advertisements dating back to the 1930s have now become collector's pieces. "K.B." is still going strong among Tooth's considerable range of products, and is Sydney's best-selling beer. There is a period feeling, too, about some of Australia's drinking places. The stylish balconies of the Sir William Wallace are at Balmain, New South Wales.

Queensland

SPORTING DRINKERS who pass through Brisbane will want to toast an historic racehorse whose memory is still held dear in that city. The appropriate drink for this occasion is a glass of Carbine, a *bitter stout* which was named after the aforesaid nag. Carbine is one of the very drinkable brews prepared by the local firm of Castlemaine Perkins.

By Australian standards, Queensland's principal brewing company produces only a small range of beers, but it has made some inventive contributions to the industry in the matter of brand-names. Carbine is named after an animal of astonishing achievements. The horse was bred in New Zealand, but raced mainly in Australia, winning 33 times out of 43 starts, and being placed in all but one of its outings (in which race it went lame). Carbine won the 1890 Melbourne Cup in the then record time of three minutes, 28·25 seconds, with possibly the heaviest winning weight. Sixty thousand Australian dollars were bet on the horse, and this stake was not beaten for 25 years. Carbine was sold to the Duke of Portland for stud at a price of £26,000, and three generations of his stock won the Derby in England during the 1920s.

Regrettably, some of the other colourful names used by Castlemaine Perkins have vanished over the years. Nurse Stout has been extinguished, and Emerald Stout shines

The range of beers brewed in Queensland by C.U.B. includes a civically-named Brisbane Bitter, a light lager aimed at the young market. The label shows the city's Story Bridge, a local landmark.

no more. Boar Stout was beaten out of sight by the horse. All that remains is Mr Fourex, personification of Castlemaine's full-bodied XXXX Bitter Ale, a golden-coloured *lager* of 3·90 per cent by weight, which is Brisbane's most popular brew.

The city also has a C.U.B. brewery producing a full range of beers (including, oddly, Melbourne Bitter). Further North, C.U.B. has another brewery in Queensland, at Cairns. This plant produces Cairns Bitter Ale and NQ (North Queensland) Lager to meet tropical tastes North of Capricorn.

The People's Favourite

Western Australia

What Queensland may lack in the variety of its beers, it makes up in the personal touch. Everyone in Brisbane knows Mr Fourex, symbol of the home-town brewery's principal product, and it would be a shame if they forgot Carbine the horse.

On November 5, 1890, the "Melbourne Age" newspaper published the impression below, with a report which stretched for many columns. "Never in the history of the Australian turf," said the newspaper, "has there been such a demonstration as that which marked Carbine's phenomenal victory." Such was the enthusiasm of the spectators that the police had to clear the course. Carbine was, said "The Age," the "people's favourite"... "the greatest horse that has ever been seen in Australasia." There were tributes to the man who brought Carbine to Australia, a Mr D. O'Brien, and to the horse's owner, "an honourable, straight-going sportsman."

Perhaps it is Carbine's ill-luck to be remembered in a style of brew which commands only a minority market, but it would be sad if such a winner were in the future to be trodden underfoot by beers with less colour, individualism and character. It is the unusual which requires preservation, not the commonplace.

THE BLACK SWAN symbol of Western Australia is familiar in many other parts of the world for its appearance on beer cans. The Swan Brewery Company of Perth, which was incorporated in 1887, has for many years been a vigorous exporter. Swan is the only brewing company in Western Australia. Apart from the well-known Swan Lager, Swan Draught, and the premium Swan Special Bond, the company pays its respects to the State's other indigenous bird with Emu Export Lager. All of these beers have an alcohol content of 3·85 per cent by weight. Emu Bitter is a drier *lager*, with an alcohol content of 3·60. The Emu brewery, with a history dating back to 1837, is now the company's main plant. The Swan brewery still exists, but is primarily used for fermentation and storage. The company has another brewery in the State, at Kalgoorlie, brewing a *stout* and a *lager* under the name of Hannan's.

Swan is a diversified company, with extensive involvements not only in the drinks and hotels industries, but also in radio and television. Its beers are also produced in association with the San Miguel company at the former Territory United Brewery of Papua New Guinea.

When the engraving below of the Swan brewery was made in the late nineteenth century, the company had 36 competitors within the State. Today, it has none. Even the Emu belongs to the Swan.

Swan also owns Hannan's . . . the "K" is for Kalgoorlie. The starry Swan and the San Miguel are both products of the joint brewery in Port Moresby. Swan also has a joint brewery with C.U.B. in Darwin.

New Zealand

CAPTAIN COOK BREWED New Zealand's first beer, in 1773. He had landed at Dusky Sound, which is at the South-Western corner of New Zealand's South Island. One of the first things he did upon landing was to "make a strong decoction of the small branches of the spruce and tea plants by boiling them for three or four hours." Then, his journal records, he added molasses, and fermented the mixture with yeast. After a few days, he had what he considered to be a drinkable beer. The brew may sound less than appetizing, but it helped prevent scurvy among his crew. This achievement was recognized in England by the award of the Royal Society's gold medal.

A healthy tradition of beer-drinking was thus implanted by the explorer, himself from the great beer-drinking county of Yorkshire, long before the islands were settled. Beer-drinking has since grown to great proportions in New Zealand, but not without a titanic and colourful struggle. The inheritors of Cook's thirst have helped their country into a place among the world's top half-dozen beer-drinking nations (ahead of Denmark, Ireland and Britain), but there are still a handful of "dry" areas dating back to the Prohibition era.

Temperance, too, came remarkably early. There was a Temperance Society in 1835, even though settlement of the islands did not begin in earnest until after 1840. Ships were searched by temperance zealots, rum dumped in the sea, muskets loosed, people tarred-and-feathered, but the establishment of breweries could not be stopped. In less than 50 years, 89 breweries were set up, the majority on the South Island, where gold-diggers helped boost demand. The ravages of competition and recession quickly reduced their numbers, and there were only a dozen substantial breweries at the beginning of the twentieth century. Then ten of them joined hands, the

As early as 1907, the Captain Cook Brewery, in Auckland, introduced beer which was filtered, pasteurized, and artificially carbonated. "Modernization" is a constant theme.

better to fight Prohibition pressures. The resultant company, New Zealand Breweries, remains one of the country's three brewing groups. The shape of today's brewing industry was, in this way, determined by the temperance movement.

Women were to the forefront of Prohibitionist agitation to such an extent that brewers and publicans became leading opponents of universal suffrage. The Women's Christian Temperance Movement was an astonishingly powerful voice in the 1890s, and the future of the brewing industry was in the balance until the late 1920s. Prohibitionists persuaded the Government to introduce regular polls, every three years, on licensing laws. These polls operated on a local basis. Between 1894 and 1910, no new liquor licences were issued, and the number of existent licences was reduced by 25 per cent, rendering "dry" not only country districts but also some main urban areas. The issue echoed the same "Local Veto" or "Local Option" question which had been debated in Britain for half a century. In the Mother Country, the measure was finally passed by the House of Commons only to be thrown out by the Lords. A near escape. In New Zealand, immigrants wanted to build a new society without the alcoholic squalor which had accompanied the explosive growth of Britain's industrial cities. As in Britain, the temperance movement was strongly Protestant, and not without Scottish and Welsh influence.

Prohibition won the support of 49 per cent of the population in the 1914 poll, and after the First World War, temperance campaigners persuaded the Government to hold a "once and for all" vote. The result, when votes were first counted, indicated that the liquor trade would have to be completely dismantled. Then the soldiers' votes came in, and the final tally for "continuance" was 51 per cent. Soldiers had voted four-to-one in favour of drink.

Beer won, but it was a Pyrrhic victory. With ten of the country's 12 brewers now concentrated into one group, the options for the discriminating drinker had been drastically curtailed. The brewers had indulged in

some shady lobbying tactics during their struggle against temperance, and there have been obsessively defensive streaks in the industry ever since. By the same token, the drinking public – who still have only three brewing groups from which to choose – continue to view the "beer barons" with some suspicion.

New Zealand's original *Colonial* beers were very similar in colour and palate to those of Britain, more so than the Australian brews, according to a report from that country in 1900. "We must give the New Zealanders credit for producing a first class bottled *ale*," wrote August J. Metzler, of Sydney's Scientific Station for Brewing. He went on to discuss "taste, smell and general wholesomeness." He talked about beer being stored in the cask for six or eight months before being put on sale for draught consumption, or being bottled. The beers were apparently very malty. Since they were bottled without finings, they were left for an additional four months or so to ferment further, and they were still slightly hazy.

Lager was first brewed in the same year. A Swiss brewer called Conrad Breutsch was brought to New Zealand for this purpose by Moss Davis, proprietor of the Captain Cook brewery. Whether Captain Cook himself would have approved of such foreign influences is open to doubt. In fact, the brewery

The firm of Staples
(left), in Wellington,
was merged into the
New Zealand Breweries
group in 1923, along
with Captain Cook and
eight other companies.
A wide variety of brand-
names (below) is used
by the country's three
brewing groups.

was not named directly after the explorer, but after the Captain Cook Inn.

Today's beers offer a curious compromise. Many of them, especially when served on draught, have the translucent copper colour of traditional *ale*, but they are produced by bottom-fermentation. The colour is largely achieved by the use of caramel.

The Captain Cook Brewery, in Auckland, became part of New Zealand Breweries. So did the same city's Lion Brewery, the name of which was given new life when New Zealand Breweries launched a "national" brand, in full-blown Madison Avenue style, in 1972. Lion was given the total marketing treatment, its corporate style emblazoned on everything from bar-mountings to trucks, and sportsmen were used to promote the beer. Older brand-names, often with local associations, have nonetheless stayed in use. New Zealand Breweries has plants on the North Island at Auckland, Hamilton, Palmerston North and Wellington. On the South Island, its plants are at Christchurch and Dunedin, and in Southland.

Lion Brown and Lion Red are sweet, copper-coloured beers, with an original gravity of 1036. They have a light palate, are highly carbonated, and are served very cold (1–3°C; 33·8–37·4°F). These characteristics are said to have been arrived at after extensive test-marketing. There is also a more hoppy and stronger (1045) golden-coloured version called Lion Super. The company's pride of Lions is completed by a *Mild* and a *sweet Double Stout* (both 1036) under the same name. Similar brands are marketed under the Red

Band name, originally a Wellington favourite (Red Band Export is one of the drier brands in the group's range, along with Rheineck), and the Speight's name in Dunedin. James Speight was an immigrant from Yorkshire who started brewing in 1876. A beer known as Bavarian (1036, sweet, copper-coloured) was originally a local product from the group's Christchurch brewery, but has achieved considerable national popularity. Ward's is a similar beer, also originating from Christchurch. Waikato Draught (1039, hoppy, copper-coloured) and Waikato 4X (1036, hoppy, copper-coloured) are from the group's brewery in Hamilton. The Bitter Beer produced in Southland is, in fact, sweet. So is the group's "*Pilsner.*" New Zealand Breweries' strongest beer is Steinlager, a full-bodied and well-balanced golden-coloured brew with an original gravity of 1052.

New Zealand Breweries has 60 per cent of the market, plus a share in the ownership of the country's smallest and oldest brewing company, Leopard, which is run quite independently in Hastings. The joint owners of Leopard are Heineken and Malayan Breweries.

Like Australia, New Zealand used to have a "Six O'Clock Swill." (Since a referendum in 1967, hours have been, in general, 11.00 am to 10.00 pm). The "Six O'Clock Swill" was likely to take place in bare, crowded public bars, which were among New Zealand's main drinking-places at that time. Perhaps because the drinking was fast and mechanical, these were cynically known in the trade as "engine-rooms." The tiny Leopard Brewery, with no

chain of tied houses, turned its attention in other directions – towards the restaurant and take-home trade, and even towards exports. It has thus nurtured a more "sophisticated" image. Leopard was the first brewery to introduce canned beer in New Zealand, and the first to produce a low-cal brew. Half of its brands (Export, DeLuxe, Leopard Lager) have original gravities of 1045; so does the darker "Strong;" but Continental Lager, the darker Premium Draught, Black Velvet (Sweet Stout) and LoCal have original gravities of 1036. Leopard beers are exported to Samoa, the Cook Islands, Tonga, Fiji, Norfolk Island, the New Hebrides . . . and to Britain and North America. The links with Heineken (and, through Heineken, with Whitbread) are being used to further this export trade. The brewery uses yeast supplied by Heineken, and brews by batch-fermentation, with a six-week lagering period. Both of the other brewing groups use continuous fermentation.

The third group, with 34 per cent of the market, is Dominion Breweries. This group, often known as "DB," is the most conservative of the three, and best typifies the defensive attitudes which are a legacy of the temperance era. It has fewer brands than New Zealand Breweries, and its best-selling beer is Dominion Bitter. Other brands include Waitemata, Diploma, and Tennents, made under licence from the Scottish brewery. Dominion has four breweries, and has acquired and closed another three.

Dominion is also "credited" with having invented continuous fermentation.

Asia

Over it all had brooded thirst, thirst for a warmish bottle of Tiger Beer. Or Anchor. Or Carlsberg.

from *Time for a Tiger*, by Anthony Burgess

THE TIGER OF SINGAPORE; the *Singha* lion-legend of Thailand, and the red-tongued wolf; the *Kirin* dragon-horse of Japan; the Flying Horse of Bangalore; the Golden Eagle of Himalayan India; the Bulldog of Malaysia, and the Cat of Hongkong . . . a magic menagerie of animal life haunts the coffee-houses, girlie bars, nightclubs, men's hairdressing salons and massage parlours of the East.

Tiger is the most famous creature in the menagerie. *Time for a Tiger*, by Anthony Burgess, may have helped its prowling progress, but the beer was of some assistance to the author, too. *Time for a Tiger* had been an advertising slogan for the beer since 1946, and Burgess sought the permission of the management before he used it as the title for his book. The beer permeates the pages of the *Time for a Tiger* trilogy. Tiger was the brew not only of Burgess's Singapore, but also of Maugham's. In Colonial days, it was the thirst-quencher of the British Armed Forces much as "33" became decades later for the American troops in Vietnam. And Tiger is still going strong.

The famous brew is produced not only in Singapore, but also in Kuala Lumpur, Malaysia. It is a *Pilsener*-type beer, with an alcohol content of four per cent by weight. While Tiger has an international reputation, it is outsold on its home territory by Anchor Beer, a product of the same two breweries. Anchor is of the same strength, but less well-hopped. In tiny Singapore, where the handling of the beers can easily be monitored, the draught versions of both beers are served without having been pasteurized.

Tiger and Co are in Singapore by accident. The breweries were established after Heineken had failed to reach agreement with the Dutch Colonial Government of Java in 1929 to set up there. Heineken turned its attentions to Singapore, and established Malayan Breweries in association with the local soft-drink firm of Fraser and Neave.

Carlsberg is also brewed locally in Malaysia, where the Danish group has an associate company. The brewery produces a *Pilsener*-type Carlsberg Green Label, with a similar gravity to that of the other local beers, and the much stronger Carlsberg Special (about 6·6 per cent alcohol by weight).

Gold Harp Light Special, an all-malt brew of some quality, is another local beer. This brew was launched in 1975 to replace Gold Harp Lager Beer. Neither of these cumber-

some names survived for long over the bar, where the beer is known simply as "Goldie." By whatever name, Gold Harp is brewed by an associate company of Guinness. The locally-brewed Guinness itself is of the distinctive and splendid style which the company knows as "Foreign Extra Stout." This is a high-gravity beer with an alcohol content of at least 6·25 per cent by weight. It is also one of the world's most unusual beers, combining a powerful body and dry roasted-malt palate with a sharp acidity. Its full body ensures its local reputation as a beer which will build health and vitality, while its acidity is most quenching. All Guinness in South-East Asia is of the Foreign Extra Stout style.

The Chinese population of this region are especially keen beer-drinkers, and demand rises during periods like the Eighth Moon

(August/September) and the New Year (January/February). *Stout* is believed to have a healthy, and perhaps aphrodisiac, effect. It is also thought to be beneficial to the complexion, and is sometimes poured into a newly-born baby's bath for this reason. According to yin-and-yang theory, *stout* is "heaty," while *lager* is "cooling."

Bitter stout has been popular in this part of the world since it was first imported from Dublin, via Liverpool, in the late 1800s. Different shippers used to label the bottles with their own signs, usually animals. In Singapore, Guinness was identified by a Wolf's Head, sometimes known as "the Red-Tongued Dog." In peninsular Malaya, there

were Bulldog and Dog's Head brands, competing with each other. Years later, when Guinness tried to resolve this dogfight, peace was impeded by fierce brand-loyalties. Guinness settled for gradualism. The Bulldog's stance was subtly altered, in successive re-drawings, until only its head was visible.

The Wolf's Head is also used in Thailand, where it made a play on words with the name of the original shippers. They were called Blood, Wolfe and Company. The red-tongued creature on the Thai Guinness bottle is often referred to as the Blood Wolf. Guinness Foreign Extra Stout ("F.E.S.," for short) is produced in Thailand under contract by the local Amarit Brewery. The same brewery produces a well-hopped draught beer with a *Pilsener*-style palate, and 4·5 per cent alcohol by weight, called Krating. It also brews a 4·8 per cent Amarit Lager. A bigger market share in Thailand is held by the Boon Rawd brewery, which produces only Singha Lager (also about 4·8), named after the elegant but fearsome Lion-like creature of local mythology. Another cat, of more domestic proportions, is used by Guinness on the labels for the F.E.S. which is exported from Dublin to Hongkong and the Philippines, and brewed locally in Indonesia.

The Philippines is the home of the world's major brewing groups, San Miguel. This group has three breweries in the Philippines, one in Hongkong and one in Papua New Guinea. Outside of Asia, "San Mig" is better known for its huge sales in Spain, where it

has three breweries. The Philippines is the headquarters, and Spain the offshoot; the Colonial roles have been reversed. San Miguel produces the same *lager* in all of its markets: a *Pilsener*-style beer of 13 degrees Balling, 4·3 alcohol content by weight, 5·4 by volume. It has also been known to produce the odd drop of *Münchener*-style *cerveza negra*, though the continued existence of this beer is in some doubt. In the mid 1970s, a stronger *lager* called Selecta XV was launched in Spain. The numerals were derived from the beer's strength: 15 degrees Balling, which in this instance provides an alcohol content by weight of 5·1 and by volume of 6·4. San Miguel started brewing in 1890, in Manila, and is now a huge conglomerate, producing soft drinks, dairy products and packaging materials, and trading in commodities.

Dutch colonial links are still evident in Indonesia, where Heineken eventually did establish an associate company in Java. The brewery produces a *Pilsener*-style Heineken beer of conventional strength, and a Bintang Lager, of the same gravity. The Dutch link also persists in the Anker beer, from Djakarta ("brewed in co-operation with Breda Breweries"). Since Breda is now part of the British group Allied Breweries, it comes as no surprise that Skol, too, is brewed in Djakarta. The same brewery also produces a *stout*. A far-flung outpost survives even for the "33" beer of South-East Asia. The Paris-based group better known as Brasseries de l'Indochine translates into Sumatra's Brasseries de l'Indonésie, producing "33" Export (12·8 degrees Balling), Galion Pilsener (12·6) and Baris Lager (12·0).

My Goodness...!

Guinness owes its remarkable Eastern menagerie to the imaginations of rival shippers who originally handled the product. Messrs Blood and Woolfe were metamorphosed into a red-tongued creature of questionable ancestry. The blood-wolf of Thailand became the red-tongued dog of Singapore. An altogether more British canine roams peninsular Malaya. The dog's body and its head were in deadly rivalry for some years (far right), but eventually a happy medium was devised. The cat of Hongkong seems to present fewer problems. Such simple, colourful devices make good sense in multi-lingual countries, but an animal neck-label may be accompanied by a more explicit description of the contents. The label in the bottom row informs the consumer that, "this stout can make one feel lively, and is good for the blood. It could increase the appetite, and is good for the digestive system. It is especially good for those who feel weak." The Malayan on the right clearly agrees.

Japan

Beer, Peking-style

The brewery above is in Peking, but every major city in the People's Republic has its own local beer-brands. All of the breweries produce Pilsener-style beers, and some of them also have porters. Beer is a popular drink in China, and some very acceptable brews are produced. Only Tsingtao is widely available in the West.

THE WORLD'S BIGGEST BREWER, and by no means the least interesting, may one day be Kirin, part of Japan's Mitsubishi conglomerate. Figures vary from year to year, but Kirin produces about 23 million hectolitres per annum. This places the Japanese brewery clearly ahead of Heineken, and up with the top two or three American giants. Kirin has nine breweries in different parts of Japan, but no production elsewhere in the world. It exports widely, especially in Asia and the United States, but in relatively modest volume. Only Japan's anti-monopoly legislation has inhibited the further growth of the company, which already has 60 per cent of local sales. Both the total market, and demand for Kirin's products, continue to grow. Nor is Kirin without local competition. There are four other major brewing groups in Japan, and a lone minnow in Okinawa, with 25 breweries between them. After two thousand years of *sake* rice wine, the Japanese have taken to beer with almost the same enthusiasm which they are well known to show for whisky.

Japan's principal beer-style is a *lager* which is only very lightly hopped. At least one brewery regards as a different type its even milder and lighter "draft." Like Australian "draughts" this beer is also available in the bottle and the can. A distinctive brew known as Black Beer is also produced, and promoted as being "the choice of the sophisticated drinker." Black Beer is not dissimilar from the traditional *Münchener*, but very marginally stronger, with an alcohol content of five per cent by volume. Its palate tends to sweetness, but only slightly so. Its colour, derived from caramel and roasted malts, is rather less than black. *Bitter* and *medium stouts* are also popular. Guinness is the biggest-selling imported beer (a high-gravity Export version rather than F.E.S.), followed by Löwenbräu, Heineken and Tuborg. The Japanese brewers, in descending order of size, are Kirin, Sapporo, Asahi and Suntory.

Kirin produces a *lager* beer with an alcohol content of 4·5 per cent by volume, which is available unpasteurized on draught; a Black Beer; a very dark *medium-bitter stout*; and a premium *lager* called Mein Bräu of a respectable 6·4 per cent.

The huge beer industry of Japan has its roots in an experimental brewery started by the American firm of Wiegand and Copeland at Yokohama in 1869. Soon afterwards, the Japanese Government sent a researcher to Germany in search of technical knowhow, with a view to establishing a local brewing industry, and the Copeland operation subsequently passed to Japanese management,

Even in China, imperial influences helped create a beer-brewing industry. When the Germans enjoyed a colonial "concession" in Shantung, they established a brewery at Tsingtao. Despite the vicissitudes of history, brewing prospers at Tsingtao. The brewery's light, dry *Pilsener*-type beer is well-known outside the People's Republic, being notably popular in Hongkong, and is also exported to the West. A Chinese magazine article described the local origins of Tsingtao beer in the following idyllic terms:

"Laoshan is a celebrated beauty spot near the lovely coastal city of Tsingtao. Here, picturesque mountains, luxuriant with green foliage and flowers, loom up in fascinating view. Flying waterfalls and bubbling springs

and brooks add charm to many a mountain cranny. Tsingtao beer is brewed from the sweet springwater of Laoshan . . . issuing from a stratum of granite . . . limpid and soft. It has a remarkably refreshing and delicious taste. A classical Chinese proverb says that advantageous natural conditions make for excellent products, but this is not entirely so. Excellent flavour and taste depend primarily on the creative labour of the working people. This is true of Tsingtao beer."

The magazine also pointed out that, since the post-Revolution blockade cut off supplies, the Chinese had started to grow their own hops, as well as using their own barley. China also exports Tsingtao Porter, and Snowflake and Yu Chuan beers.

Once their enthusiasm has been fired, the Japanese are not given to half-measures. As with whisky, so with beer. Among several different drinking places which flourish in Japan, the rooftop beer-garden enjoys great popularity.

The graphic art of the brewer

Brewers the world over have made lavish contributions to graphic art. Many of them have foolishly abandoned such glories in favour of bolder yet less distinctive designs. The Japanese remain steadfast.

It would be sad if the splendour of Sapporo or the sacred symbol of Kirin were to be extinguished in the name of corporate identity. A fine label cannot save an indifferent brew, but it can enhance a good one.

taking the name of Kirin in 1888.

The Kirin is a mythical creature, half horse, half dragon, which features in a legend more than 2,500 years old. One evening, the story says, a Chinese woman called En Chen Tsai was strolling in her garden when she was confronted by the creature. "The Kirin enveloped her in its sacred breath. They both became attached to each other, and two nights passed before the Kirin reluctantly disappeared." Less than a year after this mysterious encounter, En Chen Tsai gave birth to Confucious. Thereafter, whenever a Chinese Saint was born, legend maintains, the mother had previously been visited by the Kirin. Thus the creature is regarded as the harbinger of happy and festive events, especially when it arrives with a beer.

The history of brewing in Japan may be relatively short, but it is no less subject to contention for that. Kirin claims to be Japan's oldest brewer, but so does Sapporo, with at least equal determination. It is really a question of interpretation. According to Sapporo, the idea of brewing in Japan first arose when the United States paid its celebrated Naval visit to Japan in 1853, with a view to opening up trade with the country. A Japanese who was an "ardent student of all things foreign" visited one of the smoky "Black Ships" commanded by the legendary Commodore Perry, and tasted a glass of beer while he was aboard. The same person later discovered a Dutch textbook on brewing, which he was able to translate, and he produced some beer for his own consumption. He is credited with having first created interest in beer in Japan. Just over 20 years later, a Government mission which had been deputed to develop

The beers and brewing towns of Asia

Almost every capital city in Asia has its own brewery, and some have more than one. The levels shown here are merely a selection, a sample from the vast number of beers which are available across this great continent. Each label is captioned with its city and brewery of origin. The world-famous names in Asian beer come from the nations of the Pacific and the South China Sea, but there are also brewing industries in the Eastern Mediterranean and the Indian sub-continent.

THE MIDDLE EAST

The beer which links Europe and Asia is Efes, brewed in both Istanbul and Izmir (Smyrna), and thus straddling the Bosporus. Izmir also has a Tuborg brewery, and Ankara the Tekel brewery. *Pilsener*-style and dark, *Münchener*-style beers are both produced. Although it is in practice an Islamic country, Turkey has been nominally secular since the time of Ataturk. Its people are hardly great beer-drinkers, but it has few inhibitions about the existence of a brewing industry. In more orthodox Islamic countries, attitudes vary. Some such nations deny the existence of alcoholic drink, but most brew on a modest scale.

Beer is becoming more widely available in Syria, for example. The Al-Chark brewery, established there in 1954 and nationalized in 1965, produces 20,000 litres a day, all in the form of a *Pilsener*-style beer (12 degrees Balling). Iraq has a government-owned brewery producing three *lagers*: Golden (11·5); Jawhara (12·5) and Kuhrmana (13·5), the latter in cans. The same country also has a joint-stock company producing Ferida Lager (12·1) and Amstel Gold (14·0). Iran has had a brewing industry for more than 30 years, with *lagers* like Setarah (11·0) and Shams (11·5), both from the Sarkissian and Sahakians company; Tuborg (12·0); and the medium-palate, dark-brown Majidieh (11·0), from a brewery backed by the Board for the Protection of Industries.

Israel has a Canadian-financed brewery which produces three *lagers*: Nesher (10·0), Abir (11·0) and Maccabee (12·0); a *Pilsener*-style beer called "O.K." (11·5); a low-alcohol malt beverage; and an *ale*-type beer called Goldstar (12·0).

THE INDIAN SUB-CONTINENT

Memories of the British Raj survive in Pakistan at the Murree Brewery, Rawalpindi, where London Lager (10·4 degrees Balling) is labelled with an illustration of Nelson's Column. Murree also brews an Export of 11·4, and a bottom-fermented *medium stout* of 14·2.

Although attitudes towards alcohol vary from State to State, India has a lively brewing industry, stretching from the Simla Hills in the North to Hyderabad and Bangalore in the South. In the Simla Hills, at Solan, the firm of Mohan Meakin produces five *lagers*: Baller (with an original gravity of 1040), Gymkhana (1045), Lion (1046), Krown (1048) and Golden Eagle (1050). In Hyderabad, the Vinedale Breweries produce three *lagers*: Regal (1042), Black Beard (1044) and Crazy, with a hefty gravity of 1064. In Bangalore, United Breweries produce three *lagers* with specific gravities of 1046, two premium *lagers* under the Flying Horse and Jubilee names (both 1052) and two *bitter stouts* (1046), under the London and Kingfisher names.

Sri Lanka has two breweries. One of them, marketing all its beers under the name Three Coins, has a *lager* (12·0 Balling), a *Pilsener*-type beer (12·25) and a *bitter stout* (13·8). The *stout* is also known as Sando. The other firm, Ceylon Breweries, has a Lion Lager (1042), a Pilsner Special (1050), a *bitter* "Double Strength" *stout* (1060) and two top-fermented sweetish *ales*, Pale (1044) and Jubilee (1060).

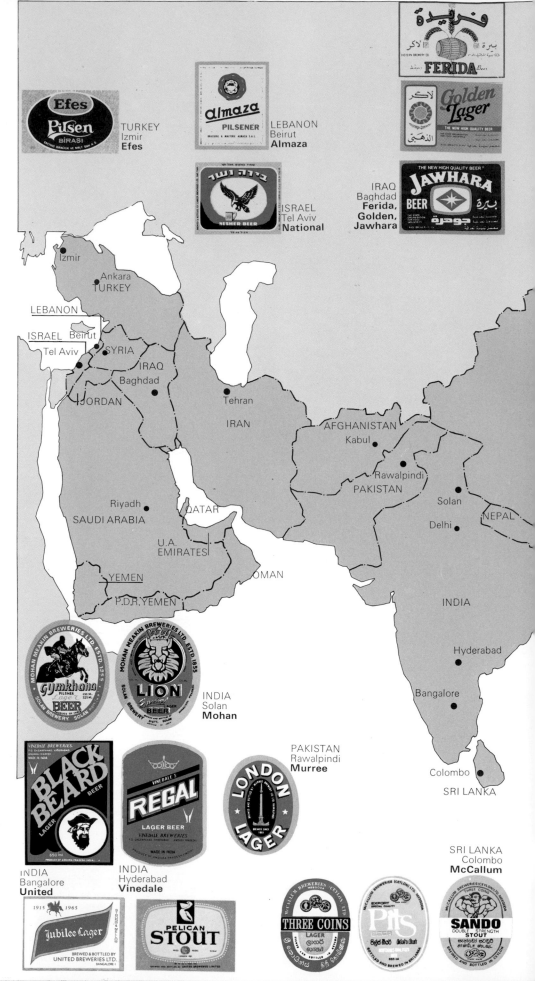

A

ASIA

The paintings on the left were originally reproduced as posters for the Sapporo brewery during the 1920s and early 1930s, and later as postcards. The set shown is from a larger collection, which can be seen at the company's museum.

The Americans, British and Dutch all had a hand in the popularization of beer in Japan, but the first brands to be sold on a wide scale were German imports, and that no doubt influenced researcher Nakawara. Once the Japanese brewing industry got under way, today's big names quickly emerged. The first lithographic poster produced in Japan was (right) for Kirin beer. The same brewer also took advantage of the Japanese flair for automotive engineering even in the early days.

THE A... first b barley and to durab time, where believ are ce and ar found brews chief's These cassav not to . . . co severa people cordin (John

Bee in som in ever of hop style i contin countr such la

Whe temple Egypt Société North its alc found in Kha British the Sta Camel pian G produc but als owns a ery, in duces a Meta B

"Sou an orig "Sourc gravity brands, cribed though called " an orig leader I in his re is own Genera take ov

industry on the Northern island of Hokkaido capitalized upon this interest by establishing a brewery there, at Sapporo, in 1876. Hokkaido's soil was ideal for the cultivation of hops and barley, and the Sapporo brewery soon prospered.

The company is proud to be located in what is now one of Japan's older cities, and further glamorizes its position by adding that Sapporo is, near enough, on the same latitude (45°N) as Munich and Milwaukee. In 1899, the company took a pioneering step by establishing the first beer-hall on the Ginza, Tokyo's most famous street. The original Ginza beer-hall is still in business. German-style drinking-places are popular, especially if they have bands, and rooftop beer-gardens are fashionable in summer. Two other large Japanese brewers were taken over by Sapporo in 1906, and the company bought the Tsingtao brewery in 1916. Subsequent events finally placed Tsingtao under Chinese control. Breweries which had been established in Manchuria and Korea were also later relinquished by Sapporo. (There are still two breweries in Seoul, producing sweetish *lagers*, with about 4·0 per cent alcohol: Crown, brewed by Chosun, is fractionally the stronger of the two beers, though the difference is inconsequential; Oriental Breweries' "O.B." is ahead in sales, but again only by a nose.)

Today, Sapporo has six breweries, all in Japan. Like all Japanese brewers, Sapporo uses rice as well as barley. Given their location, it is hardly a surprising or entirely inappropriate choice of adjunct. Sapporo uses rice in its regular *lager*, but it also offers the drinker the choice of an all-malt beer called Yebisu (both have 4·5 per cent alcohol by volume). The company also brews a Black Beer, and imports Guinness. *Lager* and Guinness are available in half-and-half packs of a dozen, ready to make a Japanese-style Black-and-Tan. All of Sapporo's draught, and bottled beer in some areas, is unpasteurized.

Also in Sapporo is the Hokkaido Asahi brewery, which takes justifiable pride in its pioneering work with unpasteurized bottled beers on the Japanese market. Asahi has six other breweries in Japan, producing both light and dark beers.

Suntory produces only one beer, called "Real Draft," with an alcohol content of slightly less than four per cent by volume, but its entire output is unpasteurized. The company attributes to its beer a "Danish" light and mild palate. Suntory only started brewing in 1963, opened a second brewery two years later, and has since moved into

Mexico. It is the only Japanese group to have a brewery overseas. The company was founded in 1899 as a wine-producer, subsequently started to distil whisky, became Japan's largest producer of spirits, and now has the fastest-growing beer. It remains a family-controlled firm, and its shares are not quoted on the stock market. Suntory has a wine museum in Yamanashi, a whisky museum in Hakushu, and a beer museum in Musashino. It also has several philanthropic projects, including a museum of historic Japanese art, a classical music award, and a

wild bird preservation campaign.

The public face of the brewing industry has adopted a rather more sophisticated air since the days when a "beer-grove" (a turn-of-the-century rival to the tea-garden) announced:

"*To English and Generally Foreign*: The beer of this establishment is made with most purest spring waters that flow. It will be satisfied to the tastes in all respects, and our proprietors guarantee politeness to each and every one. Inside within we present samples of this purest truth, and can be tested at all times."

At its longest, the Nile rises among the lakes of East Africa. More than one nation can make a claim to be its source. Uganda says it with beer. The same medium was used during the confrontation with Kenya in 1976 (top).

Ale, with a copper-brown colour and a yeasty palate, and a full-bodied, medium palate Castle Milk Stout. The latter is stronger than might be expected for a *milk stout*. Castle and Lion brands, including *ale* and *stout* are also produced by Rhodesian Breweries Limited. The original South African Breweries was founded in 1895, though its component parts include Ohlsson's Cape Breweries, which was established a few years earlier. Today, it is the biggest brewing group on the continent and one of South Africa's largest industrial companies. It has diversified into hotels, property, stores, foods and other manufacturing industries.

The only other beers in the Republic of South Africa are produced by Intercontinental Breweries, a challenger which was set up in 1973 by Rupert International, best known for its Rothmans tobacco interests. Ruperts' brewing operations elsewhere in the world describe some circuitous patterns. In Denmark, Rupert has a substantial interest in Carlsberg (United Breweries). In Southern Africa, Carlsberg operates a brewery in association with the Government of Malawi. The local brands there are Malawi Carlsberg Lager (10·9 Plato) and Carlsberg Beer (10·7). Another round-trip goes via Canada. Such are the tangles of international marketing that, while Rupert controls the original Carling company in Canada, the same brand in South Africa resides with a rival.

The beers brewed by Intercontinental are all *lagers* in the 1040–1050 range of original gravity. They include the mellow Sportsman Lager, which the company describes as being "full-strength," and the slightly darker, sweeter and fuller-flavoured Heidelberg Lager. Beck's Bier, something of an inter-national brand before war interrupted its progress, returned to Southern Africa via a tiny brewery in Swaziland. It is now brewed under licence by Intercontinental. So is a Bavarian beer called Kronenbrau "1308," which is described as being "oak-mellowed." Kronenbrau is delivered by dray-horses, the pride and joy of Intercontinental, and the brand is promoted in an annual Johannesburg "Oktoberfest."

The German colonial influence in Africa is still evident in the brewing map, most especially in the South, but less in the Republic than in Namibia. Hansa Pilsener comes from Namibia, along with the same brewery's Export and Tafel brands, all three quoted at an original gravity of 1040. A more unusual offering is the dark Hansa Urbock, at 1080. Nor is this the only *bock* in Namibia. The rival South-West Breweries Limited produces Windhoek Mai-Bock, at 1072, as well as a *bitter stout*. The latter, Windhoek Extra Stout, has an original gravity of 1050. An Export and a Lager, also named after the capital, are brewed at 1044.

Although the South is the most economically-advanced region of Africa, it does not lead in beer output. For some years, Central Africa (the region, not the Republic) could claim that distinction, by way of Zaire's sizable brewing industry. Then, in 1974, Nigeria took the lead for West Africa.

Such is the size of Zaire that in some cases the different administrative divisions have their own local beer-brands. The biggest national brand is Primus, brewed with the technical assistance of Heineken. Primus is also brewed in Rwanda and Burundi with the backing of Heineken and the Banque Bruxelles Lambert. Heineken is active in both Central and West Africa, sometimes in association with the United Africa Company, part of the Anglo-Dutch Unilever grouping. Predictably, French brewers are also active in this part of the world, notably Union de Brasseries (formerly Brasseries et Glacières de l'Indochine). Swiss brewing interests have also traditionally retained several footholds in the North-West corner of Africa. Guinness has associate companies in Cameroun, Nigeria and Ghana, and its Foreign Extra Stout is brewed under contract elsewhere in the West. Such arrangements usually operate in association with local private interests or Governments, which in some cases hold a majority stake.

The traveller in Africa may find interesting beers in surprising places. A *Pilsener* with the unusually high density of 14·0 degrees Plato, and an alcoholic content of 6·0 per cent by volume, is brewed by Société des Brasseries

Time for a Tusker

There was a pioneering spirit about the early days of East African Breweries. The setting up of the original plant in 1922 was largely the work of a former gold-prospector, who was then farming in Kenya. He and two partners imported their brewing equipment from Britain, and later hired a brewer from Burtonwood, in the North-West of England. Hops were imported from Kent, and the brewery's products were ales and stout. The group picture (inset) shows the staff in 1929, and the photograph of the company's fleet in front of the brewery was taken around the same time. Lager-brewing was introduced in 1930, and today's yeast-culture is imported from Denmark. In 1968, the company won two gold medals and one silver at the World Beer Competition in Nürnberg. When a new headquarters was built in 1970, the foundation stone was laid by President Kenyatta, and he was later presented by the managing director with a bronze cast of a famous Kenyan Tusker called Ahmed.

Index

Picture credits